Java™ Tools

Java™ Tools

Using XML, EJB,™ CORBA,™ Servlets and SOAP

Andreas Eberhart
Stefan Fischer

JOHN WILEY & SONS, LTD

John Wiley & Sons Ltd,
Baffins Lane, Chichester,
West Sussex PO19 1UD, England

National   01243 779777
International   (+44) 1243 779777
e-mail (for orders and customer service enquiries): cs-books@wiley.co.uk
Visit our Home Page on http://www.wiley.co.uk

Other Wiley Editorial Offices

New York, Weinheim

Library of Congress Cataloging-in-Publication Data

Eberhart, Andreas
    Java tools : using XML, EJB, CORBA, Servlets and SOAP / Andreas Eberhart, Stefan Fischer.
        p. cm.
    ISBN 0-471-48666-3 (alk. paper)
    1.   Java (Computer program language) 2. Electronic data processing--Distributed processing. I. Fischer, Stefan. II. Title.

    QA76.73.J38 E24 2002
    005.13'3--dc21

                                                                          2001058127

British Library Cataloguing in Publication Data

A catalogue record for this book is available from the British Library

ISBN   0 471 48666 3

Translated and typeset by Cybertechnics Ltd, Sheffield
Printed and bound in Great Britain by Biddles Ltd, Guildford and King's Lynn
This book is printed on acid-free paper responsibly manufactured from sustainable forestry, in which at least two trees are planted for each one used for paper production.

CONTENTS

Section II

Section V

Chapter 15 XML – the new ASCII 283

Chapter 1

Introduction

1.1 Motivation

Distributed applications are programs which run on several computers connected to a computer network and which together perform a specific task. An example of such an application would be a flight booking system. Such a system consists of different components, e.g. one or several databases in which all available flights and reservations are filed, a management system, and tens of thousands of user programs which enable interactive enquiries on places available, and their direct booking through a graphic or text-oriented interface.

In such a scenario, each subprogram has its individual components which contribute to the total functionality of the system. Communication occasionally has to take place between individual subprograms in order to inform the partner program about the intermediate results, user input or simple status modifications. It is this communication element that makes the development of distributed applications a complex matter.

This book deals with the design and implementation of distributed applications. Obviously, distributed applications, just like simple local applications, have to be programmed. This is precisely the topic of this book. In addition to actual program logic, i.e. the part of the program which solves application problems, communication code has to be implemented between subprograms in distributed systems.

Distributed applications have been a topic of information technology since the 1970s, i.e. since the advent of high speed networks and the exchange of large amounts of data between computers. It was initially very difficult and less convenient to program such applications and make them work properly. The programmers had to know exactly the kind of networks, computer hardware or operating system with which they were dealing, in order to be able to use the functions of the communication libraries.

However, increasingly more powerful and user-friendly programming techniques and paradigms were developed, which today enable the communication part of distributed applications to be created entirely automatically.

Network applications aroused increasing interest among the general public and a further impetus was provided with the explosive development of the Internet and the World Wide Web. Nowadays, with the "network of networks," a global communication medium is available used by an increasing number of businesses and authorities, but also by more and more private individuals. In addition, organizations develop their own applications, tailor made for their special needs, such as the flight booking systems discussed previously, hotel reservation systems or bank applications.

Two technologies currently play a very important role in the creation of such programs on the Internet. On the one hand, these are applications which enable the user to access the World Wide Web, and which the reader has already experienced in some way or other. A typical property of such systems is the fact that a standardized *Web browser* works as a user interface. The actual communication technique has also developed rapidly in this field during recent years. Initially, it was possible to create static Web pages using *HTML*, but soon afterwards, it became possible to create dynamic pages, using CGI programs at first, and then Java applets. Applets are small programs written in the Java programming language. They are placed on a Web page and executed by the browser after the page has loaded. *Servlets* represent a further development and a fusion of these two techniques. Servlets are Java programs which are not executed by the browser, but by the Web server. Servlets build a powerful and simple tool for creating distributed applications, and are one of the main topics of this book. If servlets are combined with an extension of the HTML page description language, the *eXtensible Markup Language*, *XML*, some extremely advanced applications can be built. The book will focus on this topic in one of its main sections.

On the other hand, a programming method described as object-oriented programming has become increasingly important. Its basic idea is modeling a program as a collection of objects, which respectively represent the image of actual objects of the application. In order to fulfill the task of the application, these objects communicate with each other, i.e. an object sends messages to other objects to activate particular functions in this object or send new information to it. Object-oriented programming is also described as data-oriented, while procedural programming languages are regarded as process-oriented.

Object-oriented programming can also be applied to distributed environments. The result of this transfer is *distributed object computing*. In such programs, application objects can be placed on different computers. Communication between application objects has to be mapped on a communication connection over the network. On the other hand, as you can imagine, explicit programming of this communication can become extremely complex. Today, however, programming environments are available which completely hide the communication from programmers, allowing them to concentrate on the application logic.

The most prominent representative of this kind of distributed object environments is the *Common Object Request Broker Architecture (CORBA)*. CORBA is not an architecture developed by a particular firm, but is standardized by an independent organization. Using CORBA, all sorts of distributed applications can be created on the Internet, from simple Web applications using applets to database access in an enterprise network, to embedding non-Internet applications on the Internet, so-called *legacy software*. CORBA is therefore addressed in another main section of this book.

After some experience with available techniques, there has been some criticism of these approaches or their combinations. For instance, CORBA was considered too complex; in many systems the extensive functionality and very generalized approaches were not necessary. The cost of using CORBA for these applications was found to be too high. Furthermore, the Servlet solution which, as we will see later, was the combination of application development logic with the production of HTML pages, was considered too unsafe, and sometimes too complex. A new approach, suitable for solving these problems, was consequently developed. This is Enterprise Java Beans (EJB), which will be introduced in this book.

In order to explain clearly to the practitioner the use of these four technologies, we will illustrate all the procedures with an example from electronic commerce. We will develop an Internet bookshop step by step, and it will become gradually easier to understand how the techniques of servlets, CORBA, Enterprise Java Beans and XML can be used properly and can complement one another. In case of contention, we will not take sides in reaching a solution, but will try to show which techniques are available for each particular situation.

1.2 Structure of the book

The book is subdivided into several sections. After this introduction, the first section (Chapters 2 to 5) deals with the most important principles for understanding the following sections. Chapter 2 initially offers an introduction to the general idea and operation of distributed systems and applications. We will focus in particular on the Internet and Web applications, introducing such things as Web servers and Web browsers. At the end of the chapter, we will describe the sample application which will accompany the reader throughout the book.

In *Hypertext Markup Language (HTML)* and the *Java* programming language, Chapters 3 and 4 introduce two basic techniques used in the creation of Internet-based distributed applications. Chapter 3, dealing with HTML, shows the most important and basic means required to write Web pages, i.e. those files shown by a browser (at least in most cases), when the user enters and sends a *Web address* or clicks on a *link*.

Java, the topic of Chapter 4, is described as the Internet programming language, as it was first used for the development of applets. However, Java is a fully functional language and is used in many organizations as a standard programming language. The chapter argues in favor of using object-oriented languages by explaining their basic principles, and then shows how these features are realized in Java. We do not aim to provide an in-depth introduction to Java, but the material presented should be sufficient to enable a fairly experienced programmer, who has previously dealt with languages such as Pascal, C or C++, to understand the examples introduced in this book.

Chapter 5 addresses database access on the Internet. Databases are an important technique for all distributed applications in which data processing and storage play a role. A basic understanding of this technique is therefore not only helpful for this book, in which databases are required to develop the central example, but is necessary in any case for the developer of distributed applications. The chapter concentrates less on the actual configuration and administration of databases, and more on access of stored data. Two central aspects here are the standardized and well-known query language SQL, and embedding SQL queries in Java using *JDBC*. The latter will also establish the bridge between the central technologies, servlets and CORBA, and the databases.

After the introduction of the basic principles, the second section of the book addresses the servlet technique (Chapters 6 to 8). Chapter 6 analyzes the ideas behind servlet technology as well as its operation. Chapter 7 then tackles the practical part. Different development tools are represented here, with which servlet applications easily can be created. Chapter 8 will conclude the servlet section. We will implement the first part of the sample application using servlets, developing a Web-based user interface, as well as the corresponding servlets for a database connection. At the end of the chapter, a fully functional Internet bookshop will have been implemented, in which books can be searched, placed in a virtual shopping basket and finally ordered by the user.

As previously mentioned, not all distributed applications are Web based. The CORBA architecture therefore enables a more general approach for the development or integration of distributed applications. CORBA can display its strength in particular in the integration of existing software into Internet environments. This certainly plays an important role in practice in most information systems. CORBA is therefore the topic of Chapters 9 to 11 in the third section of the book. After a general introduction to distributed object-oriented programming, a detailed introduction to the architecture of the *Common Object Request Broker,* and a representation of the approach in creating CORBA-based applications in Chapter 9, Chapter 10 focuses on the tool support for the development of such applications. Tools for the Java programming language are prominent here. In Chapter 11 we will extend the existing bookshop application to explain the operation of CORBA, adding a possibility for credit card payment.

In the fourth section (Chapters 12 to14) we will consider the Enterprise Java Beans technique. To begin with, we will show in Chapter 12, using examples, the criticisms that can be applied to the use of servlets or CORBA. This leads us directly to the EJB design criteria, which will be described at the end of the same chapter. Its central section represents the EJB technique in detail. In Chapter 13 we will consider the tool support available for EJB. In particular, we will analyze the reference implementation Java 2 Enterprise Edition (J2EE) from Sun. To conclude this section, Chapter 14 sets EJB in the context of our bookshop application and shows how the Servlet approach developed in Chapter 8 can be improved by means of EJB.

Using servlets and CORBA or EJB in this context, we already have created a powerful application. However, the options which are now available for users can be considerably increased, using XML in place of the HTML page description language. The fifth section (Chapters 15 to 18) deals with this topic. After an introduction to the basic principles of

XML with a motivation for their application in Chapter 15, Chapter 16 introduces a series of tools which facilitate the use of XML. In Chapter 17 we will extend the sample application further using these tools. In this way, customers can draw price comparisons between individual bookshops without having to browse all Web pages. It immediately becomes clear how suitable XML is for this kind of task. In a later chapter we will demonstrate how useful it is to create another class of e-commerce applications. Up until now, we have fundamentally dealt with the applications for final consumers, the *B2C* applications (*Business-to-Consumer*). However, nowadays *B2B* applications (*Business-to-Business*) play at least an equally important role: they enable business partners to communicate with each other and to exchange goods and services. Many virtual marketplaces have been developed on the Internet, e.g. for steel or for chemical components. In this last chapter we will show, from section five onwards, how the techniques previously introduced can be used to create such a marketplace.

To conclude, the last part of the book summarizes the results of the three previous sections. First, in Chapter 19, the differences between the techniques introduced are explained. We will also include other approaches, such as RMI, COM+, CGI and *Active Server Pages*. Finally, Chapter 20 generalizes the example of Internet bookshops, showing which technique is best used in each kind of application.

The book ends with a series of appendices. They have to be seen as a reference to the most important themes presented in the book, and they allow programmers to create their own distributed applications. For obvious reasons, these appendices will not be able to provide a complete reference, so consulting additional sources will become necessary from time to time. The start-points are contained in a separate appendix which gives many literature references.

In addition to the book you can find also a Web page which, as well as up-to-date information and links to relevant and relating themes, also contains the files with complete source code of examples introduced here. Appendix H provides a brief introduction to the use of the Web page.

Chapter 2

Distributed applications

The aim of this chapter is to familiarize ourselves with the concept of distributed applications. We will first give a brief summary of how information technology has developed towards distributed applications over the past few decades. We will describe in detail the basic characteristics and design principles, as well as the advantages and disadvantages of the use of distributed systems. We will then be able to address such applications in their most popular current form, namely applications on the Internet or World Wide Web. Several examples will be used here to put theories acquired earlier into practice. The chapter ends with an introduction to the sample application developed in this book, an Internet bookshop.

2.1 A short history of information technology

Distributed applications are currently the latest development of information technology, which began about 50 years ago and is still developing. The first computers available in the 1940s and 50s were reserved for special applications, like military tasks such as the encryption and decoding of messages.

The 1960s witnessed the advent of *batch processing*, in which several users could pass their tasks to the computer operator. Once processed, the results were returned to the client by the operator. As there was no interactivity at that time, computers were used for numerical applications, in other words for solving problems that required little user input but resulted in a high computation effort.

With the advent of mainframes, with which several of our readers will no doubt be familiar, interactive applications came into play. Several users could finally use one computer simultaneously in *time-sharing* mode. Tasks were no longer completed in sequence as in batch processing, but part of the job would be processed, and the computer would then switch to the next job in the queue. It started to make sense to process especially data-intensive processes such as business applications. At the time, companies such as IBM were in their heyday.

The next trend, beginning with the introduction of the PC in 1980, was the shift in computing power from the central mainframe to the desktops. Computer performance, undreamt of previously, was now available to employees directly at their workstation. Every user could install his or her own applications on the computer, and create – in principle – an optimally configured work environment. So began the age of standardized office packages, which enabled office automation to be driven forward considerably. Companies such as Microsoft and Intel made huge profits.

Since the 1990s, the trend has shifted increasingly from distributed information processing to *enterprise computing*. Previously autonomously operating workstations were integrated together with central file, database, and application servers, resulting in huge decentralized clusters, which were used to handle tasks of a more complicated nature. The defining sentence characterizing this phase and coined by Sun Microsystems reads "The network is the computer."

What led to this (ever increasing) greater importance of distributed applications? There are several reasons:

- The cost of chip manufacturing dropped sharply, enabling cheap mass production of computers.
- At the same time, network technologies were developed with higher bandwidths – a necessity for the quick transfer of large amounts of data between several computers.
- Response times became increasingly longer due to heavier use of large mainframe computers, resulting in excessive waiting times. A company would think twice before purchasing a more powerful computer due to the high cost.
- The availability of a comparable distributed work environment quickly gave rise to the desire for new applications which were not possible in a central environment. This development led from the first e-mail applications via the World Wide Web to common use of information by people in completely different places. *Groupware*, tele-cooperation systems and *virtual communities* are the current keywords here.

The following section gives detailed information on the construction and properties, as well as the advantages and disadvantages, of distributed systems and applications.

2.2 Principles and characteristics of distributed systems

2.2.1 Definition of a distributed system

What actually constitutes a distributed system or a distributed application? The basic task of such a system is to solve a particular problem. As the system is described as "distributed," the problem solving obviously does not occur in a central place, but through the cooperation of several components. Countless definitions have been drawn up over time, most of which are fairly to the point. However, there are several central components that a distributed system definitely must contain:

■ a set of autonomous computers;
■ a communication network, connecting these computers
■ software integrating these components with a communications system.

The first point is quite clear. Computers are used in information technology so that problem solving occurs in a distributed system using computers. As this solution should not be produced centrally, other computers have to be involved. So why the demand for "autonomous" computers? This point reflects the necessary differentiation with respect to a central computer, to which several terminals are connected. These terminals are unable to solve any tasks independently as they have no computing ability; they can only display data sent by the central computer on the screen, or send user input to the computer. However, a configuration that would meet this definition of "a set of autonomous computers" would be a collection of PCs.

A communications network is the second important component. No communication can occur without some type of connection between computers. A problem cannot be mutually solved without communication. Partial tasks which have to be solved cannot be distributed to the individual components, and nor can partial solutions be sent to a coordination component later.

The task of the software, finally, is the virtual integration of all computers into one computing device which solves the problem posed. On the one hand, it takes over the coordination of the different partial components, and on the other hand ensures that the system looks like a real unit to a user. This so-called *distribution transparency* is an important characteristic of distributed systems. It will be discussed again in detail in the following section.

Figure 2.1 shows the cooperation of the three components graphically.

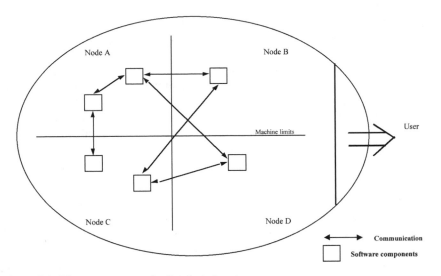

Figure 2.1: The components of a distributed system.

In short, a distributed system could be described as a collection of autonomous computers, connected together via a communication network, running software which coordinates individual partial components.

A distributed application is therefore an application A, the functionality of which is subdivided into a set of cooperating subcomponents $A_1, .., A_n$, with n elements of IN and n > 1. The partial components A_i are autonomous processing units which (can) run on different computers. They exchange information over the network, controlled by the coordination software. Coordination and application software are often physically integrated.

There are three levels in a distributed system, as shown in Fig. 2.2.

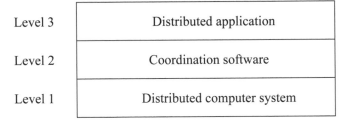

Figure 2.2: The levels of a distributed system.

The application on level 3 will ideally 'know' nothing of the distribution of the system, as it uses the services of level 2, the administration software which takes over the coordination of all the components and hides this complexity from the application. In turn, level 2 itself uses the available distributed computing environment consisting of several computers and the network.

There also are, by the way, several interesting and amusing definitions. One of the most well known was put forward by Leslie Lamport, who defined a distributed system as a system "in which my work is affected by the failure of components, of which I knew nothing previously."

2.2.2 Important characteristics of distributed systems

We will now look at several other important characteristics of distributed systems based on this very simple definition. All these properties refer to the concept of *transparency*. In information technology, transparency literally means that something is transparent, or invisible. In distributed systems, certain things should be invisible to the users. The complexity of the system should remain hidden from them, as they would not wish to concern themselves with solving other implementation questions. Rather they would prefer to solve an application problem. The way in which the solution is finally achieved is relatively irrelevant to these users. For this reason, the following transparency properties play a large role in achieving this characteristic of a distributed system:

- *Location transparency*
  Users need not necessarily know where exactly within the system a resource is located which they wish to use. Resources are typically identified by name, which has no bearing on their location.
- *Access transparency*
  The way in which a resource is accessed is uniform for all resources. For example, in a distributed database system consisting of several databases of different technologies (relational and object-oriented databases), there should also be a common user interface such as the SQL query language.
- *Replication transparency*
  The fact that there may be several copies of a resource is not disclosed to the users. The latter do not know whether they are accessing the original or the copy. Altering the status of a resource also has to occur transparently.
- *Error transparency*
  Users will not necessarily be informed of all errors occurring in the system. Some errors may be irrelevant, and others may well be *masked*, as in the case of replication.
- *Concurrency transparency*
  Distributed systems are usually used by several users simultaneously. It often happens that two or more users access the same resource at the same time, such as a database table, printer, or file. Concurrency transparency ensures that simultaneous access is feasible without any mutual interference or incorrect results.
- *Migration transparency*
  Using this form of transparency, resources can be moved over the network without the user noticing. A typical example is today's mobile telephone network in which

the device can be moved around freely, without any loss of communication when leaving the vicinity of a sender station.

- *Process transparency*
  It is irrelevant on which computer a certain task (process) is executed, provided it is guaranteed that the results are the same. This form of transparency is an important prerequisite for the successful implementation of a balanced workload between computers (see below also).
- *Performance transparency*
  When increasing the system load, a dynamic reconfiguration may well be required. This measure for performance optimization should of course go unnoticed by other users.
- *Scaling transparency*
  If a system is to be expanded so as to incorporate more computers or applications, this should be feasible without modifying the system structure or application algorithms.
- *Language transparency*
  The programming language in which the individual partial components of the distributed system or application were created must not play any role in the ensemble. This is a relatively new requirement, only supported by more recent systems.

An important aim of distributed systems or applications is to fulfill as many of these transparency characteristics as possible, so as to make the system as uncomplicated and smooth-running as possible.

2.2.3 Communication models

Communication between the individual components of a distributed system can occur in two basic ways: using either *shared memory* or *message passing*.

The former is an *indirect* form of communication, as both partners exchanging information do not communicate directly with each other, but via a third component: the shared memory. This may be an area of the main memory. The term *common variables* is also used in this case. Another variant is the use of a common file system. The sender then writes the information in a file, the name of which also is known to the receiver. As soon as the data is placed in the file, the receiver can read it.

On the other hand, message passing is based on the direct communication of information between the sender and the receiver by means of the communication medium. Two functions are generally available for the execution of message exchange, usually labeled *send* and *receive*. They are defined as follows:

- send(r: receiver, m: message)
  This function sends the message to the receiver r.
- receive(s:sender, b: buffer)
  This function waits for a message from sender s and writes it in buffer b (part of the memory made available for the application process).

The basic form of exchange of a single message can be combined with more complex models. One of the most important models of this type is the *client–server model*. In this case, the communication partners adopt the role of either a *client* or a *server*. A server is assigned to administer access to a certain resource, while a client wishes to use the resource.

A line of communication in the client–server model consists of two messages, as shown in Fig 2.3.

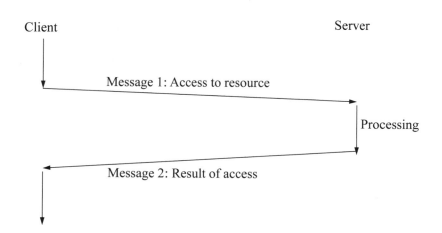

Figure 2.3: Message exchange in the client–server model.

The first message goes from the client to the server, in which the client requests access to a certain resource. In a database application, this could be an SQL query accessing a particular database table, for example. On receipt of the message, the server edits the request (if not busy with other queries). As soon as a result is determined, it is sent to the client in the form of a second message.

The client–server model is the most popular communication model, and plays a prominent role on the Internet.

2.2.4 Advantages and disadvantages of distributed systems

Compared to other technologies, distributed systems have a series of advantages, yet are not entirely devoid of problems. The technology is compared below with the two previous approaches, i.e. mainframes and standalone workstations.

Compared to mainframes, distributed systems offer the following advantages:

- They are essentially more economical, as comparable computing power is available at a much lower price.
- As previously mentioned, response times are typically much shorter.
- Distributed systems often are a better model of reality than a centralized computer. Such an example here would be the information infrastructure of a multinational company, to which a mainframe would not adjust, or robots on a production line assembling a product, or simply people working with each other, who need not necessarily be located in the same room or building.
- Distributed systems essentially can be made more reliable than a central system. There are two aspects to consider here: on the one hand, the availability of individual components can be increased by means of replication; if the working component fails, it can always be replaced by the replica. On the other hand, the failure of a non-replicated component does usually not lead to a total system failure, as the other parts can continue working independently. This is not the case with mainframes.
- Finally, distributed systems easily can be extended and adapted to increasing requirements. Distributed systems can be extended on almost any scale, whereas a mainframe is subject to strict constraints as far as memory and processor extension is concerned.

A comparison of distributed systems with conventional PC technology produces the following:

- Generally speaking, communication between computers can only occur using a connection. Applications such as e-mail, network news, or even video conference systems are only possible using these means.
- The networking of PCs allows a common use of both resources and data (such as the aforementioned flight booking system), hardware such as printers and hard drives, as well as software such as applications installed on an application server.
- Computer capacities in particular are used more efficiently. Imagine a situation where a user is running two compute-intensive applications, while another user is currently not working at his terminal. As a way of evening things out, in a distributed system one of the two applications can be transferred to the "quieter" computer and executed there. This process would not disturb the user in any way, as this produces a more rapid result. Another aspect of this idea is the more simple use of special-purpose computers from an individual workstation.

▣ Finally, system maintenance is simplified considerably, as it can be carried out for each individual PC using the network. In isolated cases a system administrator would have to treat each individual computer separately and carry out the work required.

The most important problems which arise with distributed systems are the following:

▣ The entire system is extremely dependent on transmission performance and the reliability of the underlying communication network. If the network is constantly overloaded, then the aforementioned advantages are soon canceled out, as in relation to response times.

▣ Distribution and communication always are an increased security risk in many ways. For example, as soon as two computers have to communicate with each other, this communication can be listened to, or its messages can even be modified. Another point is decentralized control, produced through distribution. The individual components are now typically controlled directly by their users, meaning that the machines are no longer part of a locked computing center, controlled by one or more system administrators. Users of the distributed system can often modify it, for instance by installing new software, by which viruses can be smuggled in to the computer.

▣ Finally, software both for applications and for the coordination of application components essentially is more complex and so more likely to produce programming errors. It is not easy to write the correct software for the management of distributed systems.

2.3 Applications on the Internet and the World Wide Web

Distributed systems on the Internet or World Wide Web are the central theme of this book. There are several reasons for this: The Internet is quickly becoming the global medium of communication. Nowadays it is quite simple to connect to the Internet using a computer. It often suffices to insert the CD-ROM of an Internet service provider (ISP), wait for the program to start, and type in the desired name for an e-mail address. The installation then runs automatically, and familiar services such as e-mail and the Web soon can be used.

This section provides a short introduction to the technology of the Internet and the World Wide Web. This knowledge is essential for later development of distributed applications on the basis of the Internet.

2.3.1 The development of the Internet

The Internet, nowadays a huge worldwide communication network, began as a collection of four computers, or hosts, connected to each other. At the time, in 1969, the US Ministry of Defense invited several Californian universities and research facilities to develop a new network which was less prone to the failure of network components such as lines and switches than ordinary networks (such as the telephone network). One reason for this task was the fear that, in case of a Soviet attack on the communication network, there would suddenly no longer be a connection between the command center and the individual units, and blind action would have to be taken.

The solution developed by the participating universities was the *packet switching technique*. Packet switching means that the information to be transferred is broken down into many small *packages*. Each packet is individually sent to the receiver, and under certain circumstances can take a completely different route from both its predecessor and successor. The packet intentionally may look for an alternative route if a certain section of the network suddenly fails during transmission.

A larger network soon developed from this small yet successful experiment. Until the end of the 1980s, it was used exclusively for military purposes and by universities. It was only with the development of the World Wide Web, a new Internet application, that the need for the commercial success of the network of today was created, as the previous text-based and cryptic user interface for Internet applications such as e-mail or file transfer was replaced by a graphic interface, controlled entirely with a mouse. Companies quickly recognized the opportunities behind the new medium, and developed Web programs and protocols to become ever more powerful tools. Today the Internet is a multimedia communication medium, in which the still extremely popular e-mail is used, as well as films being transferred and even telephone calls being made. The Internet is currently becoming a huge marketplace for every type of product and service imaginable. The latest figures (January 2001) show that 110 million computers are currently connected to the Internet, on many of which several users often work at once. Figure 2.4 shows the rapid development of the net in the 1990s.

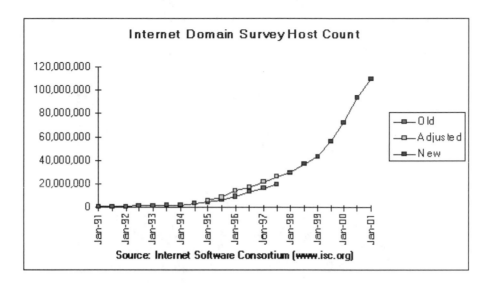

Figure 2.4: Internet growth since 1991 (number of connected computers).
Source: Internet Software Consortium (`www.isc.org`)

2.3.2   Technical principles of the Internet

Communication systems such as the Internet are best described using *layered models* because of their complexity. Every layer within the model has a certain task, and all layers together produce a particular communication service for the user. The layers are arranged in hierarchical form. It is said that layers lower down the hierarchy produce a service used by the higher layers. The uppermost layer finally combines all lower services and constitutes the interface for applications.

In the case of the Internet, the so-called Internet reference model is used, as can be seen in Figure 2.5. The model consists of four layers:

- The *Link Layer* describes the possible subnetworks of the Internet and their medium access protocols. These are, for example, Ethernets, token rings, FDDI, or ISDN networks. To its upper layer, the link layer offers communication between two computers in the same subnetwork as a service.
- The *Network Layer* unites all subnetworks to become the Internet. The service offered involves making communication possible between any two computers on the Internet. The network layer accesses the services of the *Link Layer*, in that a connection between two computers in different networks is put together from many small connections in the same network.

■ The *Transport Layer* oversees the connection of two (or more) processes between computers communicating with each other via the *Network Layer*.

■ Finally, the *Application Layer* makes application-specific services available for inter-process communication. These many standardized services include e-mail, file transfer and the World Wide Web.

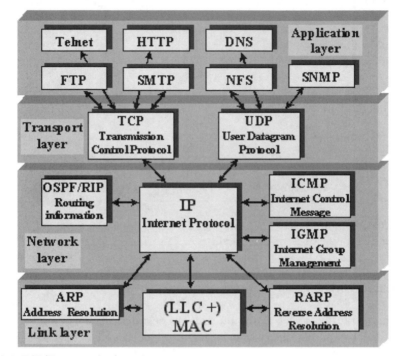

Figure 2.5: TCP/IP protocol suite.

Within the layers, *protocols* are used for the production of a service. Protocols are instances which can be implemented either in hardware or software, and communicate with their partner instances in the same levels, but on other computers. It is only this cooperation which enables the service to be produced for the next level up.

The *TCP/IP Protocol* constitutes the core of Internet communication technology in the transport and network layers. Every computer on the Internet always has an implementation of both protocols, TCP (*Transmission Control Protocol*) and IP (*Internet Protocol*). The task of IP is to transfer data from one Internet computer (the sender) to another (the receiver). On this basis, TCP then organizes the communication between two processes on these computers.

Figure 2.5 shows another protocol, UDP (*User Datagram Protocol*), alongside TCP on the transport layer. UDP and TCP are used for different tasks because of their respective properties. TCP is a connection-oriented protocol and therefore is able to ensure a reliable transfer. When using TCP, the sender can rest assured that the data sent will be received in its original sequence. Should data go missing, the sender is always notified. TCP therefore is suitable for applications where all data has to be transferred entirely correctly and in full, such as e-mail or file transfer. On the other hand, UDP is connection-less and has no control over whether data is transferred in its original sequence, or at all. UDP is therefore used for very short connections, or if reliability is not of paramount importance. Such an example would be a video conference system. Not every individual pixel transferred has to be displayed correctly for a video representation of adequate quality.

The most important protocols of the application layer on the Internet are also shown in Fig. 2.5:

- *Telnet* makes a terminal emulation available on a remote computer. The protocol enables logins to other computers using the network.
- *HTTP (Hypertext Transport Protocol)* is the underlying protocol of the World Wide Web. It is responsible for the transfer of hypertext documents.
- *SMTP (Simple Mail Transfer Protocol)* is the protocol used for the transfer of e-mail messages.
- *FTP (File Transfer Protocol)* is able to manage filestores on a server, and enables clients to access files.
- *SNMP (Simple Network Management Protocol)* is used for network management on the Internet.
- *DNS (Domain Name Service)* is responsible for the mapping of symbolic names such as www.bbc.co.uk to IP addresses such as 192.168.0.1. DNS is the name service for the Internet. We will get to know another name service for CORBA in Chapter 9.
- *NFS (Network File System)* makes the basic functionality for a distributed file system available.

The advantage of distributed Internet applications for users is that they have practically nothing to do with all these complicated-sounding protocols. These protocols are hidden using the actual application programs. The next section addresses some of the most popular Internet applications.

2.3.3 Internet applications

The huge popularity of the Internet is not due to such details which, although interesting, are extremely technical; it acquired such popularity because of the many applications which are either useful or entertaining (or both). Here we can differentiate between standardized applications, which typically use one of the aforementioned protocols of the application layer, and those developed individually, which either build directly on the transport layer, or use a standardized protocol such as HTTP as a form of higher-order transport protocol, on top of which, however, they still place a protocol of their own.

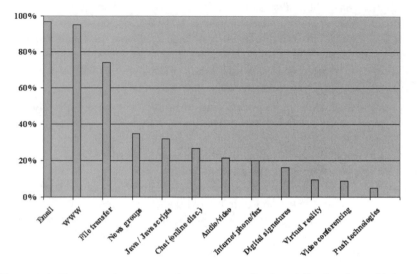

Figure 2.6: The currently most popular Internet applications (allowing for multiple mentions).

The leading Internet communication model is the client–server model as introduced previously. An Internet server usually administers certain resources which an Internet client wishes to access. Access occurs through an exchange of messages, in that the client first sends a query which then is answered by the server. For example: with file transfer, a server manages a large amount of files. If a client now sends a request for a certain file to the server, then, provided the file is available and the user has corresponding access rights, the file is sent to the client in response.

The most important applications nowadays include e-mail, the World Wide Web, and file transfer. However, multimedia data transfer is becoming increasingly popular. This includes video conference systems, for example, and also *Internet telephony*. Figure 2.6 shows the results of a recent survey of businesses who were asked which Internet applications they used.

A brief outline of the most important of these applications is given below:

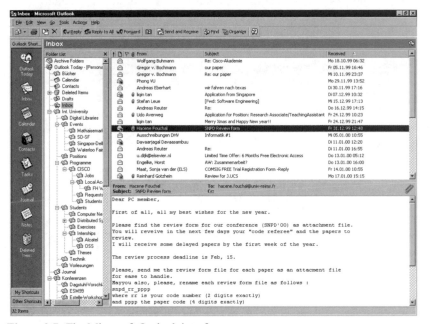

Figure 2.7: The Microsoft Outlook interface.

- *E-mail*

  Electronic mail is the oldest application on the Internet, and still the most popular today. In the 1970s, no one other than scientists at universities had an e-mail address, whereas an e-mail facility nowadays comes as standard. The first e-mail applications, still popular in the UNIX environment today, were not exactly user-friendly, and could only be used with cryptic and cumbersome keyboard commands. On the other hand, the windows-based applications available today are much easier to use, such as Microsoft Outlook or Netscape Messenger. Figure 2.7 shows the windows-based interface of Outlook. Further functions also often are included in current e-mail clients, such as a calendar, address book or task manager.

- *World Wide Web*

  Due to its importance to the content of this book and the support of specialized distributed applications, the World Wide Web is discussed in detail in sections 2.3.4 and 2.3.5.

- *File transfer*

  The transfer of files between computers is an important means for exchanging all types of electronic data. The FTP programs used, so called because of the file transfer protocol used, were initially used for small text files or PostScript documents, with which scientists exchanged their findings. Today the focus has shifted toward the transfer of large program packages, since software manufacturers have switched to selling their products over the Internet. Due to development in the e-mail sector, FTP

clients have gradually become easier to use. Figure 2.8, 2.9 shows the standard UNIX
FTP client, operated using ASCII entries. By contrast, the operation of the WS-FTP-
Light client as shown in Fig. 2.9 is essentially more advanced.

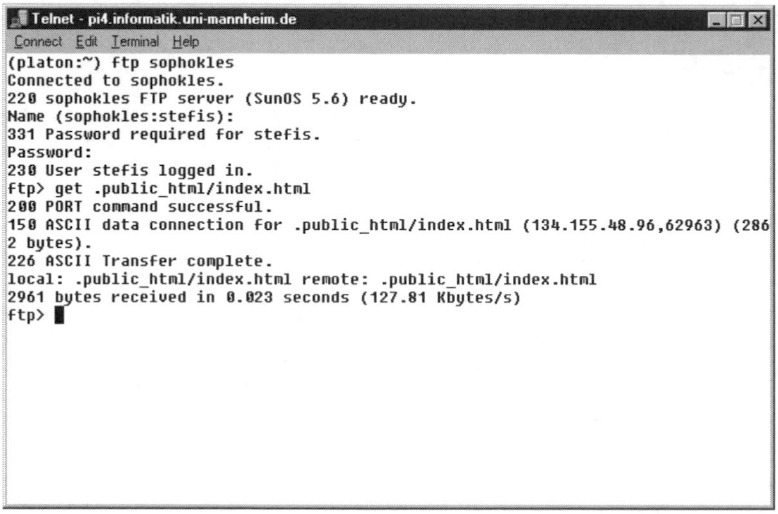

```
Telnet - pi4.informatik.uni-mannheim.de                          _ □ ×
Connect  Edit  Terminal  Help
(platon:~) ftp sophokles
Connected to sophokles.
220 sophokles FTP server (SunOS 5.6) ready.
Name (sophokles:stefis):
331 Password required for stefis.
Password:
230 User stefis logged in.
ftp> get .public_html/index.html
200 PORT command successful.
150 ASCII data connection for .public_html/index.html (134.155.48.96,62963) (286
2 bytes).
226 ASCII Transfer complete.
local: .public_html/index.html remote: .public_html/index.html
2961 bytes received in 0.023 seconds (127.81 Kbytes/s)
ftp> █
```

Figure 2.8: A simple FTP client in UNIX.

■ *Video Conference Systems*
One of the new trends in Internet-supported applications is the transfer of audio and
video data streams. As many PCs today are equipped with cameras, microphones,
loudspeakers and powerful graphics cards, the actual recording and representation no
longer pose a problem. However, the transfer of large amounts of data over the
network is fairly tricky. Different companies or research facilities have come up with
the most diverse solutions in order to minimize the amount of data or transfer in a
more effective way. The *Real Products* company was a forerunner, the same
company which undertook pioneering work with the *RealPlayer*. Many current audio
and video transfers use this technology. Video conference systems enable different
partners from all over the world to meet virtually, and both talk and exchange images
with each other. Video transfers are usually of unsatisfactory quality, but as the
Internet is constantly expanding, it is only a matter of time until Internet videos will

be no different from television pictures. This form of communication will therefore gradually be accepted more widely.

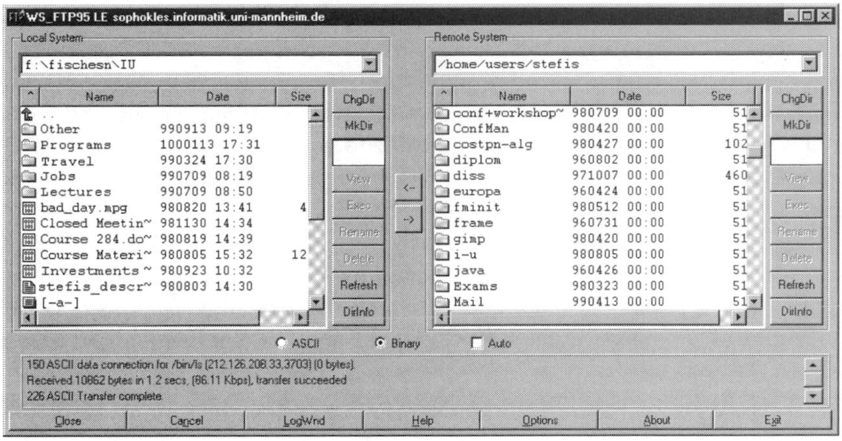

Figure 2.9: The WS-FTP-Light client.

Apart from these familiar and standardized applications, there often is the need in organizations for special, made-to-measure distributed applications for solving quite specific problems appearing in the organization. At the same time, development is constantly leaning toward offering the user a uniform and familiar interface. At this point the World Wide Web and the Web browsers used today move into the foreground. To put it simply, the idea is to give the user the results of the execution of distributed applications in the form of Web pages. As the Web service plays a decisive role, this will be explained in detail in the following sections.

2.3.4   The World Wide Web

The World Wide Web or WWW is one of the more recent Internet developments, which has contributed most to the rapid increase of the Internet to a mass communication medium.

The WWW was developed in 1989 by a physicist named Tim Berners-Lee at CERN in Geneva. The idea was to create a *hypertext system*, using which nuclear physicists could mutually inform each other of their research results efficiently. In contrast to a *linear text*, a hypertext system gives the option of jumping from one selected position to another within a document, or even of switching to a completely different document. It is therefore very easy to refer readers to further information, without actually forcing them to read all the information, in which they may not be interested or with which they may already be familiar.

The initially small system, already established by the definition of the HTTP protocol on the Internet, soon gave rise to a worldwide networked information system. Today the

WWW consists of many million documents (Web pages), and very few organizations want to be without Internet access, or "Web access," for marketing reasons.

Much work has been done in the field of layout of Web pages over the course of the past ten years. The first documents were purely text-based, but soon possibilities were created to embed graphics in Web pages, but more importantly to transfer and represent these graphics. Pioneering work was made in this respect using the "Mosaic" program, the first graphical *Web browser*. Web browsers are programs with which Web pages are displayed to users. They therefore act as clients on the Web. Mosaic was developed by Marc Andreesen, among others. On the basis of this development he later formed the Netscape company, one of the large browser providers. In the meantime, the representation possibilities for pages became ever more refined, and today there is almost nothing that cannot be achieved by a graphic designer on a Web page. In fact, Web access is regarded by many companies as so important that a large proportion of their advertising budget is invested in it.

In order to access the Web, several software components and tools are required, which will now be addressed in more detail.

2.3.5   Basic constituents of Web applications: client and server

In order to access the Web, first a *Web server* is required. The server administers the entire data material intended for publication on the Web. Part of the hard drive should be set aside to function as the file repository for the Web server. A directory tree then can be constructed according to the needs of the provider.

Other tasks include replying to client access, by delivering the desired documents according to the entitlement of the client. These access rights can be configured individually by directory in most Web servers, so parts of the service are open to all users, while others are only accessible to individuals or certain groups.

Web servers usually record all Web files accessed, so different analyses can be made using the *log files* created, from the simplest of tasks such as how many hits have been made in a certain time, or an analysis of the geographical distribution of users, right through to monitoring attempts at unauthorized access.

Finally, Web servers might start other programs, with which additional information can be obtained or generated. It is this capability that forms the basis of all distributed applications on the WWW. This will be discussed in far more detail later in the book.

There are a great number of Web server products. By far the most popular server is the Apache server. It is freely available and has a substantial share of the market worldwide. It resulted from the early NCSA server, and is characterized by a number of patches, or improvements made over time – hence also the Indian-looking name: *A PATCHY server*.

Correspondingly, Web clients are the programs with which users can access a Web provider. Web clients are generally known as Web browsers. Browsers usually provide users with the following functions:

- The user can enter the address of a document, the so-called *URL (Uniform Resource Locator),* using the keyboard. The browser then looks for the server on which the document is placed, to which it sends a document request.

- As soon as the document (or at least the first parts of it) has arrived, the browser displays it in the main window.

- The user can now click on *Hyperlinks* in the document using the mouse. These are references to other documents in the Web. In principle, every hyperlink represents another URL. After a click the browser then repeats the above process and loads the document requested.

- Almost all browsers have a number of storage functions for previously called documents or URLs, as, in all probability, users will wish to reload a document they have already seen. These functions include the list of *Favorites* or *Bookmarks*, in which users can of course enter URLs they wish to retrieve quickly. The *History* function works in a similar way. Here the browser keeps a log, in which all URLs accessed by the user are listed according to date, so that URLs not stored in the *Bookmark* list can also be accessed quickly.

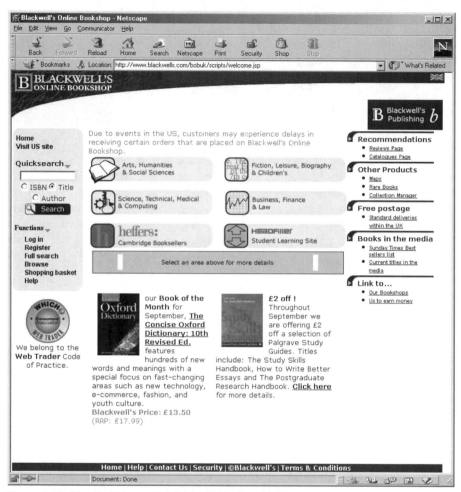

Figure 2.10: The Carl Hanser Publishing Web site with Netscape.

- The user will almost always be provided with an e-mail client, as e-mail is usually provided with Web access, in order to request further information or order something, for example.
- Finally, a number of other useful functions also are included, such as printing a Web page, an integrated page editor, with which Web pages can be adapted for one's individual needs, and built-in search functions which can find search strings on a page, or anywhere on the Web.

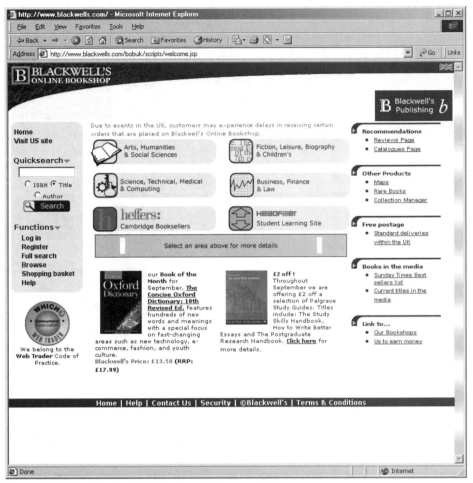

Figure 2.11: The Blackwells Web site with Internet Explorer.

The browser market is dominated by two products, Microsoft Internet Explorer and Netscape Navigator. Their user interfaces are shown in Figs 2.10, 2.11 using the Blackwells homepage as an example.

Initially, it is quite striking how similar appearance these two browsers are. This should actually be the case, even if both browser manufacturers, in constantly competing for a share of the market, are trying to introduce new, and more importantly, original formatting options not yet implemented by the other's product. If a provider uses these options, a page is no longer compatible with the respective product of the competitor.

Also the other functions, accessible using both the menu bar and the icon interface, look very similar. Overall, Navigator is the more powerful package, as it offers a number of other modules, such as for video conferences, chats and e-mail. Microsoft also offers these products, but not in this integrated form.

The communication between client and server on the WWW takes place using the HTTP protocol. As the details of the process of this protocol are not vitally important for further understanding, we will address only the most important characteristics of the protocol.

HTTP is a purely text-based protocol. This means that requests for a document are transferred by the client to the server using a "readable" command such as "get". The server responds to the request by making the document requested available to the client, together with a header giving further information. The server may sometimes respond with an error message, such as if the requested document is not available or the user does not have the rights required.

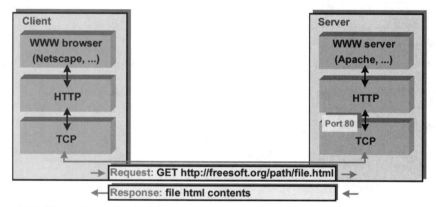

Figure 2.12: The architecture of a Web service.

This protocol process is represented graphically in Figure 2.12. HTTP uses the TCP service for the actual transfer of data between client and server. For every transfer of a Web document, a TCP connection is first established, via which HTTP protocol messages then are transferred. Actually, in the newer version of HTTP, TCP connection can last over several HTTP requests.

Until now we have not addressed how Web pages are actually written. The most important medium for this purpose is the language HTML, which because of its significance, both in general and for the fifth section of this book, is outlined separately in the following chapter. The next section addresses the general construction of Web applications, based on the client and server components outlined above.

2.3.6 Construction of Web applications

The simplest form of an application on the World Wide Web is that in which the provider places a static number of documents on a server. We call a document "static" if it is only modified from outside, by human intervention.

This simple form is the prototype of the provision of information on the Web. It is easy to see that its form is not flexible. As soon as available information has to be modified on the server, a painfully slow and cost-intensive editing process is required. For many applications, this process is simply not an option. One need only consider a provider wishing to publish current stock exchange quotations. As these change constantly, an employee would always have to be on standby to enter the current values onto the Web page.

The question is therefore whether this process of modifying documents can be automated. As you can imagine, the problem was quickly identified and resolved. Today there are a number of approaches which allow the dynamic creation of Web pages, some of which are already fairly old, and others relatively new:

- CGI scripts or programs
- Server Side Includes
- Active Server Pages
- JavaScript
- Java applets
- Java Server Pages
- Java Servlets

CGI scripts are programs placed on a Web server and arranged by the client for execution. A CGI script contains a number of variable names and their values, usually set by the client or user. The script is executed with these inputs. Most scripts generate a new Web page as the output, which then is returned to the client. CGI scripts are traditionally written in the PERL script language, but solutions in C or other compiled programming languages also are feasible and are actually used.

Active Server Pages and their forerunners, *Server Side Includes*, follow a slightly different approach. HTML pages are not generated entirely from scratch in this case. Templates tend to be used more, which when called by a client have to be modified by the server. Apart from normal HTML code, these templates also contain special commands, executed when the document is read. The result of the execution is then inserted into the HTML document instead of the command. Let us consider a simple example from Server Side Includes in order to gain a better understanding. The commands #fsize and #flastmod indicate the size of a file and the date it was last modified. To do this for the file sample.html, the following command has to be entered in an HTML document:

```
The file<tt>sample.html</tt> is
<!-- #fsize file="sample.html"--> bytes in size and
was last modified on:
<!-- #flastmod file="sample.html"-->
```

The document is processed when called by the client, and all commands are replaced by their call results, where the client's screen could look something like this:

The file sample.html is 15342 bytes in size and was last modified on Monday, 24.01.2000, 1.44pm.

These two basic approaches achieve the dynamic effect by executing a program on the server side of the application. However, Applets and JavaScript technology, in contrast, rely on changing the page contents using program execution on the client side.

Applets are small programs written in the Java programming language. They are firmly anchored in a Web document. As soon as the document is loaded by an applet-supporting browser, the applet displays its results in a pre-assigned position in the document. The execution then is done through the browser, which has to be equipped with a *Java Virtual Machine* to do so. Applets do not have full rights on a computer, unlike other programs, as this would be too large a security loophole. The only resources which can be used on the guest computer are the processor for execution, the monitor for output, and the keyboard and mouse for input. Hard drive access is strictly forbidden. However, applets can also establish network connections to the server from which they were loaded in order to retrieve further information and relay it to the client.

JavaScript can be compared to the technology of Active Server Pages. With this approach, small commands are also embedded in a Web page. Firstly, however, these have the form of function definitions in JavaScript, and, secondly, they are executed on the client side, according to the action of the client and corresponding definition of functions.

Java Server Pages and Servlets are the newest variants for dynamic creation of Web pages. They combine the ideas and advantages of earlier approaches, especially Active Server Pages, applets, and CGI programs. They will be a central theme of this book, so we will not go into detail at this point.

Furthermore, an essential basis of all these approaches is the page description language HTML. The results of the aforementioned programs, be they servlets or CGI programs, are still HTML documents, sent to the client after being generated by the Web server. And even user input, which is sent to the server, is done via documents written in HTML. Here the usual approach is to let the user make several of the inputs required for the program flow, and then send these inputs to the server using HTTP, and from here to the program for processing. As a result, the client finally receives the HTML document generated and displays it in the browser window. The user inputs are collected using formulae, in other words editable documents. HTML provides features to create forms.

HTML obviously plays an important role, for which reason a basic knowledge of HTML is very useful for understanding Web applications.

2.4 The architecture and characteristics of Internet and Web applications

Based on basic components such as Web servers and Web browsers, and the different methods of programming dynamic Web pages, different structures for Internet and Web applications can now be used. This section introduces the principal methods and addresses in particular security and scalability issues.

2.4.1 N-tier architectures

Let us consider the components which can or should constitute a distributed application on the World Wide Web or the Internet. They are the following:

- presentation interface to the user, as well as access programs to server components
- access interface to server components;
- server application logic;
- file storage (databases etc.).

In distributed applications, these four generic components are distributed on the physical nodes of the system in different ways. The term *n-tier architecture* was coined for the different variants produced. The term indicates the number of levels on which the components are distributed. In practice, 2-, 3- and 4-tier architectures are used, consisting of two, three or four levels correspondingly.

The simplest version is the 2-tier architecture in which the presentation components are placed on client computers, and all other components on one server computer Figure 2.13.

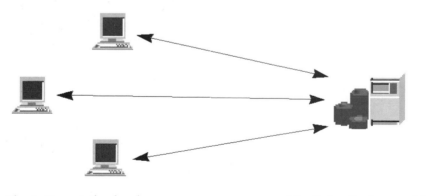

Tier 1: Presentation level   Tier 2: Applications and data

Figure 2.13: Two-tier architecture.

A typical example of this form of distributed application is TCP-based client–server applications, which access potentially available databases directly from the server process.

The 3-tier architecture ventures one step further, as shown in Figure 2.14. The important principle here is to divide the server components further, so that the actual applications are separated from data stocks and possibly non-distributed legacy applications (applications which already exist in the IT infrastructure of an organization and have to be integrated into the distributed environment). This is currently the dominating architecture, which the majority of servlet and CORBA applications follow.

Finally, 4-tier architectures have another division, in that they also partition the server interface from the applications. The resulting basic framework is shown in Fig. 2.15. The first level is formed by the graphical user interface to the client, usually represented by Web browsers. Clients only make contact with the Web server, which is only responsible for handling the HTTP protocol and for translation of queries into other protocols. For example, servlets on the Web server could be entrusted with this task. The actual application logic is located on the third level, represented by CORBA objects, for example. Only these objects can access the actual data stocks, available on the fourth level in databases or legacy applications.

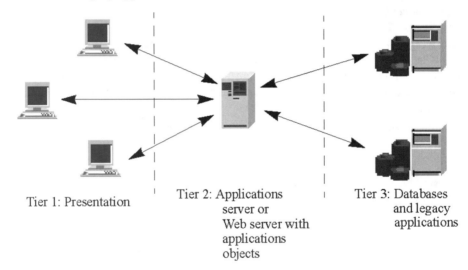

Tier 1: Presentation   Tier 2: Applications   Tier 3: Databases
                                      server or   and legacy
                                      Web server with   applications
                                      applications
                                      objects

Figure 2.14: Three-tier architecture.

The examples developed over the course of this book will essentially come from 3-tier architectures. However, we will also demonstrate how 4-tier architectures are built using servlets and CORBA objects.

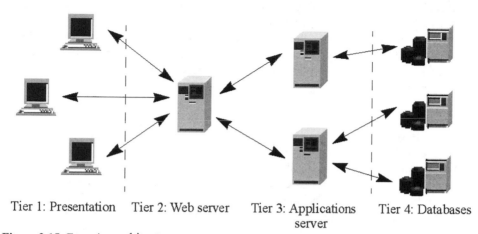

Tier 1: Presentation   Tier 2: Web server   Tier 3: Applications server   Tier 4: Databases

Figure 2.15: Four-tier architectures.

The question now arises of why server components in particular are partitioned into different logical or physical components. The following three sections answer this question by addressing the topics of *thin clients*, security and scalability.

2.4.2 Thin clients

The extensive partitioning of the architecture of a distributed system into different components with respectively different areas of responsibility basically allows the creation of simpler and therefore more controllable individual components. The result on the client side is the development of *thin clients*. A thin client is a client program which contains almost no application logic, but offers only the presentation interface to the actual application program, which may run in a distributed fashion on different servers. While the application is executed and the graphical interface is in use, application logic is partly loaded on the client computer and executed there locally. However, it is not loaded from the local hard drive, but always by a server via the network.

The most common version of a thin client nowadays is a Web browser. A Web browser has no information whatsoever on specific applications. It is only able to represent Web pages, and possibly execute applets. If a certain application is to be used, then the corresponding Web pages have to be loaded by a Web server.

The use of thin clients has many advantages:

■   The installation of program components on the client computer is unnecessary. Neither a reconfiguration of the computer nor regular updates of client software are necessary.

■   Users do not have to adjust to a new user interface for every distributed application. Access is always made using a well-known Web browser interface. This renders a substantial amount of training unnecessary.

■   Client computers can on the whole be equipped more inexpensively, as large, expensive hard drives for storing application programs are no longer necessary. Thin clients are therefore an important step in the direction of *network computing* instead of *personal computing*.

2.4.3 Security aspects

Another important reason for distribution into different areas of responsibility lies in the demands for data security. Data security here means in particular the protection of data from unauthorized access and accidental corruption or destruction. In N-tier architectures, an increase in data security is caused by the introduction of well-defined interfaces between the presentation of application results, the actual processes of applications, and access to the data stock. However, this alone is not enough. It has to be accompanied by an exact specification of who may access which interfaces and components. Figs. 2.14 and 2.15 already show how access is usually restricted: presentation components can usually only access the application server or Web server. In turn, these so-called *middle-tier components* take over access to the data stocks.

It can therefore be guaranteed that only well-defined and tested programs can access sensitive areas such as data. A client program, whether it be *thin* or not, does not have the option of direct access. Even if, for example, a client could establish a direct connection to a database (which is quite possible), it would usually lack the information required such as user number and password in order to actually open the database and read or modify data. On the contrary, middle-tier components such as servlets or CORBA objects, usually written by data suppliers themselves, or at least software houses who work together with the suppliers, have access information and use it on the client's behalf, but only in a certain way as defined by the application logic of the servlet or CORBA object.

2.4.4 Scalability

Another important point is the *scalability* of the N-tier approach. It is obviously the case that the more tiers are used, the more clients can be supported. A small example: If clients access databases directly, every client has to establish a TCP connection to this database computer. Furthermore, every client on the database computer is often given a separate process, assigned to complete the client query. However, bundling the client queries via an application server is sufficient, if the application server operates a single connection to the database computer and completes all client database queries via this connection. Valuable resources on the database computer therefore are spared.

It can generally be said that especially 3- and 4-tier architectures currently gain acceptance because of these advantages.

2.5 The sample application of the book

The sample application which will accompany us throughout the course of the book will now be introduced in order to conclude the chapter.

As applications from the *electronic commerce* area are at present considered to be the future of the Internet and World Wide Web, and also produce the most varied scope for consideration, we have selected an example from this area. Most of our readers will no doubt already have had contact with one or more online bookshops. This is one of the hottest electronic markets, to which suppliers are constantly adding something new in order to retain existing customers' interests and attract new customers. The leading addresses on the market are currently Amazon (`http://www.amazon.com` or `http://www.amazon.co.uk`), who only operate online, as well as Barnes & Noble and Waterstone's, both of whom also try to extend their traditional bookselling business to the electronic arena. But here is something of an oddity: none of these booksellers actually makes any profit from selling books online. Existence alone in this important market, and above all, beating other sectors of the market is considered so important that the current profit situation is regarded as almost negligible.

Which functions should such an online bookshop have? We will consider the appearance of one of the leading suppliers on the Internet, that of amazon.co.uk. Figure 2.16 shows a typical situation in which customers may find themselves.

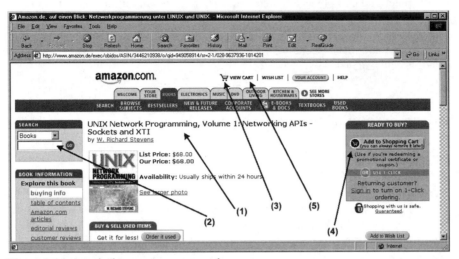

Figure 2.16: A typical page at amazon.co.uk.

The situation displayed is that the customer has just found information on a certain book
(1). So, there is first a catalog in which the user can browse. The search typically occurs
using a keyword entered in a search field (2). If you wish to order a book, it is placed in a
virtual shopping basket by clicking (4), and the contents of the shopping basket can be
displayed at any time (3). Once buyers have finally found everything they wish to buy,
they proceed via the shopping basket function to the checkout and pay. Modern e-shops
offer different methods of payment, from check to credit cards. Furthermore, Amazon sets
up an account for every customer (5), which shows the amount yet to be paid, books yet to
be delivered and books already sent.

These functions will be implemented in an exemplary manner in the book in hand. We will
develop our own electronic bookshop, which uses a similar user behavior. We wish to
familiarize our readers with the essential features of the development of such an
application. Of course, not all details which constitute such an electronic bookshop can be
addressed at this point, but at the end of the book, the reader will be able to open an
Internet bookshop, by following the example, and also to transfer these ideas to other
application areas.

Chapter 3

Hypertext markup language (HTML)

HTML is a page description language and is used mainly to create documents on the World Wide Web. We therefore could say that HTML is the Web language. Nowadays nobody need be able to write HTML code "by hand" in order to create Web pages as there are a large number of authoring tools, removing the need for a detailed knowledge of HTML. However, we should familiarize ourselves with HTML a little for the purpose of this book. There are two reasons for this: Firstly, many complex programs created from HTML code are introduced in later chapters, and a basic knowledge of HTML is required to be able to follow these programs. Secondly, XML is introduced as an extension of HTML, and a knowledge of HTML would be helpful in order to follow the progress of XML.

This chapter is structured as follows: After a short introduction to the origin and basics of HTML, the most important constituents are introduced. In conclusion, some of the most well-known tools currently used to create HTML pages are described.

3.1 Basics of HTML

HTML is related to the document description language SGML; in fact, HTML is an application of SGML. This, and the fact that there is a DTD (document type definition) for HTML, provides the whole world of SGML tools for the HTML author, such as editors and parsers.

Further document description forms, such as PostScript or ASCII, are also used on the Web. However, these cannot exploit the full strength of a hypertext system as represented by the Web. Documents not created in HTML are (with some exceptions) a cul-de-sac, since they do not contain the possibility of jumping to other documents.

The document description language HTML also enables the organization of Web pages as hypertext. Generally speaking, it enables both the description of the content of a Web page, the formatting of the content itself, and the instruction of references to other Web pages.

HTML uses *tags* to describe a Web page. A tag gives the browser, which calls up an HTML document, information about the formatting of particular text sections, states where each component is to be inserted, or establishes where a reference to another document should be introduced. A tag in HTML usually consists of the symbol <x>, where x stands for a character or combination of characters. The formatting information of this tag is valid for the entire text which follows, up to the point where the function of the tag is terminated with a further tag </x>. Some tags do not require this final tag.

Tags can be extended using parameters. An extended tag takes the form <x param1=y param2=z ...>. The value of the parameter, i.e. the text after the equal sign, can also be put in inverted commas. The meaning of such a parameter varies. Some contain more detailed formatting instructions, while others hold important information on navigation in hypertext documents.

What languages such as HTML, SGML, or LaTeX have in common is that they essentially describe the logical structure of a text or document, which allows the programs to assign a specific layout that will be applied to the document. In the case of HTML, the Web browsers usually display a document received by a Web server on the screen of a user. So a browser may decide to interpret the tag for a first-level heading as 24 point Times Roman, while another browser would display the same text in 18 point Courier and colored red.

As you can imagine, it is a nightmare for any graphic designer and marketing manager to think that the pages they have designed may be displayed differently from what was intended. For this reason, there are a range of HTML extensions which restrict the choice of the browsers as to representation. This contradicts the spirit of HTML, but the power of marketing was in this case clearly stronger than the noble aim of the original HTML inventor.

3.2 Language elements

The most important elements of the HTML language are introduced in this section. This will enable you to understand the majority of a HTML document. If you wish to see how a similar document actually appears, proceed as follows: Each Web browser has a function for displaying the *source text* of a Web page, or its HTML representation. In Internet Explorer, you can view this representation by going into the "View" menu and then clicking on "Source text." So, if a Web page has an interesting component and you do not know how it was created, consulting the HTML representation using this browser function is usually enough. In the common browsers there is an even easier version which enables the reader to view the page with a special HTML editor with more precise analytical and modification functions.

3.2.1 Structure of an HTML document

An HTML page consists of three sections: the *head*, *body* and *signature section*, where the latter is not strictly necessary. These sections are enclosed between the tags `<HTML>` and `</HTML>`. Using these tags, a browser determines that this is an HTML document which ends at a specific point. The individual sections between the tags have the following functions:

- The *head section* contains information about the document, such as its title or instruction of a path to other files referenced in this document. This section is framed with the tags `<HEAD>` and `</HEAD>`. The document title is given between the tags `<TITLE>` and `</TITLE>`; in many window-oriented browsers, the title of a document is shown in the upper window bar.
- The *body section* represents the main part of the document. All the information to be displayed by the browser is located here – that which is most interesting to the reader. The body is framed with the tags `<BODY>` and `</BODY>`. The following sections deal with the different tags which can be used in the body part of a document.
- The *signature section* is not strictly speaking an integral part of an HTML document, but it is often used to indicate who created the document. Usually the author's name is included here. However, the e-mail address and date last modified may also be displayed.

3.2.2 Text paragraphs

The simplest way to format text is to feed the required text into the computer without any tags. The browser then displays the text on the screen. But it will ignore any kind of "formatting" which may be contained in the text, such as text insertions or blank lines, rather than a blank space, between two words etc. It just strings words together, and a line break is inserted at the end of the line *of the browser* on the screen.

In order for a simple line break to be inserted, the tag `<BR>` needs to be inserted in the HTML text. Several `<BR>` in sequence lead to the corresponding quantity of empty lines.

The use of the tag `<P>` (for *paragraph*) begins a new paragraph. It is for the browser to decide how such a new paragraph should be represented, such as a simple line break, indenting the following sentence, inserting blank lines, or other formatting methods.

`<P>` can be extended and framed with a final tag. The advantage of describing paragraphs in a `<P>` container is that similar paragraphs can be influenced in their alignment. The `ALIGN` parameter is useful for this purpose: the command `<P ALIGN=CENTER>xxxx</P>` indicates that the text "xxxx" is centered in the browser window. The same effect can be achieved using the container `<CENTER>xxxx</CENTER>`.

Headings represent a special paragraph format: HTML makes different heading levels available. The uppermost level is created with the tags `<H1>` or `</H1>`, whereas `<H2>`,

<H3> and so on represent lower levels. A document can easily be divided into meaningful paragraphs using these headings. However, HTML does not number the headings; this is left to the author of the document. But this function may be available if a specific HTML editor is used.

3.2.3   Text formatting

A range of formatting features are familiar from popular word processing programs. Many of these features can also be applied in HTML. Here are some examples:

- Bold type can be obtained by putting the corresponding text in between the tags <B> and </B>.
- Similarly, italic type is indicated with the tags <I> and </I>, and underline with <U> and </U>.
- The <FONT> tag has different application options. For example, it enables the type, size, and color of characters to be determined. Corresponding parameters are used for these restrictions. The FACE parameter establishes the type to be used, e.g. Arial. SIZE specifies the size of characters, indicated in points. SIZE=12, for example, determines the size as 12 point. The parameter for the color is given with COLOR. The colors are given as RGB values. The first byte determines the red, the second the green, and the third the blue portion. A value COLOR=FF0000 specifies the color as red.

3.2.4   Lists

Lists are another important way of structuring a text. HTML makes these different lists available.

- *Unordered lists* are lists of very different items, where no specific sequence for the individual list items is given. Usually, each item on the list is introduced with the same symbol used for all the other items (a *bullet,* so an unordered list is often also called a *bullet list*). The list containing this text is unordered, and in this case the bullet is a little grey square. Generally, each symbol can be used to remove the list items. This is why the HTML tags do not prescribe how a list item has to be represented, but provide more information concerning the logical structure. An unordered list is introduced in HTML with the tag <UL>. Accordingly, the end of the list is indicated with </UL>. However, a list made up of a single item begins with the tag <LI>. No final tag is required here, because a list item is regarded as concluded, when either a new list item begins or when the list is completed.
- On the other hand, *ordered lists* allow the creation of a specific sequence. These lists are recognizable because they include numbered list items. However, HTML does not define how such numbering must be structured. Parameters which determine the

method of numbering can also be given here.

Ordered lists are introduced with the tag `<OL>` and completed with `</OL>`. Single list points are also separated here with the `<LI>` tag.

- In conclusion, *definition lists* enable lists to be described, where symbols are used to separate list items that do not consist of a single character, but of any arbitrary text. These lists are often used to explain a concept.

Such lists begin and end with the tags `<DL>` and `</DL>`. The concept to be explained in this type of list is introduced with the tag `<DT>`. Finally, the text which explains the concept begins with the tag `<DD>`.

Lists can be boxed. In this way, items on a list can be divided more accurately. In doing so, different lists can be combined together to achieve a flexible text layout.

A selection of formatting options previously introduced is given in Figure 3.1.

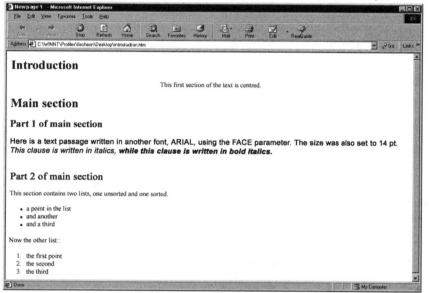

Figure 3.1: Simple formatting methods in HTML.

The source codes of this Web page are as follows:

```
<html>
<head>
<title>new page1</title>
</head>

<body>
<h1>introduction</h1>
<p align="center">this first part of the text is centered.</p>

<h1>main body</h1>
```

```
<h2>part 1 of the main body</h2>
<p><font face="Arial" size="14">here is a text section which is assigned
a different type using the FACE parameter, namely ARIAL. The size was
defined as 14 points. <I> This second sentence is italic, <B> while the
second part of the sentence is bold </B></I>.</font></p>

<h2>part 2 of the main body <h2>
<p>this part contains two lists, one unordered and one ordered.
  <li>one list item</li>
  <li>another item</li>
  <li>a third item</li>
</ul>

<p>now the other list:
<ol>
  <li>the first item</li>
  <li>the second</li>
  <li>the third</li>
</ol>
</body>
</html>
```

3.2.5   HTML links

References or *links* are actually the language feature of HTML which determines the
hypertext part of the language. References are just address entries of another Web
document, which is the URL we discussed previously. If the reader of a document chooses
such a reference, by clicking on the corresponding text, the browser is ordered to load and
show the document stored at this address. In this way, you can access all documents on the
WWW, provided this access is not limited by the rules of the information provider. In
addition to these *external* references, *internal* references can also be used. These indicate
another part of the document. If they are clicked, the browser skips to this space and shows
the content of the document in this position.

In HTML, a link is created with both tags <A> and </A>. The text (or graphic) between
these two tags represents the link on the screen. It is usually represented by a browser in a
different color and may also be underlined, for example. Now the user can click on any
word of the reference text to activate the link. The address at which the browser now
searches the new document is given using the HREF attribute. It is represented with a
URL. A typical link with environment text would appear as follows:

```
The <A HREF="http://www.cybertechnics.co.uk">Cybertechnics digital
studio</a> is based in Sheffield.
```

The browser represents the word "Cybertechnics digital studio" underlined and in a different color. If you click on the link, the homepage is loaded (as can be seen in Fig. 2.11).

The `NAME` keyword can be used as another parameter for the tag to give internal references. A tag such as `<A NAME="reference1">...</A>` marks a space known to the browser, which can be accessed by other links. Indeed, such a marked text is not particularly emphasized; it is formatted just the same way as the environment text or as other formatting instructions assign it.

The link which when clicked leads to a jump to a particular position in the document uses the HREF parameter and its exact text is `<A HREF="#reference1">...</A>`.

3.2.6 Graphics

Embedding graphics is one of the most important stylistic elements inserted into a Web page. For the most part, graphics determine the image of a page and should be embedded appropriately with care. A balance must be found between the effect of one or more pictures, and the effort involved in loading the individual pages, mostly related to the size of the graphics. If the page is accessed frequently by a large number of Internet users, graphics should be used moderately.

Graphics are embedded with the `<IMG>` container. The name of the file in which the image was stored is given with the SRC attribute. Any path can usually be given here. For example, to create a graphic in a document contained in one of the HTML files of the parent directory, the following should be used:

```
<IMG SRC="../graphic.gif">
```

Existing Web browsers support GIF and JPEG graphic formats as standard. We need not describe in detail here how these formats are defined. However, we can generally say that the GIF format is more suitable for smaller graphics, and the JPEG format for larger ones.

Controlling the position of a graphic on the page can be done using the `<P>` and `<BR>` tags, as well as using the `ALIGN` attribute. If a graphic is to be represented without being placed within text either to the right or the left, it should be enclosed by `<P>` or `<BR>` tags. However, if the text is to be copy-fitted to the graphic, the position of this text can be determined using the `ALIGN` attribute within the `<IMG>` container. `TOP`, `CENTER`, `BOTTOM`, `LEFT`, and the `RIGHT` are the most important commands available. The first three commands specify height of the graphic at which the text begins. The latter two establish whether the text is to be shifted to the left or right of the page.

Graphics can also be used as a link. In this case, the `<IMG>` instruction need only be embedded in the `<A>...</A>` environment, which refers to the document to be loaded when a link has been selected. Browsers then surround these graphics with a frame if not instructed otherwise. The new document is loaded once the link has been clicked. This option makes sense if icons are used as graphics, which clearly show what the user can expect by clicking on this symbol. Arrows, for example, are frequently used to represent references to the following, previous, or parent document. Return to the initial page of a group of documents is often symbolized by a little house (Homepage!).

Image maps are an advanced combination of graphics and links. An image map is a graphic whose surface is divided into different zones. Each zone is associated with a reference. If a user clicks on this zone, the corresponding document is loaded. In order to define such an image map, the author essentially needs a description of the zone coordinates. The coordinates are then placed in the <MAP> environment.

3.2.7 Tables

The first version of HTML did not give the option of representing numbers or other data in tabular form in Web documents. Tables were adopted after the Netscape browser started supporting tables, and became gradually more widespread. HTML tables offer many parameters, with which it is easy to format different types of tables.

Tables consist of data fields arranged in rows and columns. In HTML, table fields can contain almost anything, such as text, numbers, or graphics. A table is introduced with the tag <TABLE> and concluded with </TABLE>. A row begins with the tag <TR> and finishes with </TR>. Within a row, each table field and each single column therein can begin with the tag <TD> and end with </TD>. The content of the field has to be placed between these two tags.

In many tables, rows and columns have titles. These titles usually describe the content of the table field more precisely. For this purpose, HTML makes the tags <TH> and </TH> available. The browser usually emphasizes the content of the corresponding fields, making it easy to see the difference from the usual table fields.

In longer texts, it is often useful to assign a name and a number to tables, to be able to refer to them more easily. The tags <CAPTION> and </CAPTION> are available for this purpose. Using the attribute ALIGN, you can enter whether the table name is to appear above (ALIGN=TOP) or below (ALIGN=BOTTOM) the table.

Figure 3.2 gives an example of a table consisting of four cells, i.e. two rows and two columns, in which the different formatting options are displayed. The corresponding source text is as follows:

```
<table border="1" cellspacing="9" width="320">
  <tr>
    <td><p align="right">A simple text in field1, right-aligned.</td>
    <td>Finally, the lower right-hand field contains an image.</td>
  </tr>
  <tr>
    <td><font face="arial" size="4">Below another text in a
                     different size and type.</font></td>
    <td><p align="center"><img src="smiley.gif" width="32" height="32"
    alt="smiley.gif (978 Byte)"></td>
  </tr>
  <caption valign="bottom">Table1: example</caption>
</table>
```

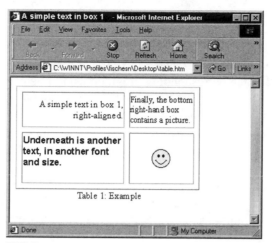

Figure 3.2: Tables in HTML.

3.2.8 Applets and scripts

Applets and scripts were briefly described in the previous chapter as features to bring interactivity and dynamics to a Web page. The corresponding tags with which these elements can be established in a page are <APPLET> and <SCRIPT>. Since these components should be only discussed on the side, the format of the <APPLET> tag will now be explained in brief.

Different parameters can be given within the tag. The most important is the parameter code which specifies in which file the program code for this applet is located. The width and height of the applet on the screen can be set using the parameters width and height. Further parameters determine, for example, the behavior of animated applets. We need not go into any further detail at this point. In order to insert an applet, whose code is given in the file example.class and which has a height and width of 300, the following entry needs to be placed in the corresponding HTML file:

```
<applet code="example.class" width=300 height=300>
</applet>
```

If the Web page containing this applet is now loaded by a user, not only is the HTML file transferred over the net, but also the file example.class. The browser shows the HTML file and also executes the code given in the applet program file within the virtual Java processor. The outputs of the applet are carried out in the document at the place determined by the position of the <APPLET> tag in the document.

3.2.9 Forms

It was explained in the previous chapter that information has to be exchanged between participating components in distributed applications. This means that with Web applications, some information is transferred from the user of the Web browser to the server which then calls the corresponding program, using this parameter transferred. *Forms* are used for the interactive input of such data in HTML. *Forms* are parts of a Web page and contain modifiable input fields of different forms.

A form in HTML is enclosed by <FORM> and </FORM> tags. It may appear at any place in the document. The elements of the form need to be defined within this environment.

The <FORM> tag can have many parameters. The most important is the ACTION parameter, with which the name of the program (CGI script, Servlet) which evaluates the form content is given. A further parameter, METHOD, allows into specify how parameters are transferred. Both the GET and POST options are available, identifying the transfer methods of the HTTP protocols. If no parameter is given, the GET method is used automatically.

For example, if a CGI script evaluation.pl and the method POST are used for evaluating a form, the <FORM> tag needs to be written as follows:

```
<FORM ACTION="/cgi-bin/evaluation.pl" METHOD=POST>
```

HTML provides the following input elements in a form for user interaction:

- text fields
- selection fields
- input fields

A text field is introduced using the tag <TEXTAREA>. It is used for the input of text which first and foremost applies to rows, but also to many columns. The appearance of the field can be influenced by the parameters ROWS and COLS, which give the number of any visible row or coloumn. A field with an 80-column width and 5 rows is defined as follows:

```
<TEXTAREA ROWS=5 COLS=80> </TEXT AREA>
```

Selection fields allow the representation of many options, from which the user can choose. The option chosen is usually represented in a specific predetermined field. If you click on this field, a menu opens and you can choose new options from it. Other representation options are lists with sliding bars.

Such a selection field is opened with the tag <SELECT> and closed with </SELECT>. The Web browser is informed that more than one choice is available using the MULTIPLE parameter. The SIZE parameter gives details of the options. The browser uses this information to supply a sufficiently large field for representation, and to avoid using sliding bars.

A single option is introduced in a selection field with the tag <OPTION>. Within the tag, the parameter VALUE is used to send the value to be transferred to the CGI script, if this option is chosen. The original text that appears in the selection field is given behind the <OPTION> tag.

Finally, the input field itself offers a wide selection of options. You can choose from single text and password fields, check boxes, radio buttons, file selection dialogs, submit and reset buttons. An input field is specified with the tag <INPUT>. The field type is given above the TYPE parameter. The name of the field is very important here because related fields are identified by it (e.g. check boxes that belong to the same selection option). It is entered via the NAME parameter, as for the other form elements. Input fields may also have a VALUE parameter, with which a default value of the field can be entered.

Figure 3.3 gives an example of a typical form with three different input fields, a button to send the form content to the corresponding program, and a button to set all form fields to the initial value. The source text for this form is as follows:

```
<h3>A simple sample form</h3>
<form method="POST" action="http://dummyserver/cgi-bin/evaluation.pl">
<p>Please enter the surname: <input type="text" name="T1" size="20"></p>
  <p>Are you<br>
  <input type="radio" value="M" checked name="R1">masculine or<br>
  <input type="radio" value="W" name="R1">feminine?</p>
  <p>Please check everything you consider interesting:<br>
  <input type="checkbox" name="C1" value="holiday">holiday<br>
  <input type="checkbox" name="C1" value="TV">television<br>
  <input type="checkbox" name="C1" value="domestic animals"></p>
  <p><input type="submit" value="send" name="B1"><input type="reset"
  value="reset"name="B2"></p>
</form>
```

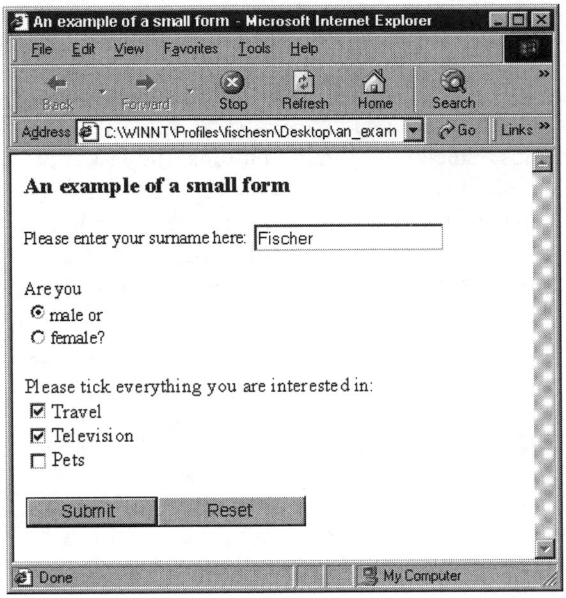

Figure 3.3: Example of a form.

Once sent, both the field names and the content are transferred to the server, or to the script/program that needs to be called. In the case of Fig. 3.3, the following information is transmitted to the server :

```
T1:    Hudson
R1:    M
C1:    Holidays, TV
```

The difference between a radio and an option field easily can be seen in this example: the C1 field can have many values, while the R1 radio field has just one value, this being M or W. The task of the script/program is to process this data. The chapters on servlets will describe in detail how this is done.

3.3 HTML tools

A basic knowledge of HTML is certainly useful for understanding the structure of Web pages. However, in the era of WYSIWYG (what you see is what you get) nobody hand-codes in HTML any longer. Furthermore, there are a large number of programs which relieve an author of most formatting work. These *HTML editors* are often available in tool packages available all over the World Wide Web. For example, image processing software should be mentioned here, as should other important programs, including site management software which carries out the management of a complete Web site from the creation of the first index page to publishing the result. However, we will only mention briefly the basic functions of HTML editors here, as this book does not focus on Web site management.

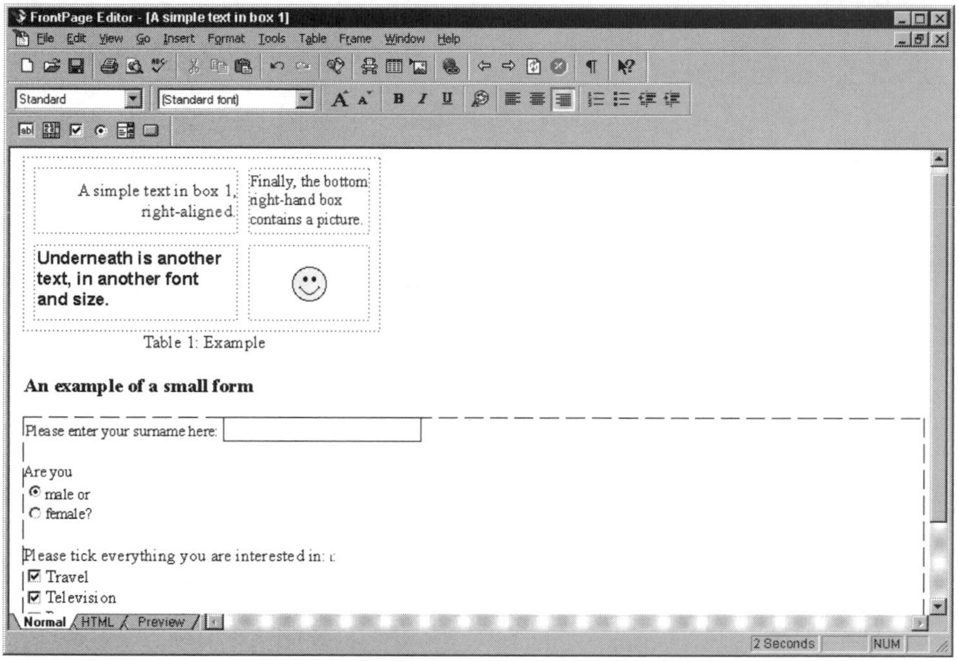

Figure 3.4: Normal view of the FrontPage editor.

In this chapter, we shall take the editor of Microsoft FrontPage 98 as an example. The editor displays the currently edited document in the main body of its window. It offers three different views: normal view, HTML view, and preview. Figure 3.4 shows the normal view.

The document easily can be edited using this view. The view follows the WYSIWYG principle, to a large extent. This means that the individual page elements are not displayed as HTML, but are displayed the way they appear in the browser. However, the author is supported with a series of help tools, such as lines for the demarcation of tables or forms. In Fig. 3.4, for example, you can see dotted lines for the four table fields. This is very helpful while working on single fields, if the table comes out in its final representation without any separation line.

Figure 3.5 shows the second view. This is an actual HTML view with all tags that contribute to the formatting of the document. Here the editor is syntax controlled, meaning that it represents keywords, tags and the content itself in different colors. In addition, the text is made more legible using insertions. An unusual feature is that, in order to find a specific place in a document, you can click on this place in the normal view. If you then turn to HTML view, the place is marked in the source text (as can be seen in the image). More simple form modifications can then be carried out directly in HTML.

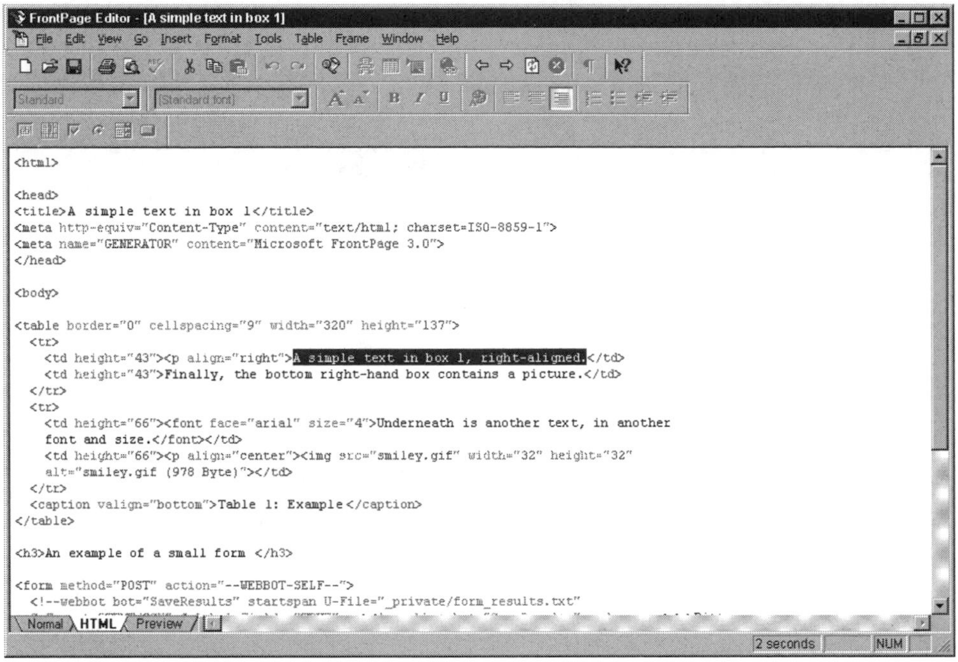

Figure 3.5: The HTML view of the FrontPage editor.

Finally, Figure 3.6 shows the third view. In this preview, the page is represented exactly as it will appear later in the browser window, i.e. without any layout assisting tools. In comparison with Fig. 3.4, you will notice that the table does not actually contain any separation line. Also, the framing of the form in the lower part of the main window has been omitted. From this view, the final result easily can be checked. The view is not suitable for editing, but there are further important functions, including, for example, the option of following possible links directly in the source text, e.g. of checking whether the reference provided actually leads to the document required. In this case, the FrontPage editor also works as a Web browser:

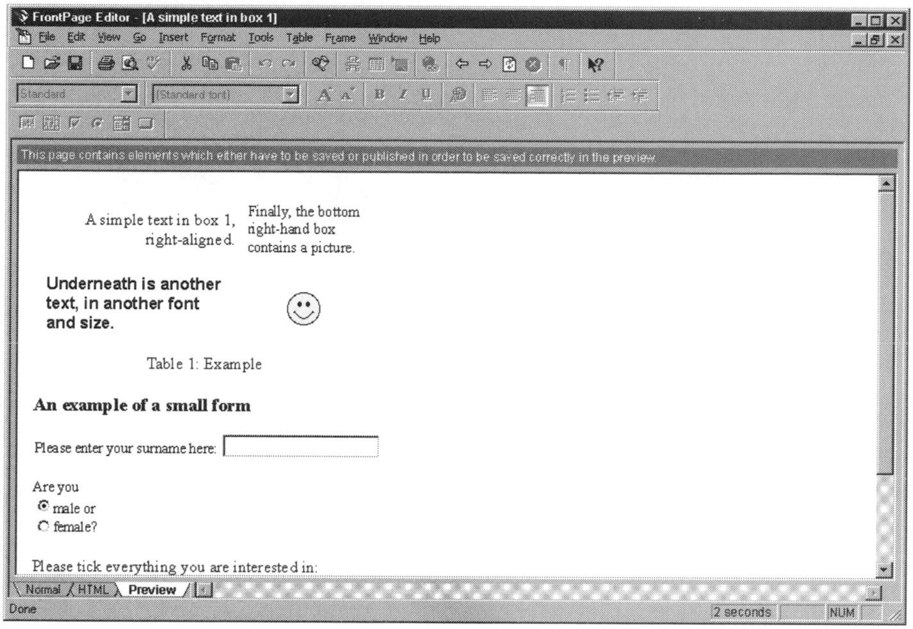

Figure 3.6: The preview of the FrontPage editor.

The upper part of the three figures shows all menu items and icon bars that help the author during the editing of a document. Together with the usual file functions such as load, save, and print, most editors have the option of inserting almost any HTML element with a mouse click, whether they are tables, forms, or images. Normal text can easily be created as in a word processing program, and the text is formatted (bold, italic, etc.) using buttons from other well-known desktop applications. Simple paragraphs can be reshaped in ordered or unordered lists. References also can be embedded in documents. The browser function is very important; it lets the author search for a reference in the file system or on the Internet. In this way, any mistakes made during the editing of the URL are reduced to a minimum.

To conclude, editors have become so advanced that no HTML author could manage without one. However, HTML is only one element that plays a role in the construction of Web pages. The Java programming language is becoming increasingly relevant for dynamic Web pages. This is the topic of the next chapter.

Chapter 4

Java as a programming language for distributed applications

All the programs in this book are written in the Java programming language. The principles and examples introduced will not be understandable without at least some basic knowledge of programming. However, we do not assume either that all our readers have already worked with Java. Therefore, the most important fundamentals of the language are introduced in this chapter in such a way that a fairly experienced Pascal, C, or C++- programmer will have no problems following the rest of the book.

The first section deals with the history of Java. Following this, the most important elements of object-oriented programming are introduced, because Java belongs to the category of object-oriented languages. Thus, even those readers who up to now have only dealt with procedural languages such as Pascal or C should manage the move on to Java. The third section deals for the first time with concrete examples, explaining how Java programs are generally constituted. Here, a series of construction elements for programs is introduced, in which the text concentrates on those elements that will be needed in further chapters. Building on this, it is shown how, once they are developed, Java objects are assembled into programs and executed. At the end of the chapter, some development environments are briefly introduced, with whose help Java programs can be implemented.

This chapter does not attempt to provide a complete introduction to the Java language. In the appendix, however, you will find some references to detailed Java books which we can recommend.

4.1 Development of Java

Nowadays, Java is certainly the programming language which is receiving the most attention worldwide, not only from programmers, but also in particular from the media. Java is regarded as "the" programming language for the World Wide Web. It is a central device to create Web pages dynamically and it is used primarily in the programming of applets and servlets. But Java is not limited to this field of use; rather, it is a fully functioning programming language, with which the same problems can be solved as with languages such as Pascal, Fortran, C, or C++.

Java was developed by Sun Microsystems, or, more precisely, by a team led by James Gosling, famous in the Internet and UNIX community notably for the development of the text editor Emac. In the original project, Java (still called *Oak* in the original version) had not been conceived as a language for the Internet, but as a device to control all types of household equipment such as toasters, microwaves, televisions, or stereos. Common languages like C or C++ were hardly suitable because of their size, but also because of the fact that programs written in them had to be compiled specifically for each processor. Hardware manufacturers have to orient themselves decisively to costs and performance and therefore often have to switch to newer control processors when new product variations are introduced. In this case the software had to be recompiled every time with great effort.

Therefore, the language developed since 1990 had the necessary features, i.e. it was relatively small, was reliable due to its strict typing concept, and in particular, it was processor independent, since Java programs are not translated but *interpreted*. This meant that only one runtime environment had to be available in a processor and each Java program that observed the language standard was immediately executable without any modification.

When the World Wide Web began its triumphal march in the first half of the 1990s, the developers soon realized that their language was exactly what they needed in order to create Web pages dynamically. If you wanted to execute any program on the user's Web browser, in order to modify the content of the pages on the client side, further requirements had to be imposed on the programming language:

- The programs had to be executable on any processor architecture because they would be stored on a server and loaded for execution by a Web browser. In principle there could be no limitations on what type of computer the browser would run on.
- The programs had to be as small as possible because they had to be transferred over relatively slow networks. The larger the programs, the longer the user would have to wait for the page to be displayed.
- The language should leave as few safety holes open as possible, because communication security plays an important role in a network environment.

Java fulfilled these conditions quite well. In 1995 Java technology was announced officially and at the same time a Web browser was provided, which could execute Java programs and represent the results on the screen. Moreover, Netscape announced it would support the Java technology also in its own browser. This led to the definitive breakthrough of the language.

Today standardization of the language lies in the hands of Sun Microsystems. Over the course of time Sun and other providers have written an extensive range of class libraries for the solution of all possible application problems. With the Java Development Kit (JDK) Sun provides the heart of Java, namely the class libraries as well as some tools for creating programs, at no cost, which is a further reason for the rapid spreading of the language. However, nowadays there are also countless commercial offers, ranging from further class libraries on integrated development environments, to applications written completely in Java.

4.2 Object-oriented programming

We have already established that Java is an object-oriented language. So what does this mean exactly? We want to have a brief look at the different approaches to solving a problem using a computer program. In the course of time, the following approaches arose:

- In *declarative programming* only the problem is described. A so-called *inference mechanism* that is provided by the respective program development environment tries to solve the problem described.
- A program is described as *event driven* when it reacts to events from outside and executes relevant actions. Typical programs that are developed using this procedure are those with graphical user environments that react to user inputs or control programs that react to external environmental conditions such as temperature variations.
- *Procedurally* described programs represent a sequential algorithm, which is executed step by step. The development of the algorithm is controlled by data that also can be modified using the algorithm.

You do not usually use one single form, but rather a combination of forms. In particular, event-driven and procedural programming are often used together.

An important extension of procedural programming is *structured* programming. The idea consists of dividing the main problem into several subproblems, and then of solving each subproblem. One advantage which arises is a substantial simplification of the individual partial algorithms (usually defined as *functions*, *procedures*, or also as *modules*), and also the maintainability of the complete program. Nowadays this option is available in all procedural languages.

Clearly, in structured programming, the algorithm or the program flow is most important. Data is modified through the execution of program steps, and procedures and functions actively access the passive data. This approach presents two important disadvantages:

- The programmer is responsible for choosing the right procedure or function for the data type that has to be processed. He or she therefore must know all possible functions and procedures.
- This approach is limited for modeling problems from the real world. Real problems or situations can be much better described as a collection of objects, which interact with each other, whether these are concrete "things" such as human beings, cars or computers, or abstract entities such as flight bookings.

Because of this weakness, object-oriented programming (OOP) became popular again at the end of the 1980s. We say "again" because the idea was not new, but, when it had originally started being considered, the powerful computers that are necessary to execute object-oriented programs were not yet available.

In OOP, the objects of real problems are the center of attention. The task of the programmer is to model these objects in the programming language used. The description of the *state of an object* as well as the detailing of the options available to a programmer for the *inquiry and for the modification of this state* are both part of the modeling process. What is interesting and new is the fact that both components are combined in one data unit, which is described as an object. The task of programmers is no longer to execute actions on data themselves by giving an algorithm, but to instruct the corresponding object to execute the corresponding action. In other words: an object, which is the model of an object belonging to the real world, usually "knows" best itself how it may change its state. It informs the programmer which methods are available and the programmer can only choose one of the methods and can no longer access the data directly in any way. Thereby, programming is greatly simplified, at least when object models for many real-world objects are available. OOP is generally much less prone to faults than other methods of programming.

To be able to describe a language as object-oriented, it needs to have the following characteristics:

- Abstraction
- Information hiding
- Encapsulation
- Inheritance
- Polymorphism

4.2.1 Abstraction

Abstraction means that only the relevant characteristics of an object are described, and details are neglected or at least concealed. For the users of an object, i.e. the programmers who want to use the object for a particular task, only the so-called *interface* of the object is interesting. The interface indicates which information is available about the object and which actions are executed on the data. For programmers, *how* a particular action is executed is completely irrelevant. They are only interested in which inputs they need to give to the object for the execution of the action and which outputs are to be expected.

At this point we have to add some information about terms in OOP: the definition of a data type (status description and actions) is described in OOP as a *class,* while the instances of a class are defined as objects. Compared with structured programming, you could equate classes with types.

4.2.2 Information hiding

The internal representation of the status of an object should not be visible to the outside, in other words, to the programmer. An example: it is irrelevant for the user of a queue object whether the queue is modeled by an array or a linked list, as long as the object behaves as a queue. The hiding of internal information is also described as *information hiding*.

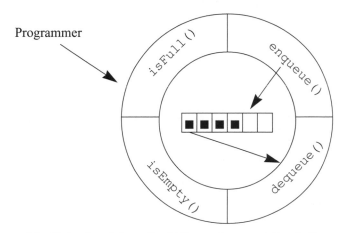

Figure 4.1: Abstraction, information hiding, and encapsulation in the example of a queue.

4.2.3 Encapsulation

All data and methods belonging to an object are integrated into one single *container*, which is described as an object. This procedure is called encapsulation.

Figure 4.1 represents these first three properties of OOP using the example of a queue. Only the outer circle of the object is visible from the outside, all the rest is hidden using information hiding. The programmer can execute the four actions `enqueue()`, `dequeue()`, `isEmpty()` (is the queue empty?), and `isFull()` (is the queue full?), which modify or check the internal representation of the queue.

4.2.4 Inheritance

One problem that arises from the encapsulation of data with its access methods is that of *redundancy*. In principle each single data type also needs its own access method even if the methods are very similar to each other in their behavior. As an example, the reader may consider a class for the modeling of a square and a rectangle, respectively. In both classes the methods for calculating the area are the same, namely by multiplying the length by the breadth. However, the method would be both programmed and stored in both classes because of the encapsulation, which is obviously a superfluous effort.

The solution in OOP consists in introducing `class` or `object hierarchies` with the help of the inheritance principle. Hierarchies consist of many tree-like ordered classes. A class placed in a superior level in the hierarchy is described as superclass, and one in a lower level as subclass. A subclass possesses all the methods and status variables (i.e. all features) of its superclass as well as possibly having its own in addition. Moreover, if necessary, it can overwrite the methods of the superclass. This is described as `overloading`.

Figure 4.2 shows a typical example of class hierarchy as it could be used in a graphics program. The aim here is the modeling of geometrical forms. The superclass is simply the class `Form`. In this example, there are two forms, namely, polygons and ellipses. Polygons can be divided further into triangles, and all the other polygons. Rectangles and parallelograms are regarded as special quadrilaterals and the square as a special rectangle. A circle is here a special type of ellipse.

The internal representation of a polygon consists of a list of corner points. A generic method for calculating the area of any polygon would consist of dividing the area into triangles and adding up their areas. This representation can be modified for special polygons, for example with a rectangle if the programmer adds both side lengths as a description of the status and then calculates the area using the product of the two sides. If a method is not overwritten in a subclass, the superclass is used to invoke the method. Therefore a method, which is the same for all classes, only needs to be written once so that redundancy is eliminated.

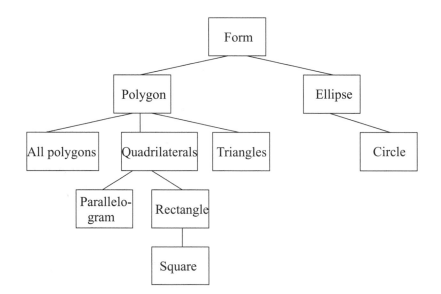

Figure 4.2: Class hierarchy of forms.

4.2.5 Polymorphism

Polymorphism describes an object's ability to behave differently, depending on the instantiation carried out by an object of a subclass, even though nothing has changed in the invocation of the corresponding methods.

As an example, we would like to consider the case in which a variable of type `Form` has been defined in a program. Polymorphism enables you to instantiate these with objects of, for example, the type rectangle or circle. If another object invokes the area method of this Form instance, in the case of instantiating with a circle, the corresponding method of the `circle` class is invoked, while in other cases the rectangle class is used. In this way very powerful programs can be written very easily, since the necessary case distinctions for different types are no longer carried out by the programmer but by the runtime environment of the programming language.

The next situation shows how Java fulfiles these five conditions for object-orientation with its main structural elements.

4.3 The most important language elements of Java

Currently, Java is a fully functioning programming language, the explanation of which can easily fill whole books. Since in many structural elements Java is similar to the C++ language, and moreover, knowledge of the complete language area is not necessary for a basic understanding, only the most important elements are introduced in this section. In order to make the following explanations a little clearer, they have each been accompanied by simple examples.

4.3.1 Classes, methods, and variables

A class definition in Java consists of variables and methods. The variables describe the internal status of an object instantiated with the class definition, while the corresponding methods enable you to initialize, query, or modify the status.

A class definition is introduced with the keyword `class`, followed by the names of the class and a curly bracket that shows the beginning of the data field definition. For a queue, it would look something like the following:

```
class queue {
```

Normally, the variables (also called *instance variables*) of the class, which describe the status, are defined next. In Java, for each variable the type is always given first, and lastly its name.

How can the status of a queue be described? A field that can hold the elements of the queue is necessary. In addition, we need a pointer both at the beginning and at the end of the queue in order to record the point for insertion or removal. Here an array that is able to store real number values, described in Java as `double`, is used:

```
double    elements[];           // elements of the queue
int       maxsize;              // maximum length of the queue
int       front, rear;         // beginning and end of the queue
```

The so-called *constructors* are responsible for the initialization of the status of an object. In this case we are dealing with special methods that can be invoked when an object is created. A constructor is assigned the same name as the class to which it belongs. It is possible to have several constructors all with the same name, and only the call parameters distinguish them. The parameters are named in round brackets after the constructor's name. As with normal methods, the actions that the constructor executes when called are described inside the curly brackets of the constructor.

We will look at two constructors for the queue. The first is a completely generic constructor without any input parameter, which sets the status of the queue to a standard value. Here the maximum size can be set as 10:

```
queue() {
    elements = new double[10];
    maxsize = 10;
    front = rear = 0;
}
```

Using the `new` operator (more about this topic in paragraph 4.3.3 on page 63) you can create a new array whose elements are of the type `double`. There are exactly 10 elements in this array. The beginning and end pointers both point to the first element of the array, which is indicated by 0 (as is the case in most languages). `Elements[0]` thus contains the first element, `elements[9]` the last element. At the beginning, however, the queue is empty, which is why `rear` also has the value 0.

The second constructor lets the caller, i.e. the creator of the object, determine what the maximal length should be. An integer parameter is used for this:

```
Queue(int queueLength) {
    elements = new double[queueLength];
    maxSize = queueLength;
    front = rear = 0;
}
```

There are also methods to query or change a status. In Java, methods are described in a similar way to constructors, with the difference that they have a different name from that of the class and they also have a return value, which is returned to the caller after invoking the method.

The queue in Fig. 4.1 has four methods: Enqueue() and dequeue() change the status of the object, by adding an element to, or removing an element from, the queue. IsEmpty() and isFull() merely check the status without making any modifications. Enqueue() uses a double value as an input, which is inserted in the queue, and answers by sending a boolean value back, i.e. either the value true or false:

```
boolean enqueue(double insertItem) {
    // exact definition remains open here
}
```

Dequeue() does not require an input value but returns the element that is in first place in the queue as an output. Therefore the return value should be a double:

```
double dequeue() {
    // detailed definition remains open
}
```

IsFull() and isEmpty() do not need an input either and provide a truth value as an output, which indicates whether the corresponding condition is fulfilled or not:

```
boolean isEmpty() {
    ...
}

boolean isFull() {
    ...
}
```

Now we just need to complete the class definition using curly brackets:

```
};
```

The next paragraph shows how the bodies of the methods which are still empty can be filled, i.e. how the real actions of a method are described.

4.3.2 Sequences, loops, and conditions

The simplest form of describing an algorithm is the sequence, in which commands are described one after the other. Such an example already has been given in the definition of queue constructors. Single commands are separated with semi-colons.

Conditions are expressed in Java, as in any common programming language, with the *if-else statement*. The general form is:

```
if (condition is true) {
   // statements for this case
} else {
   // statements for the other case
};
```

where the else-part can be dropped.

The method `isEmpty()` can be modelled very easily and elegantly using an `if`-statement, by checking whether `front` and `rear` have the same value:

```
boolean isEmpty() {
   if (front==rear)
      return true;
   else
      return false;
}
```

Some further points, which are important for the understanding of Java, leap to the eye. First, you can notice that the testing of equality is executed using the operator "==". As in C and C++, it is very important to pay attention to mistakes with the simple "=" because the most unexpected results arise. The reader will also have noticed that the curly brackets around the commands `if` and `else` are missing. Java allows this if there is just one single statement in the statements block, here the `return` statement. Finally, the `return` statement itself: using this the programmer describes which value the method sends back, in this case either `true` or `false`. Return values do not have to be constants, but they can also be determined through the value of variables.

Finally, loops, the third important element, used by every procedural programming language for the description of algorithms, are available in Java in three different flavors: *while, do-while,* and *for loops*. The three basic forms are as follows:

```
while (condition is true) {
   //statement
};

do {
   //statements
while (condition is true);
```

```
for (initial value;terminal condition;increment) {
   // statements
};
```

These forms also correspond to those used in C and C++, therefore any further explanation is not needed. However, to conclude the paragraph, a short example is given to show how loops are used.

If an element is removed from the queue using dequeue(), all the elements of the remaining queue have to move up a field so that the first element of the array always builds the head of the queue (this is just one possible implementation). This can be carried out as follows with the help of a for loop:

```
double dequeue() {
   double firstElem = elements[0];
   for (int i=0;i<rear;i++)
      elements[i] = elements[i+1];
   rear--;            // rear = rear - 1
   return firstElem;
};
```

First, the for loop sets the variable i to the value 0 and runs with this value for through the statement block the first time. What is executed, effectively, is the command

```
elements[0] = elements[1];
```

Finally, the counter variable i is incremented and the next looping occurs with the new value. This continues until the abort condition is fulfilled, in this case until i is greater than or equal to rear. Effectively, this is a shifting of all array elements one field forward.

4.3.3 Object instances and references

After having learned how classes are defined, we now ask how they are used. A class definition in an object-oriented language such as Java is comparable to a type definition in a procedural language. You use types by creating *variables* of this type.

In object-oriented languages, you can speak analogously about the creation of *instances* or *objects*. In Java, in order to identify instances, references are used, which are comparable to the pointers in C, but significantly less complicated to use.

As an illustrative example, take another look at the queue class. We will assume that we have defined the class as above and we now want to use it in a new program. First of all a reference variable is needed, which will then later identify the corresponding object. The declaration of this reference is as follows:

```
Queue    myQueue;
```

The myQueue variable can be seen as a variable that can potentially refer to an object of type queue. However, it still does not do that as we have not yet created such an object with this command. A second step is needed, which inserts the new operator in order to construct a new object:

```
myQueue = new Queue();
```

The command assigns the reference variable a new object of type Queue. Pay attention to the format of the new operator. What is given here after the keyword new is the constructor of the corresponding class. In the example above, the standard constructor is called which creates a queue of length 10. Obviously the other constructors can also be used. To create a queue of different length and to assign the reference variables the following command sequence can be used:

```
int length;
// now feed in a value for the variables
length = 5;
myQueue = new Queue(length);
```

In Java, objects are always accessed using references. When objects are handed over, for example as parameters to a method, this always happens by Call by Reference. This kind of handing over is essentially more efficient than the complete handing over of the entire object. But it also means you have to be careful not to change the value of an object inadvertently!

One thing which is not possible in Java is the use of the pointer arithmetic so popular in C. In C it is possible simply to add a value to a pointer variable and in doing so reference a new object. An example: Let us assume that an array a is given, whose individual elements are denoted by a[0], a[1], etc. The first element of the array can also be denoted using a without the index. With a pointer size of 4 bytes the next element, a[1], also can be denoted via the value a+4. With this kind of programming, efficiency can increase but the program will no longer be portable. In Java, this procedure therefore is strictly forbidden.

Simple data types, which are already predefined in Java, such as int, char, short, etc., are *not* handled as references. The command

```
int length = 0;
```

immediately creates an integer variable that has a value of 0 without having to trouble the new operator.

4.3.4 Input and output

Input and output in Java are done via streams. The most simple form of output is screen output on the console window, which is done via the `System.out` object, predefined in the IO library (see also paragraph 4.5, page 77 about libraries). This object is an instance of the `PrintStream` class which allows screen outputs. To do this, it has `print()` and `println()` as the most important methods, which analyze the expression given in brackets and display the result on the screen (with or without line feed). Both the above methods are overloaded and are able to print all simple Java data types as well as strings. Consider for example the following program section:

```
String s = new String(„The result is „!")
int n = 5;
System.out.println(s + n + „!");
```

When executing the program the following output arises:

```
The result is 5!
```

The data input from the keyboard in the console environment however, is significantly more inconvenient. The best thing to do is to read any input as a string and then continue using it. Here is a suggestion of what a method of reading a string might look like, based on the counterpart of the `System.out` object, `System.in`:

```
public static readstring() throws IOexception {
   Inputstreamreader is= new inputsreamreader(system.in);
   bufferedreader br = new bufferedreader(isr);
   string s = br.readline();
   return s;
}
```

On this basis further methods can be implemented that are able to receive simple data types as input. For example, the method for reading an integer could have the following appearance:

```
public static readInt() throws IOexception {
   string s = readstring();
   return integer.parseInt(s);
}
```

The input and output work in the same way from and to files. Different Reader, Writer and Stream objects are used here.

To output data to an ASCII file you can proceed as follows: First, a `FileOutputStream` is created, which enables general access to the file. In order to arrange the type of access in a more convenient way, this stream is only used as a basis for a `PrintWriter`, which provides the normal methods `print()` and `println()`:

```
FileOutputStream ostream = new FileOutputStream("data.txt");
PrintWriter pw = new PrintWriter(ostream);
```

```
pw.println("this is a test-text");
pw.flush(); // writes all buffered data
ostream.close()
```

The reading of an ASCII file is done analogously via both `FileInputStreams` and `BufferedInputStreams`. A `BufferedInputStream` offers the `read()` function which reads one character after the other from the file:

```
FileInputStream istream = new FileInputStream("data.txt");
BufferedInputStream bis = new BufferedInputStream(istream);
int c = bis.read();
while (c != -1) { // not equal
    System.out.print((char) c);
    c = bis.read();
}
bis.close();
```

There are further input and output options concerning, for example, the writing of binary files or input and output in window environments. However, since these options are not required here, we will not explain them.

4.3.5 Interfaces, abstraction, and inheritance

In order to build class hierarchies, Java offers the `extends` instruction. In the general notation

```
class class2 extends class1{ ...}
```

`class2` represents the subclass and `class1` the superclass. `Class1` already exists and provides a particular generic behavior that will be extended in the definition of `class2` over further methods and/or instance variables. In Java each class inherits implicitly from the `Object` class without this having to be given explicitly.

If in the example of the queue a more particular unit should be created, which offers in addition the `peek()` function to be able to look at the element at the head of the queue, then the following definition can be used:

```
class SpecialQueue extends Queue {
    double peek() { ...}
}
```

`SpecialQueue` possesses all the methods and features of `Queue`, like for example `enqueue()` and `dequeue()`, as well as the new `peek()` method.

Java only permits the so-called *single inheritance*, i.e. a class can only inherit features from one other class. In opposition to this is the concept of *multiple inheritance* which allows subclasses to inherit features from several superclasses. This is possible, for example, in C++. However, it is possible to overcome this constraint by choosing a construct that is actually used for the modeling of *abstraction*. We are dealing with the interface construct and the `implements` instruction connected to it.

An interface only describes the interface of an object, not the implementation of the individual methods. This is up to the user of the interface. Let us consider, for example, the following interface definition:

```
interface AbstractQueue {
   boolean enqueue(double d);
   double dequeue();
   boolean isFull();
   boolean isEmpty();
}
```

The designer of this interface only states which methods have to be implemented by a class that wants to behave like this interface. What the implementation itself looks like is left completely up to the user of the class. The advantage of this method is that the designer of a program can state in advance which classes and methods have to be used, but without dictating to the application developer exactly how he or she should implement the methods. In the chapters about CORBA we will show how helpful this procedure is.

The keyword `implements` is used to implement an interface. The following program extract creates a new class `OtherQueue`, which uses a different implementation of the queue than the one suggested above:

```
class OtherQueue implements AbstractQueue {
   LinkedList l;
   boolean isEmpty() {
      // check if the interlinked list owns another element
   }
   ....
}
```

To go into multiple inheritance once more: through the coupled use of `extends` and `implements` a class can inherit from a superclass and at the same time implement an interface:

```
class class1 extends class2 implements Interface3 {
   // new methods and
   //implementation of methods of the interface 3
}
```

It often happens that superclasses and subclasses as well as interfaces are written by different people. Existing classes are usually offered in Java as class libraries, and can be included into own programs using the import command.

The most important class libraries, called packages by Sun, are the *Java Foundation Classes* which are offered directly by Sun. These classes provide most of the important functionalities required every day. There are classes for simple text input and output, for the creation of graphical window environments, the treatment of strings, for mathematical functions, for distributed applications, and much more. The documentation of these libraries is usually retrievable online, so that programmers can find out quickly which class is predestined to which task and which methods are the best to use.

In order to include the input and output functions of Java and at the same time the relatively new Swing classes, which allow the programming of graphical user interfaces, you need the following commands:

```
import java.io.*; // „*" means: all classesof this hierarchy
import javax.swing.*;
```

In order to define your own package, the class definition simply has to precede the package command:

```
package MyAuxiliaryClass;

class AuxiliaryClass {
    ...
}
```

The class file `AuxiliaryClass.java` must additionally be stored in the directory `MyAuxiliaryClass`. Then `AuxiliaryClass` can be referenced, assuming the correct storing of files and importing, in two ways:

```
import MyAuxiliaryClass.*; //import all classes of the package
// Variant 1:
AuxiliaryClass hk1 = new AuxiliaryClass();
// Variant 2:
MyAuxiliaryClass.AuxiliaryClass hk2 =
      new MyAuxiliaryClass.AuxiliaryClass();
```

The second variant should primarily be used if there is the danger that classes with the same name are contained in different packages. By using the package name the class is identified uniquely.

Let us speak briefly once more about the concept of polymorphism and consider the example of geometric forms. We can assume that there is a quadrilateral class that derives from the basis class Form. Let's also assume that there is a createform() method that provides an object of type Form. How can we use polymorphism, for example to get a form, using the createform() method, that has to be stored as a quadrilateral?

C and C++ programmers already know the solution, which merely consists of what is defined as casting. With casting, a special variant, namely a superclass, is, so to speak, "put over" a more generic object. For our example, it appears as follows:

```
quadrilateral v;
v = (quadrilateral)(xxx.createForm());
```

In the later chapters on CORBA we will consider the application of casting in even more detail.

4.3.6 Information hiding: `public` and `private`

How can we distinguish in Java between publicly available and private data within a class?

For this purpose, it is possible to equip instance variables and methods with keywords. The keywords that play a role in information hiding are the following:

- `public`: a variable or a method of class A that is declared public can be read and modified or executed by any method using class A.
- `private`: a variable or a method of class A that is declared private cannot be read or written or executed by methods using class A. It is only visible within objects of type A and within all classes that are sub classes of A.
- `protected`: a variable or a method of class A that is declared protected can be read and modified or executed only within instances of class A.

Let's consider a simple example that defines a few public and private methods:

```
class A {
   private int a;
   public int b;
   private void test1() { ... }
   public void test2() { ... }
}
```

Assume that class B uses class A. In this case four different instructions that refer to the elements of A are used:

```
class B {
   public static void main( ...) {
      A ainst = new A();
      ainst.a = 5;
      ainst.b = 3;
      ainst.test1();
      ainst.test2();
   }
}
```

When compiling the classes, we will be given two error messages because B cannot access the variable `a` and the method `test1()` from A. The commands

```
ainst.a = 5;
```

and

```
ainst.test1()
```

are therefore irregular and can not be used like that.

A further use of public consists of the declaration of whole classes. Within a package only the classes indicated as public are publicly available. All other classes are used internally in the package, but are not recognized externally.

4.3.7 Exceptions

By *exceptions,* in Java or in any programming language, we refer to the announcement that a problem has arisen in a program. Such problems should be intercepted by the programmer.

The simplest procedure for handling such error conditions consists in installing instructions for the handling of errors in the program codes in the places in which errors can occur. A simple example: If a file is opened, it may happen that this file does not exist at all. The opening of a non-existing file leads to an exception that can be intercepted using an if instruction:

```
...
FileOutputStream fos = new FileOutputStream("Test.txt");
If (fos == null)
   System.out.println("file does not exists");
```

This is indeed a practical thing, because the programmer immediately sees which errors are intercepted. On the other hand, the program is "dirty" due to error treatment routines, so that particularly in cases when many errors can arise and have to be handled accordingly, the actual aim of the program is not immediately obvious any more.

The alternative is to describe the error treatment routines by concentrating them in one place. This is exactly what happens in Java in *exception handling.* The general procedure is as follows: When a piece of code can produce an error, it should be included in a `try` block. At the end of such a block, you can find one or more `catch` blocks that handle any possible exceptions. Each `catch` block is responsible for the handling of a particular type of exception. In addition, it is possible to give instructions within a `finally` block that should be executed in any case, i.e. independently of the type of exception that has arisen:

```
try {
   ...
   // now here fault-prone codes
}
catch (Exception e) {
   ...
}
finally {
   ...
}
```

The basis class for exceptions in Java is `exception`. However, there is an entire hierarchy of possible exceptions for which further classes exist. Therefore, it is also possible to use many `catch` blocks that handle different classes of exceptions.

A method cannot always handle an exception by itself. In these cases, the method needs to indicate that the exception must be handled by the calling method. This happens in the `throws` instruction which has to be written in the head of such a method. Let's assume that a method `parse` cannot treat an exception `NullPointerException`. In this case, the method must be defined as follows:

```
void parse() throws NullPointerException {
    ...
}
```

Finally, a method can generate its own exception and throw it to the calling method. The `throw` instruction is used for this purpose:

```
// within parse
throw new NullPointerException();
// has to be handled by the calling method
```

Practically, this means that when `parse` is called by another method, this call needs to be encapsulated in a `try` block:

```
void other method() {
    ...
    try {
        ...
        o.parse();
        ...
    }
    catch (NullpointerException n) {
        ...
    }
}
```

There is much more to be explained about exceptions, but for a good understanding of the examples in this book, the information introduced here should be sufficient.

4.3.8 Concurrency using threads

In many programs, it is necessary or at least sensible to execute different instructions at the same time. An example is network applications that also have a graphical user interface. The client should be able both to read and to process messages from the net, and also to receive user inputs.

The standard solution for such problems in most sequential programming languages consists of processing all functions to be executed in a large loop (almost) simultaneously. In a normal case this is probably the quickest solution but it also leads easily to chaos because the individual functions can not be clearly separated from each other anymore.

As a better solution, you can use concurrent programming, in which many so-called *threads of control* (or just *threads*) run within a single process. Threads actually represent what is usually associated with the execution of a program, namely the running of the program with the simultaneous execution of the corresponding commands.

Threads often also are described as lightweight processes because they do not require the entire effort of managing a complete process. Unlike processes, threads do not have their own virtual memory area and this considerably reduces the administrative effort. As a result, many threads can work within a process in the same memory. This makes the communication between the different parts of a program considerably easier but can also lead to problems if the programmer does not work carefully. In particular, the simultaneous access of many threads in the same memory should be avoided.

Fig. 4.3 shows the difference between conventional processes and threads. The diagram explains that the two models only differ from each in the number of threads. In the old process model there is a virtual memory area in which exactly one thread works. In the new model processes can have many threads that work simultaneously on the data of the process.

A word should be said about the concept of "simultaneity": real simultaneity can only be achieved if several processors are available and each processes a thread. If a program runs with several threads on one single processor, the multitasking of the processor or that of the operating system is used to give the impression of simultaneity. In this model each thread is assigned the processor for a certain period of time, during which it can execute its actions. When this time is up, it is the turn of the next thread. Therefore, only one command is really executed "simultaneously."

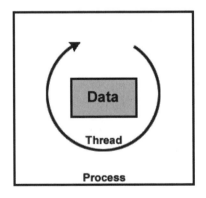
Usual Model

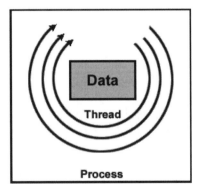
Lightweight: threads

Figure 4.3: Processes and threads.

The thread implementation of the example cited above is represented in Fig. 4.4. One thread is responsible for querying the user interface, the other for the management of the network interface. Both work on the internal data of the process so that a *synchronization need* occurs here in order to avoid a simultaneous data access of both threads.

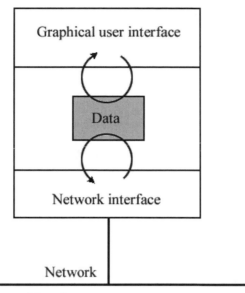

Figure 4.4: Example of the use of threads.

The use of threads in Java is relatively easy. In the *Java foundation classes* there is a thread class, from which a new class, which we would like to be executed as a thread, can inherit. Two classes can be defined for the example above:

```
class GUIChecker extends thread {
    ...
}
```

and

```
class NetChecker extends thread {
    ...
}
```

Everything that the thread has to execute has to be packed into the run() method. For the net checker this method could, for example, appear as follows (without Java codes, programmed only as comments):

```
public void run() {
    for (;;) {                    // endless loop
        // check if message has arrived
        // if so, write message in a buffer memory
    }
}
```

At this point, in order to write the complete client, you have simply to create an instance of the `NetChecker` or of the `GUIChecker`:

```
class SampleClient {
   NetChecker  nc;
   GUIChecker  gc;

   public SampleClient() {
      nc = new NetChecker();
      gc = new GUIChecker();
   }
   ...
}
```

To execute the thread you have to use the start() method, which in turn calls the `run()` method:

```
// add SampleClient() to the constructor
nc.start();
gc.start();
```

The thread is completed when the `run()` method ends.

If you look carefully, you will notice that it is sometimes impossible to implement a class as a thread, namely when this class already inherits from another class. We have to remember that Java does not allow multiple inheritance. In the previous paragraph the use of an interface was suggested as a possible solution to this problem. And indeed in the foundation classes there is such an interface, `Runnable`, which permits the execution of a class as a thread, if this class implements particular methods.

If, for example, the `GUIChecker` class has to be implemented as `Runnable`, it should be defined as follows:

```
class GUIChecker extends otherclass
implements Runnable {
   ...
};
```

The method that has to implement `GUIChecker` is the `run()` method, as in the `thread` class. The method looks the same as in the previous case:

```
public void run () {
   // work steps of the thread
}
```

Now, in order to also be able to execute the `GUIChecker` class simultaneously as a thread, you have to explicitly create a thread, to which an instance of `GUIChecker` is assigned for execution. This happens in the following way:

```
class SampleClient {
   Thread t;
   GUIChecker gc;

   public GUICHecker() {
      gc = new GUIChecker();
      t = new Thread(gc);
      t.start();
   }
}
```

Also, in this version of the use of threads the invocation of `start()` of the thread leads to the execution of the previously defined `run()` method.

We have already said that the simultaneous access of two threads to one and the same variable can lead to problems. In particular, this kind of access can make the value of the variable change incorrectly. This is primarily due to the characteristics of multitasking, i.e. the tendency to interrupt threads in unforeseeable places (without going into too much detail here).

How can this problem be solved in Java, i.e. how can we prevent two threads from simultaneously accessing the same data?

For this purpose Java makes the `synchronized` construct available. It is possible to declare a method as synchronized. As a result, this method can execute only one thread at the same time. Consequently, at a time when a thread executes a method declared as synchronized, no other thread can execute any other method which is also declared as synchronized. Thereby the programmer of a data structure that can be used by several threads can establish which methods are critical and should only be used by single threads.

Let us take another look at the example in Fig. 4.4 and assume that both threads `gc` and `nc` already have been created. Both threads want to access a common data buffer, in which `nc` writes the data from the net. `gc` reads the data in order to put them at the disposal of the user by means of a GUI (Graphical User Interface). This buffer could be described, for example, as follows:

```
class Buffer {
   private char[] data;

   public synchronized char readChar() {
      // read a character from the buffer
   }

   public synchronized writeChar(char c) {
      // write c in the buffer
   }
   ...
}
```

Obviously here we are dealing with the need for synchronization, since both threads want to access the buffer. Both methods that work with the private data field are declared synchronized. If one of the threads wants to call a method (e.g. nc wants to call the method Buffer.writeChar(), then the virtual machine first checks whether another thread is using one of the methods. If not, the thread can begin immediately with the execution. But if this is the case, then the thread has to wait until the other thread informs it that it has finished its execution of the method. All this happens automatically and in the background so that the programmer of concurrent applications does not have to deal with this.

4.4 Creation and execution of Java programs

We should now be in the position both to be able in principle to write classes ourselves and to create class hierarchies and use existing classes. But what does a complete Java program actually look like and how is it executed?

A Java program is just a collection of different objects that are executed together and carry out a particular task. One of these objects has a certain characteristic: it contains a method called main(). This is the "main program," i.e. the program begins its execution in this method.

In Java each individual class is usually stored in its own file. In the Java development environments available today (more about this in Section 4.5 on page 77) all the classes required are automatically found and translated during the conversion and execution of a program, if this has not yet been done.

We would like to consider, as an example, an application that uses a queue object to simulate certain processes. For this purpose two objects should be used, namely one object of type queue and another object that represents the application, here called QueueApp. The programmer creates two files, called Queue.java and QueueApp.java respectively, both being situated in the same directory for reasons of simplicity. The definition of queue has already been discussed above. QueueApp appears, for example, as follows:

```
public class QueueApp {
    public static void main(String[] args)) {
        Queue myQueue = new Queue(15);
        myQueue.enqueue(3.5);
        myQueue.enqueue(7.2);
        System.out.println("Dequeued value: " + myQueue.dequeue();
    }
}
```

First the program creates a new queue of length 15, then inserts two values and finally removes the first value in order to show it on the screen.

4.5 Java development environments

In order to be able develop Java programs you need at least a minimal development environment. Such an environment must contain at least three components:

- a *text editor* with which Java programs can be written. Instead of a special Java editor you can also use a "normal" editor such as Notepad in Windows or Emacs in UNIX;
- a *Java compiler* that checks the correctness of the Java program and translates the Java source code into a more compact representation, the so-called byte code. Byte code is still completely machine independent and can be executed in all computers that have a virtual Java machine;
- a *Java interpreter* or a virtual Java machine that can execute the generated byte code, and therefore the Java program, on a computer.

Nowadays there are a range of development environments; here the most important and most common are briefly mentioned or described.

4.5.1 Sun Microsystems Java Development Kit

The Java Development Kit or *JDK* from Sun forms the most important basis of all the Java developments. Sun, as the inventor of Java, also drives forward the language development, by introducing new versions of the JDK from time to time. At the moment we are up to Version 1.3 which is also called *Java 2*. Initially, there was only one JDK version, but in the meantime Sun has launched packages for different markets. In addition to the Standard edition, there are also a Micro Edition and an Enterprise edition.

The JDK consists of a range of tools which offer very helpful support for program development, the very extensive and already repeatedly mentioned class library *Java Foundation Classes*, and a virtual Java machine (*JRE, Java Runtime Environment*) which is used, for example, by Web browsers or other Java development environments.

However, the JDK is not an integrated development environment (*IDE*). It is necessary to start each tool separately from a DOS or UNIX command shell instead of being made available in a graphical menu-controlled user interface. This makes working with the simple JDK relatively difficult, but on the other hand it offers a very good basis for further developments.

Because of its significance for Java, our readers should install the JDK in any case in order to be able to follow the examples in the book. In the following, a brief explanation of installation and use is given.

The JDK is available on Sun Web pages under `http://java.sun.com/` (or indirectly via the Web page of this book) and can be downloaded after registration for the respective operating system in a compressed form. Attention: the file is relatively large, so it can take a while for it to be downloaded by modem or by ISDN.

The installation process itself is very simple. In Windows, for example, the file has to be executed after loading and saving to disk, simply by double-clicking on the file name. All the rest happens more or less automatically.

Let's assume that a developer has written a class `queue` and a class `queueApp` which contain the queue itself and the application of the class respectively. Correspondingly, both classes are stored in the files `Queue.java` and `QueueApp.java` in the directory `c:\java\examples\queue`. The next stage consists of converting the classes into byte code. To do this you have to open a DOS window (in Windows) or a terminal in UNIX and perform a directory change into the directory of the source files.

The corresponding tool for conversion is called javac. Figure 4.5 shows its invocation and effect. At first, only the two source files are in the directory. After the invocation of > `javac *.java` it contains a further two .`class` files which contain the byte code of the two classes.

```
MS-DOS                                                                    _ □ ✕
06.03.00   09:25           <DIR>          .
06.03.00   09:25           <DIR>          ..
06.03.00   09:27                       18  Queue.java
06.03.00   09:28                       21  QueueApp.java
                 4 File(s)              39  bytes
                                 246.480.896  bytes free

C:\java\examples\queue>javac *.java

C:\java\examples\queue>dir
 Volume in drive C has no label.
 Volume Serial Number is 3028-16EE

 Directory of C:\java\examples\queue

06.03.00   09:25           <DIR>          .
06.03.00   09:25           <DIR>          ..
06.03.00   09:27                       18  Queue.java
06.03.00   09:28                       21  QueueApp.java
06.03.00   09:29                      184  Queue.class
06.03.00   09:29                      190  QueueApp.class
                 6 File(s)             413  bytes
                                 246.415.360  bytes free

C:\java\examples\queue>_
```

Figure 4.5: Invocation of the Java byte code compiler.

In order to start the application, you have to enter the line

```
c:\java\example\queue> java QueueApp
```

assuming that the `QueueApp` class contains the `main()` function of the program.

An important notice: a very important environment variable for all the Java programs is called `classpath`. The variable informs the compiler and interpreter where the already existing Java classes are. In the installation of a development environment this variable is always set to a standard value, which correctly references the corresponding classes of the package. But if you have to write and use your own classes, then the path of these classes must be added to the value of the environment variables. The `set` instruction is used for this in DOS and Windows:

```
set CLASSPATH= existing_path;path_to the own _class ess
```

The command should be found in the `autoexec.bat` file (or under the different UNIX variants in the corresponding configuration file of the shell used). A correct modification (if necessary) is extremely important to guarantee the correct functioning of the Java program.

4.5.2 Netbeans or Forté for Java Community Edition (Sun)

NetBeans (`http://www.netbeans.com`) is, or was, one of the first companies to offer a graphical Java development environment written completely in Java. Netbeans is available for free on the Web page of the company, although recently bought up by Sun. Sun not only took over the company, but also the product, and changed its name to Forté for Java Community Edition. Forté is still available for free and can be obtained on Sun's aforementioned Web page. Compared with Netbeans, Sun has meanwhile carried out some modifications on the product.

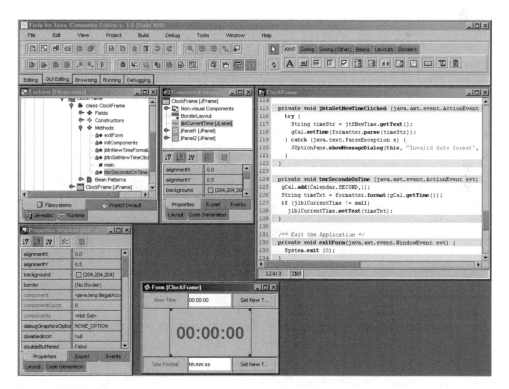

Figure 4.6: Forté for Java.

The advantage of writing a Java development environment in Java itself is obvious, if you consider that the Java code runs in all platforms without any reconversion. The developers of NetBeans only have to maintain one version (so not one for Windows, one for Linux, one for Solaris, etc.) and the users buy (or load) the package just once and can install it in any platform. The installation effort itself is strictly limited, because only some (or, rather, numerous) Java files have to be copied into the computer.

Netbeans or Forté contains all the fundamental components that can also be found in commercial products. In particular, these are an editor with a colored identification of the source code, a debugger, a tool for drawing up dialogs, menus, and windows (*Form-Editor*) and finally also a series of class templates, i.e. code patterns that can be used for your own creations. Figure 4.6 shows a screenshot in which you can see the most important components, with the main window on the upper edge of the screen, the class browser on the middle left, the graphic form editor below, and the syntax-controlled text editor on the middle right-hand side. In the right-hand side of the main window you can see an important option to simplify the graphic development of user interfaces. With the menu placed there for all possible types of window elements such as menus, dialogs, lists, buttons, etc., new components can be inserted very easily in the existing forms, like that shown on the lower margin. Parallel to this, the code, which should be executed in a form by pressing the buttons, is entered in the syntax-controlled editor. Here the ice-blue background of the code which is not to be changed is very practical, clearly showing the designer which part should not be modified, if you do not want to affect the functioning of the program.

4.5.3 Further IDEs

Nowadays many traditional manufacturers of development tools also of course offer IDEs for Java. Many manufacturers go a similar way to Sun, providing simple versions that can be downloaded free from the Internet, while the more professional tools can only be installed if you pay a license fee. These exclusive versions are typically called *Enterprise Editions* because they usually offer all the necessary features and components for the easiest development of distributed applications. However, all IDEs contain the components already described, such as syntax-controlled editors, form editors, etc. In the following, some of these IDEs are briefly introduced:

■ Forté Enterprise Edition (Sun)
   The Enterprise Edition by Forté is offered to the public by its own company Forté
   (`http://www.forte.com`).
■ Symantec Visual Café (Symantec) (`http://www.symantec.com`)
   The company Symantec was one of the first companies to offer graphical IDEs for Java. Therefore the name Visual Café has had a good ring to it for a long time among Java developers. Symantec has also followed the trend of offering versions of different powers with the *Standard*, the *Professional* and the *Database Edition*. The last offers the complete functionality necessary for the development of 3- and 4-tier architectures.

▨ Visual J++ (Microsoft)

Even Microsoft, with Visual Studio or the "subroutine" Visual J++, has an IDE for Java. If you know Microsoft then you know that the company does not necessarily always support the standards, as they believe they can be more successful with their own developments. As a result, unfortunately, not all Java-2 compatible applications can run under J++ and vice versa. In particular, in the field of distributed programming it can be relatively difficult to adapt a program to any other standard. Instead of using the JDK *Java Foundation Classes* Microsoft adopts the so-called *Windows Foundation Classes*. On the other hand, Visual J++ is relatively mature and supports program development well. The simple creation of installation procedures makes the distribution of developed programs and their installation on the user computer almost child's play.

▨ JBuilder (Borland/Inprise) (`http://www.inprise.com`)

Borland or Inprise is also one of the most important players in the market of development tools. JBuilder has also been available for a short time for free and is called *JBuilder Foundation Edition*. JBuilder supports the Java-2 Standard 100 per cent and for this reason it is the only one that can be considered recommendable.

In this paragraph only the fundamental features of Java have been analyzed in detail. The possibilities for the creation of professionally distributed programs are described in full in the remaining chapters. Accordingly, the chapters also analyze the respective support through the development environments, where we limit ourselves to the use of JDK and *Forté for Java Community Edition*.

Chapter 5

JDBC – database access with Java

In this chapter we will address databases and the *Java Database Connectivity* (JDBC) interface. Although these topics do not fall directly into the Internet context of this book, we believe that there is hardly any Internet application which operates without a database. Online bookshops, travel timetables, or pages with the latest share prices are examples of database-supported applications. Servlets which generate Internet pages dynamically based on information from a database create a direct link to the central information system for the customer. This technique is also an enormous relief for the site operator since the frequent update of static pages with new information is omitted.

The chapter initially addresses the relational data model and the technology of the database server, which represents an important component within a database-supported distributed application. Databases are stored and queries processed on such servers. SQL is a powerful language available for processing this task – this is the topic of the second section. An understanding of SQL will help us both to familiarize ourselves with database technology and to recognize the possibilities of distributed applications when accessing external databases. The chapter concludes with a description of JDBC, which allows SQL access to databases from Java programs.

5.1 Features of database servers

Commercial database servers are very powerful software packages which relieve the developer of many complex tasks:

■   Efficient reading and saving of data
Saving information in files is still a commonly used method. However, databases enable a much quicker and more reliable access, and are usually easier to handle. With the wide availability of products such as Microsoft Access or MySQL, databases are also used increasingly for smaller software projects.

■   Data consistency checks
    Saved data should reflect reality, and for this reason can only assume certain values.
    The developer of a database-supported stockkeeping program can, for example,
    define an integrity constraint which reports an error as soon as a stock level falls
    below zero. The application is automatically informed by the database system, and
    the action which caused the error (a large purchase order in this case) is canceled.

■   Multi-user capability
    The data of several participants needs to be able to be read and written in distributed
    systems. The extremely difficult task of synchronizing access is undertaken by the
    databases. Every user is fully protected from the actions of other participants.
    However, *database management* software is able to process different queries at once,
    and thereby also support multi-processor architectures, and partly even clusters. It
    should be noted at this point that multi-user capability is fully transparent to
    application developers. The functionality of the program is not affected when other
    users work on the database.

■   Transactions
    A transaction is a fundamental construct in the database context, which among other
    things ensures that a group of operations is handled *atomically*. This characteristic
    means that either all or none of the operations are executed. The classic example is a
    transfer. Debiting one account and crediting another may only be executed together.

■   Fault tolerance
    In case of a system failure or power cut, a database system has mechanisms which
    restore damaged data to the hard drive and undo interrupted write operations. This is
    a decisive advantage over saving information in files. If a traditional file-based
    application should crash during the write process, the entire file often will be
    damaged. This is something that most users will have already experienced with word
    processing software.

It is therefore obvious when application developers revert back to this wide range of
functionality. The two following sections outline how files are read and can be saved using
SQL, and how databases are accessed by a Java program using JDBC.

5.2 The relational data model

Relational databases work with tables. Every row represents a data set. If, for example, a
project description table is involved, then there will be a row for every project. For
example, the project table in Figure 5.1 contains information on two projects. For every
characteristic of a project, a column is created and the data type of the information
specified. If the project budget and project name are to be saved, the columns are selected
as character strings and floating point numbers. In addition, every project is assigned a
specific identification number. This number is also known as the key.

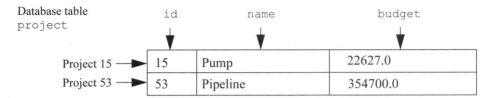

Figure 5.1: The basic data structure of relational databases is tables. The table displayed here contains the project data of a company: an identification number, the name, and the budget. The individual projects are placed in the rows.

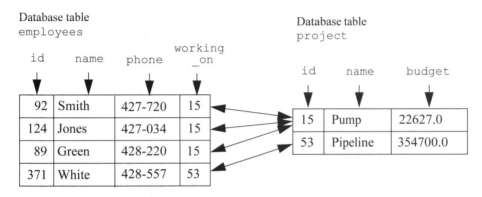

Figure 5.2: The `employees` and `project` tables are connected via the foreign key attribute `works_on`.

In order to make connections (or relations in database jargon) between tables, a table can reference the primary key of another table. This reference is also known as the foreign key. Figure 5.2 shows an example in which another table, `employees`, is defined, which stores the names and telephone numbers of staff. In order to show which employees are working on which project, the key `working_on` is defined. As several people can work on one project, yet in this company every employee is assigned only one project, the relation between `employee` and `project` is called an n:1 relation. This also explains why the foreign key is defined in the employee table and points to the primary key of the project. As Fig. 5.2 shows, the value 15 appears in the foreign key column three times. This means that three employees are working on the "pump" project.

There would be a lot more to add to this topic, but you now have sufficient knowledge to implement the sample application.

5.3 The SQL query language

Structured Query Language (SQL) is an international standard, supported by practically all database systems. Quite a number of books have been written which concentrate on this topic alone. We will focus on the most important commands here for creating tables, as well as inserting, deleting, modifying, and reading data sets.

The SQL instruction `create table` creates the `project` table in the database. The names and types of columns are indicated in brackets. Appendix A on page 416 contains a table listing the most important SQL data types with their equivalent Java types.

```
create table project (id int primary key, name char(20), budget float)
```

There are several methods of saving data sets in a table. The simplest is using the `insert` command. A value has to be assigned to every column when this is used. Of course, data types have to be considered, meaning that the format of the value declaration has to be compatible with the corresponding type of a column. Note that the character string is enclosed in inverted commas.

```
insert into project values(53, "Pipeline", 354700.00)
```

The SQL instructions are entered using an *SQL client*, usually supplied with the database software. Figure 5.3 and 5.4 show the *SQL Query Analyzer* of *Microsoft SQL Server 7.0*, and the command line tool for accessing MySQL. Certain data from the `project` table is displayed here using the `select` command. The `where` clause, in this case `budget >= 10000`, indicates the condition a row has to satisfy to be included in the result. The *projection* indicates which columns are displayed. The asterisk (*) is an abbreviation for all columns in the table. This selection therefore displays all attributes of the project with a budget of 10,000 or more.

```
select * from project where budget >= 10000
```

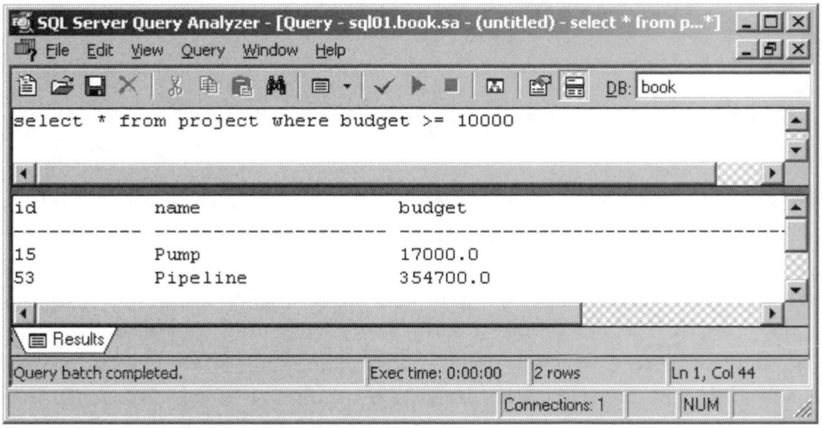

Figure 5.3: Access to the Microsoft SQL Server 7.0. The client program sends the SQL query to the server and presents the table of results.

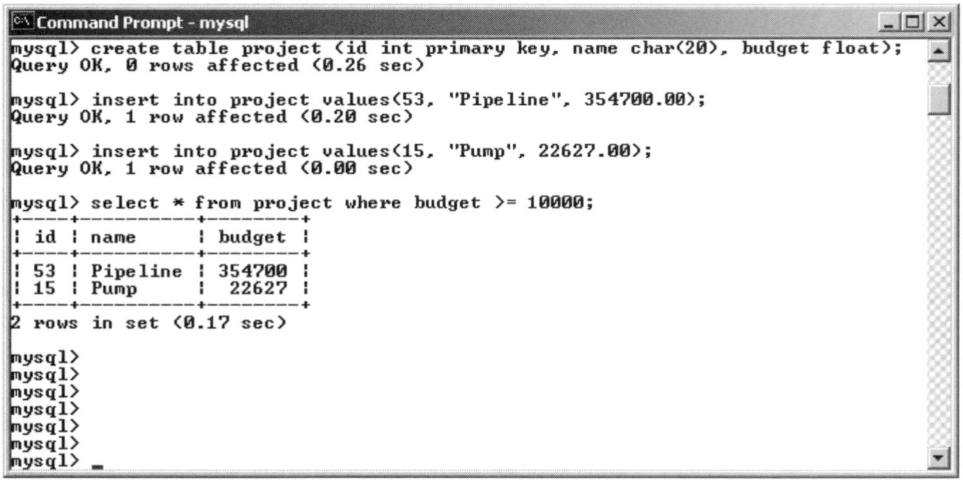

Figure 5.4: Access to MySQL with the command line tool. This example shows the commands for creating the table, inserting the data and the select query as shown in Fig. 5.3.

As well as queries which only refer to one table, there is also the option of using defined relations between tables. If we base the table structure on that of Fig. 5.2, it may be of interest to distribute the names and telephone numbers of all employees working on the "pump" project. This is done using a join query consisting of the information of both tables:

```
select
   employee.name, employee.phone
from
   employee, project
where
   employee.working_on = project.id and
   project.name = 'Pump'
```

Both tables are now listed in the From clause of the query. In order to guarantee that the foreign key reference is retained, the equality of foreign and primary keys is examined with employee.working_on = project.id in the where clause of the join. In the result table, all tuples not referring to the pump project are now filtered out.

A where clause is also used when deleting and modifying data sets in order to indicate the data sets concerned. Data sets are deleted using the delete command. In order to delete project 15, the following SQL instruction has to be entered:

```
delete from project where id = 15
```

The values of individual columns can be modified using update. The following command is used in all projects with a budget under 25,000 to increase the budget amount by 10 percent:

```
update project set budget = budget * 1.1 where budget < 25000
```

As previously mentioned, SQL offers many more options, ranging from the combination of several tables in a *join query* to the complex *Online Analytical Processing* query *(OLAP)* for the analysis of customer behavior. However, the SQL commands reviewed correspond to the functionality required for our example, as well as most of the applications in *Online Transaction Processing (OLTP)*. The following example shows that not only can SQL queries be started by a special tool such as the *Query Analyzer*, but also by every Java program and every servlet.

5.4 Database access via JDBC

The *Java Database Connectivity* interface enables any Java program to send SQL queries to any database, and receive back result tables with the desired data. As with the basic idea of Java in writing a program for all hardware platforms, JDBC enables the development of programs which function with nearly all database products. Apart from the general popularity of Java, this is surely the main reason for the widespread acceptance of JDBC.

In order to guarantee the general database access, JDBC defines a certain core functionality supported by all databases. This common denominator can be implemented by JDBC. This naturally implies that different product characteristics and manufacturer-specific optimizations have to be ignored in the JDBC standard.

One prerequisite for the use of JDBC is the availability of a *JDBC driver* for the database used. For example, one such driver is already available for MySQL in the `org.gjt.mm.mysql.Driver` class. This JDBC driver translates the JDBC queries of the Java database client into the respective supplier-specific calls. The simplest version on the Windows platform is the *Open Database Connectivity* interface *(ODBC)*. ODBC also enables different databases to function via a uniform interface. JDBC and ODBC are both based on the same idea. Using the JDBC–ODBC bridge, it therefore is possible to access an ODBC datasource via JDBC.

Figure 5.5 gives a summary of the different options of accessing a database. The client software supplied by the manufacturer usually communicates with the server via a proprietary interface. The drivers translate JDBC or ODBC commands into the respective database-specific calls. As shown in the previous section, the user can also access the database directly using an SQL tool, as well as the JDBC and ODBC programming interfaces. This version is represented in the top box in Fig. 5.5. Queries can simply be typed in an SQL tool. A Java program can run queries against the database via either a JDBC driver or the JDBC–ODBC bridge. The software supplied by the database manufacturer is summarized in the gray box.

One disadvantage of the ODBC solution is that for every computer on which a Java database application is to run, the ODBC connection has to be configured. This contradicts the Java principle *"write once, run anywhere."* However, this does not pose a problem in our case, as will be demonstrated in later chapters, as database access is made centrally by the servlets. The ODBC connection therefore only has to be configured on the computer on which the servlet engine is run.

If a database application is installed on several computers or even distributed as an applet, the JDBC–ODBC bridge is not an option as the ODBC connection would have to be configured on every computer.

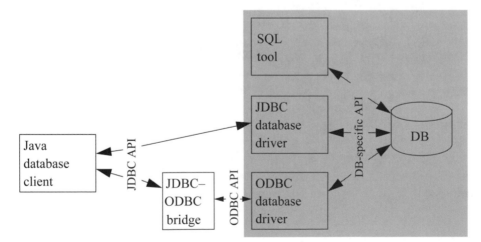

Figure 5.5: Different methods of database access.

5.4.1 Configuring the ODBC connection

Let us assume we wish to create an ODBC connection to an Access database. We open the 32-bit ODBC control panel in Windows and select " System DSN" (Figure 5.6 rear image). After clicking on "Add," the view of the front image is displayed, with a selection of possible database drivers. We will select the Access driver and click on "Finish."

It is important that the connection be created as a system data source so access is not limited to the user currently logged in. Figure 5.7 shows the next procedure. Clicking on "Finish" opens another dialog window in which the database to be accessed is selected. The selection is made easier with the browser window displayed in the foreground. Clicking on "OK" after selecting establishes the connection.

Similar steps are required for ODBC connections to other database products.

The book.mdb file, referenced by the process displayed, contains the data required later for developing the sample application. You can also refer to the site of this book. If you wish to use another database software, configure a book database using the respective management tool. The SQL instructions for creating tables and test dates are explained in Section 8.1.3 on page 128.

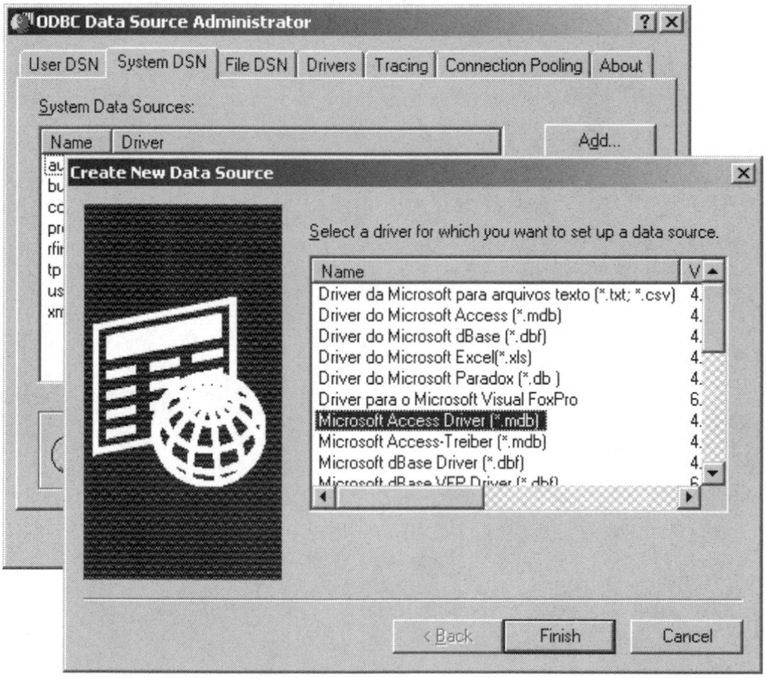

Figure 5.6: Dialog for selecting a database driver.

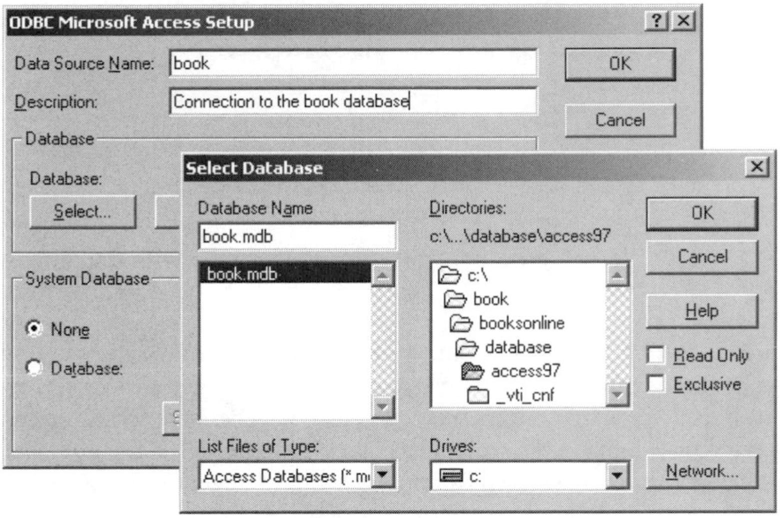

Figure 5.7: Other dialogs for ODBC configuration.

The use of the JDBC–ODBC bridge does not restrict you to a Windows platform. If the server, complete with application, is to be hosted on a Linux or Solaris computer later, this is not a problem. Another database driver need only be loaded. The name of the driver can also be indicated with a configuration parameter so the program code need not be modified.

5.4.2 The Connection, PreparedStatement, and ResultSet objects

If you process the work with an SQL tool, the sequence involves three steps:

1. First it is indicated on which computer the database server is located. After the login name and password have been entered, the connection is established.
2. An SQL command is typed in.
3. If it is a Select command, the results table is read and analyzed.

It is also possible to create tables using a Java program. However, as this is a unique process, we recommend using the respective database tools to create the tables instead of developing a separate program to send the respective commands. Fig. 5.4 shows how the `create table` command is sent to a MySQL server.

The functionality of each of the three steps is captured in an object of the `java.sql` package. The `Connection` object represents the connection to the database server. The connection is actually established by the DriverManager class. The database driver, login name, and password are provided for this process. In the sample program the JDBC–ODBC bridge and ODBC data source will be used with the name `project`.

The following program intially creates an empty `Connection` object. This then is initialized using the `DriverManager`, so that a connection to the project source exists for the user "user" after `getConnection()` has been executed:

```
import java.sql.*;
public class Select {
   public static void main(String[] args) {
      Connection con = null;
      try {
         Class.forName("sun.jdbc.odbc.JdbcOdbcDriver");
         con = java.sql.DriverManager.getConnection(
                  "jdbc:odbc:project", "user", "passwd")
```

The `Connection` object offers a number of methods. Two of the most important ones are `close` for ending the connection and `prepareStatement`. Using this method, an instance of the `PreparedStatement` class can be generated, which corresponds to typing in an SQL command. The argument of the `prepareStatement` method call contains the query for information on all projects with a budget over a certain value. With `preparedStatement` these constants can be replaced by question marks and inserted later. The point is that the command in the database server is precompiled and saved. The query can be repeated efficiently in the same way for several parameters. This makes no difference in our case, as the query is only placed once and the program then breaks off the connection. However, it is recommended that `preparedStatement` be used here:

```
PreparedStatement pstmt;
double budget = 10000.00;
pstmt = con.prepareStatement(
             "select * from project where budget >= ?");
```

We now have to inform the system which data type it should expect for the first (and only) parameter, `double` in this case. A parameter is inserted by calling the `setDouble` method. Here the first parameter indicates the parameter's index in the query, whereby the first index is one. The value of the variables used in the query is given in the second parameter.

```
pstmt.setDouble(1, budget);
```

Corresponding methods such as `setString` or `setInt` are used for parameters of other data types, such as if the `where` clause refers to the project name instead of the budget. The `Statement` class offers an alternative. However, the search parameter, in this case the variable `budget`, then has to be appended to the query string:

```
pstmt = con.prepareStatement(
             "select * from project where budget >= " + budget);
```

Especially with string parameters, which have to be placed in SQL quotes, the variant with `preparedStatement` is far more elegant and less prone to error. Another advantage is that the data types of the parameters are retained, eliminating another source of potential errors.

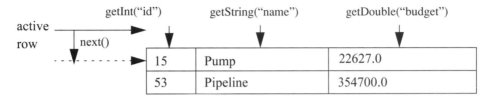

Figure 5.8: Methods and operation of the `ResultSet` class.

The actual execution follows the preparation of the database command. If it is a select query, this is started by calling `executeQuery`. `executeUpdate` is used for deleting, inserting, or modifying data sets. Only the `executeQuery` method has a `ResultSet` object as a result. As shown in the third step, the results table is included in this object

```
ResultSet res;
res = pstmt.executeQuery();
```

Figure 5.8 illustrates the operation of the `ResultSet` class. The data is always read row by row from the active row (also known as the cursor row). In order to activate the next row, the `next` method has to be called. The flag returned indicates whether the results table is at an end. If the entire table is to be read, the `while(res.next())` construct also used in the sample program is applied. The individual numbers in the columns of the active row are referenced using column names or column numbers, counting from 1 upwards. It is decisive here which columns are selected in the select instruction, and in which sequence the columns are entered. For example, the first column of the results table contains the project budget with the `select budget, name from project` query, and the second column contains the project name. As with `preparedStatement`, the corresponding methods (`getInt`, `getString`, and `getDouble` in this case) are selected, depending on the data type of the column. Detailed information on the mapping of SQL data types in Java can be found in Appendix A on page 411.

```
while (res.next()) {
   System.out.print(res.getInt("id") + "\t");
   System.out.print(res.getString("name") + "\t");
   System.out.println(res.getDouble("budget"));
}
```

If the `while` loop is processed, the three objects still have to be closed. When working with the database, as when accessing a file, errors can occur. Therefore, the statements are included in a `try` block. The causes of errors can very greatly. They range from database drivers not being located, through non-existent tables to the violation of an integrity constraint defined in a database. This example simply reports an error message, as well as the SQL and driver-specific error numbers:

```
            res.close();
            pstmt.close();
            con.close();
        } //try
        catch(SQLException e) {
            System.out.println(e);
            System.out.println(e.getSQLState());
            System.out.println(e.getErrorCode());
        }
        catch(ClassNotFoundException e) {
            System.out.println(e);
        }
    } //main
} // class Select
```

The applications introduced in the following chapter will show how SQL errors are interpreted and how one should react to them. A list of SQL errors as generated by different databases is also located in Appendix A on page 413.

5.4.3 Inserting, deleting, and modifying values in the database

We will now show examples for operations which access the database in writing, i.e. inserting, modifying, and deleting data sets. The ResultSet object is no longer required, as the executeUpdate method has no return value, as opposed to the executeQuery method. The construction of the SQL query and setting the parameter are identical to the select example.

```
import java.sql.*;
public class Insert {
    public static void main(String[] args) {
        Connection con = null;
        PreparedStatement pstmt;
        try {
            Class.forName("sun.jdbc.odbc.JdbcOdbcDriver");
            con = java.sql.DriverManager.getConnection(
                            "jdbc:odbc:project", "", "");
            pstmt = con.prepareStatement(
                            "insert into project values(?,?,?)");
```

As with the `select` query, the data types of the three expected parameters now have to be determined. This is done using the three methods mentioned previously:

```
pstmt.setInt(1, 22);
  pstmt.setString(2, "Rampe");
  pstmt.setDouble(3, 10000.00);
  pstmt.executeUpdate();
```

The remaining commands can then be taken from the `select` version of the program:

```
    pstmt.close();
  con.close();
}
catch(SQLException e) {
System.out.println(e);
System.out.println(e.getSQLState());
System.out.println(e.getErrorCode());
}
catch(ClassNotFoundException e) {
    System.out.println(e);
}
}
```

Update and delete queries function analogously. Only the lines for creating and the method call of the `pstmt` object are modified. Here is the `update` example:

```
pstmt = con.prepareStatement(
            "update project set budget = budget * 1.1 where budget < ?");
pstmt.setDouble(1, 25000.00);
pstmt.executeUpdate();
pstmt.close();
```

The code to execute a `delete` statement is no longer surprising:

```
pstmt = con.prepareStatement("delete from project where id = ?");
pstmt.setInt(1, 22);
pstmt.executeUpdate();
pstmt.close();
```

Chapter 6

Principles of the servlet technology

Now that the most important basic techniques of the Internet and WWW environment have been introduced in previous chapters, we will explore the practical development of distributed applications. The second part of this book, beginning with this chapter, concentrates on the topic of servlets. Servlets are a technology specially geared toward the use of the World Wide Web as a basic technique. The aim of this chapter is initally to familiarize ourselves with the basics of the servlet technique, assuming we are already familiar with technologies previously outlined, such as WWW, Java, HTML, and JDBC.

We will begin with a short introduction to the "historical" development of servlet technology, insofar as this topic can have a history. We will then demonstrate how the architecture of distributed applications, as already explained in detail in Section 2.4 on page 31, will look with servlets, with special emphasis on 3-tier architectures.

In order to be able to execute servlets, a servlet engine is required in the Web server. The next section explains this, before we start on the real technical things – servlet objects in Java. HTTP servlets as a subclass of generic servlet objects are perfectly adjusted to the use of HTTP as a transport protocol. It will be seen that this variant already offers a convenient application programing interface. To conclude this chapter, the session model will be introduced, which enables clients and servers to maintain more long-term associations on the basis of servlets.

6.1 The development and task of servlet technology

Servlets actually have two main roots from their development into an important technique for the creation of distributed applications, firstly the concept of the *Common Gateway Interface (CGI)*, and secondly that of *applets*. Both technologies have already been briefly mentioned in Chapter 2 on page 7. They represent two fundamentally different approaches, as CGI is a server-sided technology, while applets are small application programs which run on the client side. With CGI, program calls and parameters are passed via a standardized interface to the Web server, which controls the execution of respective programs as separate processes of the operating system. Applets are loaded by the Web server into the browser on the client side and then executed.

Like Java, servlets are a development of Sun Microsystems. The name "servlet" already bears a resemblance to the name "applet." Servlets are principally the equivalent of an applet on the server side. They are also written in Java, yet like CGI scripts, are executed on the server after being called by the browser. However, in contrast to CGI, the Web server does not actually initiate a separate process; rather the servlet is executed using a *servlet engine* integrated in the Web server. Today there are great number of Web servers able to execute servlets; more information can be found in Chapter 7 on page 113.

Other important properties of the technology should be noted at this point:

- Sun makes servlet technology available as an application programming interface (API) using a class library.
- The programmer can access the contents of the client request as well as other environment variables using the API.
- The API supports *cookies*, with which servers place user-specific information on the client computer, and which can be downloaded again during the next session.
- The API supports *sessions*, using which an association between client and server survives a single HTTP request. Section 6.6 on page 107 gives further information on cookies and sessions.
- The API does not determine whether the actual application, accessed using servlets, runs in the same process as the Web server, or perhaps even on another computer. Section III will demonstrate how, using this feature, very powerful applications can be built in combination with CORBA.

Servlets act, as CGI scripts do, in creating an interface between the World Wide Web and existing (or also yet to be rewritten) non-Web-based applications. In other words, the aim is to provide services available in the distributed environment via one standardized and familiar interface, namely the Web browser.

6.2 The architecture of distributed applications with servlets

We have already seen different architectures of distributed applications in Chapter 2 on page 7. Servlets help implement 3-tier architectures elegantly. Figure 6.1 shows the servlet-based version of this architecture.

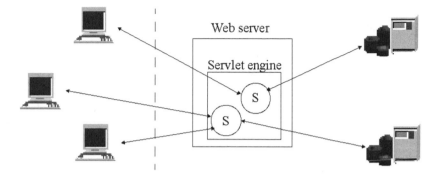

Tier 1: Presentation   Tier 2: Web server/servlets   Tier 3: Legacy applications

Figure 6.1: Three-tier architectures with servlets.

In tier 1 on the client side, Web browsers run as presentation programs. Requests are transferred to the Web server by entering a URL or clicking on the corresponding links. The Web server recognizes that a servlet call is coded by the URL received. The call is transferred to the servlet engine, which in turn starts the execution of the servlet. The most common task of the servlet now is to translate the parameters received by the client into the language of the actual application, and to forward this request to the application in tier 3. This processes the query, usually produces some result and returns it, via the Java method used in the servlet, back to the server itself. This re-encodes it into the language of the Web browser, HTML, and sends it to the client, which eventually displays the results in its output window.

One of the most typical types of application to be implemented using the architecture represented in Fig. 6.1 is that of the database application. A Web form is usually made available to the user, with which different database queries can be made. The query's content is transferred to the servlet by sending the form (usually by pressing a button on the form). This decodes the parameters, translates them into an *SQL query*, and sends the query to the database using *JDBC*. The database processes the query, collects the results, and also returns them to the servlet using JDBC. It remains only for the server to format the database tuple into HTML and send it to the browser as a results page.

6.3 Servlet support in Web servers

6.3.1 Servlet engines

The central component for executing servlets is the servlet engine. Such an engine is required in order to be able to install and execute servlets on a Web server. It is in principle a virtual Java machine, able to execute certain methods of objects which are servlets. Servlet engines easily can be embedded into Web servers which are already written in Java, as servlet class files easily can be saved together with the server's class files. The Java Web server from Sun is one example. Mounting in "traditional" Web servers such as Apache or the Netscape server is somewhat more time consuming, but most available servers nowadays also have a servlet engine.

6.3.2 The execution of a servlet call

In the 3-tier architecture described above, there is a relatively precisely determined sequence of operations of how servlets are executed or how they contact other programs and deliver results. This process is shown in Figure 6.2.

A servlet is usually accessed via a Web form represented in the browser window of the client. The user fills in this form and sends it to the Web server by clicking the mouse. The server recognizes that it is a servlet call, and activates the selected servlet via the servlet engine. As servlets are nothing other than Java objects, a certain object method must of course be called. These details will be addressed later in this chapter.

Calling a servlet mostly involves translating parameters transferred by HTTP into a format legible to the application in tier 3. The information is then transferred to the application by calling an API function.

As soon as the application receives a call, the desired program function is executed and the results are in turn delivered back to the servlet by the API function. The servlet, normally waiting for the result from the application at this point, encodes the API-formatted results into HTML and sends them to the client as a Web document. This then represents the received document in the browser window.

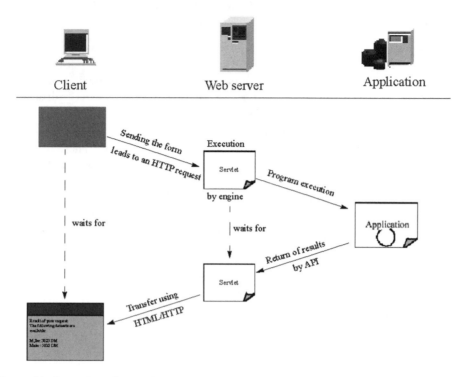

Figure 6.2: Execution of a Servlet.

6.4 Generic servlet objects in Java

Now what do the servlet objects that do the work in tier 2 of the architecture look like? This section explains the general appearance of the servlet library in Java in order to give a clearer picture of the life cycle of servlets. Furthermore, the special request and response objects will be addressed.

6.4.1 The servlet library in Java

The servlet library in Java is available in the `javax.servlet` package. The central component is the `interface Servlet`, which has to be implemented by all objects working as a servlet. Only the most important class components will be introduced in this chapter; a comprehensive summary of all classes and methods can be found in Appendix B on page 419.

The most important method of this interface is called `service()`. Its tasks are accepting, processing, and answering the requests of clients. This has the following appearance:

```
void service(ServletRequest request, ServletResponse response);
```

The servlet has access to input and output data streams using both objects of the types `ServletRequest` and `ServletResponse`. These provide the servlet with data from the server, or allow it to return the response data to the client.

In order to make the work of the programmer simpler, two additional abstract classes were provided which implement the interface and offer additional functions. These two classes are called `GenericServlet` and `HttpServlet`. The former also is located in `javax.servlet`, and the latter in `javax.servlet.http`. As the classes are declared as abstract, they cannot be instantiated directly. Rather you have to write an individual class yourself, inherited from one of these classes, and implement the `service()` method. The `HttpServlet` will be addressed in more detail in Section 6.5 on page 105. The `GenericServlet` complements the `interface Servlet`, in particular with methods for monitoring and logging accesses.

In order to implement a new servlet, a class has to be created which either

- implements the `interface Servlet` itself, or
- inherits from the `GenericServlet` class, or
- inherits from the `HttpServlet` class.

A typical class definition could look as follows:

```
class NewServlet extends GenericServlet {
    // service() has to be implemented
    public void service(ServletRequest req, ServletResponse res) {
        // read req
        // carry out work
        // write res
    }
```

Applications generally use the `GenericServlet`; for applications based on the use of HTTP as a transport protocol and HTML as a page description language, it is recommended that the additional properties of `HttpServlet` be used. Let us now consider the general operation of servlets.

6.4.2 The life cycle of servlets

Similar to applets, servlets also run through a certain life cycle. They are initialized at the beginning of this cycle. This occurs by calling the method `init()`, executed by the servlet engine after the servlet was created. The servlet is then available for client requests, handled by an arbitrary number of calls of the `service()` method (one call per client). At the end of the life of a servlet instance, the method `destroy()` is called. The three methods are already defined in the `interface Servlet`. `Service()` has to be implemented, as mentioned, while standard implementations of `init()` and `destroy()` already are available through the abstract classes. The methods have to be overridden if other or additional actions are required.

6.4.3 Request objects

The servlet gains access to the actual client request arguments via the `ServletRequest` object, submitted when the `service()` method is called, but also to other environment variables. This results in an interface similar to the *Common Gateway Interface.*

The query object has a number of methods as its most important components, with which the input parameters of the client can be made accessible to the servlet. These methods have the following signature:

```
Enumeration    getParameterNames();
String[]       getParameterValues(String name);
```

The first method delivers all parameter names of the filled-in form as an enumeration. The second delivers a field of character strings for a given field name (identified by the input parameter name), as every parameter can have several values. If the parameter names are known in advance and only one parameter value is relevant, the method

```
String         getParameter(String name);
```

also can be used, which simply delivers a value to a given parameter.

The following describes a standard method of how a servlet may decode the individual parameters and their values. The parameter names first have to be determined:

```
public void service(ServletRequest req, ServletResponse res) {
    ...
    Enumeration e = req.getParameterNames();
```

Then you can browse the parameters and output all the parameter values in the following way:

```
while (e.hasMoreElements()) { //practical loop for Enums!
    String name = (String)e.nextElement();
    String values[] = req.getParameterValues(name);
    System.out.print("Name: " + name + " value:");
    if (value != null)
        for (int i=0;i<value.length;i++)
            System.out.print(value[i] + " ");
```

```
        else
           System.out.print(" (none)");
        System.out.println();
    }
    ...
} // End of service()
```

In the case of Web forms, the corresponding values equate to the user form entries; during the further course of the `service()` method, the entries have to be processed further. Chapter 8 on page 125 gives a more detailed explanation.

Environment variables can also provide servlets with interesting information. `ServletRequest` has a range of other methods used to question these variables. Such examples are:

■ String `getServerName()` for querying the host name of the server;
■ int `getServerPort()` for querying the TCP port of the server process;
■ String `getRemoteAddr()` for querying the IP address of the client computer;
■ String `getRemoteHost()` for querying the host name of the client computer.

The request object also has other methods, listed in detail in Appendix B on page 419.

6.4.4 Answer objects

The counterpart of the request object is the response object, defined in the Java class `ServletResponse`. Its main task is to enable the servlet to deliver results to the client. Two output data streams are used for this:

■ On the one hand, a `ServletOutputStream` can be used which allows binary data to be sent. `ServletResponse` offers the `getOutputStream()` method here.
■ Alternatively, a `PrintWriter` can be requested which allows the transfer of text. The method for requesting this object is called `getWriter()`.

Before these methods are used, the MIME type of data should be determined using `setContentType()`. "text/plain" is predefined. You may rather wish to use "text/html" for Web applications. In this case the method should be called before the output data stream is requested.

The following section of code shows a typical procedure in coding the output of a servlet. The MIME type is defined first and then the output data stream requested:

```
public void service() {
    ...
    res.setContentType("text/html");
    ServletOutputStream sout = res.getOutputStream();
```

Usual methods such as `print()` and `println()` can be accessed on the stream:

```
sout.println("test output...");
sout.close();
```

It is interesting to note that both `ServletRequest` and `ServletResponse` are actually `interface` types. For this reason, both have to be implemented somewhere before they can be used. However, the servlet programmer need not take care of this; rather it is the task of the servlet engine to implement these.

6.5 Special servlets for Web applications

Generic servlets are fairly easy to use, yet when working in a restricted environment, different improvements can be made. Servlets are especially used in the World Wide Web, in which HTTP is used as a transport protocol for Web documents written in the HTML language. Special classes and interfaces of the `javax.servlet.http` package are provided for such environments, which make use of the availablility of the HTTP protocol. This section describes the three basic classes with `HttpServlet`, `HttpServletRequest`, and `HttpServletResponse`.

6.5.1 HTTP servlets

The `HttpServlet` class is a subclass of `GenericServlet` and so inherits its methods. However, it defines other methods which make use of the advantages of HTTP.

As explained earlier, HTTP is a text-based transport protocol for hypertext documents. The most important protocol commands are `GET` und `POST`, with which a document can be requested or information sent to the server. In addition to the `service()` method, `HttpServlet` now offers the `doGet()` and `doPost()` methods, with which the respective client requests are processed. The `service()` method still remains, but its only responsibility is to distribute the incoming requests to the correct methods, these being `doGet()` or `doPost()` (there are also others, but they are not relevant here). It should therefore not be overridden.

Nothing different from the `service()` method happens within the new method: the client inputs are read and processed accordingly. Other external programs may possibly be called, and results are then sent back to the client.

Let us consider an HTTP servlet as an example, `NewServlet`, which we assume uses the `GET` command of the HTTP protocol:

```
class NewServlet extends HttpServlet {
   ...
   public void doGet(HttpServletRequest req,
                     HttpServletResponse res) {
      ...
      res.setContentType("text/html");
      PrintWriter sout = res.getWriter();
      sout.println("<H1>output of a servlet<H1>");
      ...
   }
}
```

The client would receive an HTML document using GET as a servlet output, which outputs a level-1 heading in the browser window.

In the line in which the method doGet() is executed, it can be seen that the query and answer objects also have special HTTP versions. Both will be described now.

6.5.2 HTTP query objects

The special object for handling HTTP-based requests is described in the HttpServletRequest interface. As compared with the generic ServletRequest, the improvements are mainly due to the extended access of environment variables and to typical HTTP components such as a document header. Otherwise, superclass methods are available which enable access to field names and values sent by the client. They are then used in the same way.

Additional environment information includes, for example, the URL, which is coded in the servlet call, or the username, provided it has been authenticated. getCookies, which will play an important role in Section 6.6 on page 107, represents an interesting way of establishing longer-term relations between client and server.

6.5.3 HTTP answer objects

The HTTP-specific answer object HttpServletResponse is more interesting. It inherits the methods and properties of ServletResponse. The same output production methods then are available to the programmer, especially a PrintWriter or ServletOutputStream.

The new components of HttpServletResponse consist of a number of constants, which represent HTTP status codes. The user sees these status codes of Web pages if a request does not function, and an error message such as "HTTP 404 - File not found" appears on the screen. There are a wealth of other such status reports which inform the user of different problems. The best case is described with the code "200" – everything worked fine.

The corresponding codes are defined as integer constants, and can be sent to the client with the functions

- `void sendError(int statuscode)` for status reports without commentary, or
- `void sendError(int statuscode, String message)` for an additional message.

Furthermore, many other methods are available for amending the HTTP header of a created document:

- `void setHeader(String name, String value)` creates a header field;
- `void setStatus(int statuscode)` only defines the status of a document, without actually sending the document itself.

Another important method which acts as the opposite to the `getCookies()` method of the `HttpServletRequest` object is offered in the `HttpServletResponse` by the method `addCookie()`. This enables the programmer to install cookies on the client computer. We will be explained in more detail in the next section.

6.6 Long-term connections

The HTTP protocol is connection-less. This means that a Web server saves no status information about a client. Even if the client requests pages repeatedly from the same server, these requests look completely new and as if made by a new "client." It is now easy to imagine a huge number of situations where a more long-term relationship between client and server makes sense, in which the server saves information about the client. The typical example of such an application, which will be outlined later, is the virtual shopping cart. An e-business customer usually has the option of placing all his or her purchases in such a virtual cart, and paying for all the selected products together at the end. But how should this memory be implemented if the server is unable to keep track of older information? Actually, every product selection would usually be processed by calling new Web pages, on the basis of building a completely new HTTP communication.

This problem is solved using *cookies* and *HTTP sessions*, which will be introduced in the remainder of this chapter.

6.6.1 Cookies

Cookies are small pieces of information which the server places on the client computer. If the client calls a Web page or servlet on the corresponding server, the cookies saved for this context are transferred to the server.

The methods which the server can use to access cookies or create them on the client side will now be outlined. A cookie is stored with the client using the method

```
void addCookie(Cookie c)
```

The class `Cookie` represents a data structure, the central components of which are the name and value of the cookie. These two variables also have to be set when a cookie is created:

```
Cookie c = new Cookie("TestCookie.counter","0");
```

creates a cookie with the name "TestCookie.counter" and value "0". Please note that cookie values can only be strings. In order to integrate the cookie into the response to the client, the `HttpServletResponse` has to be set:

```
public void doGet(...,HttpServletResponse res) {
    ...
    // The cookie is created using a new cookie here
    // then the setting:
    res.addCookie(c);
    ...
    // finally: writing the answer using PrintWriter)
}
```

Cookie values are read in the following way using `getCookies()`, possibly in another servlet:

```
public void doGet(HttpServletRequest, ...) {
    ...
    Cookie[] cookies = req.getCookies();
    Cookie c;

    for (i=0;i<cookies.length,i++)
       if (cookies[i].getName().equals("TestCookie.counter")) {
          c = cookies[i];
          break; // breaks for-loop
       }
    ...
```

The value of the cookie found can be determined using `getValue()`:

```
if (c != null) {
    String value = c.getValue();
```

and processed further appropriately. A typical action would be to modify the value of the cookie and then return it to the client.

Cookies do not have the best reputation, as many users are reluctant to let arbitrary servers place data on their computer. The lifetime of many cookies is restricted to the lifetime of the client browser. However, the server can also increase the lifetime so that the cookies are placed on the client's hard drive. The problem is that it is impossible to control the information the server delivers. The second solution acts as a remedy – the HTTP session.

6.6.2   Sessions

The procedure applied here to maintain a relationship is to create an object managed by the servlets. A servlet can place information in relation to a special client in this object. Such an object of the `HttpSession` type survives the call of a servlet, meaning that it can be used again when called by the servlet in the future. In other words: the essential information on a client–server relation is located on the server, and not on the client as with cookies.

Creating a new or accessing an existing session object is done as follows:

```
HttpSession getSession(boolean create)
```

This belongs to the `HttpServletRequest` interface. If a session associated to the calling client already exists then this session is used. Otherwise the `create` parameter is checked. If set to `true`, a new session is created – otherwise not.

Objects of the type `HttpSession` have their own base methods and variables, which retain or distribute their identification number, date of creation, and date last accessed. However, in order to be able to retain information about a client, there also has to be an option of placing parameters and their values in the session or reading them again later. This is done as follows:

- `void setAttribute(String name, Object value)` creates a name parameter in the session and assigns it the value `value`. If the name of the parameter already exists, its value is replaced by a new one.
- `Object getAttribute(String name)` reads the name parameter and sends it to the caller.
- `Enumeration getAttributeNames()` delivers the names of all parameters filed in the session and returns the enumeration of strings.

The following example shows in brief how the methods described are put into practice. Chapter 8 explains this in more detail. The code now displayed first creates a session or shows whether a session is already available.

```
public class SessionExample extends HttpServlet {
    ...
    public void doGet(HttpsServletRequest req,
                      HttpServletResponse res) {
        HttpSession session = req.getSession(true);
```

The task we want to fulfill now is to take on all parameters and values provided by the client (such as the contents of a form filled in by the client) in the session. We only read one parameter value for the sake of simplicity, from which we can furthermore assume that it is of type `String`. The `setAttribute` method is used:

```
// first read the parameters sent by the client
Enumeration e1 = req.getParameterNames();
// then run through these elements and write them in the session
while (e1.hasMoreElements()) {
   String name = (String)e1.nextElement();
   String value = req.getParameter(name);
   session.setAttribute(name,value);
}
```

We will now return all parameters saved in the session to the client:

```
PrintWriter pw = res.getWriter();
pw.println("You sent the following parameters and values:");
Enumeration e2 = session.getAttributeNames();
while (e2.hasMoreElements()) {
   String name = (String)e2.nextElement();
   String value = (String)session.getAttribute(name);
   pw.println("Parameter: " + name + "value: " + value);
}
...
   } // doGet
} // SessionBeispiel
```

We had said that a session survives the call of a servlet. Yet how are we to end the session, as a servlet will not want to keep all sessions open forever? For that purpose, a session always has a maximum period of inactivity. This period can be determined by the session using the method `setMaxInactiveInterval()`. If the specified time is over, the session is removed by the servlet engine and no longer identifies the client. This method is important in keeping servlet processing fairly efficient.

The question remains as to how the session identification number is transferred from the client to the server. This occurs via the URL, or more specifically using *URL rewriting*. After a URL containing a servlet call is sent, the URL is still supplemented with the available session number, and only then sent to the server.

```
http://192.168.0.1:8080/servlet/SessionExample
```

The modified URL:

```
http://192.168.0.1:8080/servlet/
       SessionExample?jrunsessionid=3248654786450974
```

The server can now find out whether this session number is already assigned to a client.

A second option is saving the session ID on the client side as a cookie. Both techniques can be combined elegantly in this way, without the client having to save too much information as a cookie. Our example in Chapter 8 on page 125 shows in more detail how this combination can be used efficiently.

After this introduction to servlet technology, the next chapter addresses developer support of servlet-based applications using tools.

Chapter 7

Tool support for servlets

Like all Java-based technologies, servlets also enjoy tremendous success. In view of the dynamics and speed of development, it is impossible to deal with all tools and supporting software in this chapter, so we will focus on the most important representatives in this field, which are then used in the creation of the sample project. To begin with, the Sun *Java Servlet Development Kit (JSDK)* is introduced. The JSDK is the reference implementation of the Servlet specification. The aim is to provide the developers with a tool enabling them to experiment with the new technology. However, the aforementioned dynamics initially come from the *Open Source Community* which enabled the servlet support of the popular Apache Web server with the JServ module and the Tomcat server. In conclusion, after a review of the servlet capabilities of the popular Forté or Net Beans IDE we will address the *Java Server Pages (JSP)* technology. JSP is a further development of servlets which simplifies the design and the layout of dynamic Web pages in particular.

7.1 Java servlet development kit

With regard to installation and handling, the Sun *Java Servlet Development Kit* is definitely the simplest way to get results using servlet technology. The package is excellent for experimentation, but regarding stability and performance, it is only suitable for servlet development, not for daily work on a "production" Web site. You will notice this, for example, when a Web page saved locally with its own graphics is still only displayed very slowly in the browser due to the slow Web server.

The JSDK only supports version 2.1 of the servlet specification. This is sufficient for small examples and for experimentation. The small size of the server is a particularly neat feature of JSDK. JSDK's successor, the Tomcat server, supports the more recent 2.2 specification. As the "porting" of servlets from version 2.1 to version 2.2 can simply be done by copying the servlet files into the corresponding Tomcat directory, working with the "old" JSDK is legitimate.

7.1.1 Installation

Installation is very simple. Versions 2.0 and 2.1 are currently available, and we recommend Version 2.1. All JSDK versions are available to download from `java.sun.com/products/servlet/download.html`. You will get a WinZip file or a compressed tar archive of less than 0.5 MB containing the Web server, the class libraries, the Java program sources, the sample programs, and the documentation generated with javadoc. The *Java Development Kit, JDK 1.3* provides the Java interpreter or Java virtual machine required for the execution of servlets (`java.exe`). The compiler is also required for the development of individual servlets (`javac.exe`). The Windows, Linux, and Solaris versions of the software can be downloaded free of charge from `http://java.sun.com/j2se`.

7.1.2 Handling

The Web server is started simply by executing the batch file `startserver.bat` or the script `startserver`. If you execute the Web browser from the URL `http://localhost:8080/`, an information page will appear, from which Servlet API documentation and well-documented sample programs can be reached. This page is found under the path `JSDK2.1/webpages/index.html`. If further HTML files are added to this directory, they can be accessed via `http://localhost:8080/filename.html`. If the browser is directed to `http://localhost:8080/servlet/SnoopServlet`, the Web server executes the `SnoopServlet`. The result is a dynamically generated Web page which provides all possible information about browsers and Web servers. The `class` file of this servlet is found under `JSK2.1/webpages/WEB-INF/servlets/SnoopServlet.class`.

Before setting and compiling our own first servlet in this directory we have to add the servlet base classes from the JAR archive `servlet.jar` to the classpath. To do so, the following instruction is entered:

```
set CLASSPATH=complete path to the jsdk2.1 directory \servlet.jar;.
```

We then switch to the directory `JSK2.1/webpages/WEB-INF/servlets` and place the following small test program in the file `Test.java`. If the program is compiled we can look at our first servlet under `http://localhost:8080/servlet/Test`.

```
import java.io.*;
import javax.servlet.*;
import javax.servlet.http.*;

public class Test extends HttpServlet {

    public void doGet(HttpServletRequest request,
                      HttpServletResponse response)
                throws IOException, ServletException {
        response.setContentType("text/html");
        PrintWriter out = response.getWriter();
        out.println("<html><body>It works!</body></html>");
    }

}
```

Note here that the path to the servlet classes has changed somewhat with the introduction of the concept of Web applications in version 2.2 of the servlet API. The file is placed under `tomcat/webapps/ROOT/WEB-INF/classes/SnoopServlet.class` in the Tomcat server, introduced in the next section.

When experimenting with the JSDK you take into account that the Web server does not reload a recompiled class automatically. In order to make modifications visible to the servlet class in the browser, the Web server has to be stopped and started again and then the page reloaded by browser reload. By contrast, Tomcat does load new versions automatically.

7.2 Tomcat servlet engine

Tomcat is a reference implementation of the Java servlet 2.2 and JavaServer pages 1.1 technologies (see also Section 7.5 on page 120) developed under the Apache Software license. Tomcat replaces older implementations such as the Apache JServ module.

The Tomcat server is also able to provide the client with static pages, and so is a fully functional Web server. In practice, this task is undertaken by the Apache server (see also the following section). Tomcat is configured as an Apache module. Apache then forwards calls to servlets and JSP pages to the Tomcat module.

The latest version can be downloaded from `http://jakarta.apache.org/tomcat`. In Windows, a ZIP file need only be unzipped, for example in the directory `C:\tomcat`. After the following commands, the server is started and the Tomcat homepage can be accessed from `http://localhost:8080/`.

```
C:\tomcat>set TOMCAT_HOME=C:\tomcat
C:\tomcat>set JAVA_HOME=C:\jdk1.3
C:\tomcat>bin\startup
```

The essential reform compared to previous versions is the concept of a Web application. Several such independent applications can be installed on a host. Apart from the ever-present ROOT application, several other logical applications can be reached via a certain logical URL prefix. For example, the URL `http://host/admin/usr/faq.html` corresponds to the administration application, as the prefix `admin` is assigned. The file `usr/faq.html` is then accessed within the application. With the above installation directory, the physical directories of the ROOT and admin application are located under `C:\tomcat\webapps\ROOT` or `C:\tomcat\webapps\admin`. The following structure is prescribed within these directories:

- Static components: \
  All static components such as html, jpg, and gif files are located directly in the respective application directory or corresponding subordinate directories, such as `usr\faq.html`. These static components also include the class files for applets, as these also are only delivered to the browser.

- Java Server Pages: \
  JSP files are addressed as html pages. The essential difference is that JSP files never reach the client, but only the html or xml text created by them.

- Servlets: `\WEB-INF\classes`
  As the `WEB-INF` directory assumes a special function, only servlets can be executed. Otherwise the client cannot access `WEB-INF` files. A servlet of the `admin` application in the file `Test.class` then responds via the URL `http://host/admin/servlet/Test`. A servlet s defined in the package p then has to be saved in `\WEB-INF\classes\p` and called using `.../servlet/p.S`. All help classes used by the servlets or JSP pages of this application also have to be located in the classes directory.

- Libraries: `\WEB-INF\lib`
  If a servlet or JSP page works with, for example, the MySQL JDBC driver contained in the `mysql_uncomp.jar` library, the archive jar has to be copied into the `lib` directory.

- Configuration information: `\WEB-INF\Web.xml`
  This file contains context parameters of servlets, documentation, the timeout for sessions, access rights to files for users created in the Tomcat base configuration, and other important application information.

The logical separation in Web applications considerably eases the work of the Web server administrator. So two applications which require different versions of a library can be installed. This would otherwise inevitably lead to problems.

The directory structure of an application can now be compressed in a Web application resource (WAR). A WAR file then need only be placed in the `webapps` folder of the Web server. This then automatically decompresses the files as soon as a client accesses the application.

7.3 Apache Web server

The Apache Web server boasts an incredible success story. In recent years all the important software manufacturers have tried to gain supremacy in the extremely important Web servers market (Figure 7.1). Well-known commercial Web servers include the Microsoft Internet Information Server, the Netscape Enterprise Server, and the IBM Web Sphere. However, according to a Netcraft study, the Apache Open Source Project is the most successful with a market share of 57 percent. The strengths of the Apache server include high software performance and stability.

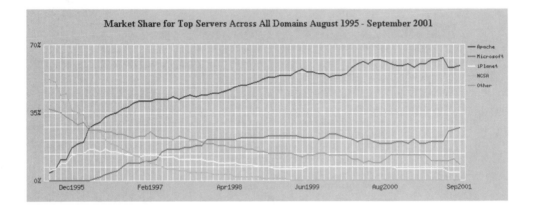

Figure 7.1: Top developers across all domains from 1995 to 2001.

The development of Web applications has long been limited to CGI-based solutions.

The above-mentioned Tomcat server is an efficient Web server with servlet and JSP support. Nevertheless, the original Apache Web server for static pages and CGI applications remains unbeatable. For this reason, the integration of the Apache server and Tomcat engine is intended. The Web server then calls the Tomcat if queries on servlets or JSP pages arise. This integration is described in detail in the Tomcat distribution.

The latest Apache version, currently 1.3.14, for the desired platform can be found at `http://www.apache.org/dist/`. "Typical installation" should be selected when installing.

7.4 Servlet development with Forté for Java

The development environment Forté for Java (Forte4J) offers some very useful features such as the simple administration of projects, a debugger, and an editor which marks different Java language elements like strings and keywords in color, as shown in Fig. 7.2.

This comfort was withheld from servlet developers for a long time, since the tools primarily support the creation of applications. Stopping and starting the Web server and switching between browser, editor, and compiler were part of everyday business.

Many developers prefer to work in this manner rather than struggle with menus and dialogs. However, there is some good news for the supporters of integrated development environments: Today most integrated development tools support servlets and JSP programming directly with an integrated Web server. The Internet Edition of Forté for Java is one example. Unfortunately, only a 30-day trial version is available for free from Sun's Web site: `http://www.sun.com/forte/ffj/buy.html`. Besides servlets there are also tools and program templates for *Remote Method Invocation (RMI)*, *Enterprise Java Beans (EJB)*, CORBA, JINI, JNDI and XML in the package.

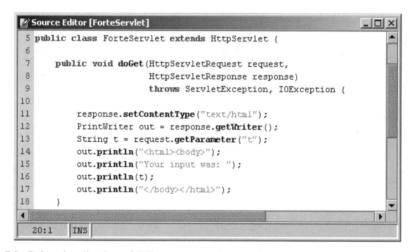

Figure 7.2: Color visualization of different syntax elements in Forte4J.

The Servlet module enables the developer to compile a Web-based project like any other application, and to start it directly from the development environment. A Web server is integrated and started if necessary. A Web browser also is included and shows the HTML output. Therefore the servlet shown in Fig. 7.2 can be developed and tested without having to use further software. Figure 7.3 shows the servlet, Web server, and browser in action. The integrated Web server is fully functional and can be accessed by conventional browsers from the same computer or other computers in the network. It usually displays some status information on its screen window. The sample servlet reads the parameter t given in the URL and outputs it on the Web page created. The URL can be edited in the integrated browser (as is usual from other browsers) in order to respond to the servlet with the values required. Of course, HTML forms also can be designed with a corresponding action attribute and used them for the value input. In comparison, the diagram also shows the output of the same servlet using Netscape Navigator.

The administration of the Web server is also managed very easily with Forte4J. If you have to edit further configuration files with the JSDK Web server or the Apache server, you can control the integrated Web server easily in a dialog, as shown in Fig. 7.4.

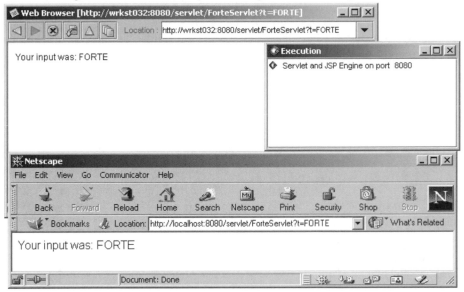

Figure 7.3: Servlet execution and representation of the results with Forte4J.

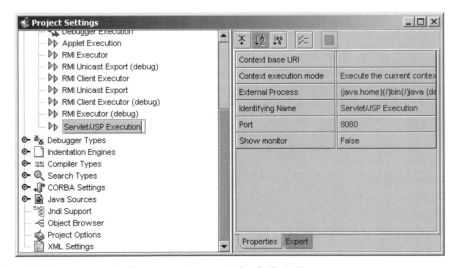

Figure 7.4: Parameter modification and representation in Forte4J.

This is a very simple entry option, particularly for important parameters and those which change from time to time, such as the root directory for Web pages and servlets, the Java virtual machine, the classpath, the port number of the Web-server, and the default page of a directory.

The root directory of the Web server shows directly in the working directory where projects are created. If several Web servers have to run on one computer at the same time, conflicts can be avoided by modifying the ports. On the level of the virtual machine you can indicate which `java.exe` is used to execute the servlet. It is also practical for the `classpath` settings to be taken over directly from the development environment. If required, the `classpath` for the servlet executions can be modified in the dialog box.

7.5 Java Server Pages

7.5.1   JSP between servlets and HTML

Java Server Pages are a new technology from Sun, building on servlets. In essence, Java Server Pages work exactly like servlets. However, the principal difference is in the relationship between Java and HTML or XML. Servlets are normal Java classes which are compiled like any other class in Java and distribute the dynamic Web content with `println` statements. The following servlet, for example, gives the present time and date:

```
public class date extends HttpServlet {
    public void doGet(HttpServletRequest request,
                      HttpServletResponse response)
            throws IOException, ServletException {
        response.setContentType("text/html");
        PrintWriter out = response.getWriter();

        out.println("<html><body>");
        out.println("It is:");
        out.println((new java.util.Date()).toString());
        out.println("</body></html>");
    }
}
```

This is the corresponding variant based on Java Server Pages:

```
<html><body>
It is:
<% out.println((new java.util.Date()).toString()); %>
</body></html>
```

You immediately notice that this file looks almost like a common HTML document. Dynamic page components, for example the date in this case, are missing. Instead you find a Java program line, enclosed by <% and %>, which generates the date, as in the servlet. If this JSP file is invoked by the Web browser, it is automatically converted into a servlet. This happens by packing all characters, not contained between <% and %>, in `out.println()` method calls. This servlet generated from the JSP file is automatically compiled, saved in the work directory of the Web server and then executed like any other servlet. Of course this also means that variables can be defined and other complex Java classes called with JSP. Fig. 7.5 shows what happens if an error is made in the JSP program.

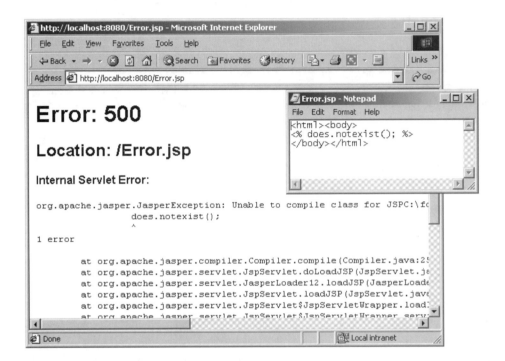

Figure 7.5: The Java instruction `does.notexist()`; leads to an error when compiling in a JSP file. This is displayed in the browser.

The advantage of this technology is obvious: the regular recompilation of the servlet, in which only one detail on a `out.println()` instruction is modified, is eliminated. It is sufficient to modify and store the JSP file in an editor.

Figure 7.6: Java Server Pages can be processed with graphic HTML editors such as FrontPage 98 here, as these ignore the Java code. FrontPage 98 interprets the <%%> characters as Visual Basic Plugin.

Since the <% and %> characters are interpreted as comments by browsers and graphical HTML editors, JSP files can be handled as normal HTML files and can for example, be edited in FrontPage or Composer, as shown in Fig. 7.6.

7.5.2 JSP language constructions

The short example outlined above shows that the `out` object is implicitly defined. Likewise with the `request` and `response` objects known to the servlets. You almost find yourself in the doGet method of a servlet. In the following text we wish to introduce several JSP-specific constructions:

The following syntax is used to import classes:

```
<%@ page import="java.util.Date" %>
<%@ page import="java.net.URL" %>
```

Using the include command it is possible to embed both static as well as dynamic elements. Any form parameters sent are passed on here to `include.jsp`.

```
<%@ include file="include.jsp" %>
<%@ include file="footer.html" %>
```

If an exception on a page is not treated, you can jump straight to a certain URL by setting the errorPage in case of an error. Again, form parameters are passed on.

```
<%@ page errorPage="error.jsp" %>
```

Branching can easily be embedded in the application using the forward instruction.

```
<% if (request.getParameter("choice").equals("yes")) { %>
   <JSP:forward page="index.html"/>
<% } else { %>
   <JSP:forward page="no.jsp"/>
<% } %>
```

When using JSP you should be sure to retain the application logic in extra classes. Sun recommends the use of beans in this case. Beans differ from other classes in their properties, private class variables that are accessed using get/set methods. However, no specific interface needs to be implemented by the bean in this case. JSP offers a syntactic variant with the use of beans in the form of the following example. A useBean tag is used to create an instance of the class. The scope attribute is practical here, which automatically places the instance in the session, and makes it available to the client's next invocation:

```
<jsp:useBean id="var" class="MyBean" scope="session"/>
<% var.processRequest(request); %>
```

Data can easily be transferred by the request object into the bean using the setProperty tag. If an HTML form parameter name is entered in the property attribute and there is a corresponding set... method, this method is called with the corresponding value. In the stern syntax used in the following example, all pairs are worked off.

```
<jsp:setProperty name="var" property="*"/>
```

It is assumed that parameters a and b are available in the request, and that `public void setA (string)` and `public void setB(string)` are defined in the bean, so the `<jsp:setProperty name="var" property="*"/>` tag causes the following two commands to be executed:

```
var.setA(request.getParameter("a"));
var.setB(request.getParameter("b"));
```

7.5.2 Servlets or JSP?

When should you use servlets and when JSP? In the end it is a matter of personal taste. If there is a formatting problem with an HTML table, the JSP format is normally preferred. However, servlets are simpler when a translation error has to be eliminated. Therefore servlets should be used in more complex tasks in which the Java part outweighs the HTML output. If the user's name from the session is the only part of a Web page that is dynamically created, then JSP is the optimal choice.

7.5.3 Tool support for Java Server Pages

As previously mentioned, Tomcat supports both servlets and JSP. JSP pages are treated as HTML pages here, and easily can be placed in the corresponding directory of the Web application. If, for example, you place our date program in the folder `tomcat/`

`webapps/ROOT`, it then can be started in the browser by typing in the URL `http://localhost:8080/Date.jsp`.

As the web server calls the Java compiler dynamically, the `JAVA_HOME` variable environment variable has to be set before starting the Tomcat server.

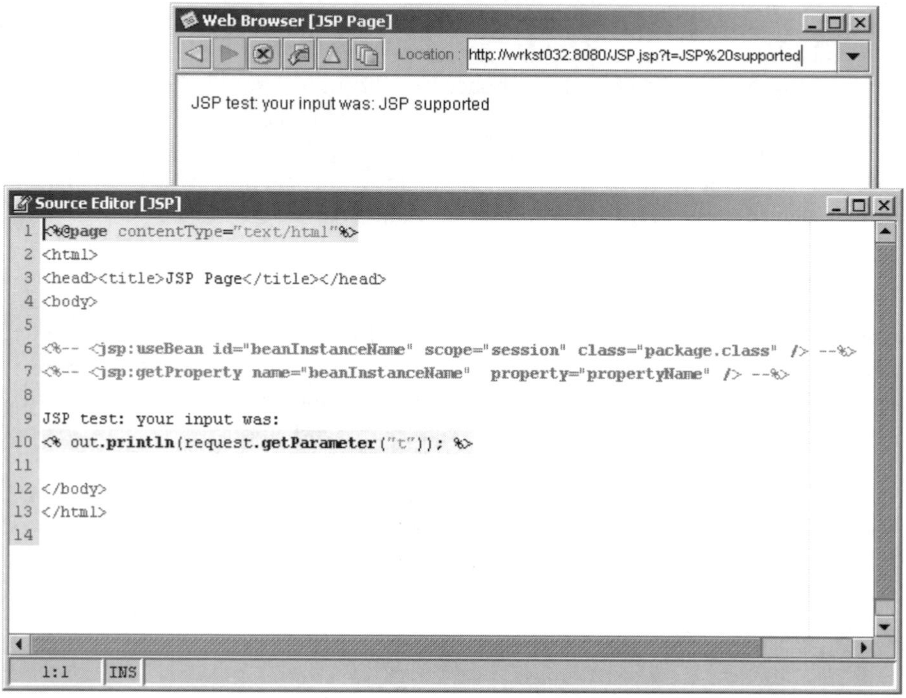

Figure 7.7: The Forte4J Web server also supports Java Server Pages.

Regarding support with tools, it should also be mentioned that Forte4J also leaves little room for improvement in Java Server Pages. A JSP program is treated by the development environment just like a normal Java Project and is managed correspondingly. You can also execute tests directly with the built-in Web server and browser, without having to use a further application. Figure 7.7 shows a small test program that, like the servlet in Fig. 7.2, issues a parameter placed in the URL, in the dynamically created Web page.

Chapter 8

A sample application with servlets

E-commerce is currently the "killer application" on the Internet. Forerunners in this field are companies such as Amazon.com or eBay. The Web applications on these sites offer a wide range of functionality such as login, search, shopping basket, evaluations, etc. In our example of a virtual bookshop, "Books Online," we intend to show what the server side may look like, behind the scenes of these Web pages. Of course, it will not be possible to reproduce the entire functionality in the context of this book. We will, however, develop a fully working Web application, which can serve as the basis for a commercial solution.

First, we will take a look at the development of a database schema for our virtual bookshop, as this represents the basis of all further considerations for the actual application. We will then carry out an analysis of requirements, in order to determine which functions our bookshop should support. The design phase will conclude with considerations of what the user interface will look like and what form the interaction with the client will take. The implementation will then follow, in which we describe in detail the development of the servlets required.

8.1 The central database

The database plays a central role, in virtual as well as in actual businesses. All relevant information, such as current stock, orders received, client data, outstanding invoices, and so on are saved in the database. Using servlets, a company grants clients controlled access to the data relevant to them, and lets them participate directly in business transactions. Since the Web application relates directly to the database, it is essential that you be familiar with and understand the information structure and features of this database. In our example, we will select the part of the database schema that deals with clients, books, and orders. We will explain which records are modified or added when, for example, a client places an order, and which SQL database queries are needed to do this. If you have never worked with databases and only want to concentrate on the development of the servlets, you do not need to understand fully the explanations in this section. However, we believe that access to databases plays a significant role in almost all server-side Web applications, be they written with servlets, CGI, or ASP. For this reason we consider it important to take an in-depth look at this topic.

8.1.1   The Books Online database schema

A database schema describes which tables there are and what relationship the records in these tables have with one another. The data for our example is stored in three tables whose relationships with one another are shown in Fig. 8.1 in the form of an entity relationship diagram. The current stock of books is stored in the `Book` table. The primary key of this table is the ISBN, which identifies each book uniquely. It therefore is not possible to place two records in the book table with the same ISBN. As is clear from Fig. 8.1, the title, the price of the book, and the number of copies in stock are stored. If a new delivery of 100 copies of a book arrive, of which there are already seven copies in stock, the amount field alone will be increased to 107.

Every registered client is represented with an address, e-mail and credit card information. In this client table, the choice of primary key is not so simple. Moreover, there is the question of the username with which the client logs on to the system. In most Web applications, the client's e-mail address is used for this. The question arises of whether this also makes a good primary key.

As long as you consider several people, who, for example, share one e-mail address in the same household, as one client, then the e-mail address is indeed clear, but not necessarily suitable as a primary key. A primary key should never change, as not only the client entry changes, but all entries in the orders table which reference the client primary key with a foreign key also need to be changed. As e-mail addresses can change relatively frequently, a database-generated client identification number should be used as the primary key instead.

It is also possible to let the database generate the number; however, the SQL syntax required for this is not standardized, and requires very database-specific program code. Therefore, we will use the following solution: for the primary key we will use a combination of the system time, measured in milliseconds since 1970, and the hash code of the e-mail address. The probability of two users registering in the system at the same time AND their e-mail addresses having the same hash code is negligible.

The client registers in the system using his or her e-mail address. This means that this table attribute also must be unique. This solution is considerably more user-friendly than asking clients to remember a long string of figures.

The order table contains a record of every client transaction. Using this information, the deliveries are sorted out in the evenings. In this process, the entries in the order table are deleted and are transferred to the archive. As a client may well happen to order the same book twice in the same day, a combination of the client identification number, the ISBN, and the time and date is used for the primary key for this table. If the client orders two different books in one transaction, then two entries with the same time are entered in the order table. The number of copies delivered and whether the client paid by invoice or by credit card is also recorded.

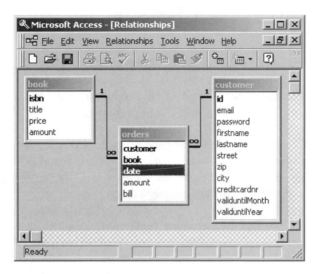

Figure 8.1: The entity relationship schema of the orders, book, and client tables.

Since the orders table contains foreign key references to the client and book tables, the corresponding client address and the price of the book can be accessed from each order. As Fig. 5.2 on page 84 shows, 1:n relationships are created. A book can appear in different orders and a client can place different orders.

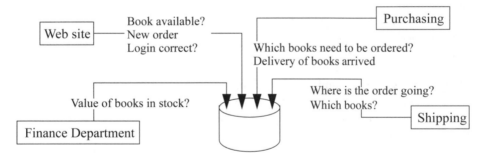

Figure 8.2: Different programs, in particular the Web, purchase, finance, and shipping applications, access the database.

For the sake of simplicity, the entity relationship diagram shown contains only the tables that are needed to operate the Web site. In addition, an orders archive, a table of information for suppliers, outstanding client invoices, and so on would also be necessary. As Fig. 8.2 shows, the Web application is only one of many programs that access the database. The enormous advantage of this architecture is that the current information can always be found on the Web pages, provided that the database correctly reflects the stock, for example. All prices, numbers of items, and other data come from the same source, which ensures consistency and greatly simplifies correct updating.

8.1.2   Choice of database software

This sample application is not dependent on a particular database product. Using the `create table` SQL instructions in the next section, the three tables used can be created on an Oracle, Informix, DB2, SQL Server, or Sybase database. Products such as Access or MySQL also can be used if no large database server is available. An Access97 file complete with the tables created and some test data to download is available on the Web site to accompany the book. You should, however, note the following: in a multi-user operation, as is the case with a heavily frequented online bookshop, problems can arise in the handling of purchases, since Access and MySQL only support limited database transactions. If, for example, two users are both interested in the last copy of a book in stock, database transactions ensure that only one is sold. This topic is explained in more detail in the development of the checkout servlet. If simple databases such as Access and MySQL are used, a small check in the program makes sure that there are no complications. The development is not interfered with in any way by this, and the example application of course also has the same range of functions with these databases.

8.1.3   Creating the tables

Using the following `create table` instructions, the book, customer, and orders tables can be created. Here you must pay attention to the choice of primary key. Furthermore, the following conditions are defined: the number of books in stock cannot be negative (check `(check (amount >= 0)`), the clients' e-mail addresses must be unique, and orders can only be placed by registered clients. In addition, the books ordered must of course also be located in the corresponding tables. This foreign key relationship is indicated by `references customer(id)` and `references book(isbn)`. Data types such as `decimal` for saving long strings of numbers such as credit card numbers or `datetime` for saving the time of purchases were intentionally left out. Instead, we will use simple strings, since special data types from the different databases are not handled in the same way and a different syntax is needed when creating the tables and for enquiries.

Unfortunately, MySQL still does not support some of the features used here. The easily modified table definitions for MySQL can be found on the Web site for this book.

```
create table book (
    isbn          char(16)    primary key,
    title         char(32),
    price         float,
    amount        int         check (amount >= 0)
```

```
);

create table customer (
    id              char(32)    primary key,
    email           char(32)    unique,
    password        char(16),
    firstname       char(32),
    lastname        char(32),
    street          char(32),
    zip             char(32),
    city            char(32),
    creditcardnr    char(16),
    validuntilMonth int,
    validuntilYear int
);

create table orders (
    customer char(32)   references customer(id),
    book            char(16)    references book(isbn),
    date            char(20),
    amount          int,
    bill            int,
                            primary key(customer, book, date)
);
```

We will now insert some test data in the table. In the insert SQL instructions, character sequences are marked by simple inverted commas. As mentioned above, the date is given in milliseconds from 1.1.1970, to prevent any problems with country and database-specific formatting.

```
insert into customer values ('568404960954083944050',
    'jon@company.co.uk', 'jonboy',
    'Jon', 'Burton', '26 Church Street','Sheffield', S10 1AB
    '1111222233334444', 1, 2001);
insert into customer values ('59646833954083902700',
    'helen@web.co.uk', 'secret',
    'Helen', 'Sharp', '5 Railway Terrace', 'Warwick', CV35 2AT,
    '4444333322221111', 1, 2003);

insert into book values
    ('3453159926', 'Atlantis', 11.00, 50);
insert into book values
    ('3446133631', 'The Name of the Rose', 9.00, 75);
insert into book values
    ('3257201184', 'Animal Farm: A Fairy Story', 3.9, 65);

insert into orders values
    ('568404960954083944050', '3453159926', '958977592291', 1, 0);
insert into orders values
    ('568404960954083944050', '3257201184', '958977678806', 1, 0);
insert into orders values
    ('59646833954083902700', '3446133631', '958977688910', 1, 0);
insert into orders values
    ('59646833954083902700', '3453159926', '958977698774', 3, 0);
```

The procedure for executing SQL instructions is explained in detail in Chapter 5 on page 90.

8.2 Functions

As is the case in the creation of a conventional application, it is also extremely important with servlets and Web applications to think first about the requirements of the program. As regards functionality, we will follow the example of Amazon.com. If you experiment with this Web application, you can summarize the usage as follows: You create a user account and log in. You receive information on books by means of a search function and can then place copies in a shopping basket. The shopping basket view enables you to remove books and change the number of copies of a book. You only complete the actual purchase by proceeding to the virtual checkout. Here, at the latest, you must authenticate yourself. The search and management of the shopping basket also can be operated in Amazon without the system knowing who the client is. From this minimal specification we can derive six menu entries for our Web application:

1. *Homepage*
   You will find general information and special offers on this page.
2. *Login*
   Clients who already have an account can authenticate themselves here.
3. *New clients*
   New clients can enter their details here and define their personal password.
4. *Shopping Basket*
   All products selected so far are shown here. In addition, the number of copies selected can be changed.
5. *Search*
   Books can be searched according to title and ISBN.
6. *Checkout*
   The client chooses between paying by credit card or by invoice, confirms the transaction and receives a summary.

Figure 8.3: In AltaVista the search result is very similar to the homepage from a design point of view.

8.3 Web design

The layout of the Web pages plays a central role, not only for esthetic but also for technical programming reasons. If an HTML form is filled out and sent off, a new page appears with the answer to the enquiry or with an error message. It is preferred that the structure of both pages be the same. Essential page elements such as the navigation menu should not simply disappear when the form is sent off. As can be seen in Fig. 8.3, by using AltaVista, for example, a new enquiry can be made straight from the results page.

A simple way of avoiding a break in the design between the form and the result is the use of *frames*. These enable several static or dynamic HTML pages to be displayed at the same time. Therefore, if it is indicated in the form definition, with the `target` attribute of the `<Form>`-tag, that the results page should appear in another frame (`target="Frame_Name"`), then the homepage remains unchanged. We will avoid this solution for the simple reason that when using frames, the URL of the individual pages is no longer apparent. If the parameters are read by means of GET, the developer can immediately tell from the URL which parameter names and which values are submitted. If necessary, these can also be edited manually.

The solution used here assumes that every page is structured according to the model shown in Fig. 8.4. The creation of this structure is encapsulated in a Java class `Page` and is used by all servlets. By calling the printMenu method all page elements except for the actual content are printed. This method has two advantages: the first is that it ensures that the page structure is uniform, and the second is that the servlet developer can concentrate fully on the task in hand, such as creating the shopping basket view. More on the different Java classes later.

Company name and logo	
Menu items	
Display of the active menu items	Individual greeting
Contents	

Figure 8.4: Base structure of all Web pages of Books Online.

8.4 Interaction with the user

The page structure and the six main categories have been established. Now we need to investigate whether there are more pages within the categories, and the nature of the pages themselves. The simplest case is a static information page. In addition, pages can contain forms and can be created statically or dynamically. Of course, our servlets are hiding behind dynamic pages. It must also be clarified which parameters will be called up in forms, and what the answer to a form that has been filled out should look like. When processing the form, it should be established whether and how the login status and the shopping basket are influenced. The search will not have any influence, a login process on the other hand will. The hyperlink structure of the pages should also be investigated.

Figure 8.5: The menu structure: homepage, display shopping basket, log in, create new account, search and checkout.

Now let us go through each of the main menu items in turn and discuss the points just mentioned. In the following diagrams, we will try to represent graphically the course of the interaction. Each page involved is represented by a box. A jump from one page to another is indicated by an arrow. The labeling of the arrows indicates the actions to be carried out by the system. The gray areas delimit the field of work of a servlet. This includes generated Web pages, actions performed by the servlet, and the application logic in the servlet. Each diagram refers to a menu item. Since the main menu is shown on every page, the six linked pages can always be accessed. It therefore should be taken into account that, next to the displayed paths of each page, it is always possible to jump to one of the six menu items. Figure 8.5 shows the design of the main menu.

8.4.1 Homepage

The homepage is a simple static HTML page. An interesting question to ask is what a special offer will look like in our sample bookshop. It would of course be preferred that the information not only be displayed as text, but also that a hyperlink be provided, which provides more detail, or places the book straight into the shopping basket with just one click. This can be achieved by putting a hyperlink with the corresponding search parameter onto the search servlet. The client then does not have to transfer the ISBN to the search field manually.

```
<a href="servlet/Search?search=3446133631">...</a>
```

Figure 8.6 shows this link once again graphically.

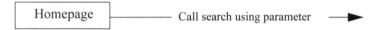

Figure 8.6: Jump to special offers from the homepage.

8.4.2 Registering and creating a new account

At the beginning of both registering and creating a new account, there is a static HTML form. If one of these forms is filled out and sent off, then either a success message or an error message can follow. Typical sources of error are, for example, incorrectly entered passwords or a letter inadvertently typed in a numerical field. The user should be alerted to the error with a message. The diagrams of these two cases are shown in Figs. 8.7, 8.8. It also should be noted, when registering, that, in the case of an error, the user who may have been logged in before is still not logged out. If the creation of a new user account is successful, the user is then automatically registered.

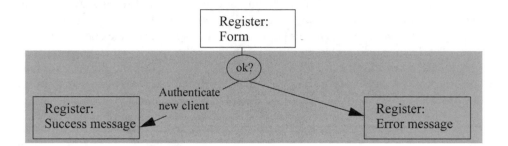

Figure 8.7: Registration procedure.

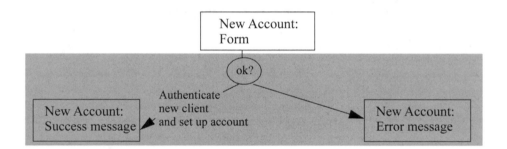

Figure 8.8: Procedure when setting up a new account.

The `Login` and `NewUser` servlets which implement the functions shown in Figs. 8.7 and 8.8 are explained in Section 8.10.2 on page 156 and in Section 8.10.3 on page 158.

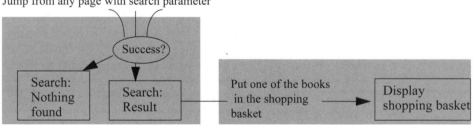

Figure 8.9: From the search result, one of the books can be placed in the shopping basket. The search result and the shopping basket are created by two different servlets.

8.4.3 Search

The search category is an exception, as the main menu of each page already contains the search form. You therefore can jump from any page to a search result, as is also the case from a special offer hyperlink. The search of course is implemented by a servlet. The books listed on the search results page can be placed straight into the shopping basket. This is done by clicking on the shopping basket symbol, which, like a special offer, is directly linked to a servlet and sends the corresponding information to it in the same way. If this option is selected, you jump from the search result to the shopping basket view. Figure 8.9 shows this process. The corresponding `Search` servlet is explained in Section 8.5.1 on page 138.

Figure 8.10: Books can be placed directly in the shopping basket from the search result.

8.4.4 Shopping basket

Primarily, the shopping basket view should show the user which books he or she has decided to purchase so far. However, you must also be able to change the quantity of books. If a book is chosen from the search view, it is standard for one copy to be placed in the basket. If you change the quantity to zero, the book should be removed from the basket. As is the case with the search result, there is an active element in each row of the shopping basket. In the shopping basket, this is a small form with the number field and a confirmation button. If the number of copies of a book is altered, you will return to the modified shopping basket view. The screenshot sequence shown in Figs. 8.10, 8.11, 8.12

clarifies the passage from the search to the shopping basket and from there to the modified shopping basket.

Figure 8.11: The number of books ordered can be changed from the shopping basket view.

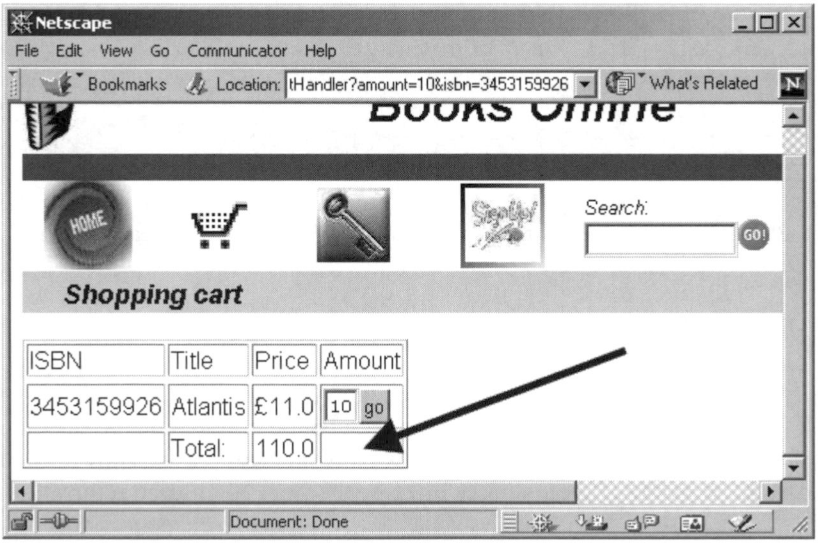

Figure 8.12: Modified number of books ordered as well as the new price.

Figure 8.13 clarifies once again the logical sequence of operations from the servlet's viewpoint. Section 8.9 on page 150 shows the implementation by the `CartHandler` servlet.

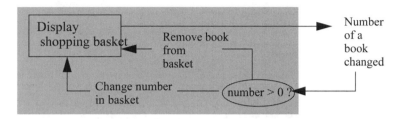

Figure 8.13: The quantity of each book in the shopping basket can be changed. If the quantity is less than or equal to zero, the book is removed. Calling this function comes from the shopping basket display and results in a modified shopping basket.

8.4.5 Checkout

When paying, there are error or success messages, as with login and the setup of a new account. However, the application logic is significantly more complex, as certain checks are necessary to ensure the correct transaction sequence: Are there enough books in stock? Can the amount be put on credit card? Is the user logged in? Figure 8.14 shows the sequence of this function. Section 8.11 on page 160 shows the checkout servlet.

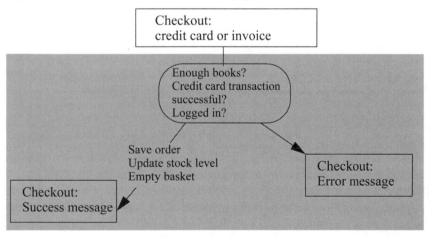

Figure 8.14: Checkout with checks of various conditions.

8.5 The first servlet

Let us begin the implementation with the search servlet, which receives an ISBN or a title fragment from the search form, searches the book table for matching titles, formats this in HTML, and returns it to the user.

8.5.1 The definition of classes

Servlets are normally derived from the `javax.servlet.http.HttpServlet` class. This class provides basic implementations for all functions to be carried out by a servlet (see also Chapter 6 on page 113 and Appendix B on page 419). Similarly, we define the `DatabaseHttpServlet` class which extends the servlet base class and defines the basic function for all servlets that have to access the database. As this is the case with the search servlet, it extends the `DatabaseHttpServlet` class, which is explained in Section 8.13.5 on page 176.

```
public class Search extends DatabaseHttpServlet {
```

8.5.2 The doGet() method

In our case, the search parameter is handed over using the GET method of HTTP. The parameter name is `search`. Reminder: this is specified in the HTML form. The basic implementation of the doGet() method is overwritten.

```
public void doGet(HttpServletRequest request,
                  HttpServletResponse response)
            throws ServletException, IOException {

    response.setContentType("text/html");
    PrintWriter out = response.getWriter();

    String search = request.getParameter("search");
    Page.printMenu(request, out, Page.SEARCH);
    out.println("Search for: " + search + "<br><br>");
```

You will find the first two lines in almost all servlets. The `request` and `response` objects handle the communication with the client. All outputs and results generated by the servlet therefore are passed on by the response object. First, it is indicated that the output will be in HTML. Then, the output channel is created. In general, the page is dynamically generated by out.println instructions. In the third line, the search parameter is read from the request object. If the search parameter does not appear in the request, for example because the name of the formula field was entered incorrectly, this call comes back with `null`. Now we can start on the output of the results page. The `Page.printMenu()` method is a static method that takes on the output of the menus for all servlets. The

`PrintWriter` used by the server is handed over just like a `Page.SEARCH` constant that indicates the active menu item. Details of this method are dealt with in Section 8.12 on page 168, so we need not concern ourselves with them at this point. The actual content of the results page then begins with a repetition of the search string.

8.5.3 Creating and starting the database query

Once the search parameter is saved in the `search` variable, the database enquiry can begin. The objects of type `Connection` and `PreparedStatement` are imported from the `java.sql` package. They contain the connection to the database and a database enquiry. Before the connection is established, the area in which a database error can occur must be defined using the `try` instruction. The connection is provided by an object of the `Pool` type. Details of this and the handling of errors are explained in Section 8.5.4 on page 140 and Section 8.13 on page 171.

The enquiry is prepared by the `prepareStatement` method. All search enquiries have the form

```
select * from book where isbn = ? or title like ?
```

In the source text, the conventional variant of the handing over of the parameter had to be accessed with the `like` operator, otherwise the regular expression `%Searchstring%` could not be interpreted correctly.

At the time of program creation, only the search parameter is not yet known, so a question mark is entered in its place. As it can search for either the ISBN or part of the title of the book, another `like` expression is also used in the `where` clause of the enquiry. This means that regular expressions can be used. In our example the two percentage signs indicate that any character strings in the title can appear before and after the search parameter. The `setString` method puts the search parameter in the enquiry and `executeQuery` then executes it.

A `ResultSet` object is consequently delivered. This essentially contains a table of the results. The table columns are defined by the `select` and the `from` part of the query. All columns of the book table are selected here. These are ISBN, title, price, and amount. Each row of the table contains a book that fulfils the conditions of the `where` clause. Data can only be read from the active row. Calling `res.next()` has two aspects. The first is to activate the next row. It should be noted that initially the first row is not yet activated. The second is to show that there are no more rows available, which is indicated by the return of `false`.

Here is the source text to be entered in the `doGet()` method:

```
      Connection con = null;
      PreparedStatement pstmt = null;
      SQLException dbError = null;


   try {
      con = pool.getConnection();
      pstmt = con.prepareStatement("select * from book where isbn = ?
                                    or title like '%" + search + "%'");
      pstmt.setString(1, search);

      ResultSet res = pstmt.executeQuery();
      if (res.next()) {
         out.println("<table border=1>");
         out.println(Book.searchTableHeader());
         Book book = new Book();
         do {
            book.dbLoad(res);
            out.println(book.toHTMLSearchTableRow());
         } while(res.next());
         out.println("</table>");
            }
         else
         out.println("No book found.");
          res.close();
          pstmt.close();
      }
```

The `if(res.next())` query checks whether the results table contains any records at all. If not, a message to this effect is printed. Otherwise an HTML table is printed. Details, about how a book or a table with books should be represented in HTML, are contained in the book object. The active row of the database results is loaded into the `book` object and then printed. This process is repeated for each row. Finally, the `ResultSet` and the `PreparedStatement` are closed.

It is extremely important in the `doGet` method that the objects of the `Connection`, `PreparedStatement`, and `ResultSet` type are defined as local variables and not as instance variables of the `Search` class. If, for example, two users invoke the search function in their browsers at the same time, two threads are active at the same time in the `doGet` method of the servlet. If the variables are defined locally, each thread has its local variables available on its stack. If the variables were defined as instance variables, it would lead to conflicts, as both threads would access only one object instance each.

8.5.4 Dealing with errors

Things can go wrong when reading files, as well as with database queries. It is essential to have a good strategy for dealing with errors. For example, resources still held must be released and a helpful error message must be passed to the user, when an error occurs. The following `catch` part of the `try` block deals with this situation:

```
catch (PoolException e) {
    out.println(e);
}
catch (SQLException e) {
    out.println("DB Error during search: " + e);
        dbError = e;
}

finally {
    pool.close(con, dbError);
    out.println("</body></html>");
}
```

If an error occurs, the error message will be printed on the HTML page. This is very practical during the development phase, but later the client should not be confronted with these types of irrelevant technical details. If an error occurs when preparing or executing the database query or when reading the results, it is communicated to the connection pool via the `dbError` variable. In every case the `finally` block is executed, in which the database connection is returned and the closing HTML tags are printed.

8.5.5 An initial test run

In order to be able to compile servlets, the environment variable `classpath` must contain the path to the servlet basic classes. This can be done by typing the following command in the command line:

```
set CLASSPATH=C:\book\lib\server.jar;C:\book\lib\servlet.jar;.
```

We will now compile the `Book`, `Page`, `DatabaseHttpServlet`, and `Search` classes. Finally, we will make sure that the `class` files are located in the servlet directory of the Web server. We will then start up the Web server and navigate our browser to the following URL:

```
http://localhost/servlets/Search?search=rose
```

The browser now shows a search result page that looks somewhat similar to the one shown in Fig. 8.10 on page 135.

8.6 Encapsulated functionality in the book class

The book class is responsible for carrying out all functions regarding books. This has the decisive advantage that each servlet can use this class. This avoids source code, for example, which creates the HTML representation of a book, having to be written redundantly in several servlets. The choice of name and data type of the book instance variables has actually already been carried out when defining the book table in the database, since all attributes are mapped directly as variables.

```
public class Book {
    public String isbn;
    public String title;
    public float price;
    public int amount;
```

If a new book object is created, there are two possible ways of setting the fields. The data can come from a database query, as with a search, but it can also originate from an HTML form when a book is placed in the shopping basket or when the number of copies of a book is changed. The two methods that accomplish the loading of the book information are outlined next:

```
public void dbLoad(ResultSet res) throws SQLException {
    isbn = res.getString("isbn").trim();
    title = res.getString("title").trim();
    price = res.getFloat("price");
    amount = res.getInt("amount");
}
```

The dbLoad method is very simple. Only the four fields of the current results table row are read. As the character sequences in the database are defined with fixed lengths, the title and ISBN of the book are filled up and returned with a corresponding number of blank characters at the end. The trim method cuts these off. Any database error that may occur is passed on, since this method does not have the right context to interpret the error correctly. This is declared using the throws keyword.

```
public void requestLoad(HttpServletRequest request) throws
    ApplicationException {
 isbn = request.getParameter("isbn");
 title = request.getParameter("title");
 try {
  price = Float.parseFloat(request.getParameter("price"));
 }
 catch(NumberFormatException e) {
  throw new ApplicationException("Price not numeric.");
 }
 try {
  amount = Integer.parseInt(request.getParameter("amount"));
 }
```

```
        catch(NumberFormatException e) {
         throw new ApplicationException("Amount not numeric.");
        }
    }
```

The `requestLoad` method sets the local variables of the book object from the values of the form with which the servlet was called. It is important for this that each component, such as HTML pages or servlets, adhere to the name conventions. For the sake of simplicity, we will use the name of the variable for the name of the form field. Form values are always strings. Numerical values must therefore be converted using the relevant parse method. If an error occurs, an application-specific error object is generated.

```
    public boolean equals(Object o) {
        if (o instanceof Book)
            return (isbn.equals(((Book)o).isbn));
        else
            return false;
    }
```

The `equals` method determines when two book objects are the same. Since the ISBN is the primary key of the book table and since two different book objects can never have the same ISBN, the testing of equality can be reduced to testing the ISBN.

The further methods of the `book` class all deal with the output of a book's data. Dynamically generated book information always appears on the Web pages in an HTML table, namely once in the search results view and once in the shopping basket view.

```
   public String toHTMLSearchTableRow() {
      String available;
      String cart;
      if (amount > 0) {
         available = "available";
         cart = "<a href='CartHandler?isbn=" + isbn +
                "&title=" + java.net.URLEncoder.encode(title) +
                "&price=" + price +
                "&amount=1'><img border=0 src='/cart-small.gif'></a>";
      }
      else {
         available = "sold out";
         cart = " ";
      }
      return
         "<tr>" +
         "<td>" + isbn + "</td>" +
         "<td>" + title + "</td>" +
         "<td>£" + price + "</td>" +
         "<td>" + available + "</td>" +
         "<td>" + cart + "</td>" +
         "</tr>";
   }
```

For the search result, the return instruction at the end of the `toHTMLSearchTableRow` method returns the HTML table row with five columns. The ISBN and the title are issued directly. The price is given in "£". Instead of directly listing the number of copies of the book still in stock, it will simply say either "available" or "sold out." If the number is greater than zero, a shopping basket icon also is displayed. If the user clicks on it, a copy of the book is placed in the shopping basket. The icon therefore is actually a hyperlink that refers to the `CartHandler` servlet, which is responsible for the management of the shopping basket. The book attributes are submitted to this server as parameters directly in the URL, in other words, a form previously filled out. The `CartHandler` servlet is explained in Section 8.9 on page 150.

Calling the `java.net.URLEncoder.encode` method has the following purpose: Unlike the ISBN and the price, the title of a book may contain special characters or blank characters. Such characters cannot appear in a URL and must be specially encoded. A blank character, for example, is represented by `%20`. It is exactly this type of encoding that is carried out by the `encode` method.

The amount parameter is set to one, as it is most common for one copy of a book to be bought. If the user would like more copies, this can be altered in the shopping basket view. The search view, and therefore also the output of this method, can be seen in Figure 8.10.

At this point, a short remark should be made about security: It is very simple for the user to modify the URL so that a book is placed in the basket at the price of, say, 10 cents. However, when paying at the checkout servlet, the price of the books in the shopping basket is compared once more with the database. If the values do not match, the transaction will not be completed.

If you look at the book information in the shopping basket view in Figure 8.11, you will see that next to ISBN, title, and price in the first the three columns, each table row contains a form for changing the amount to be bought. All forms are processed again by the `CartHandler`. Which book this form corresponds to is encoded in the `hidden` parameter ISBN and cannot be changed by the user. By using this parameter the servlet can find out which book needs its number changing. The second parameter is of course the new number, which the user can enter in a small text field. It is important here that the text field is initialized with the current number. The `value` attribute of the text field, which is set to the value of the object variable number, is used for this.

```
public String toHTMLCartTableRow() {
   return
      "<form action=/servlet/CartHandler method=GET>" +
      "<tr>" +
      "<td>" + isbn + "</td>" +
      "<td>" + title + "</td>" +
      "<td>£" + price + " </td>" +
      "<td>" +
         "<input type=text name=amount size=2 value=" + amount + ">" +
         "<input type=hidden name=isbn value=" + isbn + ">" +
         "<input type=submit value=go>" +
      "</td>" +
      "</tr>" +
      "</form>";
   }
```

As the book class defines the book attributes, the appearance of a book table must also be defined there. We have already shown the methods for creating single rows. We are still missing the header and footer rows of the tables, which are generated using the following methods:

```java
public static String searchTableHeader() {
    return
        "<tr>" +
        "<td>ISBN</td>" +
        "<td>Title</td>" +
        "<td>Price</td>" +
        "<td> </td>" +
        "<td> </td>" +
        "</tr>";
}

public static String cartTableHeader() {
    return
        "<tr>" +
        "<td>ISBN</td>" +
        "<td>Title</td>" +
        "<td>Price</td>" +
        "<td>Amount</td>" +
        "</tr>";
}

public static String cartTableFooter(float sum) {
    return
        "<tr>" +
        "<td> </td>" +
        "<td>Total:</td>" +
        "<td>" + sum + "</td>" +
        "<td> </td>" +
        "</tr>";
}
} // End of book class
```

8.7 Managing the client session

The book search is a good example of a type of stateless access. All the information needed to process the request can be provided as parameters of a single invocation. In particular, there is no dependency between the individual invocations, so that the search will always have the same result, independent of which pages have been called up previously. The situation at the checkout is different. This action is considerably dependent on whether the client has already put books in the shopping basket and whether he or she is already authenticated. This means that a session (see Section 6.6.2 on page 109) is created for each client. In our example, the session contains information about the client and the books that were put in the shopping basket. Figure 8.21 on page 128 shows how two users from two browsers are logged into the system. The Web pages displayed contain the name of the respective client and their current shopping basket.

8.7.1   Creating and deleting sessions

When is a user session created, when is it deleted, and how are sessions implemented? We would like to reiterate briefly the most important facts about sessions.

As we already have discussed, the HTTP protocol of the Internet actually has no conditions. The riddle will be answered if you turn off the automatic acceptance of cookies in the browser. Cookies are, as we know, small units of data stored on the client side which are typically used for saving names and preferences. If you disable the automatic setting of cookies in your browser, then it will ask explicitly whether a cookie can be set. Figure 8.15 shows this situation in Netscape Navigator.

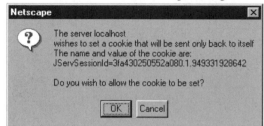

Figure 8.15: Use of cookies by the servlet engine.

If a servlet is called on the server which wants to create a session, the dialog will appear as to whether the cookie sent by the servlet engine should be accepted. This demonstrates that every browser is assigned a temporary identification, with which a connection between the browser on the client side and the corresponding session object on the server side is established. The session is destroyed as soon as a certain period of inactivity has elapsed, or the session is specifically deactivated by calling `session.invalidate`.

This mechanism is very simple to handle and enables the straightforward saving of user session data between the individual servlet invocations, such as Login, Search, Shopping Basket, and Checkout.

8.7.2   The session interface

The servlet API provides the `HttpSession` interface. The user session can be obtained from the Request object by the `doGet` or `doPost` method from the `Request` object:

```
HttpSession session = request.getSession(true);
```

We remember that the flag submitted indicates whether a new session should be created if there are none available. The `HttpSession` interface can be used like a hash table in Java, meaning that any objects can be created under a certain name and can be called again by another servlet. If the session cannot be created, or if no object with the corresponding name is found in the session, then the `getSession` or `getValue` methods return the value `null`.

```
Customer customer;
...
session.putValue("customer", customer);
...
customer = (Customer)session.getValue("customer");
```

8.7.3   Avoiding cookies with URL rewriting

In case cookies are disallowed on the client, the session ID must be transferred via the
URL. The following small sample demonstrates how this works. The URL of every
hyperlink or form action attribute, the string Session in the example, must be converted
by calling response.encodeURL. Figure 8.16 shows the effect of this technique when
cookies are denied. Looking at the HTML source of the dynamically generated page, one
can see that the first line of the form definition was modified to <form
action='Session;jsessionid=yrag475o91'>.

```
import java.io.*;
import javax.servlet.*;
import javax.servlet.http.*;

public class Session extends HttpServlet {

    public void doGet(HttpServletRequest request,
                      HttpServletResponse response)
                throws ServletException, IOException
    {
        PrintWriter out = response.getWriter();
        response.setContentType("text/plain");

        HttpSession session = request.getSession(true);
        String text = request.getParameter("text") + ", " +
                      session.getAttribute("text");
        session.setAttribute("text", text);
        out.println("<html>" + text);
        out.println("<form action='"+response.encodeURL("Session")+"'>");
        out.println("<input type='text' name='text'>");
        out.println("<input type='submit'>");
        out.println("<form></html>");
    }
}
```

This mechanism makes sure that sessions will work on all clients. It is important to note that while a session is active, no static page can be viewed. Static pages contain hyperlinks without the session ID encoded. Traversing such a link causes the session ID to be lost.

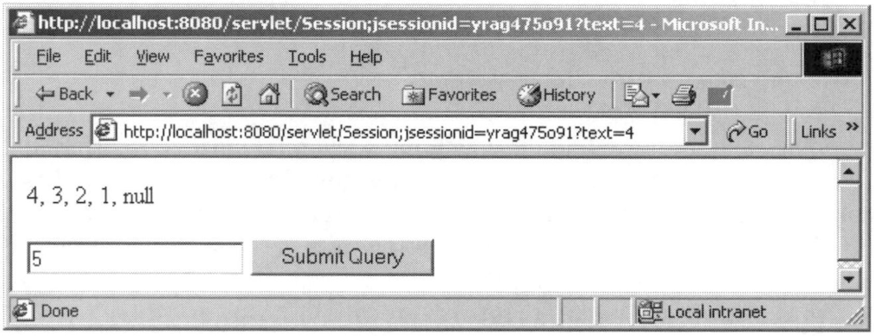

Figure 8.16: The cookie of the session-based servlet was denied. The `encodeURL` method causes the session ID to appear in the URL.

8.8 The shopping basket class

Before we explain the management of the shopping basket in the next section, we will describe the class itself. The shopping basket is responsible for the management of the books selected and offers relevant methods such as placing a book in the shopping basket. It makes sense to construct the shopping basket on the `Vector` class of the *Java Foundation Classes*, as this already provides a simple solution for managing arbitrary objects.

```java
import java.util.Vector;

public class Cart extends Vector {

    public void addElement(Book book) {
        int i = indexOf(book);
        if (i == -1)
            super.addElement(book);
        else {
            Book b = (Book)elementAt(i);
            b.amount = b.amount + book.amount;
        }
    }
}
```

If a new book is to be placed in the shopping basket, the `addElement` method is used. In this method, it is checked whether the book is available, using the `indexOf` method. You can go back to this method, since the equivalence of two books is defined by the `equals` method in the book class.

If the book is not yet there, it is inserted with the `addElement` method given by the `Vector`. Otherwise the number of copies of the book is increased accordingly.

```
public void changeAmount(Book book) {
    int i = indexOf(book);
    if (i != -1) {
        Book b = (Book)elementAt(i);
        if (book.amount > 0)
            b.amount = book.amount;
        else
            removeElementAt(i);
    }
}
```

It should be possible to change the number of copies of a book in the shopping basket. In Section 8.9 on page 150 we describe how HTML forms that pass on the ISBN and the new number are installed in the shopping basket view. The next section explains how this request is then packed into a book object by the `CartHandler` servlet. Therefore such an object appears here as a parameter. Using the `indexOf` method, we will also determine the index of the book to be changed. If the number of copies is zero, the book object will be removed from the vector. Otherwise the new number will be assumed.

```
public float sum() {
    float res = 0;
    for (int i=0; i<size(); i++) {
        Book book = (Book)elementAt(i);
        res = res + book.amount * book.price;
    }
    return res;
}
```

The `sum()` method calculates the total price of all books in the shopping basket. As we already have mentioned, the user can, by manipulating the URL in the browser, artificially influence the price in the shopping basket and therefore also the sum. When it comes to the actual purchase, therefore, the prices are compared once more with the prices stored in the database.

```
public String toHTMLTable() {
    if (size() == 0)
        return "Your cart is empty.";
    else {
        StringBuffer buffer = new StringBuffer();
        buffer.append("<table border=1>");
        buffer.append(Book.cartTableHeader());
        for (int i=0; i<size(); i++) {
            buffer.append("<tr>");
            buffer.append(((Book)elementAt(i)).toHTMLCartTableRow());
            buffer.append("</tr>");
        }
        buffer.append(Book.cartTableFooter(sum()));
```

```
            buffer.append("</table>");
            return buffer.toString();
        }
    }
} // End of shopping basket class
```

Lastly, we will define another method using `toHTMLTable`, which issues the whole shopping basket as an HTML table. This invokes the book class methods, which encode the header row, the footer row, and the individual books in HTML.

8.9 Managing the shopping basket

As Fig. 8.10 on page 135 and Fig. 8.13 on page 137 show, the shopping basket view can be called from two different places, namely from the search, if a new book arrives, and from the shopping basket view itself, if the quantity of a book is changed. The basket manager servlet, responsible for the creation of the shopping basket view, can determine which call it is, due to the form parameter. In the shopping basket view forms, only the number and ISBN are given, whereas from the search result, all the information about the book is provided. Therefore, if the `title` parameter is available and the `if request(request.getParameter("title") != null)` condition is fulfilled, then the book will be added. Otherwise the number will be altered.

```
import java.io.*;
import javax.servlet.*;
import javax.servlet.http.*;

public class CartHandler extends HttpServlet {

    public void doGet(HttpServletRequest request,
                      HttpServletResponse response)
            throws ServletException, IOException {

        response.setContentType("text/html");
        PrintWriter out = response.getWriter();

        Page.printMenu(request, out, Page.CART);

        HttpSession session = request.getSession(true);
        Cart cart = (Cart)session.getValue("cart");
        Book book = new Book();

        if (request.getParameter("title") != null) {
            try {
                book.requestLoad(request);
                if (cart == null) {
                    cart = new Cart();
                    session.putValue("cart", cart);
                }
```

```
                cart.addElement(book);
            }
            catch(ApplicationException e) {
                out.println(e);
            }
        }
```

The `CartHandler` servlet begins with the usual declarations. As was explained in Section 8.7 on page 145, the `shopping basket` object can be created in and also retrieved from the user session, which is what will be done here. The `requestLoad` method described in the `Book` class sets the fields in the book object to the parameter passed on in the URL, using the HTTP-GET method. If no shopping basket had been created in the session, an empty basket is created and saved in the session. Lastly, the book is placed in the shopping basket by calling `addElement`. An `ApplicationException` can occur if, for example, the user enters a non-numerical value for the new number. In this case nothing in the shopping basket will be changed.

```
        else if (request.getParameter("amount") != null) {
            book.isbn = request.getParameter("isbn");
            try {
                book.amount = Integer.parseInt(
                                    request.getParameter("amount"));
                if (cart != null) {
                    cart.changeAmount(book);
                }
                else
                    out.println("Your cart is empty.");
            }
            catch(NumberFormatException e) {
                out.println("The amount isn't numeric.");
            }
        }
```

If there is no title in the request object, then the number of copies is changed by the user. To execute this user request, the ISBN and the new number are copied into the as yet uninitialized `book` object. This object is passed on to the `changeAmount` method, which carries out the relevant changes in the shopping basket.

```
        if (cart == null)
            out.println("Your cart is empty.");
        else
            out.println(cart.toHTMLTable());

        out.println("</body></html>");
    }
}
```

Finally, the HTML representation of the shopping basket is called by the `toHTMLTable` method and delivered to the client via the output stream `out`.

8.10 Client management

In the following three sub-sections, we will first explain the general customer class. Building on this, we will explain the login procedure and the creation of new users in the database.

8.10.1 The client class

As is the case with the book class, described in Section 8.6 on page 142, the `client` class encapsulates functionality regarding the loading and storing of clients from and to the database. In addition, the authentication of the user is controlled in the authentication method defined here. This method is then called by the login servlet.

```java
import java.sql.*;
import javax.servlet.*;
import javax.servlet.http.*;

public class Customer {

    public String id;
    public String email;
    public String password;
    public String firstname;
    public String lastname;
    public String street;
    public String zip;
    public String city;
    public String creditcardnr;
    public int validuntilMonth;
    public int validuntilYear;
```

As in the `book` class, we also find in the `Customer` class a corresponding instance variable for each attribute defined in the database table. To prevent errors when implementing the `dbLoad` and `dbSave` methods, the Java variable names and the database attribute names are the same.

```java
public void dbLoad(ResultSet res) throws SQLException {
    id = res.getString("id").trim();
    email = res.getString("email").trim();
    password = res.getString("password").trim();
    firstname = res.getString("firstname").trim();
    lastname = res.getString("lastname").trim();
    street = res.getString("street").trim();
```

```
        zip = res.getString("zip");
        city = res.getString("city").trim();
        creditcardnr = res.getString("creditcardnr").trim();
        validuntilMonth = res.getInt("validuntilMonth");
        validuntilYear = res.getInt("validuntilYear");
    }
```

The dbLoad method encapsulates the transfer of the cursor row attributes in the ResultSet object to the object instance variables. As is the case in the book class, blank characters at the end of the character sequences delivered by the database are removed using the trim method. Database errors that may occur are passed on to the calling methods as indicated by the throws clause, so that they can be dealt with accordingly there.

```
    public void requestLoad(HttpServletRequest request)
                throws ApplicationException {
        email = request.getParameter("email");
        java.util.Date timestamp = new java.util.Date();
        id = "" + Math.abs(email.hashCode()) + "" + timestamp.getTime();
        password = request.getParameter("password1");
        if (!password.equals(request.getParameter("password2")))
            throw new ApplicationException("Password was not entered
correctly.");
        firstname = request.getParameter("firstname");
        lastname = request.getParameter("lastname");
        street = request.getParameter("street");
        zip = request.getParameter("zip");
        city = request.getParameter("city");
        creditcardnr = request.getParameter("creditcardnr");
        if (!creditcardnr.equals("")) {
            try {
                validuntilYear = Integer.parseInt(
                                    request.getParameter("year"));
                validuntilMonth = Integer.parseInt(
                                    request.getParameter("month"));
            }
            catch (NumberFormatException e) {
                throw new ApplicationException("The date is not numeric.");
            }
        }
        else {
            validuntilMonth = 0;
            validuntilYear = 0;
        }
    }
```

If a new client enters his or her information in the HTML registration form, the servlet that processes this request must be capable of initializing a customer object with this data. The requestLoad method implements this functionality, which, as shown in Section 8.10.3 on page 158, is called by the NewUser servlet. The program code is significantly longer than the `dbLoad` method that we have just explained, as the data in the `Request` object is handed over as strings. Therefore, in the example of the credit card information, these have to be converted back into numbers. This, in turn, makes some error handling necessary. However, the principle is the same in both variants. Only the client identification is generated in the method.

In the discussion in Section 8.1.1 on page 160, the combination of the hash code of the e-mail address and the system time was suggested. The implementation of this strategy can be seen at the beginning of the method. This method also checks whether the password was entered correctly, since the user has to enter his or her password twice in the corresponding formula in Fig. 8.17. If these two values do not match, an error is reported.

```java
public void dbSave(Connection con)
        throws ApplicationException, SQLException {
    PreparedStatement pstmt = con.prepareStatement("insert into client
values (?,?,?,?,?,?,?,?,?,?,?)");

    pstmt.setString(1, id);
    pstmt.setString(2, email);
    pstmt.setString(3, password);
    pstmt.setString(4, firstname);
    pstmt.setString(5, lastname);
    pstmt.setString(6, street);
    pstmt.setString(7, zip);
    pstmt.setString(8, city);
    pstmt.setString(9, creditcardnr);
    pstmt.setInt(10, validuntilMonth);
    pstmt.setInt(11, validuntilYear);

    try {
        pstmt.executeUpdate();
        pstmt.close();
    }
    catch(SQLException e) {
        if (e.getSQLState().equals("23000"))
            throw new ApplicationException(
                "Input error. Check your email address.");
        else
            throw e;
    }
}
```

The `dbsave` method is used to store a client object in the database. As the instance variables correspond exactly to the database attributes, only one `insert into` command has to be used as a parameter with all instance variables. If a database error occurs, it is more than likely that there is a conflict with another client's e-mail address. Since the e-mail address is used to authenticate the user, two clients cannot give the same e-mail address. This condition is queried in the database, as the `email` attribute is defined as a unique attribute by the SQL keyword `unique`. Table A.2 on page 413 shows that violations of database conditions are normally displayed using the SQL 23000 error. Correspondingly, in this case an `ApplicationException` with a corresponding message is generated. Otherwise the `SQLException` is passed on.

```
public static Customer authentication(
                    Connection con, String email, String password)
                throws SQLException {
    PreparedStatement pstmt = con.prepareStatement(
        "select * from client where email = ? and password = ?");

    pstmt.setString(1, email);
    pstmt.setString(2, password);

    ResultSet res = pstmt.executeQuery();

    if (!res.next())
        return null;

    Customer customer = new Customer();
    customer.dbLoad(res);
    res.close();
    pstmt.close();
    return customer;
}
```

When logging in, the user enters his or her login name, in our case the e-mail address and password. These values are then delivered to the authentication method together with a database connection for starting the enquiry. Using the select request, all clients with these attribute values are found. Since the e-mail address has to be unique, only one or no tuples can be present in the result. Instead of the otherwise usual while loop, an if request is sufficient for us here. If the result is empty, it means that there is no client with this e-mail address and this password and the login procedure fails. This is indicated to the calling method by the return of null. Otherwise, the data about the client found in the database is packed in an object of type client and returned.

```
public boolean equals(Object o) {
    if (o instanceof Customer)
        return (id.equals(((Customer)o).id));
    else
        return false;
}
}
```

In this last method, as is the case in the `Book` class, the equivalence of two clients is reduced to the equivalence of the primary key.

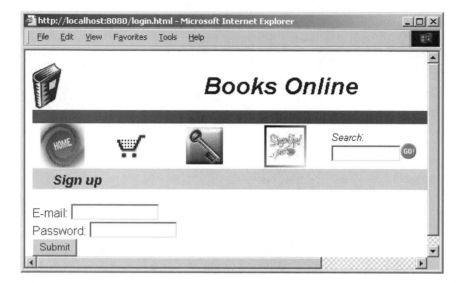

Figure 8.17: This Login form invokes the Login servlet.

8.10.2 The login procedure

The login servlet has to call the `authentication` method introduced in the previous section with the e-mail address sent from the HTML form in Fig. 8.17 and with the password. If necessary, it also has to create the client information in the session object.

The servlet itself looks like the following:

```
import java.io.*;
import javax.servlet.*;
import javax.servlet.http.*;
import java.sql.*;

public class Login extends DatabaseHttpServlet {

    public void doPost(HttpServletRequest request,
                    HttpServletResponse response)
            throws ServletException, IOException {

        String msg = "";
        Connection con = null;
        SQLException dbError = null;
```

```
String email = request.getParameter("email");
String password = request.getParameter("password");

try {
   con = pool.getConnection();
   Customer customer = Customer.authentication(
                                con, email, password);
```

After the customary variable declarations, the servlet collects the parameters from the Request object. These are handed over using the HTTP-POST method, otherwise the password would be visible to everyone in the browser display of the URL. If successful, the authentication method returns the client information, which is then stored in the local customer variable.

```
if (customer != null) {
   HttpSession session = request.getSession(true);
   Customer oldCustomer =
                     (Customer)session.getValue("customer");
   if (oldCustomer != null)
      if (!oldCustomer.equals(customer))
         session.removeValue("cart");

   session.putValue("customer", customer);
   msg = "Login successful.";
}
else {
   msg = "Authentication error. Please try again..";
}
}
```

If the return value is null, a report of the unsuccessful login will be stored in the message variable. This variant was selected with regard to the direct output of the results page, in order to be able to execute clearly all outputs at the end of the method. If a client entry is found in the database, first it is checked whether another client was previously logged in from the same browser. If this is the case, their shopping basket is removed. Before the success message is produced, the servlet stores the client information in the session. In doing so, any information about a previously logged-in user is deleted.

```
catch(PoolException e) {
   msg = e.toString();
}
catch (SQLException e) {
   msg = "DB error during authentication query: " + e.toString();
   dbError = e;
}

finally {
   response.setContentType("text/html");
   PrintWriter out = response.getWriter();
   Page.printMenu(request, out, Page.LOGIN);
```

```
            out.println(msg);
            pool.close(con, dbError);
            out.println("</body></html>");
        }
    }
}
```

Regardless of whether the login was successful or not, or whether a database error has occurred, an HTML page is returned to the user. The message variable contains the relevant information about the actions executed by the servlet. The rest of the page always contains the same text.

8.10.3 Dealing with new registrations

New clients enter their information in the form shown in Figure 8.18. Like the login servlet, this servlet also relies heavily on the functionality of the Customer class.

```
import java.io.*;
import javax.servlet.*;
import javax.servlet.http.*;
import java.sql.*;

public class NewUser extends DatabaseHttpServlet {

    public void doPost(HttpServletRequest request,
                       HttpServletResponse response)
             throws ServletException, IOException {

        String msg = "";
        Connection con = null;
        SQLException dbError = null;

        try {
            con = pool.getConnection();
            Customer customer = new Customer();
            customer.requestLoad(request);
            customer.dbSave(con);

            HttpSession session = request.getSession(true);
            Customer oldCustomer = (Customer)session.getValue("customer");
            if (oldCustomer != null)
                if (!oldCustomer.equals(customer))
                        session.removeValue("cart");

            session.putValue("customer", customer);
            msg = "User created successfully.";
        }  // End of try-block
```

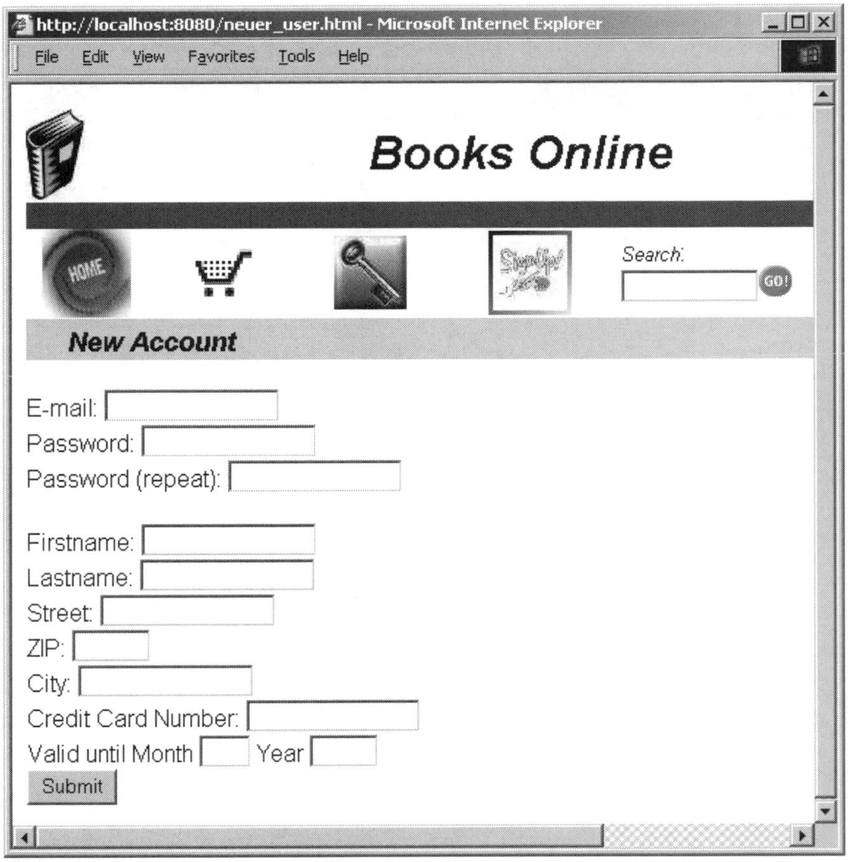

Figure 8.18: The form for new users to log in calls the NewUser servlet.

The `requestLoad` method initializes the client object using the values from the HTTP request. This information is then immediately entered into the database by means of the `dbSave` method. We want a new user to be logged in straight away, once he or she has successfully registered. To do this, the shopping basket of the user previously working on this browser is deleted and the new client information is entered in the session.

```
catch (SQLException e) {
   msg = "DB error during insertion of new user: " + e.toString();
   dbError = e;
}
catch (ApplicationException e) {
   msg = e.toString();
}
catch(PoolException e) {
   msg = e.toString();
}
```

Many errors can occur during registration. As well as the usual database problems, quite a number of incorrect user inputs, such as non-numerical credit card numbers or an e-mail address which already exists in the database, can lead to errors. In this case, an error message comprehensible to the user is provided in the form of an ApplicationException and is copied to the message variable. As with the login servlet, the results page output is only processed at the end.

```
        finally {
            response.setContentType("text/html");
            PrintWriter out = response.getWriter();
            Page.printMenu(request, out, Page.NEWUSER);
            out.println(msg);
            pool.close(con, dbError);
            out.println("</body></html>");
        }
    }
} // End of servlet
```

8.11 Completing the purchase transaction

Completing the purchase transaction is by far the most difficult task. A number of steps have to be carried out, which can all lead to errors. Besides the coordination of the database and credit card payment, the handling of errors is therefore particularly important. As the credit card payment is not shown until Chapter 11, we will leave out the necessary CORBA initialization and assume that the debit is implemented in a local transfer method.

Here is the doGet method of the checkout servlet:

```
import java.io.*;
import javax.servlet.*;
import javax.servlet.http.*;
import java.sql.*;
import CreditCard.*;
import org.omg.CosNaming.*;
import org.omg.CORBA.*;

public class CheckOut extends DatabaseHttpServlet {

    String nameserverIP;
    String nameserverPort;
    int account;

    Dispatcher d = null;

    boolean creditcardok = true;

    public void init(ServletConfig config) throws ServletException {
        super.init(config);
```

```
            nameserverIP = config.getInitParameter("nameserverIP");
            nameserverPort = config.getInitParameter("nameserverPort");
            try { account =
                      Integer.parseInt(config.getInitParameter("account")); }
                      catch(NumberFormatException e) { account = -1; }

                if (nameserverIP == null)
                    nameserverIP = "127.0.0.1";
                if (nameserverPort == null)
                    nameserverPort = "900";
                if (account == -1)
                    account = 7745;

            try {
                // create and initialize the ORB
                String[] args = new String[4];
                args[0] = "-ORBInitialHost";
                args[1] = nameserverIP;
                args[2] = "-ORBInitialPort";
                args[3] = nameserverPort;
                ORB orb = ORB.init(args, null);

                // get the root naming context
                org.omg.CORBA.Object objRef =
                            orb.resolve_initial_references("NameService");
                NamingContext ncRef = NamingContextHelper.narrow(objRef);

                // resolve the Object Reference in Naming
                NameComponent nc = new NameComponent("CreditCard", "");
                NameComponent path[] = {nc};
                d = DispatcherHelper.narrow(ncRef.resolve(path));
            }
            catch(Exception e) {
                creditcardok = false;
            }
    }

    public void doGet(HttpServletRequest request,
                      HttpServletResponse response)
                throws ServletException, IOException {

        String msg;

        HttpSession session = request.getSession(true);
        client client = (client)session.getValue("client");
        Cart cart = (Cart)session.getValue("cart");

        if (cart == null)
            msg = "Your cart is empty";
        else
            if (cart.size() == 0)
                msg = "Your cart is empty";
            else
```

```
            if (client == null)
               msg = "You must login first";
            else {
               String payment = request.getParameter("payment");
               if (payment == null)
                  payment = "";
               if (payment.equals("creditcard")) {
                  if (creditcardok)
                     msg = buy(client, cart, 0, session);
                  else
                     msg =
                        "<p>Unfortunately Credit Card payments aren't
                        possible at the moment.</p>" +
                           buy(client, cart, 1, session);
               }
               else
                  msg = buy(client, cart, 1, session);
            }

      response.setContentType("text/html");
      PrintWriter out = response.getWriter();
      Page.printMenu(request, out, Page.CHECKOUT);
      out.println(msg);
      out.println("</body></html>");
   }
```

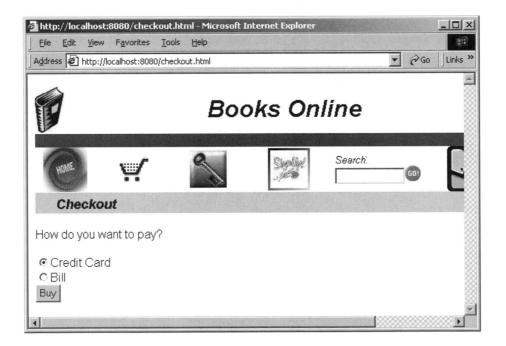

Figure 8.19: Before the order is completed, the client chooses between paying by invoice or by credit card.

If you click on the "checkout" symbol on the right-hand side of the menu structure (see Fig. 8.5 on page 132), the form shown in Fig. 8.19 will appear first. The user has to indicate whether they are going to pay by credit card or by invoice. The servlet is activated by this enquiry. First of all, it checks certain conditions needed for a successful order. The user must be logged in and the shopping basket must not be empty. If errors occur, the servlet stores an appropriate message in the `message` variable. The `creditcardok` flag indicates whether the network connection to the CORBA server was initialized successfully. If not, and if the client opted to pay by credit card, an invoice will be sent instead. Figure 8.20 shows this situation.

Figure 8.20: If the credit card server cannot be contacted, an invoice will be sent instead.

Once the necessary enquiries have been completed, the local `buy` method takes over the database and payment actions. The client information, the shopping basket, a flag that indicates the method of payment, and the HTTP session are passed on as parameters. The session is given as a parameter, so that the shopping basket can be "emptied" if the order is successful.

```
private String buy(client client, Cart cart,
                   int bill, HttpSession session) {

    boolean ok = false;
    float sum;
    String msg = "";
    Connection con = null;
    PreparedStatement select = null;
```

```
PreparedStatement update = null;
PreparedStatement insert = null;
SQLException dbError = null;
Payment z = null;

try {
    con = pool.getConnection();

    setAutomaticTransactionMode(con, false);

    update = con.prepareStatement("update book set amount =
                amount-? where isbn=?");
    insert = con.prepareStatement("insert into orders
                values(?,?,?,?,?)");
    String time = "" + (new java.util.Date()).getTime();
    for (int i=0; i<cart.size(); i++) {
        Book book = (Book)cart.elementAt(i);
        update.setInt(1, book.amount);
        update.setString(2, book.isbn);
        insert.setString(1, client.id);
        insert.setString(2, book.isbn);
        insert.setString(3, time);
        insert.setInt(4, book.amount);
        insert.setInt(5, bill);
        update.executeUpdate();
        insert.executeUpdate();
    }
    update.close();
    insert.close();
```

First of all, the servlet executes the database actions. As these actions can no longer be completed with just one SQL enquiry, the SQL commands need to be grouped in a database transaction. The `setAutomaticTransactionMode` method initiates the relevant steps relating to this. The implementation of this method continues below. Firstly, a new record has to be inserted into the orders table for each book in the shopping basket, and the number of books available is reduced. The `update` and `insert` SQL requests carry out this task. In this way, all order entries are assigned the same time of receipt, stored in the `time` variable.

```
select = con.prepareStatement(
    "select sum(price * orders.amount)
    from book, orders
    where isbn = book and client = ? and date = ?");
select.setString(1, client.id);
select.setString(2, time);
ResultSet res = select.executeQuery();
res.next();
sum = res.getFloat(1);
res.close();
select.close();
```

```
if (Math.round(sum * 100) != Math.round(cart.sum() * 100))
    throw new ApplicationException("The prices in your cart
    don't match those in the DB: " + sum + " <> " + cart.sum());
```

We already have mentioned that the information in the shopping basket can be manipulated by the user, as this is handed over by the HTTP-GET method. You can, therefore, amend the values encoded in the URL in the browser. This is no problem in the case of the title and the number. The title is not used internally and the user, of course, needs to be able to manipulate the number. However, if the ISBN or the price is manipulated, a book can be bought very cheaply. The servlet therefore compares the price in the shopping basket once again with the price in the database. The select request is a join of the `book` and `order` tables. Only the information about the order just placed is requested, as the client identification and the system time of the order are indicated in the `where` clause. The expression `sum(price * order.number)` in the enquiry gives the total sum of the order. If this does not match the sum of the price in the shopping basket, apart from errors in rounding, an error is reported.

```
if (bill == 0) {
    try {
        z = d.openConnection();
        z.transfer(client.creditcardnr,
                client.validuntilMonth,
                client.validuntilYear, account, sum, "GBP");
        msg = "Your credit card was billed with £" + sum +
            ". Thanks for shopping with us.";
    }
    catch(Exception e) {
        if (!(e instanceof CreditCardException))
            throw new CreditCardException(
                "Error communicating with the credit card server");
        else
            throw (CreditCardException)e;
    }
}
else {
    msg = "You will receive a bill for £" + sum + " shortly. " +
        "Thank you for shopping with us.";
}
session.removeValue("cart");
ok = true;
}
```

If everything has gone well until now, everything is in order as far as Books Online is concerned. The absence of database errors indicates that enough books are in stock and that both the book ISBN and the client number are recognized. Now the credit card transfer can be initiated. Here we are anticipating Chapter 11 by saying that the `transfer` method can cause specific CORBA errors similar to an `SQLException` as well as application errors (`CreditcardException`), with an invalid card for example. All exceptions are intercepted. If it is a general CORBA error, and not a `CreditcardException`, it is changed into an application error. The reason for this is to reduce the number of different errors.

If the client is paying by invoice, nothing else needs to be done except for the creation of a message, as the information to appear on an invoice is noted in the orders table. Finally, the shopping basket is "emptied" and the `ok` flag indicates that the transaction has been successfully completed.

```
catch (SQLException e) {
   msg = e.toString() + "  JDBC:" + e.getErrorCode() +
         "  SQL:" + e.getSQLState();
   dbError = e;
}
catch(CreditCardException e) {
   msg = "Credit card transfer failed: " + e.reason;
}
catch(PoolException e) {
   msg = e.toString();
}
catch(ApplicationException e) {
   msg = e.toString();
}
```

If any error occurs, a message is saved for the user. As the `ok` flag is initialized with `false` and the last instruction of the `try` block that sets the flag to `true` is not reached in the case of an error, this flag indicates whether the database transaction will have to be canceled or not. The credit card payment can not be reversed. This is no problem, however, since if the database queries started previously produce an error, the payment is not started at all.

```
finally {
   try {
      if (ok)
         con.commit();
      else
         con.rollback();
      setAutomaticTransactionMode(con, true);
   }
   catch (SQLException e) {
      msg = "Error during DB transaction: " + e;
      dbError = e;
   }

   if (bill == 0)
      d.close(z);
   pool.close(con, dbError);
}
return msg;
}
```

Finally, the `ok` flag decides whether the order is completed using a commit, or reversed by a rollback. Calling `setAutomaticTransactionMode` returns the database connection to the normal transaction mode.

So what happens in this method? In a JDBC database connection, the following options are set as default: Every query is actually a transaction. This means that a successful update takes immediate effect and can no longer be reversed. If this mode is switched off by `setAutoCommit(false)`, an explicit invocation of `commit` or `rollback` is necessary to complete or reverse the transaction. So the servlet switches off at the beginning of the automatic mode and back on again at the end. Not all databases support this, as can be seen in Table A.1 on page 412. JDBC, however, offers the option of requesting information on the database used. The `supportsTransactions` method of the `DatabaseMetaData` class provides information about whether the automatic mode can be switched off and whether several enquiries can be combined in one transaction.

```
private void setAutomaticTransactionMode(Connection con, boolean on)
            throws SQLException {
   DatabaseMetaData meta = con.getMetaData();
   if (meta.supportsTransactions()) {
      if (on)
         if (meta.supportsTransactionIsolationLevel(
               Connection.TRANSACTION_READ_COMMITTED)) {
            System.out.println(
               "Isolation Level: TRANSACTION_READ_COMMITTED");
            con.setTransactionIsolation(
               Connection.TRANSACTION_READ_COMMITTED);
         }
         else
            System.out.println("Isolation Level unchanged.");
      else
         if (meta.supportsTransactionIsolationLevel(
               Connection.TRANSACTION_SERIALIZABLE)) {
            System.out.println(
               "Isolation Level: TRANSACTION_SERIALIZABLE");

            con.setTransactionIsolation(
               Connection.TRANSACTION_SERIALIZABLE);
         }
         else
            System.out.println("Isolation Level unchanged.");
      System.out.println("AutoCommit: " + on);
         con.setAutoCommit(on);
   }
   else
      System.out.println("DB does not support transactions.");
   }
}
```

A further JDBC default setting is the *Transaction Isolation Level*. JDBC defines five of these levels. We do not wish to provide a full explanation concerning these levels, but we will say this much: the various levels indicate how restrictively the database server provides the records that have been read and written by a transaction with locks, in order to protect them from being accessed by other transactions running parallel. Restrictive levels can be set to guarantee a higher level of security. However, the performance of the server is impaired if many records are locked.

When dealing with orders, it is advisable that the most secure level (TRANSACTION SERIALIZABLE) should be used. You must also check beforehand whether the database used supports this level. At the end, the servlet restores the JDBC default (TRANSACTION READ COMMITTED). Figure 8.21 shows the method output when using Access 97, SQL Server, and MySQL. In Access, the Isolation Level can not be modified. SQL Server offers full support, while MySQL does not yet support transactions.

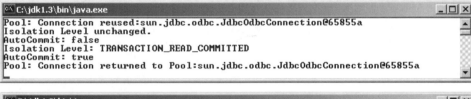

Figure 8.21: Transaction support when ordering books.

8.12 Navigation structure output

The purpose of the class Page is to relieve all servlets of the task of formatting the pages to be created. As mentioned in Section 8.3, all pages should demonstrate a uniform design. We committed to the structure shown in Section 8.4 on page 131. This structure is reflected in this class. All elements displayed in the illustration, except for the actual content, were printed using the class Page.

```
import java.io.*;
import javax.servlet.*;
import javax.servlet.http.*;

public class Page {

    public static final int CART = 0;
    public static final int SEARCH = 1;
    public static final int CHECKOUT = 2;
    public static final int LOGIN = 3;
    public static final int NEWUSER = 4;
```

The constants defined here are used to identify the active menu entry. This influences the output as the heading of the active menu entry will be shown large again.

```
private static String part1 =
    "  <tr align=\"center\">" +
    "  <td width=\"397\" height=\"1\" colspan=\"4\"
       bgcolor=\"#ffcc66\"><div align=\"left\"><p><strong><em><font" +
    "  face=\"Arial\"><big><big>    </big>";

private static String part2 =
    "</big></font></em></strong></td>" +
    "  <td width=\"310\" height=\"1\" colspan=\"2\"
       bgcolor=\"#ffcc66\"><div align=\"right\"><p><font" +
    "  face=\"Arial\" size=\"2\"><em>";


private static String part3 =
    "    </em></font></td>" +
    "      </tr>" +
    "  </table>" +
    "</form>";
```

Let's look at the output to be implemented in this class a little more closely. Apart from two points, the individual greeting and the menu entry display, the outputs are all static. We proceed with the implementation as follows: A typical page was created with FrontPage. The design used shows that the company name, logo, and navigation bar make up the majority of the HTML text, and have to be modified the most frequently. It therefore makes sense not to define this section as fixed strings in the class, but in a separate text file. This enables the source text to be edited using other tools, without having to compile the class again.

The remaining two dynamic entries are framed by three static elements. These static HTML elements are therefore saved in the strings part1, part2, and part3 for later use.

```
private static final String[] text = {
    "Shopping cart", "Search", "Checkout",
    "Sign up", "New Account"};

public static void printMenu(HttpServletRequest request,
    PrintWriter out, int page) {
try {
    BufferedReader in = new BufferedReader(
        new InputStreamReader(new FileInputStream(
        new File("webpages\\menu.txt")))));
    String line;

    while (true) {
        line = in.readLine();
        if (line == null) break;
        out.println(line);
    }
    in.close();
```

PrintMenu is the only method of this class. It receives the following parameters: The request object allows access to the client session, as the name of the client is stored there. With the out parameter the HTML text of the page to be created can be sent on its way back to the client directly. Finally, one of the constants defined above is enclosed to show to which menu entry the page belongs. The respective headings are placed in the text array.

As explained in the previous paragraph, the method issues the HTML text saved in the menu.txt file first.

```
    out.println(part1);
        out.println(Page.text[page]);
    out.println(part2);

        HttpSession session = request.getSession(false);
        if (session == null)
            out.println("Guest");
        else {
            client client = (client)session.getValue("client");
        if (client == null)
            out.println("Guest");
        else
            out.println(client.firstname + " " + client.lastname);
        }
        out.println(part3);
    }
    catch(FileNotFoundException e) {
        out.println("Menu bar not found.");
    }
    catch(IOException e) {
        out.println("Error reading menu bar.");
    }
}
}
```

The output of three predefined static strings and the two dynamic components now follows. The heading is created in the array by the simple reference `text[page]`. The index is provided by the calling method. The formatting of the heading is contained in the static strings, issued beforehand and afterwards.

The client name or "guest" (if the user is not yet authenticated) is issued, followed by the third string. The formatting also is contained in the surrounding strings here, i.e. the second and third strings.

8.13 Management of database connections

When working with databases, bottlenecks often occur when accessing the central database server. In our example, a database query is required for every search and login process. If you analyze the different components – connecting, preparing, starting the query, reading the results and disconnecting, you will see that establishing the connection takes up the most time. The following solution, which establishes a database connection for every access, though secure and technically simple, is, however, inefficient for frequently accessed Web sites.

```
Connection con = java.sql.DriverManager.getConnection(url, uid, pwd);
...
con.close();
```

8.13.1 Storing connections intermediately

One possible variant is to reserve a database connection for every user that visits the Web site. If a query is completed, the connection is stored intermediately in the user session, but remains open until required. This variant enables more secure and quicker access to the database, but treats resources such as network connections and memory wastefully. The connection is only closed once the user has fully logged out, or the session becomes damaged after a certain period of inactivity. If several users are accessing the Web page at the same time, it may happen that the database refuses other connections. This can be problematic as the open connections may hardly be used. The code for this version can look as follows:

```
Connection con = (Connection)session.getValue("Connection");
if (con == null) {
   con = java.sql.DriverManager.getConnection(url, uid, pwd);
   session.putValue("Connection", con);
}
...
```

The connection would be closed in the `Logout` servlet:

```
Connection con = (Connection)session.getValue("Connection");
con.close();
```

It is not transparent how the servlet engine creates and disposes of session objects. Therefore the use of the `finalize` method that is called on an object before it is garbage collected is not the proper way of cleaning up the session state. The servlet API offers the `HttpSessionEventListener` interface. Its method `sessionDestroyed` obtains a reference to the invalidated session and can close the connection stored there. It is important to note that in order to be called, the listener class must be registered in the deployment descriptor of the Web application.

8.13.2 Connection pooling

In order to bypass these problems, many commercial application servers and *Enterprise Java Beans containers* use the *connection pooling* strategy. Here, the application server assumes the management of connections. If a connection is no longer used, it is not closed immediately, but kept in a *pool* and used again for the next query. The difference from previous versions is that the connection is used again for the queries of different users. In this way, both the constant and time-consuming opening and closing of connections, and the poor usage of available connections, will be avoided. As several users share one connection using this strategy, all users must have the same rights. This is guaranteed in our example, as all users are clients of the book shop. System administrators and other users will not share such a connection pool with the users of the Web site.

Connection pooling makes great demands of the discipline of the programmer. If database transactions were not ended or results tables not closed, the connection could become unusable and hinder the work of other users.

```
Connection con = pool.getConnection();
...
pool.close(dbError);
```

The *connection pool* saves the open yet momentarily unused connections in the `Vector cons`. The `getConnection` and `close` methods are declared as `synchronized`, in order to guarantee that only one thread can work with the *pool*. However, this is not usually a problem, as these methods are processed very quickly. The `getConnection` method checks first to see whether there are still connections available in the *pool*. If this is not the case, a new connection is opened.

```
public class ConnectionPool {

    private Vector cons = new Vector();
    private String url;
    private String uid;
    private String pwd;

    public ConnectionPool(String driver, String url,
                          String uid, String pwd)
            throws ClassNotFoundException {
        Class.forName(driver);
        this.url = url;
```

```
      this.uid = uid;
      this.pwd = pwd;
   }


   synchronized public Connection getConnection() throws PoolException {
      try {
         if (cons.size() == 0) {
            Connection con =
                  java.sql.DriverManager.getConnection(url, uid, pwd);
            System.out.println(
                  "Pool: New Connection established:" + con);
            return con;
         }
         else {
            Connection con = (Connection)cons.remove(0);
            System.out.println("Pool: Connection reused:" + con);
            return con;
         }
      }
      catch(SQLException e) {
         throw new PoolException(
                  "Pool: Error during Connection open" + e);
      }
   }


   synchronized public void close(Connection con, SQLException dbError){
      if (con == null) return;

      boolean close = false;
      if (dbError != null) {
         close = true;
         if (dbError.getSQLState().equals("23000")) {
            System.out.println("Constraint violation");
            close = false;
         }
      }

      try {
         if (close || (cons.size()) > 5) {
            System.out.println("Pool: Connection destroyed:" + con);
            con.close();
            con = null;
         }
         else {
            System.out.println(
                        "Pool: Connection returned to Pool:" + con);
            cons.addElement(con);
         }
      }
      catch(SQLException e) {
         System.out.println("Pool: Error during Connection close" + e);
      }
   }
```

Along with the no longer used connection, the close method may also receive another SQL error caused when working with the connection. The SQLException class has two ways of analyzing the error encountered, getSQLState and getErrorCode. If a more serious error occurs, the connection is closed for security reasons. This could be an unclosed results table or an old but still active transaction. This is a safety mechanism which prevents a defunct connection from remaining in the system.

So what exactly constitutes a more serious error? An SQL error also appears with a simple database instruction violation. For example, if a new client enters an e-mail address already available in the database, the unambiguity principle is violated. This is no reason to close the database connection. Table A.2 on page 413 shows how SQL Server 7, Access 97 and MySQL react to different errors. The SQL error numbers should be standardized, but unfortunately only the number 23000, which occurs on violation of a database constraint, is used as an indicator of a not so serious error.

```
protected void finalize() throws Throwable {
    for (int i=0; i<cons.size(); i++) {
        try {
            ((Connection)cons.elementAt(i)).close();
        }
        catch(SQLException e) {
            System.out.println(e);
        }
    }
} // End of destroy
} // End of class
```

The finalize method is called by the virtual Java machine if the object should be discarded. Before this happens, all connections still open should be closed down.

It could be said that during peak times, this solution provides as many connections as main memory and the database server allow. If the number of queries decreases further, all connections apart from five (in our example) will be closed. Figure 8.22 shows the *connection pool* in use. Two browsers start a search query at the same time and are now located in the shopping basket view. The console in the lower part of the picture shows the status report of the Web server. The connection at the memory address 34a1fc is used for the first search query. The pool then creates a second connection at the address 7934ad, as the first is still in use. Finally, both objects are stored in the pool intermediately.

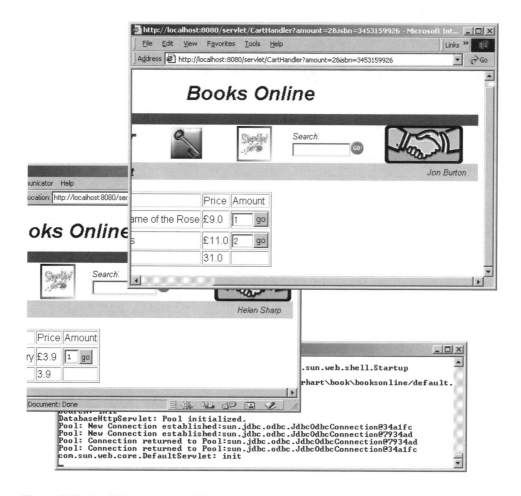

Figure 8.22: Parallel access on the Web application of two browsers.

8.13.3 Switching the pool off

If a Web site only has to handle a few queries, the pool can easily be "switched off" by the `if` query being removed from the `getConnection` and `close` methods. Thus the pool opens and closes the database connection every time.

8.13.4 Prepared Statements

Another way of optimizing the application is by reusing `PreparedStatements`. The query is compiled and saved in the database server on preparation. This process is not necessary anymore if the query is executed with another parameter. As only a limited number of different database queries are made by the application in total, you could consider using not only the connection, but also the `PreparedStatements` again. For example, you could have a search query prepared in advance at every connection. As the book search is the most frequently placed query with security, this removes the need for creating the `PreparedStatement` object with every query. We are concentrating on the optimization of the *connection pool*. However, the suggested solution is easily implemented.

8.13.5 The base class of the database servlet

In this example, all servlets related to the database are derived from the class `DatabaseHttpServlet`. These servlets all use a reference to a commonly used *connection pool*. This reference and the intialization of the pool are controlled by this class.

```
import javax.servlet.*;
import javax.servlet.http.*;
import java.sql.*;

public class DatabaseHttpServlet extends HttpServlet {

    String dbDriver;
    String dbUrl;
    String dbUser;
    String dbPass;

    static protected ConnectionPool pool = null;

    public void init(ServletConfig config) throws ServletException {
        super.init(config);

        if (pool != null) return;

        dbDriver = config.getInitParameter("dbDriver");
```

```
        dbUrl = config.getInitParameter("dbUrl");
        dbUser = config.getInitParameter("dbUser");
        dbUser = config.getInitParameter("dbPass");

        if (dbDriver == null)
            dbDriver = "sun.jdbc.odbc.JdbcOdbcDriver";
        if (dbUrl == null)
            dbUrl = "jdbc:odbc:book";
        if (dbUser == null)
            dbUser = "book";
        if (dbPass == null)
            dbPass = "book";

        try {
            pool = new ConnectionPool(dbDriver, dbUrl, dbUser, dbPass);
            System.out.println("DatabaseHttpServlet: Pool initialized.");
        }
        catch (ClassNotFoundException e) {
            throw new ServletException("DB driver not found: " + e);
        }
    }
```

In order to make this application independent of the database, the name of the database driver, the database address, login name, and password are defined as configuration parameters of the Web server. In order to port the application from one database to another, no recompilation is necessary. However, as it is not always easy to put this configuration file in the right place and format it correctly, it is recommended that default values be entered in case the parameters can not be read.

```
    protected void finalize() throws Throwable {
        super.finalize();
        pool.finalize();
    }
} // End of class
```

If the Web pages of Books Online are no longer used and the Web server wishes to free some memory, this can be done by calling `finalize`. When implementing the method only the `finalize` methods of the subordinate class and of the local variable `pool` are called.

Chapter 9

Basic principles of CORBA

Servlets are a technology used in the World Wide Web for creating Web-based applications. Obviously, nowadays, not all distributed applications run on the Web. A technology which first of all needs to be considered independently of any special implementation variant is that of the distributed object system. Here, the principle of the object-oriented approach in software construction for local applications is transferred to the wider area of distributed applications.

In this third part of the book, we will address a common standard for distributed object systems usually called *Common Object Request Broker Architecture* or *CORBA* for short. CORBA is more extensive than the servlet attachment, as with CORBA you can both create Web applications and use other base technologies. This, and the following chapters, deal with the many options offered by CORBA.

In the first section, the chapter brings together the concepts of development of distributed applications and object-oriented programming already introduced, by addressing the basics of distributed object systems. On this basis, it is no longer difficult to understand the need for a standard for such object systems, as is represented in CORBA. In the following, we introduce the structure of the CORBA approach, i.e. we explain its architecture. We consider in detail the most important architecture components, namely the *Object Request Broker (ORB)*, the *Interface Definition Language (IDL)*, *stubs* and *skeletons* as well as the CORBA services. The chapter finishes with the description of a general approach for the development of CORBA-based applications.

9.1 Distributed object systems

As the reader may remember, in Chapter 4 different programming models were introduced. In essence, all these models can also be employed for programming distributed applications. If we consider the extension of structured programming, then one of its most important concepts – dividing a program into procedures and functions (or modules) – can be found again in the popular *Remote Procedure Call (RPC)*. With RPC, you can place procedures on other computers and execute them remotely. For the programmer of a distributed RPC application, a remote procedure call does not really differ from a local procedure call, i.e. the call of a procedure in the same process. The development of a distributed application is very similar to the usual approach for the creation of a local application as the programmer does not have to deal with the communication required between the computers and processors involved. Obviously, this does not work "just like that." Much program technology is behind the realization of RPC, in order to conceal the communication from the application programmer.

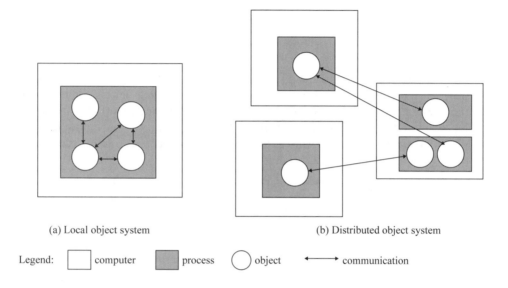

(a) Local object system   (b) Distributed object system

Legend: ☐ computer   ▨ process   ◯ object   ⟷ communication

Figure 9.1: Local (a) and distributed (b) object systems.

The application of the object-oriented model to distributed applications now leads to the concept of the distributed object system. A local application, which was developed the object-oriented way, can be described as a collection of objects within the same process in a computer. These objects cooperate with each other to carry out a task. A distributed object system is simply a collection of cooperating objects which can be distributed over many processes and computers. In order to realize the cooperation, the objects need to communicate with each other via the computer network. Figure 9.1 explains once more the difference between local and distributed object systems. Figure 9.1 (a) illustrates a local application that runs in a single process and on a single computer. On the contrary, Fig. 9.1 (b) deals with distributed objects which communicate with each other beyond the limits of computers and processes.

Certainly, it would also be very helpful in this case if the programmer of the distributed object system could avoid dealing with the communication. The next sections show how object systems of this type can be created using CORBA.

9.2 CORBA – a standard for distributed object systems

CORBA generally represents a *standard architecture* for distributed object systems. Using CORBA you can write applications consisting of a collection of distributed, heterogeneous objects which cooperate with each other. In this case heterogeneous means:

- These objects do not all have to be written in the same programming language.
- They do not all have to run on the same operating system or computer architecture.
- They do not all have to be created by the same group of developers.

CORBA is a creation by the *Object Management Group* (OMG, `http://www.omg.org`). The OMG was founded in April 1989 by eleven companies, including 3Com, American Airlines, Canon, Data General, Hewlett-Packard, Philips Telecommunications, Sun Microsystems, and Unisys. Currently, the OMG works as an independent public organization which comprises over 800 businesses thanks to its commitment to the development of technical, commercially usable and primarily manufacturer-independent software specifications.

CORBA was introduced for the first time in 1990 as Object Management Architecture (OMA). Since then, several revisions have been carried out, and now CORBA is available in version 3.0.

The next paragraphs describe in detail the architecture of CORBA and its components.

9.3 Architecture of CORBA

Figure 9.2 shows the general architecture of CORBA. The four core components are listed here:

- the *Object Request Broker*
- the *Common Object Services*
- the *Common Horizontal* and *Vertical Facilities*
- the *Application Objects*

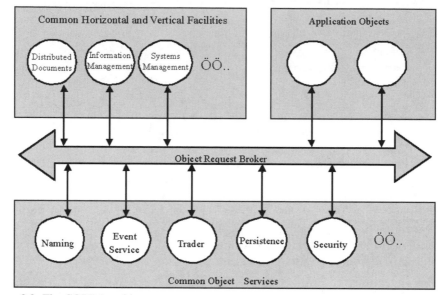

Figure 9.2: The CORBA architecture.

These components will now be explained.

9.3.1 The Object Request Broker

The *Object Request Broker* or ORB is the central component of the CORBA architecture. Its main purpose is making distributed objects communicate with each other transparently, which means that in programming objects on the level of the application, there is no difference between local and remote method calls. Compared to other similar paradigms such as the *Remote Procedure Call,* the ORB approach goes further. For example, an ORB enables you to find out other objects in the distributed system, including calls to the methods of the objects found, even if their names were not known before.

An ORB has to be available on every computer containing CORBA objects. In order to call object methods of objects on other computers, the ORBs of these computers need to communicate with each other. This communication is standardized in CORBA with the *General Inter ORB Protocol (GIOP)* or the more special *Internet Inter ORB Protocol (IIOP)* suited to the Internet. A further important result of this standardization is that ORBs of different manufacturers can communicate with each other, at least when they adhere to the GIOP standard. This forms the basis of all heterogeneous applications created with CORBA in which some objects are implemented by one manufacturer and other objects by another. Only when the ORBs used can communicate with each other, can the objects that use the ORB for communication also communicate.

9.3.2   Application objects

Application objects are those objects which use further services of CORBA in order to communicate with each other regardless of the actual distribution. Objects are created by applications programmers, and different objects can be programmed by different manufacturers and in the case of professional applications really are. Section 9.4 on page 185 explains exactly how application objects use the ORB for communication; Section 9.5 on page 191 explains the complete construction process of distributed applications based on CORBA objects.

9.3.3   CORBA services and facilities

In addition to the main components, i.e. the ORB and the general format of application objects, CORBA also defines a series of special services made available to the application objects in order to solve specific tasks quickly and easily. We can distinguish between the *Common Object Services* and the *Common Facilities.*

The task of the *Common Object Services* is to complete or extend the base functionality of the ORB. The services are implemented as objects and can be accessed just the same way as *application objects,* i.e. you can use their methods by remote call. There are currently many general services available which considerably simplify the applications programmer's work. The following list is not complete, but shows the most important services available:

- ■ The *Life Cycle Service* enables objects to be created in a computer or to be removed from it, or allows them to be transferred from one computer to another. If this service is not available, objects need to be created by the *object factories* that run on this computer. Such *object factories* must be created by the application programmer.

- ■ The *Persistence Service* allows you to save objects persistently on non-volatile memories such as in a file or database. This can be useful if objects survive the end of a program execution and have to be loaded again when a program is restarted. Even if this service easily can be realized within an application object, in any case it is better to use an existing service rather than to implement it again.

- ■ The *Naming Service* is one of the central services in a distributed object environment and no CORBA product should be without it. A *Naming Service* can be compared to a telephone directory. Objects can be found within a distributed environment on the basis of their name alone. Firstly, this name has to be registered in the *Naming Service.* If another object queries the *Naming Service* for the location of an object with this name, the service provides the corresponding address. On Internet implementations of a CORBA naming service, the address contains, for example, the IP address of the host computer and the TCP/UDP port number of the process in which the object runs. Without this service, location transparency would not be possible, and each object whose methods should be called would have to be known by the caller in all its technical details.

- Using the *Event Service*, the communication between objects can be decoupled. The service enables objects to express their interest in particular events. Events can be created by other objects. If such an event appears on the *Event Bus*, the objects that are registered for this event are informed. Accordingly, objects can afterwards react to the event. As an additional feature, anonymity can be preserved; objects do not necessarily have to know who has created an event.

- The *Transaction Service* supports the execution of distributed transactions in which many components (objects) are involved. The service implements a general form of the two-phases-commit protocol, with which important transaction features are produced; in particular, the transaction is either completed or not executed at all (atomicity).

- The *Query Service* supports the development of database applications. It enables database queries to be sent using some generic methods. The service is based in particular on the Standard SQL3 and on the *Object Query Language* (*OQL*) developed by the OMG.

- With the *Licensing Service* CORBA offers an important service for professional accounting for the use of software. The service is very flexible as regards the type of accounting, even if set up very coarsely per session or very fine per number of object instances created. Object servers can register their own services together with the accounting policy in the *Licensing Service*. When a client uses the corresponding service, the *Licensing Service* keeps track to what extent the client is using the service.

- Absolute time is a complex topic in distributed systems. Since from the practical point of view it is not possible to use two computers with the same time and in particular to keep the same time over a long period, information technology has devised a set of solutions which can at least partly solve the problem. The temporal synchronization of the processes involved is an important procedure. The CORBA *Time Service* provides an interface for this. Moreover, it allows you to specify events which are created on the basis of temporal conditions.

- Communication security gains increasing importance at a time when more and more data is exchanged on the World Wide Web. The *Security Service* in the CORBA architecture provides a considerable contribution to the increase in security, maintaining a complete framework for all important matters concerning secure communication. Namely, it supports authentication, access control lists, confidentiality, and the authenticity of the origin of messages.

- To conclude, the *Trader Service* is the counterpart of the "Yellow Pages." Objects register services, including their features, with the trader. On the other side, clients can send enquiries to the trader in which they search for services with particular features. The trader answers with a list of all known objects that offer services with these features.

The use of the standardized CORBA services, in particular of the *Naming Service*, is explained again in detail in Chapter 10 and Chapter 11.

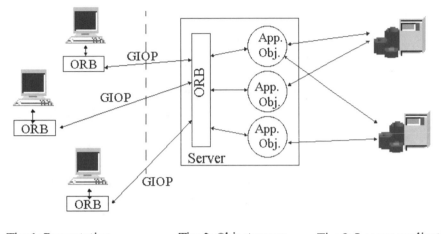

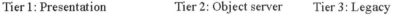

Tier 1: Presentation   Tier 2: Object server   Tier 3: Legacy applications

Figure 9.3: Three-tier architecture with CORBA.

The *common facilities* make a range of services available to application objects. However, these are mostly non-specific services, but complete frameworks for extensive tasks. Today, CORBA provides for *facilities* such as *mobile agents*, *workflow management* or *business object frameworks*.

Considering once more the general architecture of distributed applications, and in particular those organized according to the N-tier principles as introduced in Section 2.4 on page 31, we can insert the components of the CORBA architecture into the generic architecture. For 3-tier architectures, Fig. 9.3 shows the resulting more concrete architecture.

An ORB has to be available on each computer involved. The ORBs communicate via the GIOP or usually via the special IIOP. The task of many CORBA objects is the "packing" of legacy applications in object-oriented technology so that client programs in tier 1 can use the functionality of the legacy applications with method calls in tier 3.

9.4 Communication between objects

How does actual communication between objects, i.e. the call of the methods of an object over the net, take place?

Figure 9.4 illustrates the principle: there is an object implementation on a computer somewhere in the net . A client would like to use one or more services offered by this object. It then passes the corresponding enquiry to the ORB that deals with the real communication.

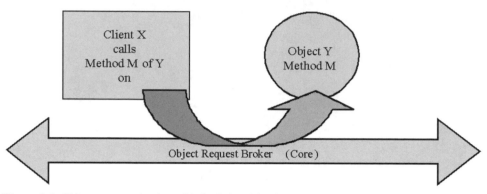

Figure 9.4: Object communication with the help of the ORB.

For a better understanding of the function of the ORB, its architecture should be further refined. In addition to the general components that are available in the ORB for any application, further application-specific parts are required. These can be divided according to the client and server side. The following are available on the client side:

- *IDL stubs*
- *Dynamic Invocation Interface*
- *Interface Repository API*
- *ORB Interface*

CORBA makes the following components available on the server side:

- *IDL Skeletons*
- *Dynamic Skeleton Interface*
- *Object Adapter*
- *Implementation Repository*
- *ORB Interface*

Figure 9.5 represents graphically the interaction of the ORB core with the application objects and other components. The following paragraphs address the most important components of this sophisticated architecture in more detail.

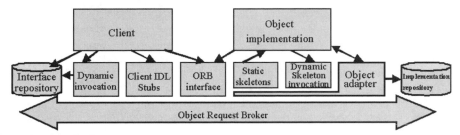

Figure 9.5: The ORB components

9.4.1 Interface Definition Language (IDL)

We mentioned in particular the implementation of *heterogeneous* object systems as one of the most important aims of the CORBA architecture, e.g. objects of different manufacturers, written in different programming languages, which are supposed to cooperate. CORBA is therefore regarded as language-independent, i.e. nothing in the architecture points to a particular implementation language such as Java or C++. However, a language is required to describe the appearance of objects. When a client has to use a remote object, it has to know which methods this object provides for public use. The ORB also has to know, so as to be able to translate the requests and responses into the proper syntax. So, what has to be known about an object is its interface.

In order to describe such interfaces in CORBA, we can use the *Interface Definition Language* or *IDL*. IDL makes some language constructs available which allow a developer of distributed objects to define the following independently of any programming language:

- data types and
- object interfaces consisting of methods and variables

and furthermore

- to combine matching interfaces into modules.

The IDL definition is the basis of any further work step in the development of distributed applications and should be carried out very carefully. For a better understanding of the fundamental IDL construction elements, we will now present a short example to illustrate how interfaces are defined using IDL. As an example, consider the data type queue with its methods `enqueue()`, `dequeue()`, `isEmpty()` and `isFull()`, introduced in Chapter 4. The job is to define an interface via which a remote queue can be accessed. To illustrate the concepts even better, we use a queue which does not contain values of type `double`, but a structured data type such as information about people.

First, we combine all definitions which belong to the same application, into one *module* of the IDL description. This is possible in IDL, creating a module context that has to be named:

```
module QueueTest {
```

Structured data types are the basis of an IDL description, as they can be employed as input and output parameters for the methods of an object interface. We will need a type `PersonalInfo`. The definition basically works as in C or C++ (without affecting the independence from programming languages!):

```
struct PersonalInfo {
    string firstname;
    string lastname;
    string address;
    int age;
};
```

At this point the keyword `interface` is used to define the actual `queue` interface:

```
interface Queue {
    boolean      enqueue(in PersonalInfo pi);
    PersonalInfo dequeue();
    boolean      isEmpty();
    boolean      isFull();
}
} // End of module
```

The experienced reader learns that, unlike method descriptions in programming languages, it must be specified in the description of the method parameters, such as the `enqueue()` method, whether it is a pure input, a pure output, or a mixed input/output parameter. This is expressed with the keywords `in`, `out` or `inout`.

We now already have a complete IDL definition. It is very important to underline that it is not a task of the IDL to specify the `object behavior` through the description of methods. The only purpose is the description of the interface in order to come to an agreement between client, server, and ORB on which method calls are available for which remote objects. The implementation of the object's functionality, i.e. what really happens in the methods, will be the task of the applications programmer.

This simple example should be regarded as just a short introduction to the field of IDL specification. In particular, Chapter 11 on page 209 will provide a more detailed explanation of the development of IDL. Appendix D on page 439 provides a complete review of all available IDL keywords.

It is interesting to note that in the previous paragraphs all *common object services* and *common facilities* mentioned have an IDL interface description. It is therefore formally defined which functionality each object offers, and through which method calls and with which parameters it has to be used. In this way it becomes very simple for the applications programmer to use existing services just the same way as "normal" *application objects*.

9.4.2 IDL compiler

A more important advantage of an electronically available formalized description of the existing object interfaces is the possibility to process it automatically. To ultimately develop distributed applications on the basis of the IDL description programming language we have to create code which in some way completes the method implementation and is finally translated with a corresponding programming language compiler.

Earlier, the usual transition procedure to proceed from specification to implementation was a manual form of the translation of the specification into programming language code. This approach is firstly prone to error, and also very time-consuming. However, if you have a tool able to read formal descriptions, to analyze and to transfer them into another representation, these two disadvantages are eliminated, at least if the tool works correctly.

One important component of the CORBA specification is thus the *IDL Compiler*. The task of this compiler is to convert the IDL interface description into programming language code such as C, C++, Smalltalk, or Java. As a result of running the IDL compiler on an IDL specification, the programmer has descriptions of the objects to be used in the application available in the appropriate programming language. Obviously, the compiler simply generates interface descriptions together with the conversions of the data types defined. In particular, it cannot generate the method functionality, since nothing is known about it in the IDL description. This functionality has to be made available by the applications programmers.

The CORBA standard does not describe the precise structure of an IDL compiler. However, it describes exactly, for every programming language, into which element of the language an IDL element fits. In particular, such conversion rules are also available for Java. For example, a `struct` in IDL is translated into a `class` in Java. An `interface` in IDL is converted into an `interface` (see also Section 4.3.5 on page 66). You need not know all the conversion rules in order to understand the rest of this chapter, though those interested should refer to Appendix D on page 439 for further information.

9.4.3 IDL stubs and skeletons

What exactly does the IDL compiler create? In order to answer these questions we need to consider Figure 9.5 again. There you can find the components *IDL stubs* and *IDL skeletons*. These two are actually the central products of the IDL conversion process.

In order to understand the tasks of both components, you should understand how the ORB sends method calls from the client to the server. In networking, the unit of communication is the *message*. This means that the ORB has to transfer any form of communication as messages. A message is in principle a sequence of bytes sent from a transmitting to a receiving computer. However, as already said, we do not want the client to deal with messages, but with methods that he or she knows how to use.

Stubs and skeletons come into play at this point. A stub represents the connection between client and ORB. It makes a method call available to the client and translates method calls to "flat" messages for the ORB. Therefore, any method call has to be converted into a message. Skeletons undertake exactly the opposite task, accepting messages from the ORB on the server side and transmitting them as a method call.

These are clearly not generic tasks, e.g. stubs and skeletons can not be part of a readily available ORB as provided by CORBA tool manufacturers. Much more of its functionality depends on the structure of the interfaces described in IDL. Stubs and skeletons have to know which methods a remote object provides, in order to make the corresponding local method calls available to the client, and finally to be able to convert a call into a correct message. But, luckily, the IDL description contains all the information required to generate stubs automatically, these being

- the name of the interface
- the name of the method
- the types of all input and output parameters.

With this information, you can generate both the local call interface for the client, and the *marshaling* methods to convert this information into messages which are transferable with the ORB. The precise structure of stubs and skeletons in the programming language Java is explained in detail in Chapter 10.

9.4.4 Dynamic interfaces and repositories

The task of stubs and skeletons is limited to the interfaces known to an application at IDL compile time. These interfaces are also called *static interfaces*. However, CORBA is defined very flexibly and also allows a *dynamic* definition and use of remote objects. To solve this task in the CORBA architecture, the *dynamic invocation interface* is provided together with the *interface repository* on the client side, and the *dynamic skeleton interface* with the *implementation repository* on the server side.

If a client has to use an object, but does not know its interface, which is, however, available in the distributed environment, it can learn the structure of the interface, i.e. the method names and parameters, by consulting the *interface repository*, but only in case the object was registered earlier. The repository provides a programming interface for this purpose. As soon as the data of the interface is known, the single methods can be called on the *dynamic invocation interface*. The latter also offers a corresponding programming interface.

On the server side, the *dynamic skeleton interface* enables objects to be supported which do not have an IDL description. Objects therefore have to register in the *dynamic skeleton interface* at runtime which stores such information in the *implementation repository* database. If queries for objects appear in the *skeleton interface,* this can find out if the object mentioned is available on this server, on the basis of the information contained in the *skeleton interface.*

These explanations conclude the description of the general architecture of distributed systems on the basis of CORBA. The next section deals with practical questions describing how the process of developing CORBA applications is usually executed.

9.5 General procedure for the development of CORBA applications

For the development of CORBA-based applications a certain procedure has been established which we will introduce on the following pages. Figure 9.6 provides a graphical representation of this process.

Professional application development usually begins with a customer's order to solve a particular problem using a computer application. Referring to the customer's requirements, the development team carries out a system analysis. As a result, a system architecture is produced which identifies the individual components and describes their individual behavior and their cooperation. Since CORBA is a standard for distributed object systems, it is advisable to use object-oriented methods already in the design process. A method which has gradually gained more support is the *Unified Modeling Language (UML)*. Basically, it allows all components of a system to be specified as objects, as well as to describe their static relations with each other and the dynamic sequences of operations in the system in a more formal way. Nowadays, there are tools that can generate IDL documents from a UML description (e.g. Rational Rose) automatically.

This mapping of the system architecture to an IDL description is actually the next step of the development process. Often, it is still executed manually except in the cases mentioned above, in which the complete development process is formalized and automated.

As soon as the IDL description is concluded, the development tasks can be distributed. This not only means that, within a software firm, separate workgroups work on the tasks.

In the same way, partial tasks can be assigned to outside companies. It often happens that a company develops just the server side, and with it specific services which are later offered in the distributed environment (e.g. on the Internet). The availability of these services is then published together with the IDL interface description. It is up to other software companies to write applications which use these services. In this case, the development process is already very much decoupled.

Each workgroup now needs an IDL compiler, as well as other CORBA components such as an ORB. To reiterate: each group can use different tools and programming languages as long as these completely support the CORBA standard. To begin with, the IDL description available is translated into the programming language selected for the implementation. Then, through hand-coding, the object methods have to be described on the server side in order to provide the object functionality. The corresponding method calls have to be integrated on the client side in the application which also has to be implemented.

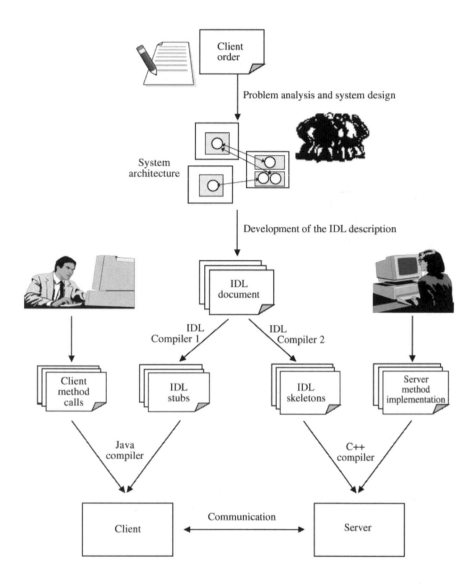

Figure 9.6: Order of the development stages in a CORBA program.

The generated files and those created manually then have to be translated (and eventually linked) with a compiler for the programming language used. To execute the distributed application, first the *Common Object Services* required, such as the *Naming Service,* should be started. Next, all servers, and possibly also some server objects, need to be started. Finally, clients have to be executed.

Figure 9.7 shows how the development tasks are shared among the manufacturers of CORBA products, the applications manufacturers, and the tools. The actual functionality of the application is described manually by the applications programmer. Stubs and skeletons are generated using IDL compilers for the communication between application objects. To exchange messages these use the generic ORBs provided by the CORBA product manufacturers.

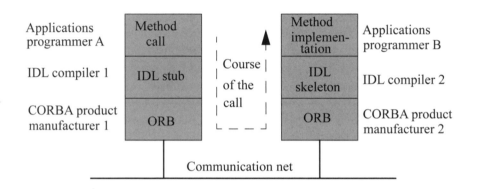

Figure 9.7: Distribution of the development tasks.

9.6 Advantages of using CORBA

The features and options described so far suggest why CORBA is perfectly suitable for creating distributed applications. This paragraph once again underlines the advantages.

■ *Distribution transparency*
  The programmer of a client does not know in principle if an object is executed as local or remote. How a method is called does not change. An applications programmer therefore does not have to deal with all the problems communication between computers and processes may raise.
■ *Location transparency*
  A user of services offered by the objects distributed in the net need not know where these objects can be found. ORBs and *Name Servers* undertake these tasks. The client simply needs to know the name of the service, or, using the *Trader Service*, the features he or she is interested in.

■ *Static and dynamic calls*
  Object interfaces do not have to be known during the development of the application. At runtime, new objects with new interface descriptions can enter the system and make their services available to the client. The advantage of static methods is the option of executing strict type checking during conversion, and so recognize errors early and avoid them. However, dynamic calls offer great flexibility.

■ *Independence of a particular programming language*
  Since CORBA is not tied to any particular programming language, you can develop CORBA solutions for all current languages. However, the application components described on the respective basis can cooperate with each other, thus achieving greater flexibility.

■ *Availability of many predefined services*
  The application developer is relieved of many standard tasks due to predefined services. Much development work is saved in this way.

■ *Separation of interface and implementation*
  With the separation of the description of an interface and the implementation of an object, CORBA is particularly suitable for the integration of legacy applications. We can also say that CORBA objects encapsulate legacy applications and give them an object-oriented structure.

9.7 From architecture to product

From the description in this chapter, it emerges that, during the development of CORBA applications, a complete series of tools and software components are used. Nevertheless, until now, we have not yet discussed products. In fact, the OMG defines just a framework with CORBA, but does not provide any product. This is the task of the software manufacturers. Their task is to develop the tools required, limited in their efforts only by the definitions of the CORBA standard. By doing so correctly, you get interoperable distributed object systems in which objects implemented by different manufacturers can communicate with each other, provided the systems are using the same IDL description.

Currently, there are many companies that create CORBA-based tools. The following chapter introduces some of the most important and useful tools.

Chapter 10

Java tools for CORBA

Several manufacturers offer products for the development of CORBA-based applications with Java. Iona OrbixWeb (`http://www.iona.com`), Inprise/Borland Visibroker (`http://www.inprise.com`), Objectspace Voyager (`http://www.objectspace.com`) and Oracle Web Request Broker (`http://www.oracle.com`) are examples of such software. ORB, IDL compiler and *Name Server* are usually offered as a bundle. These tools make the designer's work with CORBA very easy. All complex operations are completely transparent behind the scenes. The call of a method of an object residing on another computer looks exactly like the call of a method of a local object. Moreover, some products make practical extensions available. The Voyager ORB, for example, enables copies of Java objects to be submitted as *Call by Value* parameters to an object in another computer.

Unfortunately, it emerges in practical experience that different products are only partially compatible with each other. It is also unsafe to assume that CORBA applications which employ stubs and skeletons generated with the IDL compiler of the JDK can communicate straighforwardly using Voyager ORBs and a Visigenic *Name Server*. This is the result of the CORBA specification, which leaves too many details unresolved. For this reason, we stay with one manufacturer, and the sample application works complete with the tools and class libraries enclosed in JDK 1.3.

10.1 The IDL compiler

The IDL compiler converts the IDL interface definition into the corresponding Java classes and interfaces. JDK 1.3 comes with an IDL compiler called `idlj` which is located in `jdk1.3/bin`. In order to explain the Java CORBA functionality, a simple example is provided, in which a CORBA server determines the present time and passes it on to the client. The IDL interface looks as follows:

```
module Example{
   interface Server {
      string getTime();
   };
};
```

At this point, the file `Service.idl` is compiled with `idlj`.

```
idlj -fall Service.idl
```

All stubs and skeletons as well as the helper and the implementation base classes belong to the Java package `Example`, and therefore also are created in the directory `Example`.

10.2 Anatomy of stubs and skeletons

We wish to look at the files generated in more detail. The following files are located in the example directory:

- `Server.java`
- `ServerOperations.java`
- `ServerHelper.java`
- `ServerHolder.java`
- `_ServerImplBase.java`
- `_ServerStub.java`

The functionality of the single files are explained in the following paragraphs.

10.2.1 The Java interface

Once the IDL file has defined an interface `Server`, the `Server.java` file is also generated accordingly, which contains a corresponding Java interface definition. As the IDL pendant, the `Server` interface contains the method `getTime` which is inherited from the `ServerOperations` interface. Furthermore, `Server` is derived from the interface `org.omg.CORBA.Object`, as are all CORBA object references.

```
public interface Server extends ServerOperations, org.omg.CORBA.Object,
                        org.omg.CORBA.portable.IDLEntity
{
} // interface Server


public interface ServerOperations
{
  String getTime ();
} // interface ServerOperations
```

10.2.2 The server base classes

_ServerImplBase is the base class of the CORBA server. It is abstract, since the implementation of the getTime method is dictated through implements Example.server in the class definition. As described in the next paragraph, the developer must extend this class and provide the implementation of getTime.

```
package example;
public abstract class _ServerImplBase
                    extends org.omg.CORBA.DynamicImplementation
                    implements example.Server {
```

Some incidental CORBA details follow the class definition. However, we draw your attention to the following program lines:

```
private static java.util.Dictionary

    _methods = new java.util.Hashtable();

    static {
        _methods.put("getTime", new java.lang.upright(0));
    }
```

This peculiar syntax can be explained as follows: When this class is loaded for the first time in the Java virtual machine, the instruction _methods.put(...) is executed. Therefore the class registers all methods specified in the server interface in a hash table.

```
public void invoke(org.omg.CORBA.ServerRequest r) {
        switch (((Integer) _methods.get(r.op_name())).intValue()) {
            case 0: // example.Server.getTime
            {
                org.omg.CORBA.NVList _list = _orb().create_list(0);
                r.params(_list);
                String ___result;
                ___result = this.getTime();
                org.omg.CORBA.Any __result = _orb().create_any();
                __result.insert_string(___result);
                r.result(__result);
            }
            break;
        default:
            throw new org.omg.CORBA.BAD_OPERATION(0,
                        org.omg.CORBA.CompletionStatus.COMPLETED_MAYBE);
    }
}
```

invoke initiates the call of methods on the server side. A number contained in the enquiry indicates which method should be called. The number "0" in this example stands for getTime, the only method defined. Available parameters may be taken from the request object. Our server provides a string according to the definition of the method. For this result the variable __result is declared. The next line calls the local method getTime, which has yet to be implemented. In the end, the result is written to the result array of the request object. If a wrong method code is passed, a CORBA error is created in the default part.

10.2.3 The helper class

In the helper classes there are some methods which control the object serialization and deserialization. However, the narrow method is particularly interesting.

```
package example;
public class ServerHelper {

    ...

    public static example.Server narrow(org.omg.CORBA.Object that)
            throws org.omg.CORBA.BAD_PARAM {
        if (that == zero)
            return zero;
        if (that instanceof example.Server)
            return (Example.Server) that;
        if (!that._is_a(id())) {
            throw new org.omg.CORBA.BAD_PARAM();
        }
        org.omg.CORBA.portable.Delegate dup =
            ((org.omg.CORBA.portable.ObjectImpl)that)._get_delegate();
Example.Server result = new example._ServerStub(dup);
        return result;
    }
}
```

A CORBA object reference is submitted to the method. First, this is examined using the instance of operator. If the that parameter is from the server type, the corresponding casted parameter is returned. Otherwise this is an instance of the org.omg.CORBA.portable.ObjectImpl class. This class is the basis for all stubs. Therefore, a suitable server stub is created and returned to the calling method. The narrow method can be compared in its function with casts among Java classes.

10.2.4 The client stub

The _ServerStub class extends the aforementioned stub base class ObjectImpl. Furthermore, our server interface is implemented. In the source code of the CORBA client, the _ServerStub class does not appear since there the corresponding interface is always used, i.e. server in this case. If the client calls the method on the CORBA server using server.getTime(), the server is in fact an instance of the stub class obtained via the narrow method of the helper.

```
package example;
public class _ServerStub
        extends org.omg.CORBA.portable.ObjectImpl
        implements example.Server {

    ....

    public String getTime() {
        org.omg.CORBA.Request r = _request("getTime");
        r.set_return_type(org.omg.CORBA.ORB.init().
            get_primitive_tc(org.omg.CORBA.TCKind.tk_string));
        r.invoke();
        String __result;
        __result = r.return_value().extract_string();
        return __result;
    }
}
```

The getTime method generates a query object, in which space for the string return value is provided. Using invoke the call is passed to the ORB before the result is extracted and returned to the calling method.

10.2.5 The Holder class

In this example the Holder class is not required, since no out or inout parameter is used. In order to understand why this happens, let us consider part of the source code:

```
package example;
public final class ServerHolder
                    implements org.omg.CORBA.portable.Streamable {

    public example.Server value;

    public ServerHolder(example.Server __arg) {
        value = __arg;
    }

    ...
}
```

The class essentially consists of a reference to a server object. Using the methods `read` and `write` defined in the interface `org.omg.CORBA.portable.Streamable`, it can serialize this reference in order to send it over the network. If, for example, you wished to include the method

```
void getRef(out Server s);
```

in the `Server` interface, the file `Server.java` would contain the following line:

```
void getRef(Example.ServerHolder s)
```

A server holder object is derived from the server object. This holder object bypasses a basic problem: if a method has to return a result to the calling method without using the usual procedure of the return parameter, then you need to use the additional indirection of the holder. Figures 10.1, 10.2 illustrate this.

10.3 Object Request Broker

The class `org.omg.CORBA.ORB` contained in the JDK1.3 distribution is a complete Object Request Broker. An instance of this class is also created by calling the static method `init`. The IP address of the *Name Server* and the port on which the communication should occur also have to be given. In normal Java applications this appears in the command line.

```
java CorbaClient -ORBInitialHost 195.185.235.35 -ORBInitialPort 950
```

The command line arguments are represented as an *array* with four strings. The required parameters are submitted to the ORB `init` method exactly in this form. If a CORBA call is to be performed from a servlet, this array needs to be created manually. Our example is called by the command line, but we use the method just mentioned.

Figure 10.1: The reference to the result object cannot be disclosed to the client without the holder. The value of the variables on the client page is still null after calling the method `getRef`.

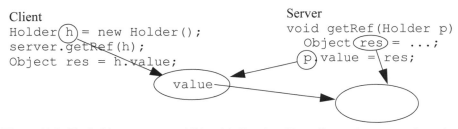

Figure 10.2: The holder creates an additional indirection. Now client and server work on the same object reference value, the client on `h.value`, the server on `p.value`.

Let us consider the program code of the server. The name of the class is `ServerImpl`. It is derived from `_ServerImplBase` which in turn implements the interface `server`. As the client does not know that the server functionality is implemented in the class `ServerImpl`, the reference to a `ServerImpl` object can also have the data type `Server`.

```
ServerImpl si = new ServerImpl();
Server s = si;
```

The class `_ServerImplBase` is abstract because no implementation of the `getTime` method defined in the server interface is available. The method `main` initializes the CORBA infrastructure. This makes up most of the source code. Obviously the `getTime` method is defined as public in order to be callable from outside.

Now let's take a closer look at the `main` method: in order to register a CORBA server object, the connect method is used. This registration process must be executed so that the ORB has a reference to the server object and can therefore call its method. Obviously, you can only register objects which implement the methods listed in the IDL interface.

Both client and server must get object references from the *Name Server* or have themselves registered there. As the ORB obtained the address of the *Name Server* on initialization, the method `resolve_initial_references` is provided to prepare the interaction with the *Name Server*.

```
import Example.*;
import org.omg.CosNaming.*;
import org.omg.CosNaming.NamingContextPackage.*;
import org.omg.CORBA.*;

public class ServerImpl extends _ServerImplBase {

    public static void main(String[] s) {
        try {
            String[] args = new String[4];
            args[0] = "-ORBInitialHost";
            args[1] = "212.126.208.32";
            args[2] = "-ORBInitialPort";
```

```
            args[3] = "950";
            ORB orb = ORB.init(args, null);

            ServerImpl server = new ServerImpl();
            orb.connect(server);

            org.omg.CORBA.Object nameservice =
                orb.resolve_initial_references("NameService");
            NamingContext namingcontext =
      NamingContextHelper.narrow(nameservice);

            NameComponent name = new NameComponent("DateServer", "");
            NameComponent path[] = {name};

            namingcontext.rebind(path, server);

            java.lang.Object sync = new java.lang.Object();
            System.out.println("Server ready");
            synchronized (sync) {
                sync.wait();
            }
        }
        catch (Exception e) {
            System.out.println(e);
        }
    }

    public String getTime() {
        System.out.println("getTime called. Thread: " +
      Thread.currentThread());
        return (new java.util.Date()).toString();
    }
}
```

Using the `narrow` method, the *naming context* object is assigned the right data type. The actual signing-in follows by calling the rebind method of the *naming context* object. The server object and the compatible name, under which the object can be found, are given. Consequently the *Name Server* can associate the name and the object reference.

The development of the communication initialization on the client side is similar. As the client does not know anything about the `ServerImpl` class, the server object is referenced via the server interface. The object reference of the *name server* is obtained with the resolve method of the *naming context,* and is converted into the right type again by calling `narrow`. After this process, the methods defined in the server interface can be called as methods of a local object. Now the variable `server` is connected with the stub which passes the call on to the correct server.

```
import Example.*;
import org.omg.CosNaming.*;
import org.omg.CORBA.*;

public class Client {
    public static void main(String[] s) {
        try {
            String[] args = new String[4];
            args[0] = "-ORBInitialHost";
            args[1] = "212.126.208.32";
            args[2] = "-ORBInitialPort";
            args[3] = "950";
            ORB orb = ORB.init(args, null);

            Server server;
            org.omg.CORBA.Object nameservice =
                orb.resolve_initial_references("NameService");
            NamingContext namingcontext =
NamingContextHelper.narrow(nameservice);

            NameComponent name = new NameComponent("DateServer", "");
            NameComponent path[] = {name};

            server = ServerHelper.narrow(namingcontext.resolve(path));

            String res = server.getTime();
            System.out.println(res) ;
            res = server.getTime();
            System.out.println(res) ;
        }
        catch (Exception e) {
            System.out.println(e) ;
        }
    }
}
```

The CORBA client and CORBA server are compiled like any other Java program. The IP address of the individual name server computer used has to be entered instead of the IP address 212.126.208.32. If the computer has no IP address, you can always use Localhost, i.e. 127.0.0.1.

10.4 Name servers

In the Java Development Kit 1.3 a *Name Server* is already enclosed. It is located under jdk1.3/bin/tnameserv.exe. The "t" in the name stands for *transient*, meaning that the *Name Server* does not store references of registered objects on the hard drive. If the *Name Server* is stopped or the computer crashes, all CORBA server objects have to register again. The port which has to be used by the *Name Server* can be given at startup. The default setting is Port 900. This parameter need only be given when another port is to be used.

```
tnameserv -ORBInitialPort 950
```

We have found that communication by CORBA did not work in a Windows95/98 network. If the *Name Server* runs in Windows NT, CORBA objects can also communicate with each other on two Windows95/98 computers. If the components communicate locally, i.e. client, server, and *Name Server* on a single computer, the system works without problems even under Windows95/98.

With each third-party manufacturer's ORB, a corresponding *Name Server* is also supplied. Unfortunately, not all *name servers* work together so easily, as they are supposed to. Object references can seldomly be exchanged between two *Name Servers* of different manufacturers.

10.5 Test run

For a test run, we copy the class files onto a computer which should host client and server. In fact, the client class and its stub are not necessary on the server, just as the server classes are not used on the client. However, having installed the System.out.println instructions, we can check that the server-side object is called, rather than a local object.

First of all, the *name server* has to be started according to the instruction described in the previous paragraph, because both client and server will contact it. The server then follows:

```
java ServerImpl
```

If the server object is registered, the message "server ready" appears on the console. Once the client is started, it calls the getTime method twice and the corresponding entries appear on the client and server console. This is shown in Fig. 10.3.

Figure 10.3: The time check server (center window) is called twice by the client (upper window). The communication follows on a name server (lower window).

10.6 A tip for working with the JDK ORB

A frequent error when working with the Sun Java–CORBA package is caused by transferring strings and data structures when a parameter or method result is `null`. This is easily demonstrated on our getTime server:

```
public String getTime() {
    return null;
}
```

If the CORBA client is started, the following error message appears:

```
ERROR : org.omg.CORBA.BAD_PARAM:   minor code: 1 completed: Maybe
org.omg.CORBA.BAD_PARAM:   minor code: 1 completed: Maybe
    at java.lang.Class.newInstance0(Native Method)
    at java.lang.Class.newInstance(Class.java:239)
    at com.sun.CORBA.iiop.ReplyMessage.getSystemException()
    at com.sun.CORBA.iiop.ClientResponseImpl.getSystemException()
    at com.sun.CORBA.idl.RequestImpl.doInvocation(Compiled Code)
    at com.sun.CORBA.idl.RequestImpl.invoke(RequestImpl.java:219)
    at example._ServerStub.getTime(_ServerStub.java:30)
    at Client.main(Client.java:23)
```

This behavior is described in the documentation. However, other ORBs can cope with the value `null` without problems.

10.7 Forté for Java

CORBA support is also included in the Internet modules for Forte4J. Figure 10.4 shows the administration options of the *name server* on the left. Unlike the previous example in which the server objects register themselves and generate a *naming context,* here it is possible to carry out this process on the *graphic* user interface.

The template is also helpful; it gives the programmer the base structure of the IDL file as well as that of the Java implementation of the client and server classes.

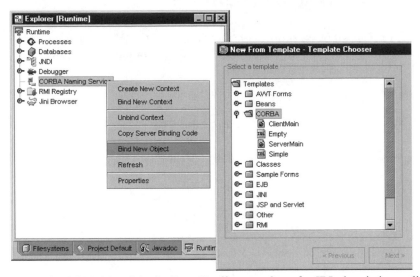

Figure 10.4: The CORBA module for Forte4J offers templates for IDL descriptions, client and server classes. A name server is also included.

Chapter 11

The sample application in CORBA

The process of transferring money from a customer credit card directly into your own account is not simple. Contracts with all large credit card companies should be made. Transactions are usually carried out via a modem or leased line to the credit card company. The respective driver software is installed and can be called via a shell or as the function of a *Dynamic Link Library (DLL)* with the e-commerce application. To carry out a payment transaction the following information is required: the credit card number, expiry date, the account number in which money has to be credited, as well as the invoice amount and the currency.

Fortunately, there are a number of *commerce service providers* which deal with the transaction details and negotiate with the credit card institutions. They offer user-friendly payment methods for their customers as CORBA objects on the Internet. Our bookshop will use the offer from *Easy Commerce*.

In this chapter we will describe the structure of the interface for this *commerce service provider* and explain how the checkout servlet uses the payment interface as a client along with its role as a server. The client–server communication using a *name server* and a possible CORBA implementation at the *commerce service provider* should also be considered. To conclude, we will show how a CORBA search interface represents an alternative to the search servlet which provides suitable data structures for further processing instead of an HTML page which is more or less useless for computers.

11.1 Overview of the architecture

In a multilevel architecture as in our scenario, a simple identification of components as client and server will soon no longer be sufficient, as a single component can operate on the one hand as a server, and on the other as a client. We want to try to illustrate the architecture with the graphic representation in Fig. 11.1.

Servlets on the Web server make sure that the clients receive up-to-date information from the database. The servlets on the Web page of Books Online are, in turn, clients of Easy Commerce, a *commerce service provider* which offers its customers payment services. The Easy Commerce server is in turn one of the many customers of the Visa central computer.

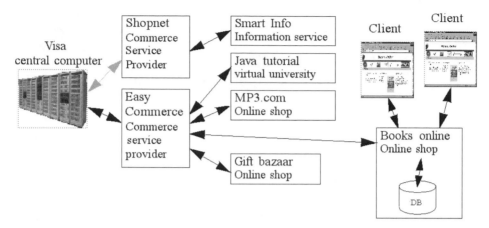

Figure 11.1: The Web site of Books Online in a network of clients and servers.

11.2 Transaction process

We will now examine the precise transaction process by a client, in this case our servlet, up to the central computer of the credit card company. We will pay particular attention to the *commerce service provider* as it plays the central role and acts as a mediator between the central computer and thousands of clients. There are different ways of examining how objects are created on an application server, assigned to the clients and removed again.

11.2.1 Fixed number of application servers

For example, the first option would be to instance four application server objects and to assign one of these four to each client *a priori*. This means that a quarter of the clients on the *Name Server* would always connect to `CreditCardServer1`, a quarter to `CreditCardServer2`, etc. Each server uses a resource to communicate with the credit card company, such as a modem or a socket connection, so it has to process transactions individually. The drawback of this architecture is, as Fig. 11.2 shows, that according to the distribution of queries, a queue forms at one server, while another has nothing to do. This solution offers parallel processing, but not an even distribution of tasks.

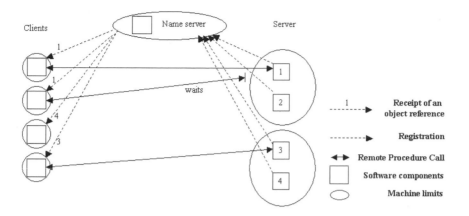

Figure 11.2: Each application server registers at the name server, and is directly available for clients. It is determined *a priori* which client uses which server.

11.2.2 A server for each client

A solution is provided by a dispatcher object, whose task is to generate a server object for each client enquiry, provided sufficient resources are available. As Fig. 11.3 illustrates, a new reference is given to the client on the new server object. When the interaction has finished, the client logs off from the dispatcher. The assigned server object is then removed again. This strategy leaves no resource untapped in case of a large workload. However, the continual creation and removal of the server objects requires time. The initialization of a resource is relatively time consuming, and it is worth using the same connection for a long time, as shown in the servlet example.

11.2.3 A pool of server objects

When the interaction with a client is concluded, it is economical to store the server objects intermediately until a new query arises, rather than removing them. Server 4 in Fig. 11.4 is not currently serving a client, but is immediately available if a new query enters. In order to avoid clogging up the memory with server objects after a short flood of queries, you can use a preferred number of server objects. More servers can be created for a short time, but these are disabled once the rush has subsided. This solution encompasses all advantages, and provides the best use and short waiting time for clients.

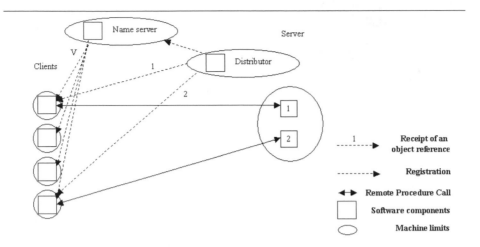

Figure 11.3: The dispatcher object creates server objects on demand.

This strategy uses the same principle as the connection pooling strategy introduced in Section 8.13 on page 171. Resources here, database connections in this case, are not simply destroyed after use, but saved and stored intermediately for later use.

11.3 The IDL interface

In each CORBA application the interface between the client and the server should always be determined at the beginning. We will now look at the file `CreditCard.idl`. You should pay particular attention to the Java–CORBA connection, especially to how the IDL constructs are translated into Java interfaces.

```
module CreditCard {
    //
    // Possible errors:
    //    error opening the connection to the payment interface
    //    invalid or expired card
    //    insufficient funds
    //    illegal account number
    //
    exception CreditCardException {
        string reason;
    };
    //
    // Payment Interface. The two services
    // verify the credit card and transfer
    // a certain amount to the account of
    // our bookstore
```

```
      //
      // Note: numTransfers counts the transfers of the current session
      //
      interface Payment {
    void transfer(in string card, in long month, in long year, in long
  account, in double sum, in string currency) raises
  (CreditCardException);
      long numTransfers();
      };
      //
      // Every payment object serves one client
      // Therefore, every client gets a payment object from
      // the dispatcher and releases it once it's done
      //
      interface Dispatcher {
    Payment openConnection() raises (CreditCardException);
    void close(in Payment p);
      };
  };
```

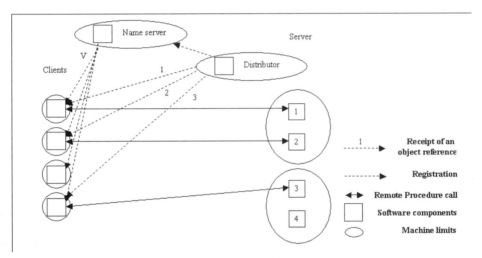

Figure 11.4: A fixed number of application servers with an enquiry dispatcher offers parallel processing and distribution of work. Here four servers are always available. However, additional servers can be made available for a short time.

This first line indicates the name of the module in which the functionality is grouped. In Java terminology this is a package. Starting the compiler idlj creates the directory containing all stubs, skeletons, helpers, and implementation base classes.

```
idlj -fall CreditCard.idl
```

All Java classes defined in the directory with this compiling process are contained in the CreditCard package:

```
package CreditCard;
```

First a specific error message for credit card transactions is defined. This contains the rejection of expired or canceled cards, invalid card numbers, and failed connections to the central computer. During the compilation, a corresponding definition of a Java exception is generated from this definition. Each of the following methods which reports an error by exception will report a usual Java exception in a Java implementation, or in other words a CreditCard.CreditCardException. In the IDL definition this is declared with the keyword raises (Exception Name).

In the following section both interface definitions follow: Dispatcher assumes the assignment and return of the object of payment, and Payment is responsible for its execution. An IDL interface corresponds exactly to its namesake in the Java world, and the files Dispatcher.java and payment.java define the Java interfaces. For those classes which implement these interfaces, we use the name of the interface plus "Impl.java" added as a name. So, for example, you should find the implementation of the Dispatcher interface in the file DispatcherImpl.java.

```
interface Payment{
    void transfer(
        in string card,
        in long month,
        in long year,
        in long account,
        in double amount,
        in string currency raises (CreditCardException);
    long number Transfers();
};
```

The method for payment handling is located in the payment interface. All necessary parameters such as the credit card number, year and month of expiry, account number of the receiver, account, and currency are placed. Error messages receive the client program through a CreditCardException. As the payment object is accessible only for the occasional user, many transactions can be completed from it. You can ask how many transactions have been completed in the present session using the numbertransfer.

```
interface Dispatcher {
    payment openConnection() raises (CreditCardException);
    void close(in payment z);
};
```

The payment interface offers two methods to reserve and release a payment object. The return value of the openConnection method and the parameter of the close method is the previously defined interface Payment. It should be noted that these are references to server objects. When the client is assigned a payment object, it remains on the server side all the same. If a method is called, the call goes to the local stub, via the network to the skeleton, from there to the original object and back again.

Before considering the implementation of client and server, Figure 11.5 illustrates once more the inheritance structure of the Java–CORBA base classes and interfaces as well as the client and server implementation. `_DispatcherImplBase` and `_PaymentImplBase` are the automatically generated abstract base classes which implement the interfaces. Our classes expand these base classes and can also be referenced as `Dispatcher` or `Payment` by the client.

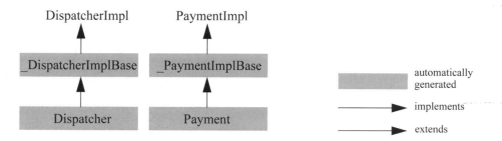

Figure 11.5: Hierarchy of base classes of interfaces and implementations.

11.4 The credit card client

First let us consider the credit card client. Client orders are executed in the `Checkout` servlet. In the temporary version this servlet checks the price and stock level, and inserts the order data record into the database. During this transaction the credit card also obviously has to be debited. Alongside the call of the methods offered by the credit card server, in particular the reference to the server object has to be obtained by the *Name Server*, as shown in the introductory examples.

11.4.1 Multithreading

As with the database connections and dealing with references to the server object connections, the question arises as to how many connections are required in order to serve threads working in parallel in the servlet. In the architecture we have chosen, each client is assigned a payment object by a common dispatcher. If two clients want to pay at the same time, a thread is active for both. Figure 11.6 shows how these two threads propagate on the same stub and skeleton on the `Dispatcher` server. A synchronization then has to be carried out in order to ensure that each client receives a payment object just for itself. This process is explained in Section 11.5 on page 219 which deals with the server. It is important for the client that all threads be able to share the same reference to the dispatcher object without problems. This reference then can be safely defined as an instance variable. However, each thread has an individual reference to a payment object. Therefore this reference is not defined as an instance variable but as a local variable in the method `buy`. This determines that not only one instance of the variable is available for each object, but one single instance for each thread.

```
public class CheckOut extends DatabaseHttpServlet {
   Dispatcher d;
   ...
   private String buy(...) {
      Payment z;
      ...
   }
}
```

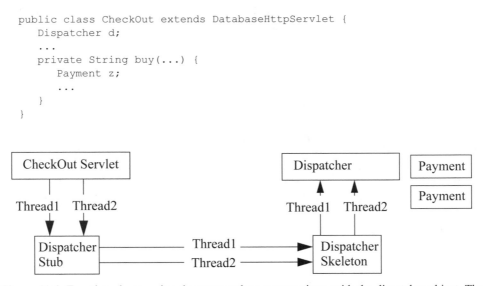

Figure 11.6: Two threads are using the same stub to communicate with the dispatcher object. The two threads are active but provide a separate reference to a payment object for the called threads on the client page.

11.4.2 Initialization of the CORBA communication

The question arises of when the ORB is to be initialized, and when the reference to the dispatcher server has to be obtained by the *Name Server*. Obviously, the `init` method of the `checkout` servlet is the ideal place to execute this. The `init` method is called by the Web server before the corresponding servlet is activated by the browser for the first time with a query.

In essence, the initialization proceeds as in the CORBA example shown in the introduction. There are merely two simple differences. Firstly, the variable `creditcardok` shows if the reference was determined correctly. If not, the client can not pay directly with the credit card and receives a bill instead. Secondly, the `init` method (such as the database connection pool) reads the necessary information about the *Name Server* from the configuration file.

```
import CreditCard.*;
import org.omg.CosNaming.*;
import org.omg.CORBA.*;
public class CreditCardClient {
    public static void main(String args[]) {
        Dispatcher d = null;
        Payment z = null;
        try{
            // create and initialize the ORB
            ORB orb = ORB.init(args, null);
            // get the root naming context
            org.omg.CORBA.Object objRef =
orb.resolve_initial_references("NameService");
            NamingContext ncRef = NamingContextHelper.narrow(objRef);
            // resolve the Object Reference in Naming
            NameComponent nc = new NameComponent("CreditCard", "");
            NameComponent path[] = {nc};
            d = DispatcherHelper.narrow(ncRef.resolve(path));
            z = d.openConnection();
            z.transfer("1111222233334444", 1, 2005, 1234, 123.99, "DM");
        }
        catch (Exception e) {
            System.out.println("ERROR : " + e) ;
            e.printStackTrace(System.out);
        }
        finally {
            d.close(z);
        }
    }
}
```

11.4.3 Payment handling

Compared to the initialization, the actual debiting is very simple. The parameter `bill` being `zero` shows that the payment by credit card has to be made. A payment object is reserved by the common dispatcher calling the `openConnection` method. This provides the `transfer` method in which credit card information, the account number of the book shop, the amount, and the currency are placed. The following source text is part of the `buy` method in the `CheckOut` servlet from Section 8.11 on page 160.

```
if (bill == 0) {
                try {
                    z = d.openConnection();
                    z.transfer(customer.creditcardnr,
customer.validuntilMonth, customer.validuntilYear, account, sum, "DM");
                    msg = "Your credit card was billed with " + sum + "
DM. Thanks for shopping with us.";
                }
                catch(Exception e) {
```

```
                    if (!(e instanceof CreditCardException))
                       throw new CreditCardException("Error communicating
        with the credit card server");
                    else
                        throw (CreditCardException)e;
                }
            }
```

If an error occurs, an exception is reported from the `openConnection` or the `transfer` method. The cause may be a technical error in the network connection to the server, which usually reports `org.omg.CORBA.COMM_FAILURE`. As there is a series of further CORBA exceptions, each type of exception is simply converted into a credit card exception in the `try` block. As the CORBA exceptions are derived from the `RuntimeException`, they need not be caught. Nevertheless, it is necessary, otherwise the Java interpreter interrupts the program.

An invalid card or an empty or overdrawn client account also causes errors. A `CreditCardException` shows such logic errors. The `if` query (`!(e instance of CreditCardException)`) preceding the conversion of the CORBA errors into credit card errors makes sure that logic errors are not declared as CORBA communication problems. If an error occurs, money is not debited. In case of errors, the client undoes previous modifications in the database using a *rollback*, as described in Section 8.11 on page 160.

To conclude, in the `finally` block after the transaction liquidation the CORBA server is released using the `close` method of the dispatcher.

```
    if (bill == 0)
                d.close(z);
```

11.4.4 Distributed transactions

The cleanest variant which guarantees fault-tolerant payment handling is a direct imbedding of the credit card server in the transaction using a *Transactional Remote Procedure Call (TRPC)*. In this case an external coordinator ensures that the direct debiting and the entry of the order take place either together, or not at all. Enterprise Java Beans (EJB) offer such a functionality. The EJB container assumes the role of coordinator here. In our case the client coordinates the process. The direct debiting is knowingly executed, as at this point it is guaranteed that no problems occurred in the order entry. If errors occur during the direct debiting, the rollback undoes any database modifications. We may well wonder what advantages a TRPC offers: Let us assume that our database server crashes when the direct debiting was executed correctly but before the transaction could be concluded using a *commit*. If the database server starts again, the incomplete order transaction is canceled. The client receives no books, irrespective of the fact that he has paid. If the direct debiting were integrated in the transaction, this would be canceled. We can assume that in practice, a similar crash with incomplete transactions rarely happens, and many online shops are therefore dealt with without TRPCs.

11.5 The credit card server

This section shows the implementation of the credit card server in CORBA. As already mentioned in the introduction to this chapter, the communication with the computer of the credit card company works on an enclosed class library or additional program. The server implementation at the commerce service provider receives the necessary data with the CORBA method call and should pass them on (possibly by *Java Native Interface*) to the components of the credit card company. This place is marked in the corresponding source text with a comment, but is not implemented.

11.5.1 Initialization and error treatment on the server side

The initialization in performed by the `main` method of the `CreditCardServer` class. Except for this method, no further functionality is available. As already shown in the simple CORBA example, the following steps are executed: the initialization of the ORB, the initialization of a dispatcher object, the registration at the ORB, and waiting for the client queries at the *Name Server*.

```
import CreditCard.*;
import org.omg.CosNaming.*;
import org.omg.CosNaming.NamingContextPackage.*;
import org.omg.CORBA.*;
public class CreditCardServer {
    public static void main(String args[]) {
        try{
            // create and initialize the ORB
            ORB orb = ORB.init(args, null);
            // create the actual object and register it with the ORB
            DispatcherImpl ref = new DispatcherImpl(orb);
            orb.connect(ref);
            // get the root naming context
            org.omg.CORBA.Object objRef =
                    orb.resolve_initial_references("NameService");
            NamingContext ncRef = NamingContextHelper.narrow(objRef);
            // bind the Object Reference in Naming
            NameComponent nc = new NameComponent("CreditCard", "");
            NameComponent path[] = {nc};
            ncRef.rebind(path, ref);
            // wait for invocations from clients
            java.lang.Object sync = new java.lang.Object();
            synchronized (sync) {
               sync.wait();
            }
        } catch (Exception e) {
            System.err.println("ERROR: " + e);
            e.printStackTrace(System.out);
        }
    }
}
```

The question arises as to which errors may occur during initialization. We will therefore subdivide the process into two logical sections: on the one hand the registration described after starting the server, and on the other, waiting for queries which, in principle, lasts as long as the server is stopped by the administrator clicking on CTRL-C.

If an error occurs in the first phase, the server terminates after the start with a corresponding message, for example when the name is not traceable. This feature is useful since the server cannot continue to work after such a serious error.

We may also wonder at this point if any errors occurring while waiting for a query will lead to the termination of the server process. We will now carry out three experiments, using the example of the date server from Section 10.3 on page 202.

1. *Errors on the server side*

In the first test we artificially create an `ArrayIndexOutOfBoundsException` in the `getTime` method of the `server` class, making an array of size 3 and referencing the fifth element.

```
public String getTime() {
    int[] a = new int[3];
    int i = a[4];
    System.out.println("getTime called.");
    return (new java.util.Date()).toString();
}
```

When you start this CORBA program, observe that the error is handled on the server side of the CORBA environment and it does not lead to the termination of the servlet. Instead the error is passed on in the form of an `org.omg.CORBA.UNKNOWN` exception. There the client breaks off with a corresponding entry, in case the exception is not handled. This also corresponds to the propagation of exceptions calling local methods, as even here an exception is passed on to the calling method.

2. *Termination of the server during the enquiry*

In the second test the server process is artificially terminated by calling `System.exit` in the `getTime` method. As in the first case, this leads to the client getting an `org.omg.CORBA.COMM_FAILURE` error since the server could not send its message back.

```
public String getTime() {
    System.exit(0);
    return (new java.util.Date()).toString();
}
```

3. *Termination of the client during the enquiry*

In the third test the client is stopped with CTRL-C after the server method has been called but before the result has come back. Obviously, for this purpose a delay has to be installed in the server. We will wait for a keyboard entry on the server console and terminate the client in the meantime.

```
public String getTime() {
   System.out.println("click key ");
   try {
      System.in.read();
   }
   catch(IOException e) {}
   return (new java.util.Date()).toString();
}
```

In this case the result returned grasps at nothing. However, this is not shown to the server with an exception.

The result from these experiments is that the error treatment in the initialization routine of the server is completely sufficient, as all errors during processing do not lead to the server crashing, but are passed on to the client via the ORB. However, in this discussion we should again observe that the experiments were carried out on the JDK ORB and surely cannot be transferable to further ORBs.

11.5.2 The Dispatcher class

We will now look at the implementation of the Dispatcher class. This class extends the _DispatcherImplBase base class created with the IDL compiler. Its operation is similar to that of the database connection pools. As shown in Figure 11.4 on page 213, the dispatcher maintains a fixed number of application server objects, e.g. of payment objects. The private field pool saves the references to these objects. This field contains status records containing object references and a flag which shows if the accompanying object is in use. The numobject constant indicates how many application server objects have to be instanced. This number depends on how many parallel credit card bookings are possible. We can imagine that this is limited by the number of ISDN channels. For the sake of simplicity, we have described this limit (here ten) just in the source text. Actually, it should be handed as a command line argument or read from a configuration file.

The implementation with a Vector like in the database connections was avoided here in order to ensure that a *local* reference is left to an object reserved by the client. This makes sure that the object is not deleted with a *garbage collection*. In the database pool this is not a problem, since the calling threads run in the same virtual Java machine.

```
import CreditCard.*;
import org.omg.CORBA.*;
public class DispatcherImpl extends _DispatcherImplBase {
    private int numObjects = 10;
    private Status[] pool = new Status[numObjects];
    public DispatcherImpl(ORB orb) {
        try {
            // prestart n DebitCredit Objects and register them with the
ORB
            for (int i=0; i < numObjects; i++) {
                pool[i] = new Status();
```

```java
                pool[i].ref = new PaymentImpl();
                orb.connect(pool[i].ref);
            }
        }
        catch(SystemException e) {
            System.out.println(e);
        }
    }
    synchronized public Payment openConnection() throws
CreditCardException {
        for (int i=0; i<numObjects; i++) {
            if (!pool[i].inUse) {
                pool[i].inUse = true;
        pool[i].ref.reset();
                System.out.println("Object " + (i+1) + " reserved.");
                return pool[i].ref;
            }
        }
        throw new CreditCardException("All connections are busy. Try
again later.");
    }
    synchronized public void close(Payment z) {
        for (int i=0; i<numObjects; i++) {
            if (pool[i].ref == z) {
                pool[i].inUse = false;
                System.out.println("Object " + (i+1) + " released.");
                return;
            }
        }
    }
}
class Status {
    PaymentImpl ref;
    boolean     inUse;
    Status() {
        ref = null;
        inUse = false;
    }
}
```

When the dispatcher object is instanced and the constructor called, the program allocates the predefined number of payment objects and stores their references in the pool with a new Status object. In the constructor of the Status object the referenced payment object is indicated as free. The calling program submits a reference to the constructor for the ORB object used. This is important in order to register the newly allocated payment object in the ORB.

```java
import CreditCard.*;
import java.util.Calendar;
import java.util.Date;
public class PaymentImpl extends _PaymentImplBase {
```

```
    // Session Variable
    private int count;
    public void reset() {
   count = 0;
    }
    private void doTransfer(String card, int month, int year, int
account, double sum, String currency) throws CreditCardException {
        System.out.println(card);
        System.out.println(month);
        System.out.println(year);
        System.out.println(account);
        System.out.println(sum);
        System.out.println(currency);
        // query VISA server
    }
    public void transfer(String card, int month, int year, int account,
double sum, String currency) throws CreditCardException {
        if (sum <= 0)
            throw new CreditCardException("Amount must be greater than
zero");
        // test the card
        Date d = new Date();
        Calendar cal = Calendar.getInstance();
        cal.clear();
        cal.set(year, month, 1);
        if (cal.getTime().getTime() < d.getTime()) {
            throw new CreditCardException("card expired.");
        }
        doTransfer(card, month, year, account, sum, currency);
    }
    public int numTransfers() {
        return count;
    }
}
```

Before the `Checkout` servlet carries out the order, a new payment object is retrieved by the dispatcher. This is done using the `openConnection` method. In order to avoid two threads getting the same object reference, this method is declared `synchronized` and consequently can always be executed by one single thread alone. Different calls to this method are stopped as long as the thread, temporarily active in this method, has left. A `for` loop checks all payment objects stored in the pool as long as one object not yet in use is found. The `reset` method sets the counter to `zero`, the object is marked and returned to the calling module. In case all objects are already busy, a `CreditCardException` is thrown:

```
synchronized public payment openConnection()
                  throws CreditCardException {
    for (int i=0; i<numObjects; i++) {
        if (!pool[i].inUse) {
            pool[i].inUse = true;
            pool[i].ref.reset();
```

```
                System.out.println("Object " + (i+1) + " reserved.");
                return pool[i].ref;
            }
        }
        throw new CreditCardException(
            "All connections busy. Search again later.");
    }
```

If the direct debiting is concluded the `Checkout` servlet logs off from the dispatcher. The payment object used is also submitted. In the `close` method the dispatcher compares the reference submitted with all objects contained in the pool. If the object previously reserved by the client is found, it is marked as being available again.

```
    synchronized public void close(Payment z) {

        for (int i=0; i<numObjects; i++) {
            if (pool[i].ref == z) {
                pool[i].inUse = false;
                System.out.println("Object " + (i+1) + " released.");
                return;
            }
        }
    }
}
```

11.5.3 The `payment` class: session managment in CORBA

The implementation of the payment class is quite simple. No multithreading problems can occur, as it is guaranteed that each time only one client gets the reference to an object. We have to check the validity and the distribution of the parameter.

However, as with the servlets, there is also the interesting issue of session handling. Sessions in the servlets were managed automatically by the Web server. Under CORBA, this has to be explicitly programmed. For example, you can assign a session identification to each client. The client sends this session ID along in each subsequent call, in order to work on its session-specific data. This variant is used also by the Web server for the management of the servlet session. As Fig. 8.15 on page 146 shows, each browser is assigned a cookie with an identification issued by the Web server. This variant could also be implemented in the CORBA server: the array data saves `SessionData` objects. Each of these objects saves the session-specific information of a client. Furthermore, there are two further arrays `timestamp` and `busy`, which show if the corresponding object is in use and when it was last used. The last piece of information is important in case the client does not completely log out. In fact, a similar functionality should also be inserted in our database and payment object pools.

If the client requires a new session, the arrays are searched and the first session data object is returned which is either unused or has not been used for longer than 15 minutes. This solution uses the index of the session object in the `data` array as the session identification. The method `query` stands for all methods of the server. Before the actual functionality is carried out, the method tests if the session identification is active, takes the session data from the array and updates the time of the last access.

```
public class Server extends _ServerImplBase {
    int maxSessions = 100;
    long sessionTimeout = 1000 * 60 * 15;

    SessionData[] data = new SessionData[maxSessions];
    long[] timestamp = new long[maxSessions];
    boolean[] busy = new boolean[maxSessions];

    synchronized public int newSession() {
        long now = (new Date()).getTime();
        for (int i=0; i<maxSessions; i++) {
            if ((!busy[i]) || (timestamp[i] + sessionTimeout > now)) {
                data[i] = new SessionData();
                busy[i] = true;
                timestamp[i] = now;
                return i;
            }
        }
        return -1;
    }

    public void query(int sessionid, int parameter) {
        if (!busy[sessionid])
            return;
        SessionData session = data[sessionid];
        timestamp[sessionid] = (new Date()).getTime();
        ...
    }
}
```

First, the clients from this server have to get a session ID which then is enclosed in each call.

```
sessionid = server.newSession();
server.query(sessionid, 6);
server.query(sessionid, 8);
server.furtherQuery(sessionid, further, parameter);
```

Another variant to manage sessions already is contained in the architecture we have chosen. Instead of making all clients always call one server which manages many objects internally with session data, you can also imagine that each client calls "its" object directly. Then, this solution represents exactly our architecture: the dispatcher assumes the role of the server which manages the session. The payment objects correspond to the `SessionData` object from the example above. In place of session identification numbers which are represented with integer values, we use references to objects of the server computer. The payment objects do not only contain data, but implement methods that can be called directly by the client. Just as the session data object offers local instance variables for information storage, a local, session-specific variable `count` is also defined in the payment object. This variable counts the bookings which are transacted by the client in the active section. We will admit that this counter variable perhaps appears not too useful and the architecture was chosen especially in order to guarantee an optimal use of resources. Nevertheless, you can file session-specific information, which is a more important aspect of this solution. The methods `reset` and `numberTransfers` enable the client or the dispatcher object to read and reset the private variable `count`.

```java
import CreditCard.*;
import java.util.Calendar;
import java.util.Date;

public class PaymentImpl extends _PaymentImplBase {

    private int count;

    public void reset() {
        count = 0;
    }

    public int numberTransfers() {
        return count;
    }
```

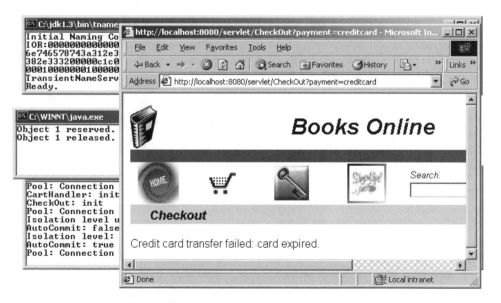

Figure 11.7: Failed credit card direct debiting. On the left you can see the consoles of the name server and Web server. The payment object is reserved and released again by the dispatcher. The Web server issues information about activities on the database.

The further source code of the class `PaymentImpl` defines another two methods, `doTransfer` and `transfer`. DoTransfer is a private method and is called by `transfer`. The credit card software has to be called there. The method `transfer` is the entry point for the client since this method is also defined in the IDL interface. The method checks if the sum is greater than zero and if the date has a legal value. Figure 11.7 shows a booking that failed because the period of validity had expired. If the direct debiting is successful the transaction data is displayed on the console again. Figure 11.8 shows an example to illustrate this concept.

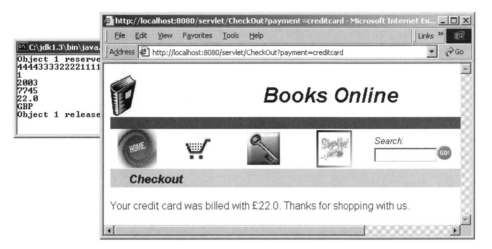

Figure 11.8: The credit card with the number 444333222111 was debited with £22. On the left is the console of the credit card server. There the data of the transfer is written on the console.

If the credit card software must be initialized, this would happen in the constructor of the class.

```
private void doTransfer(String card, int month, int year,
                  int account, double sum, String currency)
      throws CreditCardException {
   System.out.println(card);
   System.out.println(month);
   System.out.println(year);
   System.out.println(account);
   System.out.println(sum);
   System.out.println(currency);
   // Enquiry for the VISA server - check this card
}

public void transfer(String card, int month, int year,
                  int account, double sum, String currency)
      throws CreditCardException {

   if (sum <= 0)
```

```
        throw new CreditCardException(
            "The sum indicated has to be higher than null");

    Date d = new Date();
    Calendar cal = Calendar.getInstance();
    cal.clear();
    cal.set(year, month, 1);
    if (cal.getTime().getTime() < d.getTime()) {
        System.out.println("invalid");
        throw new CreditCardException(
            "The card is not valid any more.");
    }

    doTransfer(card, month, year, account, sum, currency);
    }
}
```

11.6 Why a CORBA search interface?

The Web site of Books Online has a search function which enables clients to query information quickly and comfortably from the stock database. You do not have to pick up the telephone receiver or to go to the shop and ask for a book. Just click on the mouse from your desk at home.

Nevertheless, this solution has a disadvantage. For our bookshop it is very important that we quickly reorder books that are sold out or that are low in stock. Therefore the suppliers need this information. If the query is supposed to be answered via the Web page, this is almost an impossible process. Our example lists all books in the database, provided that no search string is given in the formula. Therefore on the Web page it is relatively obvious which books are sold out. But as soon as several thousand entries are located in the database, the search result becomes incalculable to the human eye.

Moreover, it should be possible to continue to work automatically on the result of the search query through a program. For example, an *agent* could "scour" several bookshops from a supplier's computer automatically and immediately compare the sold-out books with those in its own stockpile, in order to create offers for each bookshop (Fig. 11.9).

Furthermore, you could imagine that Books Online has stores in the UK and Ireland in order to supply books quickly and at a more reasonable price. The Books Online stores in Dublin and London help each other out if a book is in short supply. To achieve this, the necessary information is exchanged using programs.

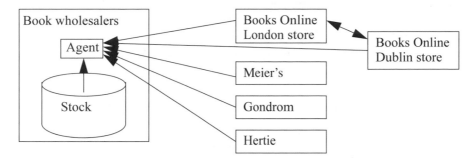

Figure 11.9: A supplier of different online and conventional bookshops checks with an agent program which books are listed to different clients in an offer.

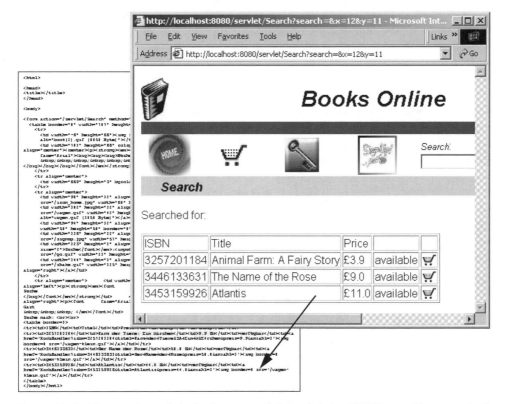

Figure 11.10: The search result in the browser and the underlying HTML text. The report in the browser is clear to the human eye. However, in the HTML the relevant piece of information (marked here) is difficult to find for the user and the machine.

Figure 11.10 hows why HTML is not suitable for the application just mentioned. The information is no longer structured but buried in the middle of HTML layout instructions. As a suitable alternative, we will introduce a CORBA solution in the following sections of this chapter. XML can also be excellent if used for this purpose and the concept of automatic information processing is picked up again in Chapter 14.

11.7 Transmission of book information with CORBA

In this section we will show a possible implementation of the search functionality based on CORBA. In principle such a solution is similar to the credit card debiting introduced in Section 11.2 on page 210. We show this example for two reasons. On the one hand, some CORBA constructs such as arrays, structs, and out parameters, not shown before, are used here. On the other hand, this sort of data transmission represents an alternative to the solution based on XML in Chapter 14 and helps you to understand the advantages and disadvantages that emerge using XML.

11.7.1 Search interface IDL: structs, arrays, and out parameters

As usual, we will begin by reviewing the IDL interface. We define two error cases at this point: the SearchException shows that something has gone wrong during the database query, while the NoBookfoundException informs the client that no book has in fact been found using the specific enquiry criterion.

```
module BookSearch {
    exception NoBookFoundException {
        string reason;
    };
    exception SearchException {
        string reason;
    };
    typedef struct BookInfo {
        string  isbn;
        string  title;
        float        price;
        long     amount;
    } BI;
    typedef sequence<BookInfo> BookList;
    interface SearchEngine {
       BookInfo searchISBN(in string isbn) raises (NoBookFoundException,
SearchException);
        BookList searchTitleFragment(in string title) raises
(NoBookFoundException, SearchException);
         void all(out BookList list) raises (NoBookFoundException,
SearchException);
    };
};
```

Similarly to the `book` class which shows an instance variable per database attribute, the IDL interface defines `StructBookInfo` with the four book attributes. This struct groups different kinds of information about a book, and so defines `BookInfo` as a parameter or as the return value of a method. Furthermore, using `sequence`, an array of book information structures can be defined. A struct is a well-known concept for C programmers. You could compare it to a Java class without methods. This assessment is confirmed when you observe the source text generated with the IDL compiler, which only contains the instance variables and constructors for their initialization:

```
package BookSearch;
public final class BookInfo {

    public String isbn;
    public String title;
    public float price;
    public int number;

    public BookInfo() { }
    public BookInfo(String __isbn, String __title,
                    float __price, int __number) {
        isbn = __isbn;
        title = __title;
        price = __price;
        number= __number;
    }
}
```

We may well wonder why we have to define a very similar structure in the class `book` again. The answer lies in the fact that actually you want to send only structured information to the client and not *references* to server objects as happens with the dispatcher object in Section 11.5.2 on page 221. We could also say that a `BookInfo` parameter in a CORBA call is submitted as a *call by value* and not as a *call by reference* parameter.

We have still to explain why a *copy* of a book object cannot simply be submitted to the client. This is because a book object could have references to other Java objects. This is not the case in our example, but you could imagine that with

```
private Vector v = new Vector()
```

a vector is used to save the data internally. This represents a problem because if a copy of the book is created and sent to the client, a vector also has to be copied and sent.

CORBA solves this problem in a less elegant way using structs, in which just primitive types are allowed. RMI and COM+ give the developer more freedom but also lead to more complex handling.

Let us now consider the interface of the search engine:

```
interface SearchEngine {
    BookInfo byISBN(in string isbn)
            raises (NoBookFoundException, SearchException);
    BookList postTitleFragment(in string title)
            raises (NoBookFoundException, SearchException);
    void all(out BookList list)
            raises (NoBookFoundException, SearchException);
};
};
```

The interface of the search engine offers three methods. First, you can search an ISBN in particular. The method `byISBN` returns a `BookInfo` struct. If the book required is not available a `NoBookFoundException` is thrown. Like searching from the Web site, only part of the book title can be given. Such a query supplies a list of information about books. Finally, the complete stock can be requested. This method has the output parameter `list` in place of a return value. The only reason for this is to present an example of an output parameter.

11.7.2 The implementation of the CORBA search engine

When dealing with the implementation of the search engine, we will rely on some classes already used for the Web application, including the `ConnectionPool` class for managing the database connections, as well as the `book` class which makes loading a record easier.

```
import BookSearch.*;
import org.omg.CosNaming.*;
import org.omg.CosNaming.NamingContextPackage.*;
import org.omg.CORBA.*;
import java.sql.*;
public class SearchEngineImpl extends _SearchEngineImplBase {
    static protected ConnectionPool pool = null;
    public static void main(String args[]) {
        try{
            ORB orb = ORB.init(args, null);
            SearchEngineImpl ref = new SearchEngineImpl();
            orb.connect(ref);
            org.omg.CORBA.Object objRef =
                    orb.resolve_initial_references("NameService");
            NamingContext ncRef = NamingContextHelper.narrow(objRef);
            NameComponent nc = new NameComponent("SearchEngine", "");
            NameComponent path[] = {nc};
            ncRef.rebind(path, ref);
            java.lang.Object sync = new java.lang.Object();
            synchronized (sync) {
                sync.wait();
```

```
            }
        }
        catch (Exception e) {
            System.err.println("ERROR: " + e);
            e.printStackTrace(System.out);
        }
    }
```

As usual, the `main` method adopts the initialization of the ORB and the registration with the *name server*. The static variable `pool` holds the *connection pool* shared among all instances of the search engine.

```
public SearchEngineImpl() {
    try {
        if (pool == null){
            pool = new ConnectionPool("sun.jdbc.odbc.JdbcOdbcDriver",
                            "jdbc:odbc:book", "book", "pass");
            System.out.println("Pool initialised"
        }
        else
            System.out.println(" Pool balready initialized "
    }
    catch (ClassNotFoundException e) {
        System.out.println("DB driver not found" + e);
    }
}
```

The pool we have just mentioned is instanced in the constructor, in case this is the first search engine object on the virtual machine.

```
public BookInfo byISBN(String isbn)
        throws NoBookFoundException, searchException {
    Connection con = null;
    PreparedStatement pstmt = null
    Book book = null
    SQLException dbError = null;

    try {
        con = pool.getConnection();
        pstmt = con.prepareStatement(
                "select * from book where isbn = ?");
        pstmt.setString(1, isbn);

        ResultSet res = pstmt.executeQuery();
        if (res.next()) {
            book = new Book();
            book.dbLoad(res);
        }
        res.close();
        pstmt.close();
    }
```

The method byISBN is one of the three methods defined in the IDL interface. The parameter submitted is inserted in a corresponding database query. The method dbLoad transfers the query result to a book object.

```
catch(SQLException e) {
    dbError = true;
    throw new SearchException(
            "Error in database query: " + e);
}
catch(PoolException e) {
    throw new SearchException(
            "Error in establishing connection : " + e);
}
finally {
    pool.close(con, dbError);
}

if (book == null)
    throw new NoBookFoundException("isbn: " + isbn);
return new BookInfo(book.isbn, book.title,
                    book.price, book.number);
}
```

If an error occurs in the database query, it is converted into the corresponding CORBA exception. A NoBookFoundException is created if no book was found. Therefore, it is guaranteed that a book object is available. Since the method returns a BookInfo object rather than a book object, the four attributes have to be copied. For this purpose the BookInfo class contains a constructor, which is simply entered with the values of all instance variables. This shows that the use of the struct does not present any relevant problem in practice.

```
public Book Info[] afterTitleFragment(String title))
            throws NoBookFoundException, SearchException {
    Connection con = null;
    PreparedStatement pstmt = null;
    Book book = null;
    java.util.Vector v = new java.util.Vector();
    BookInfo[] a;
    boolean dbError = false;

    try {
        con = pool.getConnection();
        pstmt = con.prepareStatement(
            "select * from book where title like '%" + titel + "%'");

        ResultSet res = pstmt.executeQuery();
        while (res.next()) {
            book = new Book();
            book.dbLoad(res);
            v.addElement(new BookInfo(book.isbn, book.title,
                                    book.price, book.number));
```

```
        }

        res.close();
        pstmt.close();
    }
    catch(SQLException e) {
        dbError = true;
        throw new SearchException(
            "Error in database query: " + e);
    }
    catch(PoolException e) {
        throw new SearchException(
            "Error in establishing connection: " + e);
    }
    finally {
        pool.close(con, dbError);
    }

    if (v.size() == 0)
        throw new NobookFoundException("title: " + title);
    a = new BookInfo[v.size()];

    for (int i=0; i<v.size(); i++)
        a[i] = (BookInfo)v.elementAt(i);

    return a;
}
```

The byTitleFragment method works essentially like the byISBN method. Since the select query can also list many books, each record is packed in a book object and stored in a vector. Returning the result gets more interesting. The IDL construct sequence is represented as a Java array. As at the end of the method it is known how many entries are in the vector, an array a of the same size can be created. After that, the objects are simply copied from the vector into the array. You have to take a diversion via the vector, because at the beginning of the method it is not yet known how many books apply to the query.

```
    public void all(BooksListHolder list)
            throws NoBookFoundException, SearchException {
        list.value = byTitleFragment("");
    }
}
```

The functionality of returning all books can be mapped to searching from an empty title fragment, as each book suffices the condition where title like '%%'. Therefore all simply calls byTitleFragment with the empty string as a parameter.

As we want to illustrate the programming of an out parameter, this method is defined without a return value. In its place, a holder is passed from the calling method. In order to pass the array reference on with the book information, the reference has just to be copied into the field value of the holder.

11.7.3 The implementation of the CORBA search engine client

The implementation of the client has yet to be explained. Programming with the different parameter types is the interesting issue here. The example is implemented as a simple console application, but shows all fundamental functions used in order to fulfill the ideas introduced in Section 11.6 on page 228.

```
import BookSearch.*;
import org.omg.CosNaming.*;
import org.omg.CORBA.*;
public class Client {
    public static void main(String args[]) {
        SearchEngine s = null;
        try{
            ORB orb = ORB.init(args, null);
            org.omg.CORBA.Object objRef =
                    orb.resolve_initial_references("NameService");
            NamingContext ncRef = NamingContextHelper.narrow(objRef);
            NameComponent nc = new NameComponent("SearchEngine", "");
            NameComponent path[] = {nc};
            s = SearchEngineHelper.narrow(ncRef.resolve(path));
            BookListHolder h = new BookListHolder();
            BookInfo[] a;
            BookInfo i;
            i = s.searchISBN("3453159926");
            print(i);
            a = s.searchTitleFragment("m");
            print(a);
            s.all(h);
            print(h.value);
        }
        catch (Exception e) {
            System.out.println("ERROR : " + e) ;
            e.printStackTrace(System.out);
        }
    }
    private static void print(BookInfo i) {
        BookInfo[] a = new BookInfo[1];
        a[0] = i;
        print(a);
    }
    private static void print(BookInfo[] a) {
        System.out.println("ISBN              TITLE            PRICE
AMOUNT");
        System.out.println("-------------------------------------------
--");
        for (int i=0; i<a.length; i++) {
            System.out.print(a[i].isbn + "\t");
            System.out.print(a[i].title + "\t");
            System.out.print(a[i].price + "\t");
            System.out.print(a[i].amount + "\n");
        }
        System.out.println();
    }
}
```

The search results are given in the holder h, the array a, and the struct i. As Fig. 10.2 on page 203 shows, the holder already has to be instanced by the client with `new BookListHolder()`. Three search calls follow, one for each defined method. Array and struct are assigned with the return value while the holder is simply supplied as a parameter. Two print methods are defined to print the result. The first accepts an array, the second a struct which is simply converted into an uni-elementary array internally which then is passed on to the first variant. To attain the value of the holder you just have to reference its value field.

```
    private static void print(BookInfo[] a) {

        System.out.println(
            "ISBN              TITLE PRICE NUMBER");
        System.out.println(
            "-------------------------------------------");

        for (int i=0; i<a.length; i++) {
            System.out.print(a[i].isbn + "\t");
            System.out.print(a[i].title + "\t");
            System.out.print(a[i].price + "\t");
            System.out.print(a[i].number + "\n");
        }

        System.out.println();
    }

    private static void print(BookInfo i) {
        BuchInfo[] a = new BuchInfo[1];
        a[0] = i;
        print(a);
    }
}
```

This is the output of the client. The first table illustrates the output of the search for the book with the ISBN 3453159926. The second table contains all books with an "m" in the title, and in the end all books are listed.

```
C:\book\booksonline\corba\booksearch>java Client
ISBN            TITLE           PRICE   AMOUNT
-------------------------------------------
3453159926      Atlantis        11.0    48

ISBN            TITLE           PRICE   AMOUNT
-------------------------------------------
3257201184      Animal Farm: A Fairy Story      3.9     64
3446133631      The Name of the Rose    9.0     74

ISBN            TITLE           PRICE   AMOUNT
-------------------------------------------
3257201184      Animal Farm: A Fairy Story      3.9     64
3446133631      The Name of the Rose    9.0     74
3453159926      Atlantis        11.0    48
```

Chapter 12

The basics of Enterprise Java Beans (EJB)

The fourth section of the book begins with this chapter, regarding the technology of Enterprise Java Beans. As stated in the introduction, there will be some kind of criticism of the techniques used so far, at least for certain types of application. We will address these points at the beginning of this chapter so as to motivate the development of EJB, and above all to deduce the criteria for the design of this technology. We will then consider EJBs in detail. First we will examine the typical properties of a bean, and then the two different types available to the developer, these being the Session Bean and Entity Bean. Finally, we will look at the different options available to developers if they use EJBs in their applications.

12.1 Motivation

Let us consider once more the technology examined in our application so far, both in its basic and special form, as represented in the electronic bookshop application.

We implemented the entire middle layer of a 3-tier application using servlets in the second section of this book, and so packed the complete application logic into our servlets. The sample application has already shown that servlets can quickly become large and confusing. Now imagine servlets to be the application's backbone for a full-size application! It also should be remembered that many e-commerce applications not only have to offer a certain functionality, such as ordering books, but also a certain quality to both buyer and seller. This includes the security of data transfer (i.e. protection of electronic money transactions, but also authentication of the participant) or being able to process business transactions. This primarily means that either all these processes can be processed, or none at all. Electronic travel agents are a very good example. When booking a trip, a flight, a hotel reservation, and a rental car often are required. You hardly would need a hotel room if you had no flight, and similarly you would do without the flight if you had to spend the next few nights at the airport because you had no hotel room. Transaction management is very expensive, and a separate area of IT research.

If one wished to implement these and similar properties using servlets, this would mean considerable additional expense in development. One possible solution has already been discussed, even if not yet explicitly mentioned in this context: CORBA and its predefined CORBA services offer several elegant and complete components which can be used for application development. One such example is the CORBA transaction service, which undertakes full management of a transaction. The main task of the application essentially is to indicate the beginning and the end of the transaction.

So why are we not satisfied if CORBA offers most of these features already? Well, CORBA also has its weaknesses, which can be seen from the fact that it never really became a mainstream solution for distributed applications. The CORBA approach can be compared to the ISO/OSI reference model for open systems, the main competitor of the TCP/IP model (and therefore the Internet) in the 1980s. In its standardization approach, the ISO model tried to solve too many problems in too general a way. This made it extremely complicated to implement OSI protocols, since there were simply too many exceptions to take into account. The Internet, in contrast, was not defined "from above," rather it first was implemented to show that it worked, and then was extended gradually and assigned a set of rules. In other words, a functional platform was available to developers at all times, on the basis of which they were able to develop further.

CORBA is in a very similar situation today. In the CORBA section of this book, we considered it a great advantage that objects created in different programming languages had a common IDL definition and were created using a standard tool. This is indeed true, yet considerable effort is involved in translating from one language into the standard CORBA format, and from there into other languages. For many applications this is not required, as all the code is implemented in one language, say Java. In this case, it would suffice to use the usually very efficient mechanisms available in the language for serializing objects. Nowadays there is practically no CORBA environment which fully implements the CORBA specification, i.e. together with all its services. This is a result of the complexity of the task.

Consequently, servlets are somewhat too weak to master the entire middle tier of an application, but CORBA also is only partly helpful. A technology was therefore sought with properties similar to CORBA, yet essentially less complex and easier to implement. It will no longer surprise the reader to learn that this technology has been made available with Enterprise Java Beans.

12.2 Properties of EJBs

An Enterprise Java Bean is a software component which can be used in an N-tier environment. The term "component" already has several implications: an EJB is part of an application, and so cannot run "standalone." Let us consider the multi-tier environment, where EJBs are used by components in other tiers, for example by servlets, directly by clients or possibly also by CORBA objects. EJBs themselves can contact other components. In real applications these are either other beans or components in the data layer, such as legacy applications or databases. Figure 12.1 shows a possible role of EJBs in a 4-tier architecture with presentation, Web, application, and data tiers.

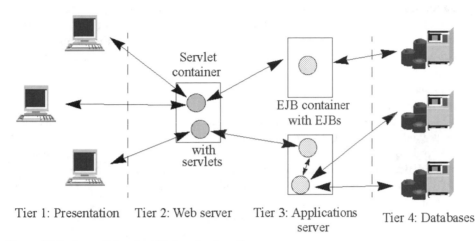

Tier 1: Presentation   Tier 2: Web server   Tier 3: Applications server   Tier 4: Databases

Figure 12.1: A possible role of Enterprise Java Beans.

As a reusable component, each EJB has a defined interface of methods with which it can be accessed. This does not mean, however, that every EJB consists of only a single object; rather it can be constructed from many different objects. However, the interface only makes one object available to the user.

CORBA objects and EJBs are fairly similar as far as we can see now. However, the specification of the *EJB container* now adds an important difference. The EJB container is the component of a software system in which EJBs "live," which manages the beans. In practice, one can imagine an EJB container as a server, which accepts the calls of the methods of an EJB and passes them on to the bean. However, different administration tasks are also involved, as mentioned previously. An EJB container actually makes all services such as security, transactions, data security, and so on available. But how does an individual EJB use these options?

Well, for this purpose, EJBs also have to fulfill another condition. They have to retain exactly the specification predefined by Sun, which prescribes the availability of several important standard methods. For example: each EJB has to implement the `Serializable` interface which enables a container to serialize a bean at any time, and convert it to a form which can be saved in a file. In the next section, we will address the conditions for the correct implementation of beans in more detail.

Which services does an EJB container offer? One can differentiate between standardized services which every container has to make available in order to be able to call itself an EJB container, and the extensions which simplify the use of an EJB container and the beans placed there.

The standard properties of a container include the following:

- Resources and life cycle management of an EJB
  A large number of beans usually run in one EJB container at the same time. Depending on the amount of tasks or number of beans, many of the resources available on the bean server might be in use (main memory, sockets, threads, etc.). The task of the container is to provide a sensible allocation of resources. Possible measures also include initiating new bean instances or removal from the memory if a bean is no longer being used, or has not been used for a long time. This is called life cycle management.

- Status management
  We have already seen from the discussion of servlets that it makes sense to establish a long-standing relation between client and server in many applications. Our example was to purchase several books and store the current selection in a virtual shopping cart. EJBs also offer the option of managing such states. One problem of stateful EJBs (we will discuss stateless and stateful EJBs in more detail later) is that they cannot be used by others during a connection with another client. The status management of the container kicks in here, which when required enables statuses to be saved and reloaded as soon as they are needed, meaning as soon as the old client becomes active once again.

- Transaction management
  The sense of transactions has already been discussed. The EJB container makes all necessary functionality available for transaction management. The EJBs themselves and also the applications do not have to take care of this; it is sufficient if the application of a transaction starts and then calls the desired EJBs.

- Security
  Based on the *Security Model* introduced in Java version 1.2 and the accompanying *Security Manager,* various security classes can be defined for the execution of an EJB, which can be broken down to individual users, and in this case, down to specific individual rights. EJBs do not need to know any API functions in this case either; rather they are executed in a context with the security properties selected previously.

- Data persistency
  This topic has also been discussed previously. A container enables an EJB object (or its status) to be saved in a file. The status can then be restored at any time, and it can be resumed at any time if required.

- Remote access and local transparency
  Just like CORBA objects, beans are developed entirely independently of a network. Each bean has its own interface, not prescribed with a language-independent IDL, but in the form of a *Java Remote Interface*. The implementation is carried out using a Java Remote Method Invocation (RMI). In principle, this effectively functions exactly like CORBA, and location transparency is also realized. Applications do not therefore have to know on which computer a certain EJB is offered.

■   Tools
     Finally, the basic equipment of an EJB container also includes a set of tools. The
     tasks include such things as the creation of necessary stubs and skeletons (also used
     with EJB) or simply the logic required for the different services.

Special features which do not necessarily have to be available in a standard
implementation include the following:

■   Load balancing
     Intelligent EJB containers can coordinate with other containers of the same type and
     divide the load between them equally, if they offer the same type of EJB. This results
     in improved performance of individual components, which in turn results in a higher-
     quality service for the user.
■   Dynamic exchange of runtime components
     Systems used in today's economic climate have to have the "24/7" feature, meaning
     they have to be available 24 hours a day, 7 days a week. This means that the system
     must not be stopped in the case of maintenance work such as testing a new version of
     the system. Containers are an advantage here in that they support the exchange of
     components or testing of new versions while the system remains operational.
■   Distributed transactions
     Transactions require relatively complex processes, but if these transactions stretch
     over several containers and servers, special support for distributed transactions is
     required.
■   Integrated XML support
     In the next part of this book, we will see how important XML has become for the
     modelling of data in distributed applications. If this new standard is supported by an
     EJB container, then many of the tasks connected with the representation of data are
     clearly simplified.
■   Integration of CORBA
     CORBA and EJB can complement each other when one compares the two
     application areas. There is a protocol for simplifying integration which enables
     CORBA objects to communicate with Java Remote Objects. This protocol is called
     RMI-IIOP.

12.3 Types of EJBs

In the specification of EJB, two main types of beans are provided which can respectively
be differentiated further. The application area of both types is completely different. We
will introduce both types in this section.

Business applications, and applications in general, can be divided into two components on
a software–technical front: the first component type comprises the active parts, general
procedures, called functions or methods, used in e-commerce applications in order to

implement *business processes*, or the process logic of the application. The other type deals with the passive parts, or generally the data of an application. There is a bean type for both, respectively the *Session Bean* and *Entity Bean*.

12.3.1 Session beans

Session beans are used for modeling business processes. They contain any type of process logic in an application. If we consider our example of the electronic bookshop, these processes include the receipt and processing of an order or loading a virtual shopping cart.

The name "session bean" stems from the fact that the lifetime of a bean corresponds to the session of a client. "Session" is to be understood in the sense of a servlet session, which usually comprises several client–server interactions. As soon as a client asks for the services of a certain session bean with an EJB container, the container first checks whether the desired type of session bean is available, and above all, inactive. If this is not the case, a new bean is created so as to make the service available to the client.

The keyword "inactive" has just been mentioned. A bean is inactive when not being used by the client. This means that session beans can only ever be used by a single client at the same time. There is also no support of concurrency, which considerably simplifies the implementation of session beans and increases performance.

We have already seen in the servlet chapter that there are business processes which can be settled with a single method call (or a servlet call), while others can extend over a greater number of method calls. An example for the first case is the query of a price of an article, while our electronic shopping cart represents an example of the second case. For this, the option of maintaining a status is required, whereas this is not necessary in the first case. As there are also considerable differences in implementation, use of resources, and efficiency, two types of session bean are available, these being *stateless* and *stateful session beans*. The use of the respective type naturally depends on the type of application, so you should check carefully to see which type is correct.

12.3.2 Entity beans

Entity beans are used for modeling data in an application. In our bookshop application the three data types were book, client, and order. This immediately stands out: there are three tables used in the database. So why remove the data from the database and model it on the EJB level? Strictly speaking, you don't actually do that: rather an object-oriented view of required data is created and stored in the EJB memory. The advantages are obvious: On the one hand, only local communication occurs when data is accessed, which essentially runs quicker. On the other hand, the data can be requested and modified in the way known to a Java programmer, using method calls made available by the corresponding bean. A direct programming of SQL commands then can be omitted.

It must of course be assured that the data view in the bean is consistent with the corresponding value in the database. This is one of the most important tasks of the container in the management of entity beans. However, the management of the persistence of an entity bean can also be undertaken manually.

Entity beans are multi-client capable, meaning that several clients can use an entity bean at the same time. The EJB container is then responsible for the correct handling of such access.

12.4 Development of EJB applications

So how should the development of distributed applications run if EJBs are to be used? In this section we will consider the typical procedure, and then address which business opportunities and markets open up through the spread of EJBs. In both cases it is important to note that EJBs are both complete and reusable components.

12.4.1 Development procedure

If one considers the usual software life cycle, roughly made up of analysis, design, implementation, test, use, and maintenance, the development of EJB applications occurs as follows:

1. Analysis of software properties
    As seen in previous chapters, this job is to be carried out carefully and thoroughly with distributed applications. This is completely independent of the techniques used, and also applies to EJBs. An error at this stage could render any work obsolete in later stages.
2. Design of the application based on a specific middleware technology, i.e. EJB
    The main aim of this phase is to create an application design which meets the requirements specified in phase 1. For this you already should have later implementation techniques in the back of your mind. As we are addressing object-oriented system development here, it is recommended that exactly the same design technique be used. A well-known and up-and-coming candidate would be UML, for example. Using this technique, the entire application can be broken down into its individual components.
3. Implementation through purchase or development of components and assembly of the entire application
    Today there are already EJBs used for many standard business transactions. It makes sense in most cases to purchase these components from a third-party supplier rather than start from scratch. According to experience, the development costs are clearly higher than the costs of purchasing the software (or even the license). Based on the interfaces of the components purchased, several other components will usually be added. These individual components ultimately have to interact according to the design, and finally be the building blocks of the entire application.
4. Testing the application or individual components
    With purchased components, you should be able to assume that at least in the case of serious suppliers, they have been thoroughly tested. In-house developments have to undergo a test phase before use, and you will surely test the application thoroughly before releasing it for use.

5.   Use
     After the tests, the beans (and other components used) are finally installed in their respective
     containers and can then be used.
6.   Maintenance
     The stability of the system should constantly be monitored.

12.4.2 Development roles

By dividing the work, there are new chances for IT companies to enter markets. The
following roles are particularly important:

- The bean manufacturer only produces beans, and no finished applications. These
  should of course be reusable so they can be sold.
- It is the task of the EJB container manufacturer to make the runtime environment for
  EJBs available. We have already seen that an EJB container has to make a minimum
  of functionality available, but there is much leeway for a difference in supply.
- Finally, the application manufacturer takes the components available, probably writes
  a few of his or her own and then assembles the application.

It is of course conceivable, and even probable, that some market contributors fulfill several
roles, such as with bean and container manufacturers.

The next chapter addresses the reference implementation for EJB from Sun, and explains
the use of the individual classes in detail.

Chapter 13

Tools for Enterprise Java Beans

In this chapter we will focus on the *Java 2 Platform Enterprise Edition*, the most important basis for the development of EJB applications. To begin with, we will concentrate on the features of this platform in order to later analyze in detail some fundamental Java classes and interfaces for the development of both session and entity beans.

13.1 The Java 2 Platform, Enterprise Edition

The Java 2 Platform, Enterprise Edition (J2EE) is a complete package for the development of professional enterprise applications, made available (in binary and source code) by Sun Microsystems. J2EE is installed as an addition to the standard version of the JDK and contains the following four components:

- the J2EE platform
- the J2EE compatibility test suite
- the J2EE reference implementation
- the Sun Blueprints design guideline for the development of distributed applications.

The most important component is the J2EE platform. Rather than an implementation, it is a specification. As such, it provides standard interfaces for the development of distributed applications, to which all product manufacturers in this field have to conform in order to be compatible. The most important components for us in this chapter are the APIs for EJB, described in the following two sections. Only by creating such standardized APIs can a market for component-based software be established.

The compatibility test suite component is used to determine if a product really satisfies the requirements of the J2EE platform. It is a configurable program package which, for example, checks if the APIs required are implemented, and if the standard EJB applications are running in the environment which has to be tested.

The reference implementation provides some of the components necessary in an EJB application. These include an EJB container or a relational database as a backend in a multi-tier application. In principle, Sun wants to show with this implementation how the J2EE model can be converted. It was not created to be used in building commercial implementations.

Finally, the design guidelines can be considered as a kind of tutorial for the development of distributed applications with the different technologies covered in J2EE.

J2EE is available at the Web address `http://java.sun.com/j2ee`. Installation in different platforms is quite simple, and is described in the instructions. For this reason we will not discuss this topic any further. In this chapter we continue to deal with the J2EE platform, while in the next chapter we will consider the reference implementation and show how you can implement our bookshop application with it on the EJB basis.

13.2 J2EE specification for Enterprise Beans

The J2EE specification explains in detail what an Enterprise Java Beans component should look like. This is done by prescribing individual constituents of such a component and the specification of *Java interfaces* which define the structure of the public interface of each component. In this section we will consider these components, and first have a look at those interfaces which have to be fulfilled by an implementation. The following are the basic components:

- the Enterprise Java Bean itself;
- the EJB object together with remote interface;
- the home object together with home interface;
- management information within the deployment descriptor and the manifest;
- the EJB Jar file.

13.2.1 The Enterprise Bean

The Enterprise Java Bean itself contains the general logic of the application which has to be implemented using this component, or, in case of an entity bean, the data that should be modeled for the application. Each EJB has to implement the following interface:

```
public interface javax.ejb.EnterpriseBean extends java.io.Serializable {
}
```

Three things are noteworthy about this interface:

1. It defines no methods which have to be made available by an implementation. In other words, this is a *marker interface* which only turns those classes which it implements into an EJB.
2. It extends the interface Serializable. This means that each class which implements the Interface Enterprise Bean is simultaneously a serializable object, and it can therefore be made persistent using the standard methods provided. This is an important feature, especially for entity beans.
3. No class implements the interface directly. There are rather specific interfaces which extend these generic interfaces, namely the interface for session beans and that for entity beans. We will discuss these two extensions below.

13.2.2 Remote interface and EJB object

A remarkable fact is that an EJB cannot communicate in the network. The examples we have previously considered show that an EJB is only defined through a class that owns some methods in which the pure application logic is implemented. But how does the communication between the server-side EJB and a client located somewhere in the net take place?

There is a kind of "representative" for the EJB which offers its interface to the outside. This representative is described as an *EJB object*. Each call of a client to an EJB does not directly reach the EJB itself, but the EJB object. The latter accepts the call and passes it on to the EJB using the container. The main purpose is to release the EJB programmer from any network programming. However, by including the container it is also possible, for example, to collect statistics on the calling behavior and modify the configuration accordingly. To ensure nevertheless that the interface presents itself to the client in the same way it would expect from a Java Bean, every EJB object that belongs to an EJB must obviously provide the same methods also provided by the EJB. The methods available in an EJB object are described in the *remote interface*. Actually, this remote interface is the one with which the client is familiar, and on the basis of which it executes method calls. Furthermore, it should be an extension of the interface EJBObject which is defined as follows:

```
package javax.ejb;
import java.rmi.*;

public interface EJBObject extends Remote {
    public EJBHome getEJBHome() throws RemoteException;
    public Object getPrimaryKey() throws RemoteException;
    public void remove() throws RemoteException, RemoveException;
    public Handle getHandle() throws RemoteException;
    boolean isIdentical(EJBObject obj) throws RemoteException;
}
```

The methods of this basic definition of a remote interface essentially fulfill management tasks. They are primarily used by the EJB container, for example via the home object, described in the next section. Another important feature of the remote interface should be enphasized: All methods described here can create a `RemoteException`. This has to be done in Java for all methods declared within an interface which extends the interface `Remote`. Such an exception always occurs when problems arise in the communication between processes on the network.

It obviously sounds like a contradiction if you say on the one hand that you should not burden application programmers with network communication questions, or generally with implementation-specific questions concerning EJB and home objects; and on the other hand that the EJB object together with remote interface also has to be made available by the programmers themselves. However, the contradiction is easily remedied: The EJB object can be generated automatically on the basis of the remote interface description, and one of the tasks of the container is to provide a corresponding tool. Also, the methods already provided in the interface `EJBObject` are all automatically generated. In fact, the tasks of the EJB object are very similar to those of the skeletons in CORBA – and these were also created automatically.

If we consider the relationship of the components examined so far, then it can be visualized like in Fig. 13.1. The EJB container provides the EJB object as an outside interface for the original EJB whose methods are made known to the object through the remote interface.

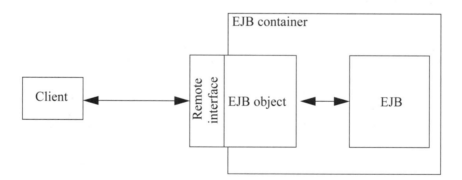

Figure 13.1: The EJB object as a representative of the EJB.

13.2.3 Home interface and home object

The question yet to be answered is: how does a client find an EJB object, or how does it create one if there is none yet that fulfiles its requirements?

Here the J2EE specification creates another indirection with the *home object*. The home object plays the role of an *object factory*, i.e. its task is to supply the client with a reference to an EJB object it requires. This could mean that the home object first has to create the reference, but it may already exist.

Obviously, a home object has to know what an EJB object looks like or which possibilities are offered if such an object is created. Accordingly, the bean manufacturer has to describe the interface of the home objects using its own interface, the *home interface*. The home object itself is container dependent and automatically generated, like the EJB object.

The basis interface for home objects defined in J2EE is structured as follows:

```
package javax.ejb;
import java.rmi.*;

public interface EJBHome extends Remote {
    void remove(Handle handle) throws RemoteException, RemoveException;
    void remove(Object primaryKey) throws RemoteException,
                                          RemoveException;
    EJBMetaData getEJBMetaData() throws RemoteException;
    HomeHandle getHomeHandle() throws RemoteException;
}
```

The most interesting are the `remove()` functions, and those which are not visible: there are no `create()` functions. Using `remove()`, you remove an EJB object previously created. But how do you create it? The solution is simple: An EJB object can have very different initialization parameters. Obviously, you cannot provide a `create()` function for each possible variant; rather, they are left open in `EJBHome`. It is only when implementing the interface that the bean manufacturer adds the necessary `create()` functions to it. An example: Let us assume that an EJB object expects an integer as an initialization value. The bean manufacturer then provides the following home interface, on the assumption that the EJB object is called `Example`:

```
import javax.ejb.*;
import java.rmi.RemoteException;

public interface ExampleHome extends EJBHome{
    Example create(int init) throws RemoteException, CreateException;
}
```

The result of calling this method (finally by a client) leads to the creation of an EJB object with the interface `Example`.

Figure 13.2 shows the extended representation of the EJB container as it appears with a home object.

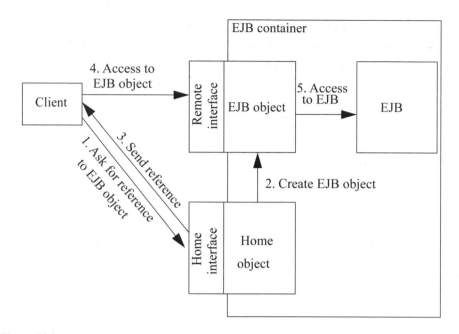

Figure 13.2: Access to the home object.

First the client is directed to the home object. This either searches an existing EJB object for the application or creates a new one. In the third step the reference to this object is given back to the client, which later in the fourth step will contact the EJB object in order to execute the application itself. We will consider some code examples for these sequences of operations in the next chapter.

13.2.4 Administration information: deployment descriptor and bean-specific properties

Besides these constituents, some administrative information has to be added to the EJB component. This is done using the two files for the *deployment descriptor* and *bean-specific properties*.

Using the deployment descriptor, the manufacturer of an EJB component can determine which service of the EJB container this bean should use. There are four fields in which parameters can be set:

- Bean management
  Here the container is informed about how the component is built. The names of the EJB and the affiliated objects and interfaces are identified. Moreover, the type of the EJB is given.
- Persistence requirements
  This primarily concerns the entity beans. It is indicated whether the bean itself takes care of the persistence management, or leaves the task to the container.
- Execution requirements within a transaction.
  Here the bean programmer can indicate how the component should be dealt with when executed within a transaction.
- Security requirements
  Using lists, the constructor can indicate who is allowed to use this component.

The parameter values set by the manufacturer have to be considered standard values, which can, however, be modified. The user of a bean can amend the deployment descriptor at will.

You can carry out your own bean configuration using the second file. The virtual machine which executes the bean reads this file in advance and passes the values contained there on to the bean itself. In this way the beans' behavior can be controlled accordingly.

13.2.5 The EJB Jar file

In order to deliver the bean, all files are packed in a single *Jar file*. Jar stands for Java archive, and is the archive format for Java libraries. All class libraries and also the EJB components are saved in this format.

We should also point out that it is not necessary to place the EJB object and home object in the Jar file. We had heard that these objects are container specific and can be generated automatically with the container in which the component is used. However, the home interface and remote interface are necessary, as objects are generated on this basis.

When everything is packed in the Jar file, the components can be delivered (the following chapter shows a concrete example of this).

13.3 Special features of session beans

In order to implement session beans there is a particular interface to be implemented, and also the program flows can be specified in a more detailed way than with the more generic enterprise beans.

13.3.1 The interface for session beans

If you want to implement a session bean with all the features we have previously considereded, you should use the following interface (or a corresponding extension):

```
package javax.ejb;
import java.rmi.RemoteException;

public interface SessionBean extends EnterpriseBean {
    void setSessionContext(SessionContext ctx) throws EJBException,
                                                      RemoteException;
    void ejbRemove() throws EJBException, RemoteException;
    void ejbActivate() throws EJBException, RemoteException;
    void ejbPassivate() throws EJBException, RemoteException;
}
```

In addition to the methods already provided in the parent interface EnterpriseBean, at least another ejbCreate() method should be provided, the signature of which, as in the home interface, depends on the respective requirements. The individual methods have the following functions:

■ setSessionContext()
This method is used by the container; it is used to enable the EJB to communicate directly with the container. After calling the method the bean owns a *session context*, in which it can access some important parameters that are available in the container.

■ ejbCreate()
The container uses these methods to create a new EJB. Their purpose is usually initialization tasks. It should be noted that a particular EJB is not always created whenever a client so wishes. It is possible that there already may be a bean instance which is then used again.

■ ejbRemove()
On this occasion we deal with the counterpart of the ejbCreate() method. The function is executed when the container eliminates the instance. Therefore the tasks include for the most part a "clearing-up operation" such as the cancelation of further objects etc.

▨   `ejbPassivate()`

The container can execute this method in order to remove a bean from the main memory. This happens when (a) the bean has not been used for a long time or (b) the performance of the system is bad.

▨   `ejbActivate()`

This is the counterpart to passivate a bean. If the bean is used again in a new client call, it is transferred again into the main memory with this method.

These administration methods also include the actual application routines. In paragraph 13.3.3 we will consider how these methods are enclosed in a bean. However, first we will briefly address the treatment of stateless and stateful session beans.

13.3.2 Stateless and stateful beans

The methods we have just discussed are employed in a different way for stateful and stateless beans. Here we will mention only briefly the most important differences without going into too much detail:

▨   Stateless session beans have no instance variables in which they can store the values. Therefore they cannot be made persistent – there is no point in this as there is no status to save.

▨   There is therefore only one `ejbCreate()` method which in this case does not accept any parameters. This is the case because there is no instance variable to initialize.

▨   The methods `ejbPassivate()` and `ejbActivate()` are not used in stateless session beans because it is not necessary to save stateless beans or load them again. Instead they are simply deleted if no longer required, or when the memory is used for other beans. They are created again if necessary.

▨   As stateless beans can be used by many clients, it is sufficient to hold a pool of instances of a bean class (similar to the pool of database connections seen in the servlet part) and assign them to new clients time and again. In this way system performance can be improved considerably. As far as stateful beans are concerned, a new bean has to be created for each client, and consequently it may be necessary to passivate beans frequently and activate them again. These differences mainly concern the manufacturer of an EJB container, whose task is to maintain system efficiency.

13.3.3 Writing our own session bean

The session bean itself, written on the basis of this interface description, supplements the interface with the business methods. Let us consider a simple example (a more complex example follows in the next chapter).

Our session bean is to calculate the price of a product. We will make the price dependent on the product itself, for which we should define a data type, and on a price policy defined with an integer. The session bean is implemented as follows:

```
public class PriceComputer implements SessionBean {
   ...
   public double computePrice(Product p, int policy) {
      // the computation routine follows here
   }

   // now all the management routines

   public void ejbCreate() {
      // the initialization code
      ...
   }

   ... // ejbRemove(), ejbActivate(), ....

}
```

13.3.4 JNDI as name server for EJB

In the previous discussion, when considering the execution of a session bean, we have forgotten an important part: How does the client know where the home interface or the home object is? The answer is that here, like in CORBA, we use a name service in which a home object registers as soon as it comes into existence and which can be queried when a particular home object is required. We do not want to consider the general operation of a name server further, as we already did so in detail in the part concerning CORBA. However, we have to mention that the EJB specification requires the use of the *Java Naming and Directory Services* (JNDI). This, too, is a specification for which implementations should be offered by third-party suppliers. However, in the next chapter, when discussing the reference implementation, we will focus on the version provided by Sun.

13.4 Special features of entity beans

We had previously explained in detail the purpose of entity beans. In short, they offer the applications programmer an object-oriented view on the database functioning as a backend in business applications. Therefore, entity beans have features very similar to those that characterize database objects, such as the ability to survive system crashes.

From the discussion about session beans, we have seen that instances were usually interchangeable (above all in stateless beans), i.e. it does not matter to a client which instance of a given EJB class it is assigned. Obviously, it is completely different with entity beans, as each bean represents a specific data item or, in other words, a particular database record. Clearly, these are not interchangeable without loss of information. However, this does not mean that during its lifetime an EJB cannot represent different database records. The EJB container is responsible for securing data consistency. For this purpose it uses the administrative functions available.

As a consequence, an EJB component contains the previously reviewed elements as well as another file which encodes the class *primary key*. As we already know from Chapter 5, the primary key is used for the unique identification of a database object. This component performs this very task with the entity beans.

Furthermore, an entity bean distinguishes itself by the use of another specialized interface, which we will now consider.

13.4.1 The interface for entity beans

This interface is called `EntityBean` and appears as follows:

```
package javax.ejb;
import java.rmi.RemoteException;

public interface EntityBean extends EnterpriseBean {
   public void setEntityContext(EntityContext ctx) throws EJBException,
                                                 RemoteException;
   public void unsetEntityContext() throws EJBException,
                                            RemoteException;
   public void ejbRemove() throws RemoveException, EJBException,
                                              RemoteException;
   public void ejbActivate() throws EJBException, RemoteException;
   public void ejbPassivate() throws EJBException, RemoteException;
   public void ejbLoad() throws EJBException, RemoteException;
   public void ejbStore() throws EJBException, RemoteException;
}
```

In addition to these explicitly indicated methods, there are further methods here which should or could be available but are not declared, as they can use different forms and parameters. These are methods of the `ejbCreate()` and `ejbFind()` type. Let us now consider the individual methods briefly:

- `ejbCreate()`
  The methods executed to create an entity do not have to be available because there is another process to get data in a bean, using `ejbLoad()`.
- `ejbRemove()`, `ejbPassivate()`, and `ejbActivate()`
  These methods have the same function as in the session beans. You can see the passivation or activation as a process in which the binding of the bean to particular database records is made or deleted. A passivated bean does not represent any particular data; this connection exists only after activation. During activation the primary key of the bean also is set.
- `ejbFind()`
  These methods are used to find a particular bean and thus a specific database record. In principle you can compare the execution of such a method with the SQL command select, which searches many database records in order to find those fulfilling certain criteria. Therefore "the" method `ejbFind()` does not exist. Rather the bean manufacturer can define many of these methods which begin with "`ejbFind`". However, at least a search method is necessary which enables a bean to be searched with the primary key. This method is called `ejbFindByPrimaryKey()`.
- `ejbLoad()`
  This method is used to load data into the entity bean.
- `ejbStore()`
  This is the counterpart of loading data; using this method, the data is written into the memory again, for example into the database.
- `setEntityContext()` and `unsetEntityContext()`
  These methods are used by the container in order to set or delete the context of the entity. The context enables access to a series of environment parameters such as the EJB object belonging to the bean or the transaction in which the bean is being used. You can access the context using a Java interface which, however, we will not look at in any more detail at this point.

The actual methods for data manipulation also have yet to be added. Apart from the ejbFind methods these are the most important methods for the user; they usually justify the use of entity beans. Otherwise you could continue using direct database access. The next section shows through a simple example how such methods are meaningfully defined.

13.4.2 A short example

Let us now consider a very short example of an entity bean. We want to model the basic framework of a billing process. The data type `Bill` has some instance variables such as the billing address, date, positions, sum, and so on. Furthermore, there are methods with which the values of the variables can be defined, and there are search methods which enable specific bills to be searched. We will begin with the class definition and instance variables:

```
public class Bill implements EntityBean {
   public String address;
   public String date;
   public Position pos[];
   double sum;
```

We find here some methods to search particular bills:

```
public Enumeration ejbFindByAddress(String addr) {
   // searches all primary keys in the calculation which go
   // to an address
   // access to the database is made here using JDBC
}
```

Finally, we will use another method which enables the sum to be calculated:

```
public void calculateSum() {
   // Loop on all positions
   // add up all component sum
   // assign the final result of the instance variable sum
   ...
}

...#
}
```

This bean is not a complete example by any means; it should merely convey a general idea about the methods which may make sense when writing entity beans.

13.5 Tools of the J2EE reference implementation

We already have mentioned that it is important to provide tool support for many of the functions described above. In fact, this is one of the markets which should be addressed by the EJB container manufacturer. We had also said that Sun itself makes a reference implementation available. For example, this package contains an EJB server or container, a tool for compiling a complete component, a database, and so on. Here, rather than describing these tools, we will show how they are used by means of an example which is described in the following Chapter.

Chapter 14

EJB example

In this chapter we will show how an implementation of our bookshop application will look using EJB. The implementation of a complete application with Enterprise Java Beans is a very complex and time-consuming task. Obviously, this only happens because EJBs relieve the clients of a lot of routine work. If programming is removed from the client side, it has to be executed somewhere else. Therefore, in the previous two chapters we have seen which tasks the individual parts of an EJB component have to perform.

If we wanted to convert our entire electronic bookshop to EJBs, or to completely explain the implementation here, this would be a whole book in itself. For this reason we will only introduce a select part of the application. However, the complete implementation will be available on the Web site for further study. For this chapter we have chosen the implementation of the virtual shopping cart. First, we will introduce the EJB component itself, also considering two corresponding modified servlets which act as a user interface, and finally we will see how the EJB component can be integrated into the J2EE reference implementation.

14.1 Development of a shopping cart EJB

In this chapter we will explain how the EJB components are developed or which functionality they can have. First we will consider the structure of the application in its entirety in order to study the three EJBs in detail, namely for modeling a book, a single position in the cart, and the cart itself.

14.1.1 Structure of the bookshop application with EJBs

Compared to the application developed in Chapter 8, we will now break down the second tier which only consisted of servlets, and replace it with a combination of servlets and EJBs. In doing so we will pass from a 3-tier to a 4-tier structure.

Figure 14.1 shows the components of the new application, in the upper section as an overall view, in the lower as a detailed view of the EJB plane. Nothing changes in the general functionality, i.e. servlets and EJBs provide the same service previously offered by the servlets alone. The tasks are now merely distributed in a different way: we can generally say that the servlets are accountable to the client for the production of Web pages, or for the user interface, while the EJBs contain the entire business logic of the application.

The EJB component of the application contains a set of entity and session beans, as you can see in the lower part of the picture. To begin with, let us examine the entity beans. We use three types of entity beans altogether, these being `book`, `client`, and `order`. The more attentive reader will immediately notice that these are precisely the entities we also used in the pure servlet application with direct access to the database. We created these very three tables in our entity-relationship diagram and the subsequent implementation using the Access database, where `order` is a relationship between the entities `client` and `book`.

Obviously, these three object classes are excellent candidates for an implementation with entity beans, as their task is to produce an object-oriented representation of the database contents.

Other objects of our EJB world are shopping carts and their contents. From the shading we can see that in this case, modeling using session beans is preferred. Why is this so? Well, we will now develop the actual application logic and place it in these objects, i.e. searching for different books, modifying the number of products in the cart, or checking out – the virtual aisle to the till. Furthermore, we do not wish to make the shopping cart permanent, i.e. saving its contents in the database. So if the system crashes, the data is lost, but this does usually not matter too much, as you can usually repeat the process fairly quickly. Saving such data permanently seems pointless, given that some clients fill their carts without proceeding to the checkout. The contents of the basket will then expire at some point.

We have yet to explain whether stateless or stateful session beans are used. In this case the answer is fairly clear, as each shopping cart should be assigned to one customer – the idea of a shopping cart is to save and collect information over a longer period of time.

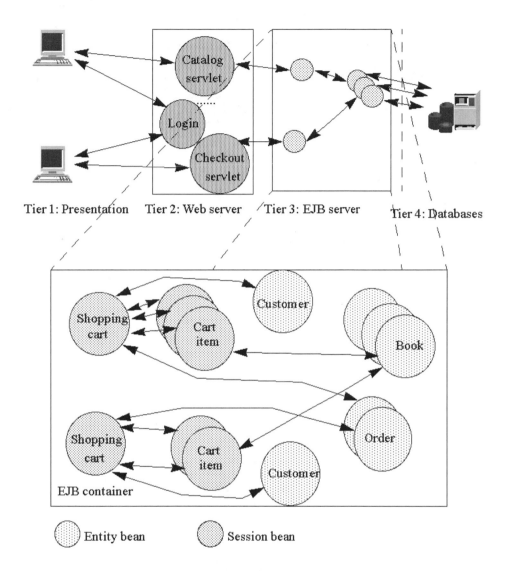

Tier 1: Presentation   Tier 2: Web server   Tier 3: EJB server   Tier 4: Databases

Figure 14.1: Structure of the virtual bookshop with EJB.

The general application process should look like follows: As soon as a customer has logged on, he or she is assigned a shopping cart using a corresponding session ID (see Section 8.7 on page 145). At the same time, the shopping cart contains a reference to the customer object which is loaded and initialized from the database. At this point the cutomer can browse through the catalog or search for a particular book. Each individual book can be placed in the shopping cart. In this way, a ShoppingCartItem is created containing a reference to the corresponding book as well as the quantity selected. `ShoppingCartItem` will contain methods for modifying the amount. Access to these methods also takes place via a servlet.

If the customer has finally decided to buy the chosen books he or she proceeds to the checkout. We will not consider the actual payment process; we saw in the CORBA example (see Chapter 11) how it could be implemented. From a technical point of view, payment means the creation of an `order` as an EJB, and saving it in the database.

Let us examine some select code fragments so as to understand more fully the basic idea of EJB programming.

14.1.2 Example 1: the book EJB

The book EJB is an entity bean. For the sake of simplicity we will leave the persistence management to the container. As a result, some of the bean methods such as `ejbLoad()` can be implemented pro forma, but will not be used.

Let us now consider the remote interface in `Book.java`, in which we declare all business methods for the bean. In this book we focus on setting and reading the actual data fields. The data fields of the book are the same we used in the table definition for `book` in Section 8.1.3 on page 145:

```
import javax.ejb.EJBObject;
import java.rmi.RemoteException;

public interface Book extends EJBObject
{
    public String getTitle() throws RemoteException;
    public void setTitle(String title) throws RemoteException;
    public double getPrice() throws RemoteException;
    public void setPrice(double price) throws RemoteException;
    public String getISBN() throws RemoteException;
    public void setISBN(String isbn) throws RemoteException;
    public int getNumber() throws RemoteException;
    public void setNumber(int number) throws RemoteException;
}
```

You will notice that the get methods return a corresponding data type, while the set methods accept the value of the required types as a parameter.

The home interface in the file `BookHome.java` contains a create method as well as two search methods. The latter are managed by the container itself and do not have to be implemented:

```
import java.io.Serializable;
import java.rmi.RemoteException;
import javax.ejb.CreateException;
import javax.ejb.FinderException;
```

```
import javax.ejb.EJBHome;
import java.util.Enumeration;

public interface BookHome extends EJBHome
{
    public Book create(String isbn, String title, double price,
                       int number) throws RemoteException,
                                            CreateException;

    public Book findByPrimaryKey(BookPK key) throws FinderException,
                                               RemoteException;
    public Enumeration findByTitle(String title) throws FinderException,
                                               RemoteException;

}
```

The task of the `create` method is to create a new database entry, while the existing objects are searched using both search methods, or created with the required entry. Method 1 searches for an object with a specific primary key, while method 2 enables one or more books with a particular title to be searched. Incidentally, this method can be generated automatically, keeping the name of the method and the parameter to conform to the name conventions given for the beans. By using the name `findByTitle` and the parameter `title`, the container knows which tasks this method has to perform, as there is also a field called `title` in the bean.

`FindByPrimaryKey` returns a reference to a book object directly because the primary key has to be explicit. On the other hand, `FindByTitle` can return a list, as many books can have the same title.

The third class to consider here defines the primary key. In essence, the task is to choose one of the bean fields as a key, and define it again as a key separately. This process is carried out in the file `BookPK.java`:

```
import java.io.Serializable;

public class BookPK implements Serializable {
    public String isbn;

    public BookPK() { }

    public BookPK(String isbn) {
        this.isbn = isbn;
    }

    public String toString() {
        return isbn;
    }
}
```

As in the database table, we have chosen the field isbn as a key. The constructors are self-explanatory and the toString method gives the class a printable representation.

Once this preliminary work is completed, we can turn to the implementation of the bean. There is not much work left, as we do not have to address persistence management. We usually focus on the implementation of the business methods. This is the file BookEJB.java:

```
import javax.ejb.*;
import java.rmi.RemoteException;

public class BookEJB implements EntityBean
{
    protected EntityContext ctxt;

    // member variables
    // must be public for container-managed bean
    public String isdn;  // primary key
    public String title;
    public double price;
    public int number;  // stock level
```

As previously explained, we define a member variable for each column name of the table. In order to enable persistence management for the container, the variables have to be defined as public. It is important to mention the variable ctxt at this point. This enables access to important context parameters such as the primary keys after they have been set using setEntityContext.

Let us now consider the business methods; here we merely describe one get and one set method, as the remaining methods can be defined in the same way:

```
//business methods
public String getTitle() throws RemoteException {
   return title;
}

public void setTitle(String title) throws RemoteException {
   this.title = title;
}

public double getPrice() throws RemoteException { ... }
public void setPrice(double price) throws RemoteException { ... }
public String getISBN() throws RemoteException { ... }
public void setISBN(String isbn) throws RemoteException { ... }
public int getNumber() throws RemoteException { ... }
public void setNumber(int ) throws RemoteException { ... }
```

We also have to define the classes required by the container. These are compulsory for defining the file correctly. The methods concerned with persistence management are defined, but as they are not used, we just use the simplest definition possible:

```
// container-required
public void ejbRemove() throws RemoteException {}
public void ejbActivate() throws RemoteException {}
public void ejbPassivate() throws RemoteException {}
public void ejbLoad() throws RemoteException { }
public void ejbStore() throws RemoteException { }
```

Setting and deleting the context requires more work:

```
public void setEntityContext(EntityContext ec) throws RemoteException
{
    this.ctxt = ec;
}
public void unsetEntityContext() throws RemoteException {
    this.ctxt = null;
}
```

These methods are called by the container in order to enable access for the bean to the context or to delete this reference.

Finally, we have to define the create method given in the home interface. Obviously, its task is to set the class member variables correctly:

```
public Book PK create(String isbn, String title, double price,
                      int number) throws RemoteException,
                                         CreateException {
    this.isbn = isbn;
    this.title = title;
    this.price = price;
    this.number = number;
    }
}
```

The definition of our book EJB is now complete.

14.1.3 Example 2: the cart content

Before defining the virtual shopping cart, its content should be considered first. The shopping cart can contain different positions, and each of those can be determined with a particular book and the number of copies to be bought. It should be possible both to select and modify the number, and to offer a function which enables the total price of the item to be calculated. This makes it easier to implement the payment function later in the shopping cart itself. Furthermore, we want to be able to verify which book we have in front of us.

The remote interface is defined in the file `CartItem.java`. According to the description above, we wish to define three business methods:

```java
import javax.ejb.EJBObject;
import java.rmi.RemoteException;

public interface CartItem extends EJBObject {
    public int getQuantity() throws RemoteException;
    public void setQuantity(int quantity) throws RemoteException;
    public double computePositionSum() throws RemoteException;
    public Book getBook() throws RemoteException;
}
```

The home interface is easier with session beans than with entity beans; we only require a create function:

```java
import java.rmi.RemoteException;
import javax.ejb.CreateException;
import javax.ejb.*;

public interface CartItemHome extends EJBHome {

    public CartItem create(Book bk) throws CreateException,
                                           RemoteException;
}
```

The method accepts a reference to a book which is used for the initialization of the `CartItem` object. We assume that the number of books is 1 by default, so that this value is only modified if necessary, using the method given in the remote interface.

It remains to provide the actual implementation of the bean, contained in the file `CartItemEJB.java`:

```java
import javax.ejb.*;
import java.rmi.RemoteException;

public class CartItemEJB implements SessionBean {

    protected SessionContext ctxt;

    private Book book;
    private int quantity;
```

The instance variables reflect the design discussed above. As in the case of entity beans, we use also a context, but of the `SessionContext` type in this case. The value is set below.

The four business methods are quickly defined and explained:

```java
public int getQuantity() throws RemoteException {
    return quantity;
```

```
    }

    public void setQuantity(int quantity) throws RemoteException {
        this.quantity = quantity;
    }

    public double computePositionSum() throws RemoteException {
        return book.getPrice()*quantity;
    }

    public Book getBook() throws RemoteException {
        return book;
    }
```

Now we have to implement the methods supported by the container. We only explain the code for `ejbCreate()` and `setSessionContext()`; the other methods remain empty as we do not wish to take any precaution for cases they would be covering:

```
    public void setSessionContext(SessionContext sc) throws
                                                RemoteException {
        this.ctxt = sc;
    }

    public void ejbCreate(Book bk) throws RemoteException,
                                                CreateException {
        this.book = bk;
        quantity = 1;
    }

    public void ejbRemove() throws RemoteException {}
    public void ejbActivate() throws RemoteException {}
    public void ejbPassivate() throws RemoteException {}
}
```

At this point `CartItem` is also finished, and we can turn to the virtual shopping cart.

14.1.4 Example 3: the virtual shopping cart

The trolley collects the different books selected and makes a method available for the checkout. The file `ShoppingCart.java` initially defines the remote interface :

```
import javax.ejb.*;
import java.rmi.RemoteException;

public interface ShoppingCart extends javax.ejb.EJBObject {
    public void addItem(Book bk) throws RemoteException;
    public void removeItem(Book bk) throws RemoteException;
    public double computeTotal() throws RemoteException;
    public void modifyQuantity(Book bk, int quantity) throws
RemoteException;
    public Order checkOut() throws RemoteException;
}
```

There are methods available for adding and deleting an entry, for modifying the anumber of copies selected for a particular entry, for calculating the total product value of the cart, and for paying.

The home interface contains only a single create function which does not accept a parameter:

```java
import java.rmi.RemoteException;
import javax.ejb.CreateException;
import javax.ejb.EJBHome;

public interface ShoppingCartHome extends javax.ejb.EJBHome {
    ShoppingCart create() throws RemoteException, CreateException;

}
```

The cart does most of the work on the EJB side. For this reason the file `ShoppingCartEJB.java` (which we do not print completely) turns out to be longer:

```java
import javax.ejb.*;
import java.rmi.RemoteException;
import javax.rmi.PortableRemoteObject;
import java.util.Vector;
import java.util.Enumeration;
import javax.naming.*;

public class ShoppingCartEJB implements SessionBean {

    protected SessionContext ctxt;
    private CartItemHome cih;
    private OrderHome bh;
    private Customer customer;

    private Vector cartItems;
```

In addition to the most important instance variables for storing the single entries, we have to consider both variables `cih` and `bh`. They help store home objects for `Orders` and `CartItems`. As we have to create them within our `ShoppingCarts`, we also need a reference to the respective home objects. Furthermore, we also wish to offer an option to store a reference to the client to whom this cart belongs. The variable `customer` fulfills this task.

An internal function follows, which enables a particular entry to be searched:

```java
private CartItem searchForBook(Book bk) throws RemoteException {
    Book currentBook = null;
    Enumeration e = cartItems.elements();
    while (e.hasMoreElements()) {
        CartItem item = (CartItem) e.nextElement();
        currentBook = item.getBook();
        if (currentBook.isIdentical(bk))
            return item;
    }
    return null;
}
```

Let us now consider the business methods. The first two deal with adding and deleting an entry. In order to create an entry, we first have to create its EJB. This is done by calling the create function of the corresponding home object. Once the reference has been received, we can insert it into our entry vector. To delete it, simply cancel the entry from the list:

```
public void addItem(Book bk) throws RemoteException {
   try {
      CartItem ci = cih.create(bk);
      cartItems.addElement(ci);
   } catch (CreateException cex) { }
}

void removeItem(Book bk) throws RemoteException {
   CartItem ci = searchForBook(bk);
   if (ci != null)
      cartItems.remove(ci);
}
```

Two more business methods are responsible for calculating the total price and modifying the number of books ordered. Since each entry of the cart already has its own method for calculating the costs of this item, you need only run through all items and call this method for each element in order to calculate the grand total. To modify the number, you first have to search the required entry and set its `quantity` parameter.

```
double computeTotal() throws RemoteException {
   double total=0;
   Enumeration e = cartItems.elements();
   while (e.hasMoreElements()) {
      CartItem item = (CartItem) e.nextElement();
      total = total + item.computePositionSum();
   }
   return total;
}

public void modifyQuantity(Book bk, int quantity) throws
                                          RemoteException {
   CartItem ci = searchForBook(bk);
   if (ci != null
      ci.setQuantity(quantity);
}
```

Up to this point we have dealt with the business methods. Among the management methods, the most interesting are `ejbCreate()` and `ejbRemove()`.

When creating a shopping cart object, not only do we create the vector to include the entries; in this method we also search for the two home objects discussed above, which we assign to the instance variables provided for this purpose:

```
public void ejbCreate() throws RemoteException, NamingException {
    this.cartItems = new Vector();
    InitialContext initCtxt = new InitialContext();

    Object obj = initCtxt.lookup("MyCartItemHome");
    cih = (CartItemHome) PortableRemoteObject.narrow(obj,
CartItemHome.class);

    Object obj2 = initCtxt.lookup("MyOrderHome");
    bh = (OrderHome) PortableRemoteObject.narrow(obj,
OrderHome.class);
}
```

When a cart object is to be removed, the vector of entries is simply deleted because they are not used any more:

```
public void ejbRemove() throws RemoteException {
    // remove CartItems as they are no longer needed
    Enumeration e = cartItems.elements();
    while (e.hasMoreElements()) {
       try {
          CartItem item = (CartItem) e.nextElement();
          item.remove();
       } catch (Exception ex) { }
    }
}
```

The other methods requested by the container are similar to the EJBs already reviewed, so there is nothing more to add here:

```
public void setSessionContext(SessionContext sc) throws
                                             RemoteException {
    this.ctxt = sc;
}

public void ejbActivate() throws RemoteException {}
public void ejbPassivate() throws RemoteException {}

}
```

We will now leave the EJB side of the application. In the following section we will see how servlets are modified so as to fulfill their new task as EJB clients.

14.2 Modification of servlets

14.2.1 New structure of servlets

We already have explained that the structure of the servlets would change substantially. This has to be attributed to the new role assumed by the servlets in the 4-tier application. If the complete business logic had previously been encoded in the servlets, and therefore been relatively large, then they merely establish the connection between the user and the EJBs. In other words, servlets are called by the user sending a form. They read the data fed by the user and call the EJBs according to their task. The results of this method call are encoded in HTML and sent back to the user.

Exactly the same happens for stateless session beans because no information about the active user has to be saved either in the servlet or in the bean. Stateful session beans are a little more complex. On the servlet side as well as on the beans' side we need to store in some way or other which user the currently used component belongs to, because on the one hand, the servlet must know which session beans it has to use when a request arrives, while on the other hand the bean must know which data needs to be assigned to the user. For example: If the user wishes to add a new entry to the cart, he or she has to call the `AddItem` servlet. This then has to find the corresponding cart, or ShoppingCart EJB used by the current user. The latter should also know to which user it belongs, if for example the products have to be sent to the right address at the checkout.

In the servlet implementation of the example we learned that servlets can store status information using sessions. Arbitrary parameters and their values can be stored in a session object. It seems obvious to use this variant in this case. The trick is to save the references to the required EJBs within the session objects. The next section shows in detail how this is done.

14.2.2 Some code examples

In this section we will consider two short code examples for the appearance of servlets in the EJB environment. The first example shows how a ShoppingCart EJB is created when a client logs in, and how it is saved in the session of the user. In the second example we will observe what happens when an item is added to the trolley.

The first servlet is to be called `LoginServlet`. We will begin with the servlet framework:

```
import java.io.*;
import javax.servlet.*;
import javax.servlet.http.*;
import javax.rmi.PortableRemoteObject;
import javax.naming.InitialContext;
```

```
class LoginServlet implements HttpServlet {
    CustomerHome   custHome;
    ShoppingCartHomecartHome;

    public void init() throws ServletException {
        // Initialization routine
    }

    public void doGet(HttpServletRequest req, HttpServletResponse res)
throws ServletException, IOException {
        // work on incomming requests
    }

}
```

After having accepted the identification data, the servlet should find out if the user already exists. For the sake of clarity we will assume that only those users who already have their own database entry log in. Otherwise, we should also consider the entire code used to create a new entry and so on. This means that we will be given a reference to a user object. Then we make a new session for this user and create a cart object. The references to the user (i.e. a customer object) and to the cart are saved in the session, and finally we send the input screen (as HTML) where the user can search for books.

The initialization routine involves a very important task: we will search the home objects for EJBs of both client type and ShoppingCart type. We will need the JNDI interface, which we use as follows:

```
public void init() throws ServletException {
    try {
        InitialContext ic = new InitialContext();
        Object objref1 = ic.lookup("e-shop/Customer");
        custHome = (CustomerHome)PortableRemoteObject.narrow(objref1,
                                          CustomerHome.class);

        Object objref2 = ic.lookup("e-shop/ShoppingCart");
        cartHome = (ShoppingCartHome)PortableRemoteObject.narrow(objref2,
                                          ShoppingCartHome.class);

    } catch(Exception e) {
        e.printStackTrace();
    }

}
```

After initialization we have references to both home objects required in the instance variables of the class. We will now use them to create or find the corresponding EJBs. This is done using the doGet method.

We first load the customer object in order then to create a ShoppingCart object:

```
public void doGet (HttpServletRequest req, HttpServletResponse res)
                   throws ServletException, IOException {

    // code for the authentication here
    // we omit this part

    // read ID from req
    CustomerID id = ...

    Customer customer = custHome.findByID(id);

    ShoppingCart cart = cartHome.create();
    cart.setCustomer(customer);
```

A session should not usually exist for the user as he or she has just logged in. The parameter `true` ensures that a new session is created:

```
HttpSession session = req.getSession(true);
```

After the session has been created, we can add both objects:

```
session.putAttribute("e-shop/cart", cart);
session.putAttribute("e-shop/customer", customer);
```

The task of printing the entry page still remains. However, we will not develop it here as we previously discussed in detail the output of HTML code using servlets in Chapter 8.

The second servlet, `AddItemServlet`, should be called when the client wants to add a servlet to the cart. With this example we will show how you can read information from the session context again. The application of this technique is necessary as the servlet does not initially know which cart belongs to the customer. We will only look at this part of the servlet:

```
public class AddItemServlet extends HttpServlet {
    ...
    public void doGet(HttpServletRequest req, HttpServletResponse res) {
        HttpSession session = request.getSession(false);
        if (session == null) {
            // error handling
        }
```

Firstly, in the `doGet()` method the session is extracted from the request parameter. Here we use the parameter false, i.e. no new session is initiated if one does not already exist. In other words: the customer is allowed to put something in the cart only when he or she has already logged in. The error treatment routine should show this to the customer.

The selection of the reference to the shopping cart object follows:

```
ShoppingCart cart = (ShoppingCart)
                        session.getValue("e-shop/cart");
if (cart == value) {
    // no trolley
    // error treatment
}
```

We now assume that the Web browser has transferred the ISBN of the book selected via URL (e.g. using the URL rewriting technique). You can then access the ISBN via the `req` parameter. Then we can provide a reference to a book bean from the book home object:

```
String isbn = req.getValue("ISBN");
InitialContext ic = new InitialContext();
Object objref1 = ic.lookup("e-shop/Book");
BookHome bookHome = (BookHome)PortableRemoteObject.narrow(objref1,
                                        BookHome.class);

BookPK bpk = new BookPK(isbn);
Book book = bookHome.findByPK(bpk);
if (book == null) {
    // this should not happen
    // if the book is not found!
}
```

Now we have only to insert the book in a `CartItem` and place it in the cart. A `CartItem` was created above in the method `addItem()`, therefore calling `addItem()` is sufficient.

```
        cart.addItem(book);
    }
```

For the full servlet codes, refer to the Web page of this book.

14.3 Installation and use of EJBs and servlets

We will now see how the beans and servlets just encoded can actually be used. However, for this purpose the components have to be packed and installed in the corresponding EJB container. Nevertheless, this process appears quite different for each EJB product. Professional packages such as BEA WebLogic offer user-friendly interfaces and powerful functionalitiy. However, we will use the relatively simple reference implementation from

Sun here. In this process we are particularly interested in two components: the EJB server itself, named j2ee, which executes both EJBs and servlets, and can also be used as a Web server, and the `deploytool` which supports the bean manufacturer when packing the different components to the JAR and WAR files (see below), and with installation on the EJB server.

The J2EE server is extremely easy to use, at least when you have set the environment variables correctly, as described in the Sun configuration instructions. You just need to call the Batch file j2ee. A Web server and EJB container are automatically made available at port 8000. The server should be started before installing any beans, as the installation tool contacts it. The server modifies the corresponding configuration entries automatically and also copies the files into the right place. We will assume that the directory of the J2EE implementation is stored in the variable `J2EE_HOME` (as the configuration instruction recommends), then the filing places for all HTML files and servlets are located under `%J2EE_HOME%\public_html` and for all EJBs under `%J2EE_HOME%\repository`. This information is not important for the bean manufacturer, but it is interesting to see where the information is stored.

The use of the installation tool `deploytool` is slightly more difficult. In the last part of this chapter we will show how the application can be converted, installed, and built available using this tool. We will go through the following steps:

1. Compilation of the EJBs and servlets created above
2. Creation of JAR files for the EJBs
3. Creation of WAR files for the HTML files and servlets
4. Installation of the complete application
5. Use of the application

For the following we will assume that all application files have been placed in the folder `d:\e-shop`, the standard Java installation is contained under `d:\jdk1.3`, and J2EE is installed under `d:\j2sdkee1.2.1`. Furthermore, we also assume that this local computer functions as a Web and EJB server.

In order to guarantee the proper work of the environment, first the following functions should be carried out:

■ The variables `JAVA_HOME` and `J2EE_HOME` should be defined in the environment. In Windows 95/98 this can be carried out in the `autoexec.bat`. In Windows NT the environment should be modified on the menu item "Settings/System." `JAVA_HOME` is set on `d:\jdk1.3`, and `J2EE_HOME` on `d:\j2sdkee1.2.1`.

■ The path for the executable files should be extended: `PATH=%PATH%; %JAVA_HOME%\bin;%J2EE_HOME%\bin`.

14.3.1 Compiling the EJBs and servlets

We will assume that for each EJB component XXX we have created three or four (for entity beans) source files, as described above (meaning that for this example we are not so interested in deployment descriptors etc.):

- the file XXXEJB.java, which contains the bean source code
- the file XXX.java for the remote interface
- the file XXXHome.java for the home interface
- the file XXXPK.java for the primary key class in entity beans

In order to translate all bean components we use the parameterized batch file, which we will call compile.bat:

```
set CPATH=.;%J2EE_HOME%\lib\j2ee.jar
javac -classpath %CPATH% %1EJB.java %1Home.java %1.java %1PK.java
```

The primary key file obviously has to be removed from the session beans. We insert the CPATH or CLASSPATH only within the Batch file. In fact, JDK 1.3 no longer requires CLASSPATH, as long as the corresponding class libraries can be found in the given paths. This is not the case here, so the CLASSPATH has to be set.

The call of the script is carried out each time with the name of the corresponding component, so for example for the book bean as follows:

```
d:\e-shop> compile Book
```

To compile the servlet, the CLASSPATH also has to be set accordingly, because the servlet libraries are also contained in the J2EE, i.e. the file j2ee.jar has to be embedded. For example, the corresponding batch file compileServlet.bat could be

```
set CPATH=.;%J2EE_HOME%\lib\j2ee.jar
javac -classpath %CPATH% %1.java
```

and the call is made using

```
d:\e-shop> compileServlet CheckoutServlet
```

In this way all preparations for creating the components are made, for which the installation tool can now be employed.

14.3.2 Creation of JAR files for the EJBs

The use of the tool `deploytool` is not so easy because, as a user, you have a series of configuration options which can considerably influence the behavior of the application. For a proper, detailed discussion of the different possibilities, we suggest you refer to the Sun J2EE tutorial, which can be found both in the J2EE documentation and under `http://java.sun.com/j2ee/j2sdkee/techdocs/guides/ejb/html/DevGuideTOC.html`. For all examples given there are step-by-step instructions for the installation of the applications.

The call of the tool is carried out with the command

```
d:\e-shop> deploytool
```

which can be called on the basis of the paths set previously. After the start you should at first create a new application, which we will call "E-shop." The tool transfers the information for this new project into a file with the extension `ear`.

When this process is carried out, you can begin to add the components to the application. For example, we want to install five EJBs and a Web component.

Each EJB consists of the three files mentioned above. In order to create the EJB you have to call the "New Enterprise Bean Wizard" which leads the user through the process. The most important information is the filenames given in the second display mask of the wizard, and the roles of the individual files contained in the files. Figure 14.2 shows this mask. You can see that the wizard wants to learn which class describes the original EJB and where the home and the remote interface are located. Furthermore, you have to give the type of the EJB since it has some consequences on the management of the component.

In other masks, different parameters can be manipulated, which are not of interest to us in this context. The sequence of the masks depends on the bean type selected, because for entity beans we have to explain, for example, how the persistence management works, whereas when dealing with session beans, for instance, you can influence the management of transactions.

We will create such a component for each of our five EJBs. The operation therefore has to be executed five times.

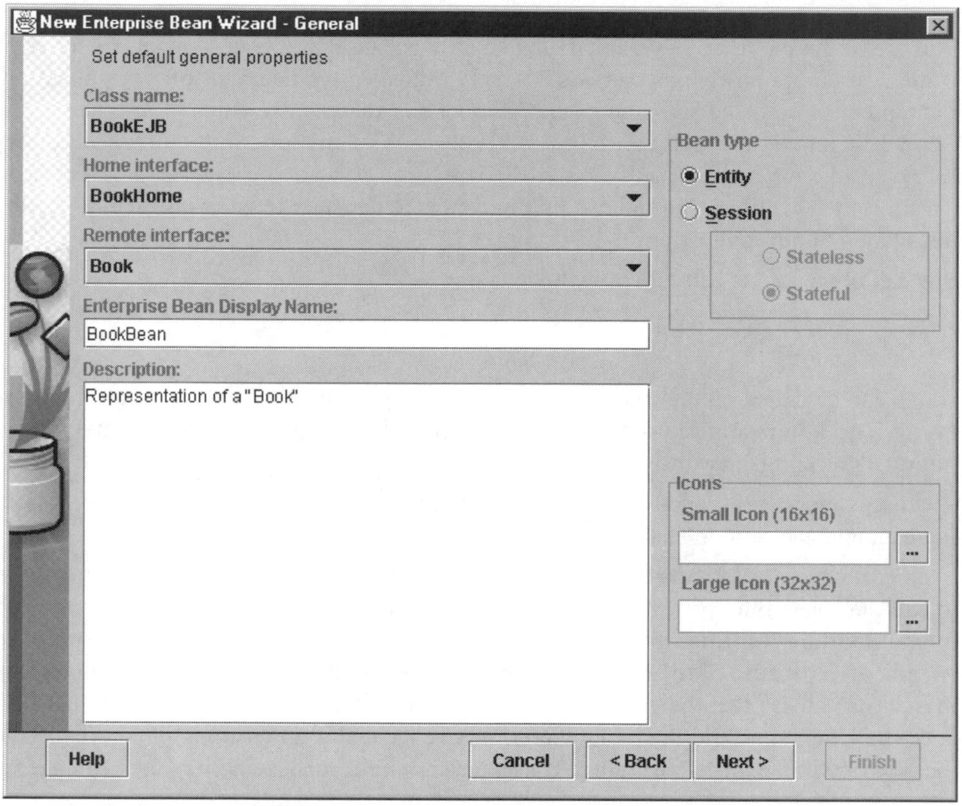

Figure 14.2: Determining the characteristics of an EJB component.

When this is done we can turn to the Web component.

14.3.3 Creating WAR files for the HTML files and servlets

Web components are not placed in JAR files, but in WAR files. The first step in creating such a Web component is to create a file in which further files are inserted later. This is done by clicking on the globe-symbol on the main screen of the installation tool.

We will add an HTML page, namely the entry page of the entire bookshop, as well as a servlet to our Web component. This process is carried out in two steps: first the Web page, and then the `class` file which contains the servlet, using the Web wizard. In the following step the component has to be informed about the component type, i.e. it has to learn whether it is a servlet or a JSP page. So the dialog shown in Fig. 14.3 has to be answered correctly.

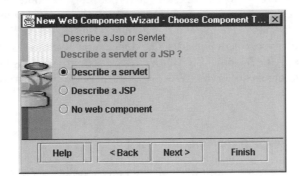

Figure 14.3: Selecting the component type.

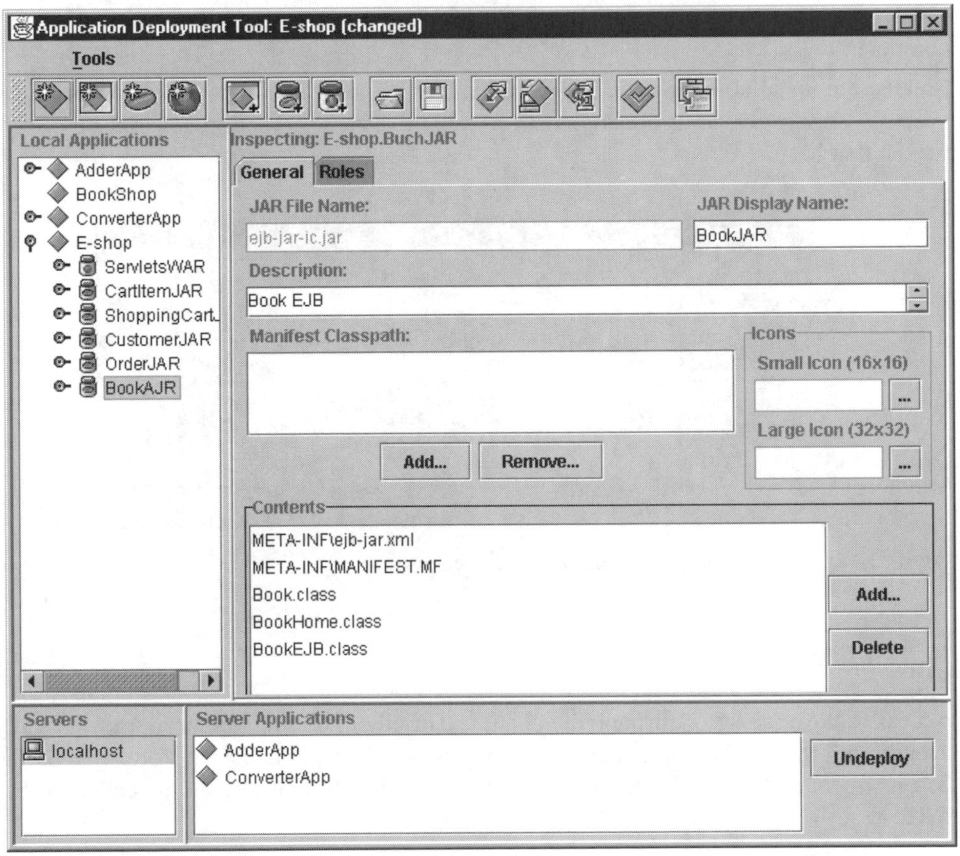

Figure 14.4: Content of the E-Shop application after the introduction of the EJB and Web components.

In the further course of the wizard the instruction of the Web context is important, as it explains in which part of the file hierarchy the Web component should be accessed. We choose the value "e-shop" here. After a successful conclusion of the Web component, the main screen should appear as in Fig. 14.4. Our application "E-Shop" contains the five EJB components BookJAR, CustomerJAR, OrderJAR, CartItemJar, and ShoppingCartJAR as well as the Web component ServletsWAR. Now the application has to be installed on the server.

14.3.4 Installing the complete application

`Deploytool` is also very useful for the actual installation. At first, using the "Deploy Application" function (third symbol from the right in the symbol bar in Fig. 14.4), you can choose the server on which the application is to be placed. In our case we can leave the given "localhost," as we carry out both development and installation on the same computer.

Finally, the installation process runs automatically. Figure 14.5 shows a snapshot of this process. `Deploytool` is already connected to the `j2ee` server and generates the stubs for the first bean.

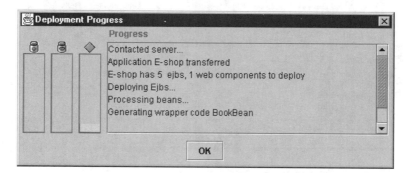

Figure 14.5: Installing the components on the server.

14.3.5 Using the application

Access to the application through the client is carried out on the Web browser, as usually occurs with the servlet application. We will contact the Web server on Port 8000 on the `localhost` and access the entry page from which the different servlets are called. So the URL

```
http://localhost:8000/e-shop/index.html
```

has to be entered into the browser.

Chapter 15

XML – the new ASCII

This chapter should answer a frequently asked question: What would I use XML for? We are not interested in showing the smallest technical details and tricks. We will leave that to the numerous books that deal with this topic alone. Instead we will show how our bookshop can be meaningfully enriched using an XML interface and we will point out the enormous advantage the client gains from this.

15.1 The development of XML

From 1996 to 1998 a workgroup of the *World Wide Web Consortium* devoted itself to writing the XML recommendation. For a while before this there was the XML predecessor, SGML. However, this was not fully recognized by Internet users. The team's purpose was therefore to analyze the reasons for this and introduce changes accordingly into the new standard.

For example, SGML is used as the documentation format in the motor industry. Small firms in particular avoided using SGML as it was difficult to develop applications and tools due to its complexity. This complexity is also reflected in the size of the standard document: the SGML specification consists of 155 pages.

Roughly speaking, many of the most complex and infrequently used SGML components were simply left out and some Internet-specific features adopted. In contrast to the 155 pages in the SGML specification, the XML counterpart requires only 42. This simplicity led to the development of tools that, together with an extensive marketing campaign led to the broad acceptance of XML today. All leading software manufacturers, from IBM, Oracle, Microsoft, Software AG, to SAP and so on have subsequently created a wider range of XML tools or have integrated XML into existing products.

15.2 XML and related technologies

"XML support" has become a key selling factor of the product. Databases, middleware, browsers, Web design tools, etc. all benefit from this attribute. Among all of this marketing information it is not a simple matter to establish what XML actually does and how it relates to other technologies. This section compares XML with more familiar and widely spread standards and products such as relational databases, HTML, or RPC.

15.2.1 XML and databases

Relational databases are the basic constituent of cyberspace. Bank accounts, stock levels, and employee information easily can be represented in *Entity Relationship* (ER) diagrams and saved in database tables. This sort of storage enables an extremely efficient search and access to the data, usually using SQL. On the other hand you can find information filed in a completely unstructured manner within a document. This includes teaching material, documentation, law, and guideline texts. The only search option in this case would be to use a full-text search of specific character strings. XML offers a representation format for semi-structured data. It is difficult and tedious to map this kind of data to a conventional ER schema, although the data exhibits a definite structure. The Internet, in particular, with its heterogeneous architecture, houses a lot of semi-structured data.

In the range of data storage formats, from unstructured documents to structured databases, XML can be placed somewhere between these two extremes. In our example in Chapter 17 a database record is formatted in XML and provided to a price comparison agent via the Internet. Therefore this application does not involve semi-structured data. However, there are numerous applications in which, for example, patients' data or insurance documents contain a certain structure using XML tags. In this way they allow access to specific information inside the document. This is the basis to be able to use such documents as a starting point for automatic data processing.

15.2.2 XML as a communication format

Let us assume that we wish to make a date with a friend for a meal and send the following e-mail:

```
From peter@company.co.uk: Let's meet at 12:30 am at Café Plaza
```

Our friend reads the e-mail and enters the appointment into his electronic appointments diary. In order to simplify this process, the relevant information can of course be highlighted:

```
From peter@company.co.uk: Let's meet at 12:30 at Café Plaza
```

Certainly in this case, instead of the proprietary format of the owner, XML could be used. The e-mail message will appear as follows:

```
<date>
   <who>peter@company.co.uk</who>
   Let's meet at
   <when>12:30</when>
   at
   < where>Café Plaza</where>
</date>
```

At this point the communication program could receive, process and register the message automatically in the appointments diary. Taking it a step further, the communication program could be seen as an object and could implement a program interface using CORBA, DCOM, or RMI:

```
setDate(String who, Date when, String where)
```

This sequence of examples shows different possibilities with increasing formality, as two people, or rather their software, communicate. In this way XML combines fundamental advantages from the two extremes. As with the method call, the XML message can be automatically processed and the date need not be entered manually. Like the unstructured e-mail, the XML message can also be read by the user. However, the definite advantage is the fact that XML is easily compatible with the existing and functioning Internet infrastructure such as e-mail, browsers, Web servers, firewalls, and *name servers*. The problems explained in Chapter 10 that we associate with CORBA show that this unfortunately is not always the case. Of course there are certain applications to which CORBA or DCOM is essential. However, in many cases XML alone can serve the necessary function. If, for instance, you have to supply information about all chemical elements, it is easy to create a corresponding XML document and to register it on a Web server. Also, dynamic information, such as up-to-date foreign exchange rates, easily can be formatted from a servlet or CGI script in XML and be sent to the client by HTTP. The corresponding CORBA or DCOM solutions are more expensive and by no means accessible to a large section of the public.

There are even ways in which XML can be used in a *Message Oriented Middleware* (*MOM*). By this process, the users send each other messages formatted in XML in order to communicate. The infrastructure provided offers important functions, for instance it guarantees message transfer and transaction support. The transaction context is sent with each message and guarantees that all operations on the computer node involved are either executed or interrupted. Chapter 14 introduces the SOAP protocol, with which you can use XML for Remote Procedure Calls.

15.2.3 XML as a document format

Organizations of all kinds have to decide in which format documents have to be saved. Postscript, Adobe PDF, Rich Text Format (RTF), and obviously HTML and SGML are popular formats. HTML has recently gained enormous importance. Nevertheless, HTML is always being enlarged, which causes problems. For instance, frames were supported relatively late. If you wish to use a new feature, all documents created previously have to be adapted.

SGML represents a powerful description language for document management, but is too complex. XML provides the most important SGML functionality, such as *Document Type Definitions* (DTDs), with a hierarchical document structure and enables you to break down large documents into smaller pieces, simplifying their management. In a book, for example, each chapter is stored in a separate file and therefore easily revised by different authors.

An important feature is also the separation of content and layout. If the same basic information has to be published in different forms, for example as a Web site, brochures, and user manuals, you can imagine that all of the publications come from one pool of XML documents, and are transformed into their respective form by means of different conversion and layout tools. This level of functionality cannot be attained from documents saved in HTML, RTF, or PDF.

As we are aware from the previous two sections, we can say that XML represents both a powerful and simple alternative to SGML, and to documents in RTF, PDF, or HTML format.

15.2.4 XML and HTML

XML is not the successor of HTML as a new representation format of static Web sites. XML can, of course, be used with stylesheets to represent Web sites. Nevertheless, we see XML and HMTL as technologies which complement one another rather than compete with each other. HTML is very common and widespread. It is improbable that in the forseeable future all Web designers will change over to XML and stylesheets. We think that XML will find its use overcoming HTML's weaknesses. These weaknesses emerge more frequently in the automatic processing, representation, and conversion of semi-structured data and, as previously mentioned, in document management, rather than in representation possibilities.

15.3 Design goals

In the development of XML the fundamental goals were as follows:

1. *XML has to be usable on the Internet.*
   Hardly any explanation is required here. Due to the worldwide availability of all documents the Internet is the ultimate market for a document format. As well as this, it should also be noted that XML uses Unicode characters and therefore it is suitable for any language.
2. *XML has to support many different applications.*
   XML should not just become a new version of HTML and be limited to the representation of documents. It should be used for all possible applications, such as databases, product documentations, address management, configuration data, and so on.
3. *XML has to be compatible with SGML.*
   The ISO committee responsible for SGML and the XML team of the W3C made some compromises. As a result, every XML document automatically obeys the SGML standard and can be read by existing SGML applications. This is relevant to the growth of XML, since some firms work with SGML extensively.
4. *It has to be easy to write XML applications.*
   Once again it is fundamental that a format is adopted only if sufficient tools are available. The aim was that a graduate student could write an *XML Parser* in a week.
5. *There should be no optional features.*
   The reason for this design goal comes from experiences in dealing with other standards. For example, when programming a database application you cannot always be sure that the respective database supports a particular optional feature. This requires much additional program code that implements support for a specific database server. On this occasion just think about the operations regarding the database connectivity of the exemplary program in the previous chapter. The automatic key generation or the variable syntax to declare a table column for date and time becomes a problem when the application has to be ported to another database management software. This situation and problems are similar in SGML. Therefore, XML has no optional features. This means that any XML parser can read any XML document.
6. *XML documents should be readable and comprehensible to the user.*
   If no tool is available for a particular operation or if a tool refuses its task, this design goal enables you to read and modify an XML document even with a normal editor, if necessary. Anyone who has ever tried in vain to load a damaged document in a text processing program will appreciate this feature.
7. *The processing of the XML standard should be concluded quickly.*
   In order to be successful in the fast-moving Internet world, the standard also has to be created rapidly.

8. *The design should be compact.*
    The development of tools is again of paramount importance — it is not helpful when reading the specification documents has already proved to be a hurdle.

9. *XML documents should be easy to create.*
    Again, it is the speedy adoption of XML that is important. If documents are easy to create, not only is it easier for the user to write the documents but also for the tool developers to create supporting editor software.

10. *Clearness transcends compactness.*
    Sometimes the length of XML documents is cause for complaint, as the actual data is enclosed in tags which very often occupy more memory, such as here: `<currency>eur</currency>`. Taking into account the particularly powerful computers and the high transmission bandwidth, this should hardly ever lead to serious problems. If you recall the millennium bug, this is definitely a good basic principle.

15.4 What XML can and can not do

With the momentary enthusiasm for XML, many products and concepts gain the stamp "XML support" just because it is "in." However, XML is very basic and simple:

■   XML enables you to subdivide a document hierarchically and to name the single parts.

■   XML is a standard format. Therefore we have chosen "XML – the new ASCII" as the title of this chapter, since ASCII is the worldwide standard format for text representation. For this reason XML has nothing to do directly with Java or e-commerce and is not object-oriented. However, it defines a standard for information exchange and information structuring which is simple to use and supported widely.

15.5 EDI and e-commerce

Why is a standard so important for the exchange of information? Let us consider the current situation for a moment with an example: Let us assume that a supplier wants to transmit the current price list to his clients electronically. This is known as *Electronic Data Interchange* (EDI) and can occur in many different ways. This could be an Excel document sent by e-mail, or an ASCII file, preformatted by both parties in the same way.

Obviously, these methods present some problems. It is likely that the price list will have to be generated from the supplier's database, and also that the processing on the client side will most probably require specific formatting work.

The experts of the Gartner Group estimate that 35–40 percent of the programming budget of a typical firm is spent on proprietary solutions for formatting documents and creating reports, which serve only to exchange data between different databases and applications.

Here XML can provide a solution: If the firms agree on a particular schema to describe the different sections of the price list, the data can be converted into the XML format. Because many databases support the data output in XML format, the supplier can directly use the result of the SQL query with which the price list can be created. The customer uses an XML parser or software with an XML import function in order to read the results. The main point here is not that XML is a more suitable format than the EDI standard. XML has simply developed the necessary impulse and momentum in order to be accepted and supported by many applications.

Most industry sectors currently work on industry-specific schemas. As an example you could imagine that all worldwide pharmaceutical patents are saved in a single given XML representation. In Section 15.17.4 on page 329 we introduce UDDI. The goal of this initiative is to provide a type of telephone book which enables companies to register Web services which support a particular EDI format.

15.6 XML documents and Document Type Definition

In this section we will consider the XML document structure and the fundamental elements of syntax in detail. In addition to this, we will familiarize ourselves with the posibilities of how formatted data can be constrained by the Document Type Definition in XML. After going through this section we should be in a position to understand all of the important terms and know how to create DTDs as well as conforming XML documents. We will not go into too much detail such as the precise mode of operation of a parser regarding blank characters, the use of different ISO language coding, or some of the special functionality adopted from SGML. We can leave this to the literature that deals exclusively with these subjects.

In the following sections we will look at the structure of XML documents and DTDs. Here it is virtually impossible to find an order to introduce concepts without jumping ahead from time to time and using a term which actually will not be explained until later on.

15.6.1 An example

All XML documents begin with `<?xml version='1.0'?>`. This can be compared with the identification normally seen with UNIX. For instance, Perl scripts begin in a similar way with `#!/usr/local/bin/perl`.

```
<?xml version='1.0'?>
<!DOCTYPE contact SYSTEM 'contact.dtd'>
<contact>
   <name>Peter Miller</name>
   <email>peter@company.co.uk</email>
</contact>
```

The `<!DOCTYPE>` tag in the second line defines the Document Type Definition of the document. Lines 3 to 7 contain the data or the document itself.

15.6.2 Internal, external, and mixed DTDs

The Document Type Definition establishes certain rules for the document. But not every document has to have a DTD. The following DOCTYPE definition is optional.

```
<!DOCTYPE root SYSTEM "http://www.books-online.com/dtd-file.dtd">
```

In this line it is established that the file `dtd-file.dtd` on the Web server of Books Online contains the DTD for the document. It is important to note that addressing the DTD-URL and setting HTML hyperlinks follow the same addressing rules. If the document is located in the same directory on the Web server, the reference to the DTD file can therefore be given relatively, i.e. just using the file name `dtd-file`. Furthermore, in comparison with the first XML line, we notice that in XML both single and double quotation marks can be used. The character string root gives us the name for the element at the root of the XML element tree. You can learn more about this in Section 15.14 on page 314.

In addition to the DTD being retrievable by the keyword `SYSTEM` from its external source, the DTD can also be saved locally.

```
<!DOCTYPE root[
    <!-- internal Document Type Definition -->
    <!ENTITY bo_url 'http://www.books-online.com'>
    ...
]>
```

How the definition of *Entity* `bo_url` is related and what DTDs generally look like will be clarified soon. The *Entity Definition* assigns a value to the constant `bo_url`. This example also uses the comment format, already known by HTML.

As well as internal and external DTDs there is also the option of combining them. Here the internal definition takes precedence over the external. If the entity `bo_url` has been defined differently in the file `dtds/external.dtd`, the external definition will be replaced with the local definition with the value '`http://www.books-online.com`'.

```
<!DOCTYPE root SYSTEM "dtds/extern.dtd" [
    <!ENTITY bo_url 'http://www.buecher-online.de'>
    ...
]>
```

All XML documents belong to one of the three classes described in the following sections.

15.6.3 Well-formed documents

All documents which obey the following syntax rules and have no DTD belong to the first class.

- Tags cannot overlap. In other words: the following example is not well formed: `<a><b></a></b>`
- The document can have just one root.
- Each tag has to be completed. Make sure that in this process you take into account the capitalization and the lower-case printing in the tag names. Even `<A></a>` is not well formed.

15.6.4 Valid documents

On the one hand valid documents have to be well formed. On the other hand they have to follow the rules defined in the DTD or in the XML schema (see Section 15.16 on page 321). Let us consider the example of an entry in an address book:

```
<?xml version='1.0'?>
<!DOCTYPE contact SYSTEM 'contact.dtd'>
<contact>
   <name>Peter Miller</name>
   <email>pete@company.co.uk</email>
</contact>
```

This document is well formed. Assuming, however, that the DTD prescribes that a contact has to contain the telephone number as well as the name and e-mail address, this would make the document invalid. In the following sections we will decribe how such rules can be defined.

15.6.5 Invalid documents

In the category of invalid documents we find all other documents which do not fall into the other two brackets, because they do not fulfill the necessary criteria. For example, we could be dealing with an XML file with incomplete tags. Also, the documents which do not comply with the DTD or XML schema rules (like the contact with the missing telephone number in the previous section) are classified as invalid, even if they follow the syntax rules.

In order to try out the examples shown in the following text you should copy the `xerces` package onto your computer. Following this, you must provide the `jar` files `xerces.jar` and `xercesSamples.jar` in the classpath:

```
set CLASSPATH=C:\book\lib\xerces.jar;C:\book\lib\xercesSamples.jar;.
```

To check if a document is well formed, enter the following command:

```
java sax.SAX2Count file.xml
```

The program SAX2Count reads the given URL using the xerces parser. To check if a document is valid, the option `-v` is included:

```
java sax.SAX2Count -v file.xml
```

The following file, `file.xml` described above, shows how a contact should appear. Let us assume that a contact must contain an e-mail address, along with the name and phone number. Then, the document above is invalid, since it is missing the `e-mail` tag.

```
<?xml version='1.0'?>

    <!DOCTYPE contact [
        <!ELEMENT contact (name, email, telephone)>
        <!ELEMENT name (firstname, surname)>
        <!ELEMENT firstname (#PCDATA)>
        <!ELEMENT surname (#PCDATA)>
        <!ELEMENT email (#PCDATA)>
        <!ELEMENT telephone (#PCDATA)>
    ]>

    <contact>
       <name>
          <firstname>Peter</firstname>
          <surname>Miller</surname>
       </name>
       <email>pete@company.co.uk</email>
    </contact>
```

For this example the validator gives the following error message:

```
C:\book\examples\xml\xml\validation> java sax.SAX2Count -v file.xml
[Error] file.xml:18:12: The content of element type "contact" is
incomplete, it must match "(name,email,telephone)".
file.xml: 591 ms (5 elems, 0 attrs, 13 spaces, 28 chars)
```

15.7 Elements

After the concept of Document Type Defininition has been used a number of times, we now have a look at which components the DTD consists of. This section deals with the definitions of elements that determine which elements will be acceptable within the document and which *parent–child relationships* are allowed between elements in the XML tree. In the following two sections entities and attributes are introduced.

What actually is an element? Because XML arranges documents in a hierarchical structure, the XML document can be viewed as a tree structure. Figure 15.1 displays the contact information graphically and in text form. An XML element corresponds to a tree node, shown in the small boxes. In the text form an element is represented by a pair of start and end tags. The bold text represents the original text of the document, i.e. all of the characters that are not *markup*, and are therefore formatting information.

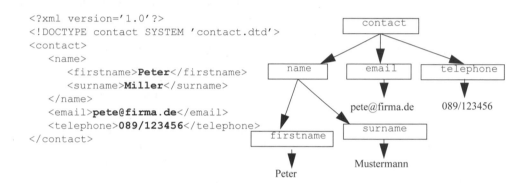

```
<?xml version='1.0'?>
<!DOCTYPE contact SYSTEM 'contact.dtd'>
<contact>
    <name>
        <firstname>Peter</firstname>
        <surname>Miller</surname>
    </name>
    <email>pete@firma.de</email>
    <telephone>089/123456</telephone>
</contact>
```

Figure 15.1: An XML document in text form and as a hierarchical tree structure. The original text of the document is bold.

15.7.1 Root element

The root element is given by the outermost tag couple. As already noticed in Section 15.6.2 on page 290 there can only be one root element. The naming of the root element is established in the DOCTYPE declaration. The name given after the DOCTYPE keyword must be the same name as the root element. In the example above, this is apparent since contact appears in both positions.

```
<!DOCTYPE contact SYSTEM 'contact.dtd'>
<contact>
```

15.7.2 Definition of the parent–child relationships between elements

The elements contained by the start and end tag of the outer element are defined as child elements. A context-free grammar in the DTD defines the constructs which are accepted.

In the case where the forename and surname are combined in sequence, the following line has to be inserted in the DTD:

```
<!ELEMENT name (firstname, surname)>
```

This ensures that the name element must have precisely two children, namely the element firstname followed by the element surname. If either of these two elements is missing, the sequence is wrong, or a different element is present, the document will be invalid.

- Assuming that we allow the surname to precede the forename, we can describe this option using an *or-clause* in the rule above:
  ```
  <!ELEMENT name ((firstname, surname) | (surname, firstname))>
  ```
  In order to avoid conflicts concerning the precedence of the sequence and or-operators, you can use brackets in order to group the subordinated expressions.
- *Optional elements* are indicated with a question mark. For instance, an optional fax number can be declared using this element definition:
  ```
  <!ELEMENT contact (name, email, telephone, fax?)>
  ```
- To make it possible to give numerous telephone and fax numbers, the operators * and + must be used. In our case, there also must be at least one telephone number available. An arbitrary number of fax numbers is acceptable, including zero:
  ```
  <!ELEMENT contact (name, email, telephone+, fax*)>
  ```
  Therefore the operator * symbolizes "0 or more elements," whereas the operator + symbolizes "one or more elements."

15.7.3 Leaf elements

All elements appearing on the right-hand side of an element definition also have to be defined themselves within the DTD. In our example the first name, surname, e-mail, and telephone elements have yet to be defined. These are leaf elements which do not have any children. Only text, or in XML jargon: *Parsed Character Data* (PCDATA), can appear between the <firstname> and </firstname> and the other corresponding tags. This is also evident in the DTD, as follows:

```
<!ELEMENT first name (#PCDATA)>
```

In addition to text elements, defining empty elements is also possible:

```
<!ELEMENT empty EMPTY>
```

The purpose of such elements will become clear in the following section. As well as by using elements, information can also be coded in attributes. Our "empty" element can therefore remain "childless" and nevertheless hold information in its attributes. The following abbreviation is defined for empty elements:

```
<empty id="c43" />
```

This is the abbreviation for:

```
<empty id="c43"></empty>
```

15.7.4 Unlimited elements

If we wish to leave it undetermined as to what structure an element will have, we can express this using the ANY keyword.

```
<!ELEMENT can_have_all_possible_children ANY>
```

This kind of element is meaningful if some sections of a document are to be rigorously checked and others are not. In such a case, a standard DTD can be developed which defines those elements not to be checked using the ANY rule. To simply not specify a DTD for the document is not an option in this case, as in so doing, any possibility of validation will be lost.

15.8 Attributes

For every element, attributes can be defined which save additional information about that element. Those who are already familiar with HTML will know about attributes from hyperlinks, such as `<a href="http:www.hanser.de">`, or from formatting instructions in tables (`<td width="120">`). XML uses the same structure. While browsers, for example, overlook the omission of quotation marks in HTML text, they must exist in a well-formed document. Furthermore, it will be explicitly specified which attributes can be assigned to which elements in the DTD. Moreover, some variations regarding the default value and features such as identification numbers and references need to be taken into account. This section provides an overview of the uses of XML attributes.

15.8.1 Character data

The most commonly used variant is the *Character Data* (CDATA) attribute, used to store simple character strings such as names or descriptions. The following example illustrates the definition of element `test` with two CDATA attributes. The attributes `att1` and `att2` are assigned to the element using the ATTLIST keyword. The attributes are given as REQUIRED. This means that the document is not valid if one of the two attributes of a test element is missing. Further details about this argument can be found in Section 15.9.1 on page 299. Even if an additional attribute, which is not defined in the DTD, occurs in a test element, this will disrupt the DTD and the document will not be valid. Unlike elements, the DTD provides no influence over the sequence in which they occur in the document.

```
<?xml version="1.0"?>
<!DOCTYPE test [
   <!ELEMENT test EMPTY>
   <!ATTLIST test att1 CDATA #REQUIRED
                  att2 CDATA #REQUIRED>
]>
<test att1="CDATA TEST"
      att2=" _ .&lt; arbitrary character strings are allowed" />
```

15.8.2 NMTOKEN and NMTOKENS

Two additional attribute types are NMTOKEN and NMTOKENS. These abbreviations stand for *Name Token* or *Name Tokens*. In this instance, a *Name Token* is a character string in which only numbers, letters and some characters such as a dot, colon, and hyphen are allowed. This restriction allows you to create a name list separated by empty characters, within an attribute value. An NMTOKENS attribute is defined as a list of *name tokens*, separated by empty characters. This kind of attribute could, for example, hold a list of a person's hobbies:

```
<?xml version="1.0"?>
<!DOCTYPE test [
  <!ELEMENT test EMPTY>
    <!ATTLIST test hobbies NMTOKENS #REQUIRED>
]>
<test hobbies="football reading sleeping" />
```

In this case it is the task of the application to separate the attribute values. In an application written in Java this is quite easy to carry out using the `StringTokenizer` class.

15.8.3 IDs and ID references

The ID attribute serves as a *unique* identification of an element within the document. The following rules apply here: if two elements have the same ID attribute value the document is not valid. As with *named tokens,* attribute values can contain only letters, numbers, and a few other characters and must begin with a letter. After elements have received their identification in this way, it must of course be possible to use them and thus refer to their identification. This can be achieved using the IDREF and IDREFS attributes. Like NMTOKEN and NMTOKENS, IDREF permits only one reference, while IDREFS contains a list of references separated by whitespace characters. The value of a reference attribute must correspond to the ID attribute of an element in the document. If a reference is given to an ID attribute that does not exist in the document, the document is classified as invalid. The name of the ID attribute does not necessarily have to be ID. However, this name is usually chosen since ID attributes are already familiar from HTML and also allow the identification of an HTML element.

This functionality enables the construction of a primary and a foreign key structure familiar from the *entity-relationship schemas*. This advantage is, however, restricted by the limitations of a document. The following example shows how IDs and IDREFs can be used for the modeling of a complex relationship between authors and their books. In this case the problem is that an author can write several books and a book can have several authors. In database jargon this is defined as an n:m relationship. If a structure such as this were to be reproduced in a hierarchical XML document, some degree of redundancy must be expected, since either the book or the author has to be chosen to be the preferential element. In the example, all author elements of a book are arranged under the book element. As a result, the author of several books would have to be listed repeatedly as well. In our example, this is "Hans." Certainly, in this case it would not be the end of the world. However, if more information about the author is saved, problems could arise because modifications made by the user or the application always have to be carried out in two places.

Hierarchical modeling does not create problems for the publishers, since every book is assigned to its own publisher. In this way, every book element is assigned a corresponding publisher element:

```
<?xml version="1.0"?>

<test>
  <publisher>Wiley
    <book>
      <author>Hans</author>
      <author>Michael</author>
      <author>Joe</author>
      ID and IDREF attributes
    </book>
```

```
<book>
  <author>Hans</author>
  All on XML
</book>
</publisher>
</test>
```

If identifications are now introduced, this allows for a different method regarding the modeling of information. Instead of heavily restricting the hierarchical structure in order to define the "is the author of" relations, references to the identifications of the author can be introduced now. The book entitled "ID and IDREF Attributes" would have, for example, an author with IDs A1, A4, and A33. The author and book elements are now arranged at the same level as each other and are linked by these kinds of references. When modeling the "has appeared in XY publisher" relation, the reference mechanism is not actually necessary because of the 1:n nature. We have actually changed this as well, in order to show the use of the IDREF attributes. A single publisher can therefore be referred to by many books; nevertheless, every book has only one publisher.

```
<?xml version="1.0"?>

<!DOCTYPE test [
  <!ELEMENT test (author+, publisher+, book+)>

  <!ELEMENT publisher(#PCDATA)>
  <!ATTLIST publisher id ID #REQUIRED>

  <!ELEMENT author (#PCDATA)>
  <!ATTLIST author id ID #REQUIRED>

  <!ELEMENT book (#PCDATA)>
  <!ATTLIST book publisher IDREF #REQUIRED
                 authors IDREFS #REQUIRED>
]>

<test>
  <author id="A1">Hans</author>
  <author id="A4">Michael</author>
  <author id="A33">Joe</author>

  <publisher id="v1">Wiley</publisher>

  <book publisher="v1" authors="A1 A4 A33">
    ID und IDREF attributes
  </book>

  <book publisher="v1" authors="A1">
    All about XML
  </buch>
</test>
```

15.8.4 Enumerated attributes

If an attribute can only assume one value from a predefined number of values, we can use *enumerated attributes*. An example of this is attribute values such as "yes/no" or "in/out." Also predefined categories such as "very good," "good," "satisfactory," and so on could be used. In the definition, options are listed in brackets and separated by the or-symbol. The following example defines the attribute `processed` which can take on either the value yes or no.

```
<?xml version="1.0"?>
<!DOCTYPE test [
   <!ELEMENT test EMPTY>
   <!ATTLIST test processed (yes | no) #REQUIRED>
]>
<test processed="yes" />
```

The advantage over a CDATA attribute is the fact that the XML validator checks whether or not the attribute has a value outside the value group defined in the DTD. When dealing with CDATA attributes, however, all that is checked is whether the attribute actually exists. The value itself is not taken into consideration.

15.9 Attribute default values

Each attribute is provided with an identification which indicates how the XML parser is to react when an attribute is missing. The following sections describe the variations in detail.

15.9.1 Required

If an attribute is provided with the keyword #REQUIRED, it has the following semantics: If the attribute is missing from one of the corresponding elements the document will be invalid. Otherwise the rules for the respective attribute type will have to be checked. For instance, whether or not an ID attribute has a legal value. An example:

```
<!ATTLIST info id ID #REQUIRED>
```

15.9.2 Implied

Information can often be derived from previous instructions. If, for instance, some sections of text are to be numbered, it is often sufficient to assign a number to the first section only. The application can determine the numbers for the rest of the sections by means of the application specifications. And so it is the task of the XML parser to inform the application about an attribute to be calculated, for example by setting up a dummy in the data structure. This appears as follows:

```
<!ATTLIST para number CDATA #IMPLIED>
```

15.9.3 Default

During the definition of an attribute, it is possible to establish a default value. If the attribute is given in the XML file, the default value of the attribute definition in the DTD is ignored. If the attribute is not available, it will be given the default value. As Fig. 15.2 illustrates, it is not relevant to the application whether the attribute in the original document was left out or not. Default values can be used for all attribute types.

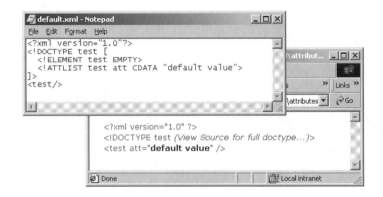

Figure 15.2: Internet Explorer displays the attribute att. Only if the XML file is viewed in an editor is it evident that the attribute has been omitted from the source text.

15.9.4 Fixed

The keyword #FIXED can be inserted after a default value. In doing so this specifies that the attribute in question must take the given value. It is also possible to omit the attribute altogether. In all other cases the document would be invalid.

15.10 When attributes, when elements?

After having introduced elements and attributes, the question arises as to whether information should be modeled as either a subordinate element or as an attribute. If the information itself is structured and relatively complex, it soon becomes obvious that the element variation needs to be chosen. However, in the following example the decision is not so easy to make:

```
<petrol engine manufacturing year="1996" mark="VW" />

<petrol engine>
   <manufacturing year>1996</manufacturing year>
   <mark>VW</mark>
</petrol engine>
```

This example shows both alternatives. As a rule, neither of the two possibilities is completely right or wrong, and the onus is on the specifier to decide which of the two structures to use. If the choice is still too difficult, you can follow the suggestions we give, which are shown in the following. Make sure, however, that under no circumstances do strict instructions take precedence over heuristics.

■ The element variant is clearer and more easily recognizable to the human eye. This makes it easier when editing and showing the "naked" documents in the browser. However, attributes allow more precise control and are therefore easier to operate from a technical programming point of view.

■ If the information is a fundamental *constituent* of the presiding element, then the use of elements is imperative. The petrol engine, for example, could never function without cylinders. If the information is inherent, such as the weight or the color, attributes need to be used.

■ If the information has been put into order, then sub-elements are most appropriate, as they also have a set structure. Therefore, attributes are more suited to the modeling of information without order on the data items.

■ Hierarchically arranged structures should be displayed as elements. Flat structures of similar capacity are kept more easily in attributes.

■ When dealing with data that describes the content, attributes should be used. An example of this is the way in which the language of a certain text is written. For the actual contents of the text, elements are certainly more suitable.

15.11 Is all this regimentation really necessary?

Naturally there is the question of whether more complex DTDs pay off or not. It depends, of course, on which application you have in mind for the XML documents. For instance, if you only want to implement an efficient search mechanism, highlighting certain relevant keywords in the domain and subdividing documents into logical parts such as question and answer, it is not necessary to have strict control on the element and attribute structure.

However, if a document is to form the basis for business processes it is extremely important to ensure that the document structure is as precise as possible. Imagine that on a telephone hotline, customers were to have their conversations documented in XML. From these documents it should be apparent whether the company has to take further measures such as sending a spare part or having an expert return the call. In this case the XML data becomes the basis for a workflow system which is ultimately very complex.

The point is that the development of the application is easier if, with a positive answer from the XML validator, a certain degree of error checking is not necessary anymore. This cuts costs and at the same time makes the application essentially more robust. In this case a similarity with database applications can be seen. Any good database schema, using key references, integrity test and unambiguity conditions, will guarantee that the saved data will be of a particular quality. As a developer, you can rely on there being a client entry for each order, for example. If we view it as such it also should be noticed that DTDs accept only relatively weaker conditions as commercial databases. However, DTDs are extremely useful and should be used. At the appropriate time, we will indicate the concrete uses of DTDs through the implementation of the XML functionality shown in the example in Chapter 17.

15.12 Entities

Entities fulfil a series of functions in XML documents. Just as a programming language does, they can be used like a constant in order to save frequently repeating text modules and to avoid listing the text repeatedly. Also, to insert special characters into the text or in order to create DTDs and documents using modules, we return to using entities.

15.12.1 Internal entities

Entities are defined as *internal entities* if the definition already comprises the value. A frequently occurring text, for example a copyright note or a contract text, therefore can be defined in one position and always be used again. In addition to the saving on typing, another considerable advantage is the fact that if the text has to be modified, you need only adapt the entity definition line. The following code line gives an example of such an internal entity:

```
<!ENTITY license 'The license holder is required to read this contract
carefully before
                declaring his agreement
                at the end of the contract. '>
```

This kind of entity declaration occurs in the DTD. In XML documents this entity can be referred to as often as desired, such as here in the text of the footer line:

```
<footer>Notice: &license;<footer>
```

However, it is also possible to use the entity in the DTD directly:

```
<!ENTITY license_complete '&license; If you are the license holder and
                do not agree with the contract in question
                express your disapproval
                clearly'>
```

15.12.2 Special characters

In order to display one of the following characters in XML text you can use the corresponding predefined entity:

```
&        &amp;
<        &lt;
>        &gt;
"        &quot;
'        &apos;
```

Entities are also used to insert symbols and special characters of different languages in the document. In this case the entity consists of one character only. In the entity definition the name of the entity will be established and the character given by its number in the *ISO Unicode Standard 10646*. The following example defines an entity for the ° character in order to be able to express a temperature:

```
<!ENTITY degree '&#176;'>

<temperature>18 &degree;C</temperature>
```

For German special characters in particular, such as umlauts, there is another, more suitable variant. In the first line of the XML document, it is possible to inform the XML parser about the language encoding of the document, using the `encoding` attribute. If the special character is available on your keyboard and supported by the editor, you can avoid a long-winded representation such as &ae; and just type the character.

```
<?xml version="1.0" encoding="ISO-8859-1"?>
```

If no special character is given, ISO 10646 UTF-8 is chosen. This standard accounts for the first 128 lines of the ASCII font. If UTF-8, which is the default setting, is chosen by the user and the document includes umlauts, an error occurs, since the application cannot interpret these characters.

15.12.3 Modular documents

Unlike internal entities, in which the value occurs directly in the definition, the value can also be retrieved from a file. In the way it functions, it resembles an include file in C that is bound in a source file by the preprocessor. Just as with the reference on an external DTD, a URL is used as a reference on the file. This can be given either as an absolute link, for example `http://www.books-online.com/component/1.xml`, or as a relative link, for example `2.txt`. This will appear as follows:

```
<!ENTITY license_complete SYSTEM "license.txt">
```

An obvious use of this technique is the partitioning of a logical document into several files. This allows different authors to work on a document at the same time without them all overtyping modifications on a file which is simultaneously open in several editors. In the following example a book is saved in four files. The main document `book.xml` contains the DTD in which four external entities are defined. Further element and attribute definitions follow this. In the root document the element `book` is found which contains the references to the individual chapters.

```
<?xml version="1.0" encoding="ISO-8859-1"?>

<!DOCTYPE book [
  <!ENTITY chap1 SYSTEM chap1.xml">
  <!ENTITY chap2 SYSTEM chap2.xml">
  <!ENTITY chap3 SYSTEM chap3.xml">
  <!ELEMENT book ANY>

  ...
]>

<book>
  &chap1;
  &chap2;
  &chap3;
</book>
```

As the individual chapters are inserted into the main document, further XML elements can appear in the files `chap1.xml`, etc. A Document Type Definition cannot exist in the file which is to be inserted, as initially only one DTD is allowed per logical document. As illustrated in Figure 15.3, the file `chap1.xml` with ISO-8859-1 uses a different encoding from the main document `book.xml`, which is coded in UTF-8.

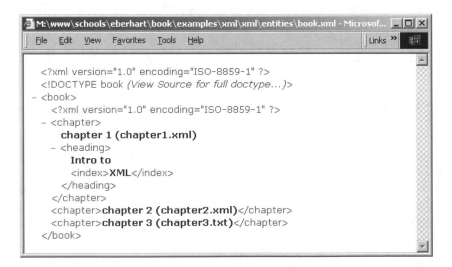

Figure 15.3: Internet Explorer shows our book document consisting of four files.

If no `<?xml?>` definition is available in the file defining the entity value, we go back to UTF-8. The file `chap1.xml` is itself a well-formed document:

```
<?xml version="1.0" encoding="ISO-8859-1"?>

<chap>
   Chapter 1 (chap1.xml)
   <headline>
      introducation to
      <index>XML</index>
   </headline>
</chap>
```

`Chap3.txt`, however, is a normal text file and has just one line:

```
<chap>chapterl 3 (chap3.txt)</chap>
```

15.12.4 Modular DTDs

There are also some functions in the DTDs which enhance the management of definitions. As shown in the previous sections, entities allow frequently occurring text elements to be saved in a type of constant and allow external files to be bound together. With regard to DTDs, the so-called *parameter entities* offer a similar functionality.

Take an insurance company as an example, whose documents are coded in XML. In the DTDs different elements are defined for different vehicles. This is necessary because every vehicle class can be very different. On the other hand, we often find that an element must have one of these vehicles as a child element. Instead of always repeating the sequence `(pkw | truck | motorbike)` in the DTD, this expression can be saved in a parameter Entity. The advantage is obvious: if, for instance, bicycles are insured in the future, a modification is only required in one location.

```
<!ENTITY % vehicle "(pkw | truck | motorbike)">
<!ELEMENT insurance (customer, %vehicle, premium)>
```

The following example shows how a DTD can be composed of several parts. On the one hand we can employ the technique shown in Section 15.6.2 on page 290, in order to supplement local definitions with an external DTD. Alternatively, a further DTD is added by means of the definition and the subsequent reference of the parameter Entity. Both possiblities enable the user to build a hierarchy of definitions to a certain extent. You could imagine, for example, that frequently used definitions such as addresses or product descriptions are established in `general.dtd`. Each section can import these definitions if it is necessary, although they can change in the local DTD or in the imported DTD `include.dtd`. Assume that the company uses a specific copyright note, defined in `general.dtd` as an entity, that is imported by all documents. If the copyright note has to be modified in the documents contained in a handbook used by the sales department, the modified definition can be filed in `include.dtd` and imported by these documents.

```
<?xml version="1.0"?>
<!DOCTYPE rootl SYSTEM "general.dtd" [
   <!ENTITY % include SYSTEM "include.dtd">
   %include;
   ...
]>
```

15.12.5 Embedding of binary files

The classic example for embedding binary files is that of graphics on HTML pages using the `<img>` tag, such as: `<img src='logo.gif'>`. The XML mechanism functions in a similar way but is considerably more strictly regulated. The `src` attribute of the element test is defined in DTD as an entity. In the following example the attribute value is `logo`. Moreover, `logo` along with the URL is allocated to the binary file as the *JPEG Notation Data* (NDATA) entity. Finally, JPEG is listed as notation with a reference to the ISO JPEG standard:

```
<?xml version="1.0"?>
<!DOCTYPE test [
   <!NOTATION JPEG PUBLIC "ISO/IEC 10918:1993//NOTATION Digital
                           Compression and Coding of Continous-tone
                           Still Images (JPEG)//EN">
   <!ENTITY logo SYSTEM "logo.jpg" NDATA JPEG>
   <!ELEMENT test EMPTY>
   <!ATTLIST test src ENTITY #REQUIRED>
]>
<test src="logo"/>
```

This can all appear very circumstantial at first glance. We should take into consideration, however, that notations are usually imported from a common external DTD. The advantage of this is that as far as the application is concerned, it is clear which format the binary file assumes.

15.12.6 Namespaces

The purpose of *namespaces* is to use tags from two "vocabularies" in one document. Let us assume that there is a document which contains medical information about patients. All tags containing the patient's contact information can belong to the namespace contact, for example `<contact:telephone>`. Medical information is allocated to the namespace "med": `<med:organ>`. The accounting software can now read the document and pick out the contact tags alone, in order to address a letter. However, a search engine for doctors uses tags relevant only to the medicine. Namespaces should make it easier to use simple XML software components in any possible scenario, such as the management of addresses.

A namespace is always defined in an element, normally in the root element, and is valid for all unordered elements.

```
<x xmlns:edifact='http://www.edi.org/edifact'>
    <edifact:price units='Euro'>32.18</edifact:price>
</x>
```

This example defines the `edi` namespace. A URL is given for the definition. Documentation could be found here, but, this is not actually necessary. The URL simply constitutes a string which identifies the namespace.

Another purpose of this development is to provide search engines, such as AltaVista, which more or less search pages randomly, an insight into how a tag should be interpreted. Through the association of a tag with one of the well-known URLs found by the search engine, it can guess the content of the tag more effectively.

In fact, in the above example the search engine does not know anything about the tag `edifact:price`. The name `price` indicates the meaning. But, since the organization edi.org deals with standards for *electronic data interchange* and EDIFACT is one of these standards, we can conclude that we are dealing with the price within the framework of the EDIFACT data record. Consequently, the search engine can now answer queries more precisely than before.

What is not clear, as far as namespaces are concerned, is how the document containing elements of different vocabularies is to be validated using DTDs.

15.13 XML schema

As well as DTDs, the XML schema gives another method of determining and checking the content and structure of XML documents. However, the XML schema reference is not yet complete, although a great deal of support has been provided. Obviously, this raises the question: What does the XML schema improve compared with DTDs? We will answer this question in the next section.

15.13.1 Why not DTDs?

DTD support has been implemented in many tools and DTDs are sucessfully introduced into many positions. Nevertheless, the following points are often criticized:

- The DTD syntax is relatively abnormal from an XML point of view. There is no reason why schema definitions themselves cannot be written in XML. Other references based on XML, such as XSL or XLink (see the following sections), require the corresponding documents to be written in XML as well. The XML schema also follows this trend.

- Because of their SGML predecessors, DTDs are strongly orientated to document management or the publishing world. The great success of XML in many other areas, such as in the development of distributed systems or in the database sector, brings to light a substantial deficit: a lack of data types. This is a fundamental feature in programming. As a result, it is left to the application to check if the element `<age>43</age>` has a meaningful value. DTDs simply enable you to ensure that the element is available. Nevertheless, you cannot check if it is an integer number between 0 and 120. The XML schema eleminates this deficit. It can use primitive data types and fix limitations according to their values.

- Section *Modular DTDs* on page 305 describes how a hierarchy of DTD definitions can be structured. The "include" style of syntax required is not exactly very natural from an object-oriented point of view. In this case, an XML schema gives us the option of defining such document class hierarchies in a clear way.

- DTDs were developed before the namespaces which are described in Section 15.12.6 on page 306. Namespaces are becoming increasingly important, and are being used more frequently. However, DTDs only support namespaces to a certain extent. As explained in Section 15.13.6 on page 313, the XML schema can offer assistance even in this case.

Instead of referring to a DOCTYPE reference, XML documents refer to the schema location attribute on the URL of the schema. DTDs should not be copied out. The XML schema reference is not yet adopted, and XML tools currently support functionality only partially. On the other hand, DTDs are in use today and are successful in many cases.

15.13.2 Combination of documents with a schema

XML documents refer to the URL of the schema on the `schemaLocation` attribute, rather than adopting a DOCTYPE reference.

```
<?xml version="1.0">
<offer xmlns:xsi="http://www.w3.org/1999/XMLSchema-instance"
       xsi:schemaLocation="offer.xsd">
 ...
```

It makes no difference to the developer of an XML application whether the document was validated by a DTD or the XML schema. The only prerequisite is that the parser in use has to support the XML schema. The structure of the document and the method used to access it (see the next chapter) remains unchanged.

Additionally, it is possible to display the URLs of several schemas in the attribute `schemaLocation`. This is particularly interesting if the document contains elements of varying namespaces. You can find further details in the Section 15.13.6 on page 313.

15.13.3 Primitive data types (simple types)

The following schema defines an element test that is assigned five sub-elements and five attributes. Other than the well-known strings, integer numbers, floating point numbers and URIs are found once again, represented in DTDs using `CDATA` or `PCDATA`. The data type `NMTOKENS` was adopted by DTDs in order to guarantee problem-free migration. Futhermore, notice that attributes and elements share the same primitive data types.

```
<schema>

  <element name="test">
    <complexType>
        <element name="integer-element" type="integer" />
        <element name="string-element" type="string" />
        <element name="float-element" type="float" />
        <element name="uri-element" type="uriReference" />
        <element name="token-element" type="NMTOKENS" />

        <attribute name="integer-attribute" type="integer" />
        <attribute name="string-attribute" type="string" />
        <attribute name="float-attribute" type="float" />
        <attribute name="uri-attribute" type="uriReference" />
        <attribute name="token-attribute" type="NMTOKENS" />
    </complexType>
  </element>

</schema>
```

With respect to the above schema, this document is valid:

```
<?xml version="1.0"?>
<test xmlns:xsi="http://www.w3.org/1999/XMLSchema-instance"
      xsi:schemaLocation="datatypes.xsd"
      integer-attribute="1234567"
      string-attribute="aabbcc"
      float-attribute="3.1415"
      uri-attribute="mailto:andreas.eberhart@i-u.de"
      token-attribute="a b c d e f">
```

```
    <integer-element>1234567</integer-element>
    <string-element>aabbcc</string-element>
    <float-element>3.1415</float-element>
    <uri-element>http://www.i-u.de</uri-element>
    <token-element>a b c d e f</token-element>
</test>
```

The document below violates some of the specific limitations fixed for the data types and creates a series of errors during validation.

```
<?xml version="1.0"?>
<test xmlns:xsi="http://www.w3.org/1999/XMLSchema-instance"
      xsi:schemaLocation="datatypes.xsd"
      integer-attribute="123.4567"
      string-attribute="aabbcc"
      float-attribute="3.14.15"
      uri-attribute="andreas.eberhart@i-u.de"
      token-attribute="a,b">

    ... (unchanged) ...
</test>
```

The ouput of the validating parser displays four errors: the number 123.456 is not an integer, the mailto prefix which represents a regular URI is missing in the e-mail address, 3.14.15 is not a floating point number and a tokenized list may not contain a comma:

```
java sax.SAX2Count -v datatypes2.xml
[Error] datatypes2.xml:8:29: Datatype error: 123.4567 has execeed the
scale Facet {1}.
[Error] datatypes2.xml:8:29: Datatype error: 3.14.15 is not a float..
[Error] datatypes2.xml:8:29: Datatype error: Value 'andreas.eberhart@i-
u.de' is a Malformed URI .
[Error] datatypes2.xml:8:29: Datatype error: Value 'a,b' does not match
regular expression facet '\c+'..
datatypes2.xml: 1202 ms (6 elems, 6 attrs, 32 spaces, 41 chars)
```

The XML schema specifies another sequence of more data types such as date, time, or even references to ID attributes. A list of every option would, however, go beyond the scope of this book. The XML schema data types Web site of the W3C is the best reference here: `http://www.w3.org/TR/xmlschema-2/`.

15.13.4 Defining custom types

The previous section shows how attributes and elements can be expressed using `<attribute>` and `<element>`. As with a programming language, a type is always specified via a declaration. Dealing with leaf elements and attributes of the test element, the data type is specified by means of the type attribute. However, this is omitted in the test element. For this purpose a subordinated element with the name `complexType` exists. In this way, the content of the `complexType` element specifies the type of the test element. The whole structure therefore defines both a new data type as well as an element which uses this data type. The new data type has no name, meaning it is an implicit definition. In an XML schema it is also possible to define a type and use it for several elements. The following example compares the two methods:

```
<schema>

    <complexType name="coord">
        <element name="x" type="integer" />
        <element name="y" type="integer" />
    </complexType>

    <element name="root">
        <complexType>
            <element name="test1">
                <complexType>
                    <element name="x" type="integer" />
                    <element name="y" type="integer" />
                </complexType>
            </element>
            <element name="test2" type="coord" />
        </complexType>
    </element>

</schema>
```

At first the type "coord" is defined as a pair of integer values (x, y). The element root contains the elements `test1` and `test2`. The declaration of `test1` uses an implicit definition, while `test2` refers to the type "coord", in a similar manner to the primative data types using the type attribute. Both coordinate elements have the same structure.

In this context the definition of a type can be compared with the definition of an element in the DTD, because this kind of coordinate type can not be used for an attribute. The corresponding DTD would appear as follows:

```
<!ELEMENT coord (x,y)>
<!ELEMENT x (#PCDATA)>
<!ELEMENT y (#PCDATA)>
```

Lists and optional constructs which can be given in DTDs as *, +, and ? are expressed in the XML schema by means of the `minOccurs` and `maxOccurs` attributes. Any limitations are possible here, for example from two to five or from one to infinity:

```
<element name="test">
  <complexType>
    <element name="student" type="studentType"
        minOccurs="1"
        maxOccurs="unbounded" />
  </complexType>
</element>
```

We wish to reiterate at this point that we have not yet explored all of the possibilities of the XML schema. Various modifiers for attributes, default values, and further features can be found under `http://www.w3.org/TR/xmlschema-1/`.

15.13.5 Extension of existing types

In larger projects, it makes sense to create hierarchies of types by deriving special definitions from generic base types. The XML schema offers two possibilities. On the one hand a type can be refined by the restriction of the range of values. On the other hand it can be extended with additional fields.

```
<simpleType name="studentid">
   <restriction base="string">
      <pattern value="[A-Z][0-9][0-9][0-9][0-9]+" />
   </restriction>
</simpleType>
```

This first example defines a data type `studentid` which refines the primitive type string. During validation, the only valid strings are those which follow the basic expression of the pattern element. Here, all student IDs begin with a capital letter, followed by a string of at least five numbers. Using regular expressions, you can structure all possible formats easily, such as those for telephone numbers, chemical formulae, product codes, and so on. The example mentioned at the beginning concerning the string of values for `age` is solved using the following declaration. Further modifications can also be made in this case.

```
<simpleType name="age">
   <restriction base="integer">
      <minInclusive value="0" />
      <maxInclusive value="120" />
   </restriction>
</simpleType>
```

Here the keyword `simpleType` means that we are dealing with a data type with only one value such as a string or a number. On the other hand, complex types can consist of many values.

With the expansion of a type, the attributes and elements of the basic type are passed on to the new type. Our example shows data types for both undergraduates and graduates; the title of their dissertation appears in the graduate student data type, and the fields of the undergraduate student are inherited.

```
<complexType name="student">
   <element name="name" type="string" />
   <element name="address" type="string" />
</complexType>

<complexType name="gradstudent">
   <extension base="student">
      <element name="degree dissertation" type="string" />
   </extension>
</complexType>
```

The resulting elements are as follows:

```
<student>
   <name>Tom Miller</name>
   <address>Campus 34, 37325 Students'accommodation</address>
</student>

<gradstudent>
   <name>Joana Smith</name>
   <address>Campus 99, 37325 Students'accommodation</address>
   <dissertation>XML Schema in Action!</dissertation>
</gradstudent>
```

15.13.6 XML schema and namespaces

A considerable disadvantage of DTDs is the limitation on one document type. Using XML schema, a document can be validated with several schemas. So, for example, an order document can be based on both the address and product description vocabulary without running the risk of losing the validation with two schemas. Of course one wonders how the connection between a schema and an element can be established within a document.

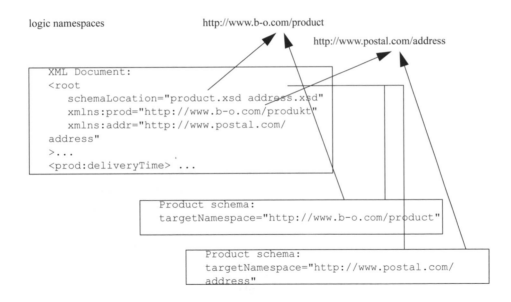

Figure 15.4: Explanation of the element-schema relationship on namespaces.

Using the `targetNamespace` attribute, you can specify which Namespace the schema refers to in the root element of the schema definition:

```
<schema targetNamespace='http://www.b-o.com/product'>
```

The schema is therefore used for all elements of this namespace. On the other hand, the prefix of the element can be reduced to the namespace within the document. In the example in Fig. 15.4 all elements are defined with the prefix `addr` (or `prod`) in the schema `address.xsd` (or `product.xsd`).

The XML schema allows for the modular formation of schema definitions. So, using the `include` element, you can specify that definitions of another schema file are used in the context or in the target namespace of the schemas.

```
<include schemaLocation='http://www.b-o.de/schema/cheap.xsd' />
```

With the `import` element, definitions can be loaded as type library with the corresponding namespace:

```
<schema targetNamespace='http://www.b-o.com/product'
        xmlns='http://www.w3.org/1999/XMLSchema'
        xmlns:addr='http://www.postal.com/address'
...
<import
        namespace='http://www.postal.com/address'
        schemaLocation='address.xsd' />
...
    <element name='receiver' type='addr:shortaddress' />
...
```

15.14 XPath

The purpose of Xpath is to establish a terminology to select the particular elements of a document. In addition, some functions are specified for the manipulation of strings and numbers. The selection of elements is the basis of the extensive Stylesheet Language (XSL) and XPointer.

A directory structure is composed hierarchically in the same way as an XML document. Therefore, it makes sense to compare the XPath syntax when navigating the file system. So, / represents the root element, .. represents the parent node, `element1/ element2` represents element two under element one under the present element. An XPath expression always refers to a context element or present element. How the context element reveals itself is determined by the application, XSL or XPointer. This will be clarified in the next sections. Several XPath examples will now be shown using the abbreviated syntax. Appendix F on page 455 shows an overview of ways of expressing normal and abbreviated syntax.

- chapter
  Selects all of the subordinate elements with the name chapter.
- @name
  Selects the attribute name of "context element."
- chapter[1]
  Selects the first chapter element of the context element.
- chapter [5][@status="ready"]
  Selects the fifth child element of the context element with the name chapter, if the attribute has the value ready.
- *[@id=a23]/chapter[5]
  Selects the fifth element with the name chapter of the element with the unambiguous ID a23.
- //chapter
  Selects all chapter elements of the tree components under the context elements.

15.15 eXtensible Stylesheet Language for Transformations (XSLT)

XSLT transforms one XML document into another using an XSL Stylesheet. XSL and XSLT are, like XML, initiatives of the *World Wide Web Consortium.* The Stylesheet documents are written in XML themselves. Each XSL document must therefore be well formed. Transformations are useful, as it is often not possible to standardize DTDs and schemas for political or organizational reasons. It also easily can occur that two groups work on XML systems in parallel and do not know about each other. Transformations are also important for representation, as will be shown in the two points below. Let us now consider the following simple example.

```
<?xml version='1.0'?>
<export>
   <person>
      <forename>Joe</forename>
      <surname>Miller</surname>
      <age>52</age>
      <contact>
         <email>j.miller@hotmail.com</email>
         <email>joe45@yahoo.com</email>
         <telephone>049-573462-700</telephone>
      </contact>
   </person>
</export>
```

This document could be the output file of the PDA of a worker from the sales department. This document should now be transferred to the customer administration department of the firm who would expect the following format for the import.

```
<?xml version='1.0'?>
<customer age="52">
   <name>Miller, Joe</name>
   <contact-info>
       j.miller@hotmail.com
       joe45@yahoo.com
       049-573462-700
   </contact-info>
</customer>
```

This transformation is most easily carried out using an XSL stylesheet and an XSLT processor. We will now look at the stylesheet. It consists of two templates. The match attribute indicates whether or not or when the template is to be used. Here we are dealing with an Xpath expression. As mentioned in the previous section, a set of elements is selected with this expression, starting from the context element. The templates then are used on each of these elements. The transformation process begins at the root. Using the root element as the context, the first template is applied, as the person is positioned directly underneath export.

```
<?xml version="1.0"?>
<xsl:stylesheet xmlns:xsl="http://www.w3.org/1999/XSL/Transform"
       version="1.0">

   <xsl:template match='person'>
      <xsl:variable name="a" select="age" />
      <customer age='{$a}'>
         <name>
            <xsl:value-of select='surname' />
            ,
            <xsl:value-of select='forename' />
         </name>
         <xsl:apply-templates select='contact' />
      </customer>
   </xsl:template>

   <xsl:template match='contact'>
      <contact-info>
         <xsl:apply-templates />
      </contact-info>
   </xsl:template>

</xsl:stylesheet>
```

The template is now used as follows. All elements within the template which do not have the xsl prefix are printed in the output document. Here these are the elements customer and name. In addition we see three XSL commands. Next, a sort of local variable a is defined, that is allocated the value of the age subtree. What exactly does this mean? In contrast to processing the subtree using the templates, all the text of subtree <age>52<age>, therefore 52, is returned. The value of a is then referable by the character chain {$a}. This technique comes into use in the generation of attributes like the age attribute shown in this case.

With the `value-of` instruction, the result is not stored in a variable, but is made part of the output document directly. The element value therefore practically takes the position of and replaces the `xsl value-of` tag itself. In this way the `name` element is filled by the forename and surname of the sub tree, separated by a comma.

Between the end tags of the elements `customer` and `name`, the command `<xsl:apply-templates select='contact' />` is executed. At this stage of the transformation process, we are involved with the action part of the first template. Up until now text was only collected from the subtrees, and no other templates were put to use. The `apply-templates` command subsequently leads to the use of further templates. This manifests itself as follows: The element that applies to the template, in this case `person`, becomes a new context element. From here on the transformation process is continued by the use of the templates. The only limitation here is that only the directly subordinate trees, with `contact` at their root, are processed.

From the context of the `person` element, the XPath expression of the second template applies to the `contact` element. In the action part of the second template, the corresponding `contact-info` element of the target vocabulary is generated and the template use is continued, this time without limitation, using the `select` attribute. Since neither of the templates applies to any of the three subtrees of the `contact-info` elements, the default template is applied. This means that elements are traversed recursively. If we come to a text node, the text will be printed to the output document. Therefore, both e-mail addresses and the telephone number will be appear in the final document. Now the whole tree structure of the initial document has been processed and the new document is constructed. It now can be imported into the customer database.

In the next section the `xalan` XSLT processor will be introduced. We want to briefly jump ahead and show how easy it is to use this tool on our example:

```
set CLASSPATH=C:\buch\lib\xalan.jar;C:\buch\lib\xerces.jar;.
java org.apache.xalan.xslt.Process
     -IN person.xml
     -XSL person-to-customer.xsl
     -OUT customer.xml
```

15.15.1 XHTML

As well as transformations between different import and export formats, stylesheets can also convert XML elements into HTML elements. Because XSL stylesheets and therefore also all template action parts are written in XML, it is impossible to generate documents which are not well formed. Pictures and graphics are imported in HTML through the `img` tag. The corresponding end tag is almost always left out. Browsers accept all attributes, excluding those without quotation marks, and those with incorrectly positioned tags. This situation and the problem associated with the implementation of browsers and other programs designed to process poorly formed HTML have led to the specification of XHTML by the W3C. XHTML basically is well-formed HTML based on XML. An XSLT transformation can therefore produce an XHTML document. For instance, let us take the example as shown in Fig. 15.5 of our bookshop's offer transformed into XHTML.

```
<?xml version="1.0"?>

<xsl:stylesheet xmlns:xsl="http://www.w3.org/1999/XSL/Transform"
        version="1.0">

  <xsl:template match="/">
    <html>
      <xsl:apply-templates/>
    </html>
  </xsl:template>
```

The first template is applied to the root element. The symbol / known from the file systems is used as an XPath expression in the template. If the expression matches, the HTML start and end tags will be issued. `<xsl:apply-templates/>` in the middle of the template tells the XSLT processor to continue by trying to apply other templates.

```
  <xsl:template match="offer">
      <xsl:apply-templates/>
  </xsl:template>

  <xsl:template match="store">
    <ul>
      <xsl:apply-templates/>
    </ul>
  </xsl:template>

  <xsl:template match="name | url">
    <li>
      <xsl:value-of select="."/>
    </li>
  </xsl:template>

  <xsl:template match="book">
    <P>
      <xsl:value-of select="."/>
    </P>
  </xsl:template>

</xsl:stylesheet>
```

The additional XSL templates dictate that elements which are subordinate to the element store should be issued as lists. As explained in the previous example, the expression `<xsl:value-of select="."/>` prints all text elements of the relevant subtree. So, the ISBN, title, amount, and currency of the book are returned directly in the last template.

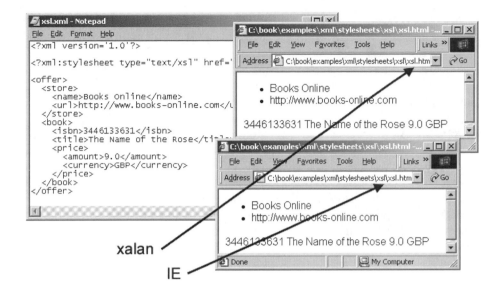

Figure 15.5: A book supply whose layout is constructed by an XSL Stylesheet and an HTML file generated by xalan.

Figure 15.5 shows the output of two methods of visualization of XML documents. The xalan processor can produce an XHTML file which can then be opened in the browser. Internet Explorer 5 also has an inbuilt XSL processor. It is therefore possible to refer to the XSL file from the XML document. This is accomplished by using the following processing instruction:

```
<?xml:stylesheet type="text/xsl" href="offer.xsl"?>
```

If the XML file is transferred to the browser, this line causes the browser to load the stylesheet referenced by its URL, and use that to display the document. The result can not be differentiated from the result produced by xalan.

15.15.2 Wireless Markup Language (WML)

The wireless markup langauge and the accompanying transport protocol, Wireless Application Protocol (WAP), makes it possible to surf specialized Web sites using a mobile phone. Figure 15.6 shows how, using WAP gateways, mobile phones are able to access WML pages which can be found on normal Web servers.

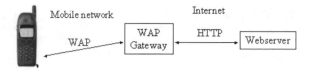

Figure 15.6: WAP gateways connect the mobile WAP world to the Internet.

Like XHTML, WML pages are also well-formed XML documents and can therefore be constructed using an XSLT transformation. The following stylesheet renders our book offer on two so-called cards. These are bound to each other by links. Links are represented by the do and go elements. In order to simplify the development of WAP and WML applications, lots of telecommunications companies have developed simulators which are provided to developers for free. Figure 15.7 shows the result of the transformation with the Nokia WAP toolkit. This toolkit can be downloaded from http://www.nokia.com/wap/.

```xml
<?xml version="1.0"?>

<xsl:stylesheet xmlns:xsl="http://www.w3.org/1999/XSL/Transform"
        version="1.0">

  <xsl:template match="/">
    <wml>
      <xsl:apply-templates />
    </wml>
  </xsl:template>

  <xsl:template match="book">
    <card id="book" title="book">
      <p>
        <xsl:apply-templates />
      </p>
      <do type="accept" label="goto store">
        <go href="#store" />
      </do>
    </card>
  </xsl:template>

  <xsl:template match="store">
    <card id="store" title="store">
      <p>
        <xsl:apply-templates />
      </p>
      <do type="accept" label="goto book">
        <go href="#book" />
      </do>
    </card>
  </xsl:template>

</xsl:stylesheet>
```

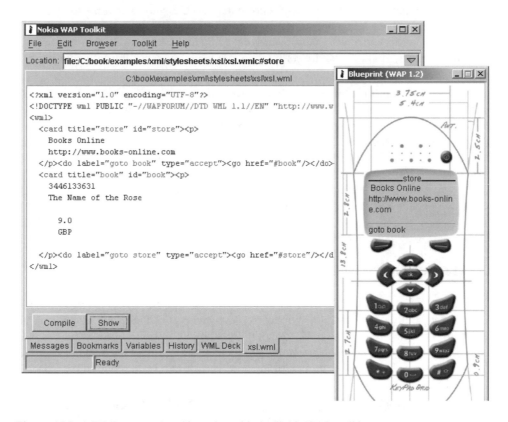

Figure 15.7: A WML page created by xalan with the Nokia WAP toolkit.

In the stylesheet processing instruction, the `media` attribute allows us to state which stylesheet should be used with the delivery medium. In this case it is shown that `wml.xsl` should be used for mobile telephones, and that in all other cases `default.xsl` should be used.

```
<?xml:stylesheet type="text/xsl" href="default.xsl"?>
<?xml:stylesheet type="text/xsl" href="wml.xsl" media="wap"?>
```

15.16 Presentation with stylesheet

Without much persuasion, it is easy to convince programmers, database administrators, and generally everybody who works with structured or semi-structured data of the relevance and usefulness of XML. However, it is more difficult to convince authors, but particularly Web designers. There are numerous ways of closing the gap between XML and the representation in the browser or the print view. In the following sections we will concentrate on the two most prominent representatives, *Cascading Stylesheets (CSS)* and eXtensible Stylesheet Language (XSL). The possibility of transforming documents into XHTML and WML had already been conceived. CSS and XSL are different from XSLT in that the formatting parameters are set by the stylesheets. Another format is not used for presentation.

In both cases we limit ourselves to a short introduction and one example. The reason for this short treatment is the following: On the one hand, professional work with CSS is very difficult due to the differing interpretations of stylesheets by Netscape Navigator and Microsoft Internet Explorer. On the other hand, parts of the XSL recommendation are still being worked on, with the result that similar products only support the new functionality to a small extent or not at all. We hope that the diverging development of CSS implementation is not repeated in XML. If the development of XSL is as fast as that of XML, we expect XSL to take huge strides in the field of document management in the coming years.

15.16.1 Cascading Stylesheets

Originally, CSS was developed in order to automate the uniform laying out of larger Web sites. If, for example, the standard style for product names is changed, it is imperative that on a pure HTML site each page be individually adapted. A CSS solution, on the other hand, gives all font tags only one common product name ID, without actually establishing the writing style. The actual definition of the writing style can be in found in the CSS file.

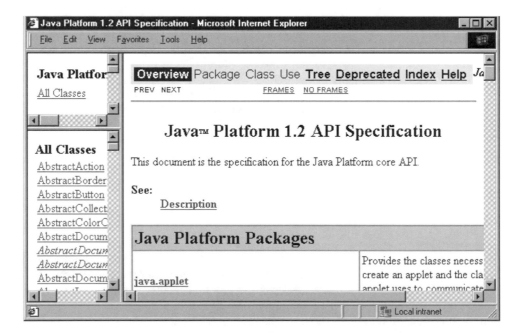

Figure 15.8: The API documentation of the JDK also uses CSS.

Sun uses the API documentation of the JDK stylesheet in order to guarantee a uniform design. The result is shown in Fig. 15.8. We can see how the HTML and CSS sources look. These sources display the currently active menu item, the overview in this case, in the first line of the main frame. The HTML file contains a reference to the stylesheet in the header:

```
<LINK REL ="stylesheet" TYPE="text/css"
      HREF="stylesheet.css" TITLE="Style">
```

The NavBarCell1Rev and NavBarFont1Rev IDs of the cell and the font below can be found in the HTML text of the table cell with the "overview" text :

```
<TD ID="NavBarCell1Rev">
   <FONT ID="NavBarFont1Rev">
      <B>Overview</B>
   </FONT>
</TD>
```

These IDs are defined in the stylesheet file with a navy blue background and white text:

```
#NavBarCell1Rev { background-color:#00008B;} /* Navy blue*/
#NavBarFont1Rev { font-family: Arial, Helvetica,
                  sans-serif; color:#FFFFFF;} /* White */
```

How can CSS be used for XML? Instead of working with IDs, the names of the elements can be assigned properties directly. We will take the XML document displayed in Figure 15.9 as an example, which contains a book offer in our shop. We will select an Arial font for the offer element. As this characteristic is inherited from other elements such as isbn, title, and price, this appears in the same font. The exception is the URL of the bookshop, for which the specific Courier font is selected, and so the default setting of the primary element is overwritten. Similarly, all information on books is indented to 13 points, as this is specified in the book element. The file css.css is shown here:

```
offer {display: block; font-family:arial;}
name {font-size: 24pt; font-weight: bold;}
url {display: block; padding-top: 6pt; font-family:courier;}
book {text-indent: 10pt;}
isbn {display: block; padding-top: 13pt;}
title {display: block;}
price {display: block;}
```

In order to present the XML file with the style features just defined, the reference to the stylesheet need only be inserted:

```
<?xml:stylesheet href="css.css" type="text/css"?>
```

CSS is relatively easy to use, but not as powerful as the XML-specific variant XSL described in the next section. It should also be noted that the CSS solution should rather be seen as a temporary solution, until XSL is fully supported by current programs.

Figure 15.9: The XML file from Fig. 15.5, represented using a Cascading Stylesheet.

15.16.2 Formatting with XSL

In contrast to XSLT, pure XSL stylesheets do not contain XML tags in the active part which are transferred in the resulting document. However, they determine the formatting attributes similar to the well-known CSS attributes, such as the fonts, colors, page layout, and so on. The following example shows an XSL rule, used on all `para` elements. These elements should be formatted in a block, the page margin set to 1.5 inches, and the spacing set to 6 points:

```
<xsl:template match="para">
  <fo:block
      indent-start="1.5in"
      indent-end="1.5in"
      space-before-optimum="6pt"
      space-after-optimum="6pt">
        <xsl:apply-templates/>
  </fo:block>
</xsl:template>
```

Working with formatting objects is still quite laborious, as support from the tools is poor. However, much will change in the near future. For example, it will be possible to display an XML document with an XSL stylesheet based on formatting objects in Adobe Acrobat Reader.

15.17 Other XML technologies

In this section we wish to discuss briefly other technologies based on XML. The corresponding W3C recommendations either have not been available for long, or are still in progress. For some of them, there therefore are hardly any programs which support and implement them. However, given the rapid technology and distribution of XML, this will soon change.

15.17.1 XLink

Hyperlinks are one of the guarantors of success of the WWW, although, or rather because, they have a very simple operation. XLink opens up several new possibilities. For example, one is no longer restricted to a link from A to B. Rather several resources can be combined in one link. If such a link is clicked, you can choose which link to follow. The following example shows a link from the homepage of a hotel. Three options are offered: you can jump directly to a reservation form, consult a map of the area, or plan the journey by train. Figure 15.10 shows how this could look in the browser.

```
Come to
<X xmlns:tourism='http//:www.woerterbuch.de/reise'>
   <L role='tourism:booking'>
      title='Places available!'
      show='REPLACE'
      href='../form/r.xml' />
   <L role='tourism:road'
      title='Journey by train'
      show='NEW'
      href='http://bahn.hafas.de/bin/bhftafel.exe/dn?bhf=8000055' />
   <L role='tourism:map
      title='Where is the hotel?'
      show='EMBED'
      href='http://www.mapquest.com/cgi-bin/find?lat=476666&lng=91833'/>
   Lake Constance hotel
</X>
```

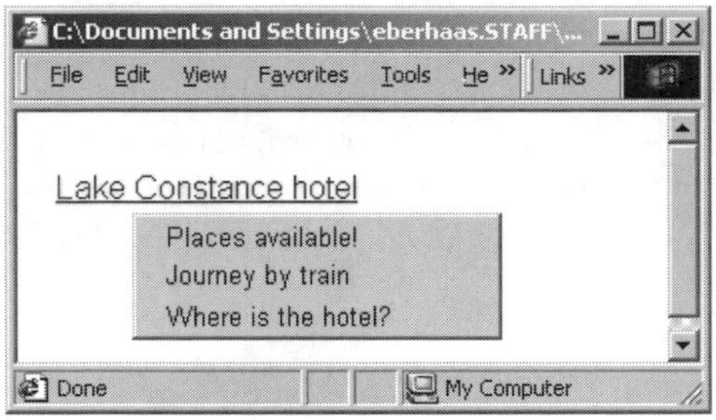

Figure 15.10: An XLink hyperlink with three endpoints.

As usual, the `href` attribute of the options indicates the URL of the linked resource. `role` indicates with which text the link is presented to the user, while `show` has a similar function to the `target` attribute in HTML. A resource can replace the current page, can be presented in a new window, but can also be embedded in the current page.

In turn, the `role` attribute can pick up a term of the namespace used, in order to give the link a semantic meaning by using a certain volcabulary. In the example, the links are assigned touristic terms such as booking and map – another way of supporting search engines.

15.17.2 XPointer

XPointers enable individual elements or a group of elements to be referred to. The basic idea is to extend the options provided with the # symbol in the URL by HTML hyperlinks. Instead of only being able to reach fixed, linearly ordered positions in a document, the entire XPath functionality is now available.

```
http://xpointer.host.com/staff.xml#xpointer(//emp[@typ="tmp"])
```

If you follow this link, you are not directed to the entire `staff.xml` document, but only reach information on temporary staff.

XPointer can also be used in an XLink. It is based on XPath and this XPointer / XPath combination is currently implemented by Software AG in the Tamino product. Tamino is an XML-based database server. The result of the query is then returned in XML format.

15.17.3 SOAP

The Simple Object Access Protocol is an initiative originally introduced by Microsoft. SOAP defines a simple, XML-based protocol for the exchange of information. It essentially consists of three parts:

- An envelope that specifies what is part of the message and how it should be processed.
- How the standard data types are to be coded in XML is specified .
- Furthermore, a convention is established for how Remote Procedure Calls and their results are to be represented.

As mentioned in the CORBA chapters, there are several problems with the use of CORBA in heterogenous systems: certain firewall ports often are not opened, or the ORBs and nameservers of different manufacturers are incompatible. SOAP should provide a solution in this case. It is entirely based on Internet standards and uses the existing nameserver and Web server infrastructure of the WWW. Furthermore, SOAP does not have many complex features such as object references, callbacks, or distributed garbage collection.

Like CORBA, SOAP is not a product but a specification, and there are a host of SOAP implementations. We will use software of the Apache project, which works in connection with the Tomcat server. The anatomy of a SOAP RPC call via HTTP is similar to the CORBA architecture displayed in Fig. 9.7 on page 194. Figure 15.11 shows the Apache implementation. The client program uses the call and response objects of the Apache SOAP library, in order to set the parameters of the RPC call. In this case the share price of IBM is queried.

```
Call call = new Call ();
call.setTargetObjectURI ("urn:stock-quotes");
call.setMethodName ("getQuote");
Vector params = new Vector ();
params.addElement(new Parameter("symbol", String.class, "IBM", null));
call.setParams (params);
Response resp = call.invoke(routerURL, "");

Parameter result = resp.getReturnValue();
System.out.println (result.getValue());
```

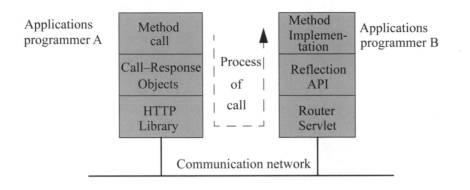

Figure 15.11: Anatomy of a SOAP call from a Java client to an Apache server.

The SOAP library converts the function call in the following XML document and then sends this via HTTP post query to the Web service specified in the `routerURL` variable. The components mentioned at the beginning are also located here. The message contains the information that the `getQuote` function of the stock-quote service should be called, that the parameter is of the string type and that the message uses the SOAP coding for the parameter.

```
<SOAP-ENV:Envelope
    xmlns:SOAP-ENV="http://schemas.xmlsoap.org/soap/envelope/"
    xmlns:xsi="http://www.w3.org/1999/XMLSchema-instance"
    xmlns:xsd="http://www.w3.org/1999/XMLSchema">
<SOAP-ENV:Body>
    <ns1:getQuote xmlns:ns1="urn:stock-quotes"
     SOAP-ENV:encodingStyle="http://schemas.xmlsoap.org/soap/encoding/">
        <symbol xsi:type="xsd:string">IBM</symbol>
    </ns1:getQuote>
</SOAP-ENV:Body>
</SOAP-ENV:Envelope>
```

The following XML document is known as the deployment descriptor, generated when the Web service is installed using the administration tool. The RPC router servlet accepts all queries and uses this information in order to pass on the call to the `getQuote` method of the QuoteService class.

```
<isd:service xmlns:isd="http://xml.apache.org/xml-soap/deployment"
             id="urn:stock-quotes">
  <isd:provider type="java"
                scope="Application"
                methods="getQuote">
    <isd:java class="mysoapapp.QuoteService"/>
  </isd:provider>
</isd:service>
```

The implementation of the Web service is very easy. As the RPC router servlet finds the corresponding function or method using reflection API, it is, in contrast to CORBA, not necessary to extend stubs. Only the desired method need be implemented.

```
package mysoapapp;

public class QuoteService {
    public float getQuote (String symbol) {
        ...
        return ...
    }
}
```

The RPC router then packs the returned floating point value into the following XML answer document. This document is then parsed by the response class of the client, and the actual result of the application is made available via the getValue method.

```
<SOAP-ENV:Envelope
  xmlns:SOAP-ENV="http://schemas.xmlsoap.org/soap/envelope/"
  SOAP-ENV:encodingStyle="http://schemas.xmlsoap.org/soap/encoding/">
  <SOAP-ENV:Body>
      <m:QuoteResponse xmlns:m="http://quotes.com">
          <Price>34.5</Price>
      </m:QuoteResponse>
  </SOAP-ENV:Body>
</SOAP-ENV:Envelope>
```

SOAP is a very interesting technology and is increasingly supported by tools. It is an integral component part of Microsoft's Dot-Net strategy. SOAP is not necessarily restricted to HTTP, although this is clearly a natural variant. So SOAP queries can also be transferred by e-mail, using POP and SMTP, for example.

It is possible to access a Web service implemented on the IIS with C# from a SOAP client written in Java. This is guaranteed using the platform-independent standards, XML and HTTP.

15.17.4 UDDI

UDDI stands for Universal Description, Discovery and Integration and is a project initiated by IBM, Microsoft, and Ariba. The idea of UDDI is as follows: The Internet offers the basis that every participant is able to communicate with all others. With XML, a widespread standard is created which enables information to be encoded. In turn, SOAP specifies how information can be exchanged. UDDI builds on this infrastructure. In the context of the UDDI project, a type of global telephone directory is implemented. All companies and organizations can register there with the following information from three categories:

- White Pages
  Name, address, telephone number, Web address, and other contact information is placed here, which could also be found in the telephone directory.
- Yellow Pages
  The organisation is categorized in the style of Yellow Pages, with a taxonomy. Branches and geographical taxonomies are provided. For example, the Microsoft company could be found under Computers > Software and USA > Washington > Redmond.
- Green Pages
  This category is the real innovation compared to previous concepts. This specifies which SOAP services the company offers, and how they can be accessed. The concept of Electronic Data Interchange was introduced in the section on *EDI and E-Commerce* on page 288. There are a number of different standards defined in this area. Oasis Open (`http://www.oasis-open.org`) and RosettaNet (`http://www.rosettanet.org`) are two of the many organizations which engage in standardization in different sectors of industry. These EDI standards are adapted by UDDI, in that they receive a unique identifier. For example, a company can then implement the RosettaNet EDI protocol with the ID "ros-net-PIP-3A5- Query Order Status," and publish the URL of the service together with the ID in the Green Pages.

The advantage of UDDI is obvious: with this global information service, our bookshop can retrieve a list of publishers in southern Germany, Switzerland, and Austria immediately, and find out which Web services they offer. All this is possible without a single telephone call or letter to the company.

UDDI is still in the early stages of development, and was only introduced at the end of 2000. However, during its brief lifespan almost all well-known companies have signaled their support. This technology could spark a revolution in the B2B sphere. More information can be found at `http://uddi.org`.

Chapter 16

Tool support for XML

As with servlet tools, this overview can convey just a limited idea of a current, rapid development. We consider only those programs that are of interest for developing the XML examples in the following chapter.

16.1 Browsers

Even if XML is much more than a language to describe Web pages, Web browsers play a central role in the display of XML documents. The most advanced is the implementation in Microsoft Internet Explorer 5. XML documents can be displayed using CSS or XSL. If no stylesheet is defined, Internet Explorer shows the tree structure of the document with color notes. Obviously a parser, which handles the conversion of the file into a corresponding data structure, is contained in Explorer. Netscape Navigator also has followed XML support in Version 6.

XML can be used also by HTML and with JavaScript. Here Microsoft uses the XMLDOM ActiveX object, i.e. the so-called *XML data island* which is defined as follows:

```
<XML ID="xmltree" src="offer.xml"></XML>
```

You can access this data island or an ActiveX object only by DOM and JavaScript. The class and method names correspond to the DOM standard. The following brief example uses the classes Document, Node, and NodeList, to create a list of all author elements contained in the XML document.

```
root = xmltree.XMLDocument.documentElement;
list = root.getElementsByTagName('author');
```

More details on this technique can be found at http://msdn.microsoft.com/ xml/default.asp. We suggest you install Internet Explorer 5.x to experiment with XML. The software is available for download at http://www.microsoft.com/ windows/ie/default.htm.

The previous version, Internet Explorer 4.0, also has a first XML implementation, but this is accessible only via JavaScript. In this case you should be careful, as the API of Version 4 still differs substantially from the DOM standard.

Generally, when dealing with browsers, you should notice that support for most of ongoing XML functionality needs more time. This refers to the XLink, XPointer, and part of the XSL recommendation of the W3C.

16.2 Parsers

When an XML document is read from a file or a Web server on the Internet, for the application this is just a series of characters. The parser analyzes this data stream and converts it into usable structured information on the basis of the XML specification. Many big companies such as Sun, Microsoft, and IBM provide XML parsers. In this book we will use the xerces-j parser from the Apache project. You will find further information on the XML developer's page `xml.apache.org`. Originally, this parser was developed by IBM Alphaworks and named XML4J, but it is now available as open source software.

XML parsers can be divided into two classes: the event-based SAX parsers and the DOM parsers, which offer the entire XML tree as a data structure. Let us first consider the DOM-based parsers.

16.2.1 DOM-based parsers

This kind of parser reads an XML document. In this case an XML document is a simple series of Unicode characters extracted from a file or a network connection. The product of the parse operation is a data structure in the main memory of the computer. In case of a Java implementation, the tree consists of node objects that have references to their subtrees. The parser interface is rather simple. The `parse` method of a parser object processes the document that is identified through the given URL. The `getDocument` method returns the data structure in the form of a DOM Document class.

```
parser.parse(url);
doc = parser.getDocument();
```

Figure 16.1 illustrates the process, executed through the two method calls.

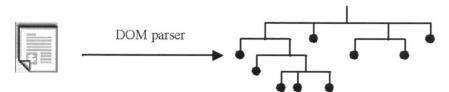

Figure 16.1: A DOM parser converts an XML file into a corresponding data structure.

As the data structure of each part in the document is immediately addressable, this is the more powerful of the two variants. The considerable need for storage is unfavorable in comparison with the SAX alternative. Our DOM example simply prints the elements of a parsed XML document recursively. This is not particularly useful but shows the different classes and methods of the DOM API. In order to demonstrate the handling of the element attributes, we use an XML file containing elements and attributes. This example describes an offer of our Books Online store.

```
<?xml version='1.0'?>
<offer xmlns:space="http://www.scheme.org/space">
  <store url="http://www.b-o.de" language="de">Books Online</store>
  <book>
    <isbn>3446133631</isbn>
    <space:title>The name of the rose</space:title>
    <price currency="DM">58.0</price>
  </book>
</offer>
```

The example program consists of the class Dom only. The parser is instanced in the `main` method and, as already explained, the parse operation is started and the document retrieved with the `getDocument` method. Then the `print` method is called. A node object and a character string are enclosed as parameters. Node is the base interface for all XML components. In the `print` method different kinds of information are printed according to the kind of the node that is dealt with. If it is a text node, its text is simply retrieved and printed using the method `getNode` Value. It is more difficult to handle elements. First, the name of the element is obtained by means of the method `getNodeName`. The element node contains a list of attribute name-value pairs as well as all subordinate nodes. This information can be obtained via the interfaces `NamedNodeMap` and `NodeList`. Similarly to arrays, these lists have to be traversed using the `item` and `getLength` methods. The subordinate nodes are fed into a recursive call to `print`. Attributes are also node objects. Their names and values are printed out in a simple `for` loop, since they are arranged in a flat structure directly below their element. All remaining DOM types such as entities, document types, and so on are not explained in this example, as they are seldom used and their application is not too relevant.

```java
import org.w3c.dom.Document;
import org.w3c.dom.Node;
import org.w3c.dom.NodeList;
import org.w3c.dom.NamedNodeMap;
import org.apache.xerces.parsers.DOMParser;
import org.xml.sax.SAXException;

public class Dom {

    public static void print(Node node, String indent) {
        System.out.print(indent);
        switch (node.getNodeType()) {
            case Node.ELEMENT_NODE: {
                System.out.print("ELEMENT_NODE: (" +
                    node.getNamespaceURI() + ")" + node.getNodeName());
                NamedNodeMap attlist = node.getAttributes();
                if (attlist != null)
                    for (int i=0; i<attlist.getLength(); i++) {
                        Node att = attlist.item(i);
                        System.out.print(" " + att.getNodeName()
                                    + "=" + att.getNodeValue());
                    }
                System.out.println();
                NodeList c = node.getChildNodes();
                if (c != null)
                    for (int i=0; i<c.getLength(); i++)
                        print(c.item(i), indent + "   ");
                break;
            }
            case Node.TEXT_NODE: {
                System.out.println("TEXT_NODE: " + node.getNodeValue());
            }
        }
    }

    public static void main(String[] arg) {
        DOMParser parser = new DOMParser();
        try {
            parser.parse(arg[0]);
            Document doc = parser.getDocument();
            Dom.print(doc.getDocumentElement(), "");
        }
        catch(java.io.IOException e) {
            System.out.println("Error in reading file: " + e);
        }
        catch(SAXException e) {
            System.out.println("Error in parsing file: " + e);
        }
    }
}
```

In DOM, the oldest version (Level 1) is different from the new version (Level 2), as DOM Level 2 supports namespaces. Interfaces are augmented with other methods, such as getNamespaceURI. As you can observe in the program output, the name of the node is given with the prefix and the corresponding namespace URL. Since only new methods are added and none removed from the interfaces, the transfer from Level 1 to Level 2 is not a problem.

When starting a DOM example on the XML file, you get the following output:

```
C:\book\example\xml\parser\dom\parse> java Dom XMLSearchAtt.xml

ELEMENT_NODE: (null)offer xmlns:space=http://www.scheme.org/space
  TEXT_NODE:

  ELEMENT_NODE: (null)store language=de url=http://www.b-o.de
    TEXT_NODE: Books Online
  TEXT_NODE:

  ELEMENT_NODE: (null)book
    TEXT_NODE:

    ELEMENT_NODE: (null)isbn
      TEXT_NODE: 3446133631
    TEXT_NODE:

    ELEMENT_NODE: (http://www.scheme.org/space)space:title
      TEXT_NODE: The Name of the Rose
    TEXT_NODE:

    ELEMENT_NODE: (null)price currency=DM
      TEXT_NODE: 58.0
    TEXT_NODE:

  TEXT_NODE:
```

Notice that, on the one hand, each text is packed again into a text node and is not directly available in the element. On the other hand, a text node with blank characters and a line break appears between the elements, for instance between offer and store. Actually, these characters should be ignored. Even in validation they are not regarded as illegal text elements. Therefore, you should pay attention to the addressing of sub-ordered nodes, since the first genuine element has the index 1 and not 0. To be sure, you should check the node type again.

If all blank characters are deleted in the XML file and all are written in a single line, the text elements are no longer inserted.

```
C:\book\example\xml\parser\dom\parse> java Dom XMLSearchAtt2.xml

ELEMENT_NODE: (null)offer xmlns:space=http://www.schema.org/space
  ELEMENT_NODE: (null)store language=de url=http://www.b-o.de
    TEXT_NODE: Books Online
```

```
ELEMENT_NODE: (null)book
  ELEMENT_NODE: (null)isbn
    TEXT_NODE: 3446133631
  ELEMENT_NODE: (http://www.schema.org/space)space:title
    TEXT_NODE: The name of the rose
  ELEMENT_NODE: (null)title
    TEXT_NODE: The Name of the rose
  ELEMENT_NODE: (null)price currency=DM
    TEXT_NODE: 58.0
```

16.2.2 SAX-based parser

SAX stands for Simple API for XML and is a de facto standard, developed by David Megginson. The SAX parsers communicate parsing events to the user, e.g. the beginning and the end of an element. The interface of a Java implementation works as follows: As with the DOM parser, the operation starts with the parse method. However, before the parsing is started, the handler object that will receive the events must be registered with the parser. This handler extends the `DefaultHandler` class containing the corresponding method stubs for all events that have to be overridden with a custom implementation. Instead of working with the complete data structure, the programmer has to establish what to do in the implementation of the methods, when a particular element is parsed.

```
parser.setContentHandler(handler);
parser.parse(url);
```

Figure 16.2 visualizes this operation again.

Figure 16.2: A SAX parser queries the application about events during the parser operation.

As the parser transfers the parsed object to the handler and immediately discards it after the call, this kind of parse requires less memory. The following SAX program example shows how an XML file can be converted to HTML. The class `MyHandler` extends the `DefaultHandler` class. As before, `DefaultHandler` offers standard implementations for all handler interfaces and is the base class for all actual handlers. The methods of the events that have to be begun are overridden in the custom handler class. At the beginning and end of the document we print the <HTML> and <BODY> tags. Character strings are printed without further coding. This is a name element, so it is printed in bold.

```
import org.xml.sax.helpers.DefaultHandler;
import org.xml.sax.Attributes;

public class MyHandler extends DefaultHandler {

    public void startDocument() {
        System.out.println("<HTML><BODY>");
    }

    public void endDocument() {
        System.out.println("</BODY></HTML>");
    }

    public void startElement(String uri, String name,
                             String qName, Attributes att) {
        if (name.equals("title") && (uri != null&&
            uri.equals("http://www.scheme.org/space"))
            System.out.println("<B>");
    }

    public void endElement(String uri, String name, String qName) {
        if (name.equals("title") && (uri != null&
            uri.equals("http://www.schema.org/space"))
            System.out.println("</B>");
    }

    public void characters (char c[], int s, int l) {
        for (int i=0; i<l; i++)
            System.out.print(c[s+i]);
        System.out.println("<BR>");
    }
}
```

The Sax class supplies the file which has to be parsed and starts the operation. The parser class and a handler class are instanced and the handler is registered with the parser.

```
import java.io.*;
import org.apache.xerces.parsers.SAXParser;
import org.xml.sax.SAXException;

public class Sax {

    public static void main(String[] args) {
        SAXParser parser = new SAXParser();
        MyHandler handler = new MyHandler();
        parser.setContentHandler(handler);

        try {
            parser.parse(args[0]);
        }
        catch(IOException e) {
            System.out.println("Error when reading file:" + e);
```

```
        }
        catch(SAXException e) {
            System.out.println("Error when parsing file: " + e);
        }
    }
}
```

Finally, we have to start the parse operation. This happens in the example with

```
java Sax XMLSearch.xml > test.html
```

You can see the result in the Web browser or in Fig. 16.3.

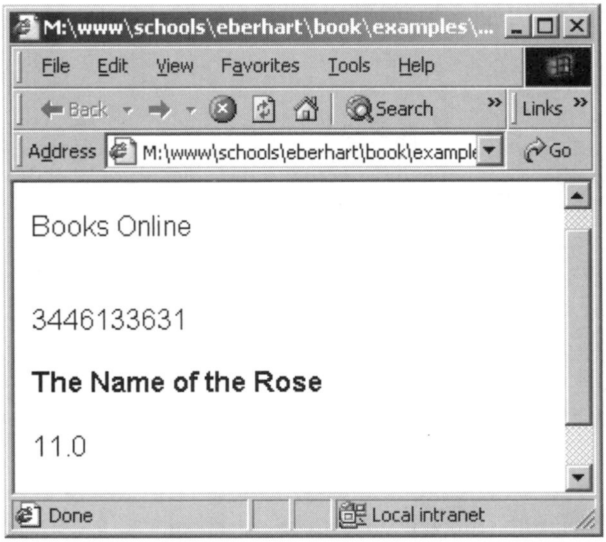

Figure 16.3: The file `test.html` generated with the SAX program in Internet Explorer.

If an error occurs while parsing the file, a SAXException is generated both in the SAX and in the DOM variants. If, for instance, $</name>$ is left out in the name element, both programs generate this error message:

```
Error in parsing file: "</name>" expected.
```

The original API was also revised in SAX for better support of namespaces. Since here, in comparison with DOM, the existing method signatures also changed, new classes and interfaces are partly defined. The previous versions are deprecated.

16.3 Validators

In the previous section we showed the DOM and SAX parsers of the `xerces-j` package which check if the XML file is well formed. These parsers can also control the validity of the document regarding the given DTDs. Even some parts of the XML schema recommendation are supported.

With the `sax.SAX2Count` tool you can call the SAX parser of the `xerces-j` package without writing your own program. In order to activate the validation of the document, simply include the option `-v`.

```
java sax.SAX2Count -v file.xml
```

As far as validation from our own program is concerned, we limit our observation to the DOM variant. In order to call the functionality of the validation option shown above, you need the following program line:

```
parser.setFeature("http://xml.org/sax/features/validation", true);
```

In addition to validation, you can insert further options and parameters which influence the operation of the parameter. In order to obtain all DTD or XML schema violations, we need to use a SAX handler. The class `MyHandler` implements the methods that are called in case of error and simply re-throw the exception.

```java
import org.w3c.dom.Document;
import org.apache.xerces.parsers.DOMParser;
import org.xml.sax.SAXException;
import org.xml.sax.SAXParseException;
import org.xml.sax.helpers.DefaultHandler;

public class DomValidate {

    public static void main(String[] arg) {
        DOMParser parser = new DOMParser();
        MyHandler handler = new MyHandler();
        parser.setErrorHandler(handler);

        try {
            parser.setFeature(
                "http://xml.org/sax/features/validation", true);
            parser.parse(arg[0]);
            Document doc = parser.getDocument();
        }
```

```
        catch(Exception e) {
            System.out.println("Error in reading file: " + e);
        }
    }
}

class MyHandler extends DefaultHandler {

    public void error(SAXParseException e) throws SAXParseException {
        throw e;
    }

    public void fatalError(SAXParseException e)
                throws SAXParseException {
        throw e;
    }
}
```

If, for instance, a second currency element is added, the parser accepts it because the document is still well formed. However, the validation process reports this:

```
C:\xml>java DomValidate Validate.xml
Error in the parsing of the file: Element "<price>" is not valid because
it does not follow the rule, "(amount,currency)".
```

16.4 Creation and serialization of documents

Up until now we have dealt with two forms of XML documents: on the one hand the serialized form, for instance a file, and on the other a DOM tree structure. Figure 16.1 on page 333 shows the parse operation, in which the document is converted from the serialized form into the tree structure. The opposite operation, creating a file from a data structure contained in memory, is called serialization.

The easiest process is to create an XML document with a text editor. If you use a general purpose editor, you need to ensure that the XML formatting rules are obeyed. A special XML editor will, for example, automatically replace a typed &-character with &. This difference also applies to creating an XML document from a program. Using println applications, you can create XML documents and write them to a file or any output stream. This technique is also used in our sample programs.

```
String title = ...;
...
out.println("<title>" + title + "</title>");
```

The following example shows the most elegant variant. As already mentioned, by means of DOM, tree structures can not only be read, but also modified. The program therefore initially uses the `getDOMImplementation` method of the xerces DOM implementation. On the `DOMImplementation` object just obtained, you can call the factory methods to create new documents, elements, attributes, and text nodes. By means of `appendChild` the nodes can be added to the tree.

```java
import java.io.IOException;

import org.w3c.dom.Document;
import org.w3c.dom.Element;
import org.w3c.dom.Text;
import org.w3c.dom.DOMImplementation;
import org.w3c.dom.DocumentType;

import org.apache.xerces.dom.DOMImplementationImpl;

import org.apache.xml.serialize.XMLSerializer;
import org.apache.xml.serialize.OutputFormat;

public class Create {

    public static void main(String[] args) throws IOException {

        DOMImplementation impl =
                DOMImplementationImpl.getDOMImplementation();
        DocumentType type = impl.createDocumentType("test", null, null);
        Document doc = impl.createDocument(null, "test", type);
        Element root = doc.createElement("root");

        Element child = doc.createElement("elem");
        root.appendChild(child);
        child.setAttribute("att", "att-value");

        Text text = doc.createTextNode("Text with & characters");
        child.appendChild(text);

        OutputFormat format = new OutputFormat(doc);
        XMLSerializer serializer = new XMLSerializer(System.out, format);
        serializer.serialize(root);
    }
}
```

In order to serialize the DOM tree we use an `XMLSerializer` object. As you can see, the text node contains a &-character. The serializer undertakes the conversion into the corresponding Entity reference and also prints the XML header as well as the start and end tags:

```
C:\book\examples\xml\parser\dom\create>java Create
<?xml version="1.0" encoding="UTF-8"?>
<root><elem att="att-value">Text with &amp; characters</elem></root>
```

16.5 XSLT processors

The xalan XSLT processor is another useful tool. The processor can be started from the command line as follows. You should ensure that both the xalan library and an XML parser are available as xerces in the CLASSPATH. In our experience, xalan.jar should also be cited before the XML parser used.

```
set CLASSPATH=C:\book\lib\xalan.jar;C:\book\lib\xerces.jar;.
java org.apache.xalan.xslt.Process -IN f.xml -XSL f.xsl -OUT out.xml
```

As previously observed in Section eXtensible Stylesheet Language for Transformations (XSLT) on page 315, in an XSLT transformation we use XML and XSL streams as input and an XML data stream as output. Both are given on the corresponding command line options. This program can be used as a rudimentary tool in the creation of XSL stylesheets. The respective output can be examined with any text editor and based on the analysis of the output, the XSL file can be corrected accordingly.

The processor can also be started from a program. Obviously, this option is useful when the processor is used in a servlet. This way the transformation is transferred from the browser to the server. This makes sense, for instance, when browsers without any XSL support or with varying XSL implementations must be supported. The servlet can supply all browsers with XHTML in this case.

```
import java.io.*;
import javax.servlet.*;
import javax.servlet.http.*;

import org.apache.trax.Processor;
import org.apache.trax.Transformer;
import org.apache.trax.Templates;
import org.apache.trax.Result;

import org.xml.sax.InputSource;
import org.xml.sax.SAXException;

public class XSLTServlet extends HttpServlet {

    public void doGet(HttpServletRequest request,
                    HttpServletResponse response)
              throws IOException, ServletException {
        PrintWriter out = response.getWriter();
        try {
            response.setContentType("text/html");
            Processor processor = Processor.newInstance("xslt");
            Templates templates = processor.process(
                new InputSource("http://localhost:8080/test.xsl"));
            Transformer transformer = templates.newTransformer();
            transformer.transform(
                new InputSource("http://localhost:8080/test.xml"),
```

```
                        new Result(out));
          }
          catch(Exception e) {
              throw new ServletException(e.toString());
          }
       }
    }
```

In the first half of the `try` block the processor is instanced and the stylesheet loaded. The actual transformation is started with the `transform` method. Here we use the `InputSource` class that allows us to read from both a URL and an `InputStream` or a `Reader` object. The result of the transformation is immediately passed to the client via the `PrintWriter` object. Figure 16.4 shows the output of the servlet.

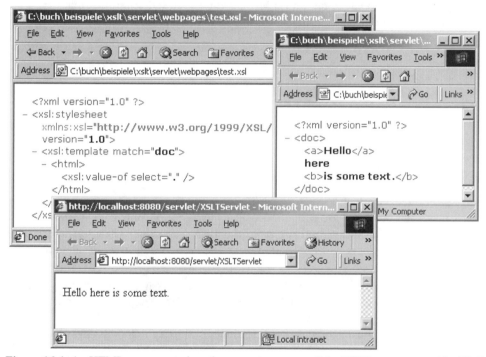

Figure 16.4: An HTML page created on the server by means of the XSLT processor and its XML and XSL source documents.

16.6 XSQL: dynamic Web pages with SQL and XSL only

The following list describes a typical program sequence in a Web application:

1.   reading the form parameters;
2.   starting a select enquiry with these parameters;
3.   conversion of the result into HTML.

The XSQL solution developed with Oracle is to execute this typical task without using any programming. In this paragraph we show how a simpler and slightly modified XSQL solution is implemented by means of the xerces-j parser and the xalan XSLT processor.

How does XSQL work? As in a JSP page, in which the server-side parts to be executed are specially marked and embedded in HTML, in XSQL the SQL enquiries that have to be executed are inserted in a query element within an existing XML document.

```
<?xml version="1.0"?>
<report>
    Projects:
    <query driver="sun.jdbc.odbc.JdbcOdbcDriver"
           url="jdbc:odbc:project"
           user=""
           password="">
        select * from project where budget >= {@budget}
    </query>
</report>
```

Further required information such as the JDBC driver class, the database URL, and the user's name and password are contained in attributes. Our example deals with the access project database, already familiar from the JDBC chapter. The character string {@budget} is replaced with the value of the corresponding form parameter by our XSQL engine.

The query element is replaced with the result table, in which the table structure is converted into a corresponding XML structure. Figure 16.5 explains this process. The resulting XML document can always be transformed by XSLT into an XHTML or WML document. At this point the three aspects mentioned at the beginning become clear.

Figure 16.5: The XSQL file after the process carried out with the XSQL engine.

So far we have dealt with the XSQL operation. The implementation is carried out using a servlet and a SAX handler. The servlet executes the transformation and coordination of the whole process, while a SAX handler carries out the JDBC part and replaces the form paramenters. To begin with, let us consider the servlet.

```java
import java.io.*;
import javax.servlet.*;
import javax.servlet.http.*;

import org.apache.trax.Processor;
import org.apache.trax.Transformer;
import org.apache.trax.Templates;
import org.apache.trax.Result;

import org.xml.sax.InputSource;
import org.xml.sax.SAXException;

import org.apache.xerces.parsers.SAXParser;

public class Xsql extends HttpServlet {

    public void doGet(HttpServletRequest request,
```

```
                        HttpServletResponse response)
                 throws IOException, ServletException {
        PrintWriter out = response.getWriter();
        String xsql = request.getParameter("xsql");
        String xsl = request.getParameter("xsl");

        try {
            SAXParser parser = new SAXParser();
            MyHandler handler = new MyHandler();
            handler.request = request;
            parser.setContentHandler(handler);
            parser.parse(xsql);

            if ((xsl == null|| (xsl.length() == 0)) {
                response.setContentType("text/xml");
                out.println("<?xml version='1.0'?>");
                out.println(handler.res);
            }
```

First, the required parameters are read, and the SAX parser and handler are instanced and connected with each other. The request object is provided for the handler in order to perform the replacing of the paramaters. The XSQL file, along with the SQL query, can be obtained after parsing from the string variable `handler.res`. You can also submit a DOM document and transfer it to the XSLT processor. This would certainly be a more efficient variant but it does not yet work reliably in the xalan version. If no stylesheet is given the XML string is returned directly to the client.

```
            else {
                response.setContentType("text/html");
                Processor processor = Processor.newInstance("xslt");
                Templates templates = processor.process(
                    new InputSource(xsl));
                Transformer transformer = templates.newTransformer();
                transformer.transform(
                    new InputSource(new StringReader(handler.res)),
                    new Result(out));
            }
        }
        catch(Exception e) {
            throw new ServletException(e.toString());
        }
    }
}
```

Otherwise let us assume that the document created is HTML. The conversion is started and the result written in the `out` `PrintWriter` object.

First, some variables are declared in the SAX handler. `res` and `request` are used to communicate with the servlet and are therefore declared as public. The variable `res` is particularly important, since the document is generated piece by piece with the query result. The five private variables save the connection information for the database. In this case `runQuery` is a flag that indicates whether the parser is currently working inside of a query element.

```java
import org.xml.sax.SAXException;
import org.xml.sax.helpers.DefaultHandler;
import org.xml.sax.Attributes;

import java.sql.*;

public class MyHandler extends DefaultHandler {

    public String res = "";
    public javax.servlet.http.HttpServletRequest request;

    private String driver;
    private String url;
    private String user;
    private String password;
    private boolean runQuery = false;

    public void startElement(String uri, String name,
                             String qName, Attributes att) {
        if (!name.equals("query")) {
            res = res + "<" + name;
            for (int i=0; i<att.getLength(); i++) {
                res = res + " " + att.getLocalName(i) + "='" +
                                 att.getValue(i) + "'";
            }
            res = res + ">";
        }
        else {
            runQuery = true;
            driver = att.getValue(uri, "driver");
            url = att.getValue(uri, "url");
            user = att.getValue(uri, "user");
            password = att.getValue(uri, "password");
        }
    }
}
```

In the start tag we specify whether we are dealing with a query. If so, the connection information is read. Otherwise the element is copied into the variable `res`. In the same way we proceed with the end tags and reset the `runQuery` flag or copy the end tag.

```java
public void endElement(String uri, String name, String qName) {
    if (!name.equals("query"))
        res = res + "</" + name + ">";
    else
```

```
        runQuery = false;
    }

public void characters (char c[], int s, int l) throws SAXException {
    String str = "";
    for (int i=0; i<l; i++)
        str = str + c[s+i];

    while (true) {
        int start = str.indexOf("{@");
        if (start == -1)
            break;
        int stop = str.indexOf("}", start);
        if (stop == -1)
            break;

        String var = str.substring(start+2, stop);
        str = str.substring(0, start) + request.getParameter(var) +
              str.substring(stop+1, str.length());
    }
```

First, the texts are saved in the `str` string. We carry out some string operations which perform the parameter replacing. All `{@parname}` character strings are replaced with the corresponding entries in the HTTP Request.

```
    if (runQuery) {
        try {
            Class.forName(driver);
            Connection con = java.sql.DriverManager.getConnection(
                                   url, user, password);
            Statement stmt = con.createStatement();
            ResultSet rs = stmt.executeQuery(str);

            ResultSetMetaData metadata = rs.getMetaData();
            int fields = metadata.getColumnCount();
            String[] names = new String[fields];
            int[] types = new int[fields];
            for (int i=0; i<names.length; i++) {
                names[i] = metadata.getColumnName(i+1);
                types[i] = metadata.getColumnType(i+1);
            }

            res = res + "<ROWSET>\n";
            while (rs.next()) {
                res = res + "<ROW>\n";
                for (int i=0; i<fields; i++) {
                    res = res + "<" + names[i] + ">";
                    switch(types[i]) {
                        case java.sql.Types.INTEGER:
                            res = res + rs.getInt(names[i]);
                            break;
                        case java.sql.Types.CHAR:
```

```
                                    case java.sql.Types.VARCHAR:
                                        res = res + rs.getString(names[i]);
                                        break;
                                    case java.sql.Types.DOUBLE:
                                        res = res + rs.getDouble(names[i]);
                                        break;
                                    default:
                                        System.out.println("unknown type");
                                }
                                res = res + "</" + names[i] + ">\n";
                            }
                            res = res + "</ROW>\n";
                        }
                        res = res + "</ROWSET>\n";
                    }
                    catch(Exception e) {
                        throw new SAXException(e.toString());
                    }
                }
                else {
                    res = res + str;
                }
            }
        }
```

The last part of the SAX handler appears the most complex. It begins by checking if a query is currently being processed. If not, the text is simply copied into the last line. Otherwise the connection to the database is opened and the query started. The problem in the conversion of the table into XML is retrieving the names and types of table columns from the JDBC metadata. This is not particularly difficult but requires a considerably long program text. In this case, you will notice that only four SQL types are supplied. However, you can insert the corresponding code easily. Moreover, let us assume that in the database no XML additional characters like <, >, &, or characters which require a particular coding are saved. This means, as explained in the section on the Creation and serialization of documents on page 340, that we have to access the XML libraries to create documents. Apart from that, the XSQL engine is able to work and can be applied on any table. Obviously, Join queries can also be processed.

Figures 16.6 and 16.7 illustrate our XSQL engine in action. In the form you can choose from three different output styles (tables, text, and XML) and also feed in the smallest budget for the SQL query.

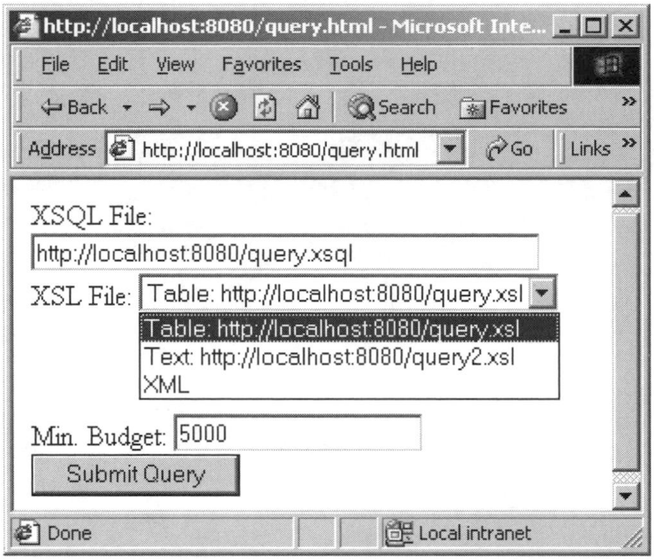

Figure 16.6: The XSQL engine requires the following inputs: the XSQL file, the utilizable stylesheet parameter, and other parameters, referenced in the XSQL file.

Figure 16.7 shows the output as a table. The stylesheet converts the ROW elements into TR and id, name and budget elements in TD, in order to create the table. The graphics come from the file system of the Web server and follow the name convention projectid.gif. The following XSL rule creates the image tag with a reference to the corresponding project image:

```
<xsl:template match="id">
  <td>
    <xsl:variable name="pic" select="." />
    <img src="/images/{concat($pic,'.gif')}" />
  </td>
</xsl:template>
```

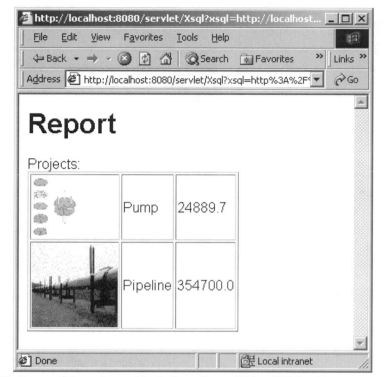

Figure 16.7: Output of the projects with a budget of over 5000 as HTML tables.

16.7 XML support in Forté for Java

The Internet module for Forte4J also contains an XML component. Figure 16.8 illustrates the corresponding dialog which offers some templates to the developer in order to create XML documents, DTDs, and SAX handler classes. These templates and the syntax-controlled editor simplify the editing of the document considerably and the automatically generated program stubs save quite a bit of search effort in the JavaDoc documentation of the `org.xml.sax` and related Java packages.

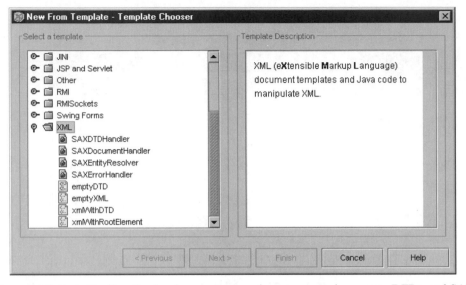

Figure 16.8: Forte4J offers the developer some templates to create documents, DTDs, and SAX handler classes.

16.8 Apache SOAP

The Apache SOAP implementation consists of two components in principle. On the one hand, the jar library `soap.jar` contains the necessary classes for SOAP clients and servers implemented in Java. On the other hand, the RPC Router Servlet is supplied; it passes on the SOAP enquiry to the implementation. This servlet can be installed on the Tomcat server by carrying out two limited modifications to the configuration files. Figure 16.9 illustrates how Web services can be registered with the RPC Router. After these operations are carried out, clients and server can communicate.

Figure 16.9: Using the administration tool of the Apache SOAP implementation, the Web services can be registered in the RPC Router.

16.9 Other tools

With the rapid development of XML applications and growing technologies, a host of XML tools are available, which usually can be downloaded free from the Internet. The following Web pages supply very good sources and starting points for the search :

- `http://xml.apache.org`
- `http://www.alphaworks.ibm.com`
- `http://msdn.microsoft.com/xml/general/xmltools.asp`
- `http://java.sun.com/xml/`

These Web pages include tools which support graphically the creation of documents, DTDs, and schemas. Many programs are useful for creating stylesheets. For instance, the user can step through the conversion process of an XML document with a stylesheet, in order to find errors in the XSL rules.

Chapter 17

The sample application with XML

How can XML be put to use in our online bookshop? From the point of view of the shop's internal information system, hardly anything else is required: the Web site is integrated directly into the central database, each customer order is carried out automatically, and price changes and new books appear on the Web site immediately. For customers, however, the automation is not quite so advanced. So what else can be done to expand this?

Today there are several dozen large online bookshops. Of course, comparing prices among these is child's play compared to comparing prices in real shops. All you have to do is log in to each shop and find the prices of the books you are looking for. Nevertheless, since all the information is already available electronically, it would be good to be able *compare it automatically* and determine which provider is offering the best price.

In this chapter we will show the development of such a price comparison agent. First we will explain the architecture, with the necessary components for customers and businesses, as well as the organizational requirements. Then follows the implementation using the XML parser from IBM.

17.1 Architecture

In order to turn the vision of a fast, worldwide price comparison into reality, there are, alongside the technical hurdles, primarily political hurdles to be cleared. It would of course make no sense if each provider only developed their own book description DTD. It would indeed be very simple to parse the different results, but a comparison of the documents would still be difficult. Some documents, for example, might use `<price>`, `<amount>`, and `<currency>`, whereas others might perhaps only use `<special-offer>`, without the divisions into the amount and the currency.

A standard book offer DTD, drawn up by an international committee, is therefore required. An example could be DIN-norms or, in our particular case, the internationally recognized ISBNs. At the time of writing this book, DTDs have been worked out for all possible sectors of industry. You can find information on these on the Internet at `http:/` `/www.oasis-open.org` or `http://www.openapplications.org`. It remains to be seen whether or how quickly such standards will be adopted. Will the interests of the different companies lead this initiative up a blind alley, or will the enormous potential of the global exchange of information at last inspire both customers and the industry? What is certain, however, is that similar models on the company level will develop quickly. The ACM information service reports that 45–50 percent of all information technology managers are currently planning XML projects.

17.1.1 The book offer DTD

The following DTD is a simple description of an offer for a book. An offer contains information about the shop that is providing the book, and about the book itself. The name and the URL of the shop are saved. You could also imagine that other information such as fees or delivery options are given. In principle, however, this does not change the solution represented in any way, and we will concentrate on this minimal amount of information.

The book is described with a title, ISBN, and price. This can be given in any currency. It is the job of the search program to convert offers in different currencies into the user's preferred currency.

The relevant DTD is relatively simple:

```
<!ELEMENT offer (store, book)>

<!ELEMENT store (name, url)>
    <!ELEMENT name   (#PCDATA)>
    <!ELEMENT url    (#PCDATA)>

<!ELEMENT book (isbn, title, price)>
    <!ELEMENT isbn  (#PCDATA)>
    <!ELEMENT title (#PCDATA)>
    <!ELEMENT price (amount, currency)>
        <!ELEMENT amount   (#PCDATA)>
        <!ELEMENT currency (#PCDATA)>
```

Figure 17.2 shows a document which is valid with regard to this DTD.

17.1.2 The role of the DTD in the example

For our example we will assume that the DTD in the previous section is a widespread standard. A modification of the DTD only requires minimal changes in the programs shown in the following, insofar as these changes are covered naturally by the structure of the database. Say, for example, the weight of a book is given. This is only possible if the corresponding information is present in the database. If a field is defined as optional, a small change would need to be made in the agent. Let us deal with the bookshop first.

17.2 The XML search interface of Books Online

The architecture of the search interface based on HTML functions as follows: The servlet sends an SQL query to the database with the attributes specified by the customer. This returns a book table in the form of a Java `ResultSet` object. One book object is instantiated for each line of this table. In the `searchTableHeader` and `toHTMLSearchTableRow` methods, the book object encapsulates the output of a book as a line in an HTML table, and the generation of the title line of a search result.

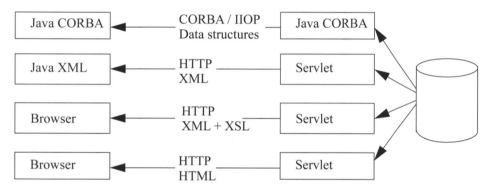

Figure 17.1: A comparison of different approaches for transferring dynamically generated data.

If the customer wants the search result in XML instead of HTML, the available structure can be reused. Figure 17.1 shows the common properties of the HTML and XML approaches. XML is flexible and, like CORBA, can be used for the automatic processing of the transferred data and, like HTML, for presenting the data to the user. The CORBA-based solution from Section 11.7 on page 230 is also included.

A further search servlet is introduced: `XMLSearch`. This servlet is identical to the search servlet except for a few small details. The HTML search works principally with titles and fragments of titles, since the user is not looking for a specific book. The XML search is different: the user probably already has chosen the book on other Web sites and is just querying the price. The XML search returns one or no book descriptions, while the HTML search can contain any number of books. The name of the servlet parameter was therefore changed from search to ISBN, and the SQL query only has the ISBN clause in the where part:

```
String isbn = request.getParameter("isbn");
pstmt = con.prepareStatement("select * from book where isbn = ?");
pstmt.setString(1, isbn);
```

Of course the *content type* is set to XML:

```
response.setContentType("text/xml");
```

The while loop can be replaced with an if query, as the ISBN is the primary key of the book table and ensures that there is a maximum of one book in the result. Just like the output of a book as a line of an HTML table, the book object capsulates the output of a book in XML format in the toXML and xmlHeader methods, concurring with the DTD described. The xmlHeader method knows where the book offer DTD is located. This would probably be on the Web server of one of the standardization organizations. In our scenario, the DTD is loaded either from the local Web server or from the Web site of this book:

```
public static String xmlHeader() {
    return
        "<?xml version='1.0'?>" +
        "<!DOCTYPE offer SYSTEM " +
            "'http://localhost/xml/offer.dtd'" +
            //"'http://www.i-u.de/schools/eberhart/book/offer.dtd'" +
        ">";
}
```

The XML output of the book object adapts itself to the DTD. The local variables are simply entered in the corresponding gaps:

```
public String toXML() {
    return
        "<offer>" +
        "  <store>" +
        "    <name>Books Online</name>" +
        "    <url>http://www.books-online.com</url>" +
        "  </store>" +
        "  <book>" +
        "    <isbn>" + isbn + "</isbn>" +
        "    <title>" + title + "</title>" +
        "    <price>" +
        "      <amount>" + price + "</amount>" +
        "      <currency>GBP</currency>" +
        "    </price>" +
        "  </book>" +
        "</offer>";
}
```

The rest of the process in the XMLSearch servlet is similar to the HTML search. The query is carried out, the result is loaded into a book object and issued as XML. If no book is found with the corresponding ISBN, an error element with a corresponding message is inserted instead of the offer element. From the violation of the DTD instructions and the lack of price, it is clear to the client that no book was found.

```
if (res.next()) {
    Book book = new Book();
    book.dbLoad(res);
    out.println(book.toXML());
}
else
    out.println("<error>No book found.</error>");
```

It is now time for the first test: If the servlet does not display a correct XML, Internet Explorer 5 must refuse to display the answer generated. If you call up `http://localhost/servlet/XMLSearch?isbn=3446133631` and the book wanted is in the database, the display should look like the one in Fig. 17.2.

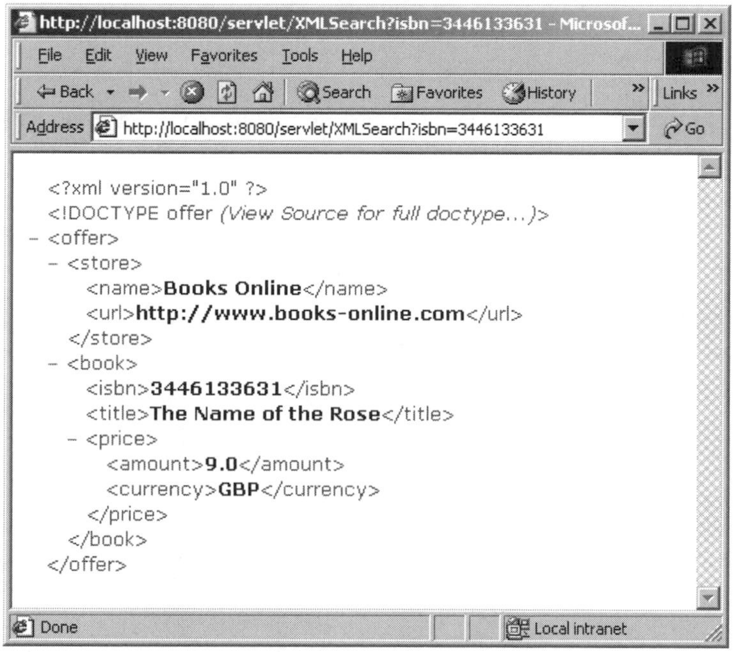

Figure 17.2: Representation of the XML book description, dynamically generated by the servlet in Internet Explorer 5.

It remains to be tested whether the document is also valid with regard to our DTD. In order to be able to invoke the validator of the xerces packages, the correct classpath must be set first. The required libraries are available on the Web site. The validation is activated using the −v option. We insert the URL, which is also given in the browser in Fig. 17.2, as the second parameter. It is not necessary to store the file specially. Like the browser, the sax. SAX2Count program starts an HTTP-GET query, activates a database query and receives the dynamic page.

```
set CLASSPATH=C:\book\lib\xercesj.jar;C:\book\lib\xercesSamples.jar;.

java sax.SAX2Count -v
       http://localhost:8080/servlet/XMLSearch?isbn=3446133631
```

The output should look something like this:

```
XMLSearch?isbn=3446133631: 230 ms
```

Of course this file can be saved locally using the "Save As..." menu item. You can then modify this file with an editor and intentionally build in an error. If, for example, the </ currency> Tag is omitted and the document is transferred in a syntactically incorrect condition, you will receive the following error message:

```
Fatal Error at (file file:/C:/xml/XMLSearch.xml, line 14, char 12): "</
currency>" expected.
```

If a second currency element is inserted in the price element, this message will appear:

```
Error at (file file:/C:/xml/XMLSearch.xml, line 15, char 13): Element
"<price>" is not valid because it does not follow the rule,
"(amount,currency)".
XMLSearch.xml: 902 ms
```

A further error occurs if the DTD can not be read, for example, if the Web server has not been started or the URL can not be reached:

```
Exception in thread "main" java.net.ConnectException: Connection
refused: no further information
```

If none of these errors occurred with the XML search servlet, the work on the server side is completed. The Web page now has a fully functional XML search interface, which generates correct XML book offer documents which are valid with regard to the standard DTD.

17.3 The XML agent

What does the program that carries out the search look like now? Again, it can assume any form. You could imagine, for example, that the agent itself is implemented as a servlet installed on an Internet price comparison portal for books. We will write the agent as a simple Java application and concentrate on the essential part. It is easy, however, to read the parameter from an HTML form instead of the command line and to structure the output as a Web page. We have already looked at how to do this.

By using efficient class libraries like the xerces package, this seemingly complex task also is made simple. We assume that all search Web pages use the GET-method. Their URLs are coded according to the following pattern:

```
http://server/path/program?parametername=searched_isbn
```

The part on the left-hand side of the = sign remains constant, as long as nothing changes on the book interface. The right-hand part is the ISBN of the book being searched for.

17.3.1 An XML directory service

The question arises as to how our agent knows which bookshops should be searched. You could imagine that an information service such as Yahoo! codes such information in XML and provides it in different categories. Figure 17.3 shows the interaction of the providers, the agent, and the directory service. The category of online book providers with an XML search interface might look like this:

```xml
<?xml version='1.0'?>
<!DOCTYPE bookvendorlist SYSTEM 'bookvendorlist.dtd'>
<bookvendorlist>
    <bookvendor>
        <url>http://www.amazon.de</url>
        <isbnsearch>http://www3.amazon.de/search.cgi?id=</isbnsearch>
    </bookvendor>
    <bookvendor>
        <url>http://www.bol.de</url>
        <isbnsearch>http://suche.bol.de/exec/find.asp?isbn=</isbnsearch>
    </bookvendor>
    <bookvendor>
        <url>http://www.barnesandnoble.com</url>
        <isbnsearch>http://www.barnesandnoble.com/ex/s.dll?s=</isbnsearch>
    </bookvendor>
</bookvendorlist>
```

Before the document is parsed, you should ensure that it is valid. This simplifies further programming, as you can be sure that certain elements are available in a definite structure. The DTD of such a category is very simple. The bookvendorlist has several bookvendor elements, which again contain the URL of the shop as well as the address of the search engine and their search parameters (isbnsearch).

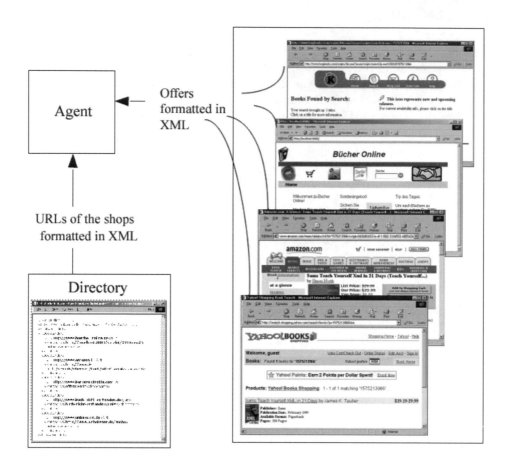

Figure 17.3: Architecture of the agent. The directory service delivers the addresses of the online shops from which offers can be requested. The whole communication runs over HTTP / XML.

```
<!ELEMENT bookvendorlist (bookvendor+)>
    <!ELEMENT bookvendor (url, isbnsearch)>
        <!ELEMENT url (#PCDATA)>
        <!ELEMENT isbnsearch (#PCDATA)>
```

We do not want to show the implementation of such a service. This could, however, be programmed in a similar way to the XML search engine, building on a bookshop database.

17.3.2 Useful classes for developing the agent

Programming the agent is a complex job. We will therefore proceed step by step and make the work easier with some useful helper classes. The use of DTDs is a great help when programming with the DOM interface. This becomes clear in Section 17.3.3 on page 365. However, you do have to take care of the validation. It would be preferable to have to give only one URL and to receive a node object, if no error occurs. Error sources in this case can be violations of the DTD, an incorrect URL, or a Web server that cannot be reached. This functionality is implemented by the following class.

```java
import org.apache.xerces.parsers.DOMParser;
import org.w3c.dom.Node;
import org.xml.sax.SAXParseException;
import org.xml.sax.helpers.DefaultHandler;

public class Validator extends DOMParser {

    public Validator() {
        super();
        try {
            setFeature("http://xml.org/sax/features/validation", true);
        }
        catch(Exception e) {
            System.out.println("Error configuring the parser: " + e);
        }
        MyHandler handler = new MyHandler();
        this.setErrorHandler(handler);
    }

    public Node parseAndValidate(String url) {
        try {
            parse(url);
        }
        catch(Exception e) {
            System.out.println("Error during Validation: " + url);
            return null;
        }

        Node root = getDocument().getDocumentElement();
        return root;
    }

    public static void main(String[] args) {
        Validator v = new Validator();
        System.out.println(v.parseAndValidate(args[0]));
    }
}

class MyHandler extends DefaultHandler {

    public void error(SAXParseException e) throws SAXParseException {
```

```
            throw e;
        }

        public void fatalError(SAXParseException e) throws SAXParseException
    {
            throw e;
        }
    }
```

The `DOMParser` class is used, as already described in Section 16.3 on page 339. The `parseAndValidate` method intercepts all possible errors. If an error occurs, null is returned, otherwise the method sends the root element back. For the agent scenario you can save yourself an exact error analysis, because it is not the responsibility of the agent to eliminate errors in the XML text.

The following class makes "descending" a valid DOM tree easier. The book offer DTDs as well as the ISBN search engines. DTDs in shops have many fixed structures. For example, a price always has an amount and a currency. The `findChildElement` method enables you to go quickly from an element e.g. price, to its children: amount and currency.

```
import org.w3c.dom.Node;
import org.w3c.dom.NodeList;

public class Util {

    public static Node findChildElement(Node node, String name) {
        NodeList list = node.getChildNodes();
        for (int i=0; i<list.getLength(); i++)
            if (list.item(i).getNodeName().equals(name))
                return list.item(i);
        return null;
    }
}
```

The element and the names of the required sub-elements are submitted to the method. This is searched for using a simple loop on all sub-elements, until the string is found.

The implementation as a static method is not exactly in accordance with object-oriented programming; however, this is the simplest variant. This is because the DOM API does not contain any implementations, only interfaces. The elegant variant would be to extend nodes, in order to define the `findChildElement` method. In order to put this into effect, however, you would also have to extend the corresponding implementation in the `org.apache.xml.dom` package.

17.3.3 Wrapper classes for DOM trees

The DOM tree structure is easy to understand, but is not technically simple to handle. It is much simpler to deal with objects, which, like our book class, only define a few instance variables. This is exactly the approach of the wrapper classes. We encapsulate all the DTD and DOM details in a Java class and provide the rest of the program access to the values in the DOM tree via `getISBN`, `getTitle`, etc. We need wrapper classes for book offers and for the list of search interfaces.

```java
import org.w3c.dom.Node;
import org.w3c.dom.NodeList;

public class Offer implements Comparable {

    private Node node;

    public Offer(Node node) {
        this.node = node;
    }
```

For the same reasons as in the `Util` class, node is not extended, but instead the root of the DOM tree is saved in the respective object and initialized via the constructor.

```java
    public String getISBN() {
        Node book = Util.findChildElement(node, "book");
        Node isbn = Util.findChildElement(book, "isbn");
        return isbn.getFirstChild().getNodeValue();
    }
```

The ISBN is reached from the node root via the book element. As the information is located in a text node under book, the string is extracted using `getFirstChild().getNodeValue()`.

We know that the sequence of the calls to `findChildElement` corresponds exactly to the DTD. Since the invoking program guarantees that the trees are validated, it is not necessary to check whether `findChildElement` has perhaps returned null. The same is true for the following methods.

```java
    public float getPrice() {
        Node book = Util.findChildElement(node, "book");
        Node price = Util.findChildElement(book, "price");
        Node amount = Util.findChildElement(price, "amount");
        Node currency = Util.findChildElement(price, "currency");
        float p;
        try {
            p = Float.parseFloat(amount.getFirstChild().getNodeValue());
        }
        catch(NumberFormatException e) {
            p = Float.MAX_VALUE;
        }
```

```
        String c = currency.getFirstChild().getNodeValue();
        if (c.equals("USD")) p = p * (float)0.64;
        if (c.equals("FF")) p = p / (float)9.35;
        return Math.round(p * 100) / (float)100.0;
    }
```

With the price of the book it is more difficult to pick out the value. As with `getISBN`, we get the amount and the currency, for which we have to take a step further into the tree structure. The amount is parsed and, if it is given in another currency, is converted into pound sterling. The only other currencies supported are US dollars and French francs. Of course the exchange rate against the dollar varies in reality and might be queried again in XML format by a bank.

```
    public String getUrl() {
        Node store = Util.findChildElement(node, "store");
        Node url = Util.findChildElement(store, "url");
        return url.getFirstChild().getNodeValue();
    }

    public String getTitle() {
        Node book = Util.findChildElement(node, "book");
        Node title = Util.findChildElement(book, "title");
        return title.getFirstChild().getNodeValue();
    }

    public int compareTo(Object o) throws ClassCastException {
        if (o instanceof Offer) {
            float a = this.getPrice();
            float b = ((Offer)o).getPrice();
            if (a < b) return -1;
            if (a > b) return 1;
            return 0;
        }
        throw new ClassCastException();
    }
} // End of Class
```

GetUrl and `getTitle` work like `getISBN`. What is interesting, however, is the `compareTo` method. As the class implements the interface Comparable, it is possible to compare two offer objects with one another with regard to their price. This is the basis for the sort algorithm predefined in the Java class library. The agent therefore issues the offers obtained, sorted according to price.

The next class delivers all the HTTP search interfaces contained in a `bookvendorlist` document. As there can be more than one of these, all ISBN search elements are obtained from the document using `getElementsByTagName` and the URLs are saved in a vector.

```
import org.w3c.dom.Node;
import org.w3c.dom.Document;
import org.w3c.dom.NodeList;
import java.util.Vector;

public class BookVendorList {

    private Node node;

    public BookVendorList(Node node) {
        this.node = node;
    }

    public Vector getSearchUrls() {
        Document doc = node.getOwnerDocument();
        NodeList list = doc.getElementsByTagName("isbnsearch");
        Vector res = new Vector();
        for (int i=0; i<list.getLength(); i++)
            res.addElement(
                    list.item(i).getFirstChild().getNodeValue().trim());
        return res;
    }
}
```

17.3.4 The program code of the agent

Due to the classes introduced in the previous sections, the programming of the agent has become considerably simpler. Let's have a look at the individual steps.

```
import org.w3c.dom.Node;
import java.util.Vector;
import java.util.Collections;

public class Agent {

    public static void main(String[] args) {
        Validator v = new Validator();
        Node node = v.parseAndValidate("bookvendorlist.xml");
        BookVendorList list = new BookVendorList(node);
        Vector urls = list.getSearchUrls();
        Vector res = new Vector();
```

The agent only consists of the main method. First a validation object is created, with which the list of bookshops is then parsed. This list comes from a fixed *directory service*. In our example, this is simply the bookvendorlist.xml file. The resulting node object converts the constructor into a new wrapper class BookVendorList. Thereby, the getSearchUrls method is now available, which delivers a vector of the URLs to be searched to the agent. A second vector, res, should then save the search results.

```
Offer offer;
for (int i=0; i<urls.size(); i++) {
    node = v.parseAndValidate(
                   (String)urls.elementAt(i) + args[0]);
    if (node != zero) {
        offer = new Offer(node);
        res.addElement(offer);
    }
}
```

Here the search engines of the individual shops are requested. To do this the ISBN entered by the user in the command line is attached to each address contained in the vector of the URL. The validator is used again to parse and validate the resulting URLs. If an error occurs, the validator writes a message on the console and returns null. If the offer is processed successfully, a new offer object can be generated and put into the result vector.

```
Collections.sort(res);

System.out.println(
  "\n\nISBN            Titlel           Price in GBP Where");
System.out.println(
  "------------------------------------" +
  "------------------------------------");

for (int i=0; i<res.size(); i++) {
    offer = (Offer)res.elementAt(i);
    System.out.print(offer.getISBN() + "\t");
    System.out.print(offer.getTitle() + "\t");
    System.out.print(offer.getPrice() + "\t");
    System.out.print(offer.getUrl() + "\n");
}
```

As offer objects can be sorted according to their price, we now only invoke the available library with the vector as an argument. Finally we issue the information in a loop using the getXXX methods of the wrapper objects.

17.3.5 A price comparison on the Internet

In order to test the agent, we will use a little trick. As in practice only one ISBN search engine is currently available (namely ours), we will lay down simple XML files, which only contain an offer for the book with the ISBN 3446133631. In this way we will simulate the dynamic output of a Web application. By using the # symbol, the attachment of the ISBN has no influence through the agent and the file can be opened without any problems. Here is the list of shops:

```
<?xml version="1.0"?>

<!DOCTYPE bookvendorlist SYSTEM "bookvendorlist.dtd">

<bookvendorlist>
   <bookvendor>
      <url>http://www.books-online.de</url>
      <isbnsearch>http://localhost:8080/servlet/XMLSearch?isbn=
      </isbnsearch>
   </bookvendor>
   <bookvendor>
      <url>http://www.amazon.fr</url>
      <isbnsearch>http://www.i-u.de/schools/eberhart/book/offer2.xml#
      </isbnsearch>
   </bookvendor>
   <bookvendor>
      <url>http://www.barnesandnoble.com</url>
      <isbnsearch>offer3.xml#</isbnsearch>
   </bookvendor>
   <bookvendor>
      <url>http://www.book-not-available.de</url>
      <isbnsearch>book-not-available.xml#</isbnsearch>
   </bookvendor>
   <bookvendor>
      <url>http://www.unknown.de</url>
      <isbnsearch>http://www.unknown.de/search?isbn=</isbnsearch>
   </bookvendor>
</bookvendorlist>
```

```
Command Prompt                                                    _ □ ×

C:\book\booksonline\agent>java Agent 3446133631
Document root element, "error", must match DOCTYPE root, "offer".
java.net.NoRouteToHostException: Operation timed out: no further information

ISBN              Title              Price in GBP   Where
────────────────────────────────────────────────────────────────────────
3446133631        The Name of the Rose        6.85   http://www.amazon.fr
3446133631        The Name of the Rose        8.85   http://www.barnesandnoble.com
3446133631        The Name of the Rose        9.0    http://www.books-online.com

C:\book\booksonline\agent>
```

Figure 17.4: Test run of the agent. Five URLs were tested, three are valid, one violates the offer DTD and one cannot be accessed. The valid offers are converted into £ and sorted according to their price.

One of the offers is created by a servlet on our Books Online Web site. One of the static files comes from an external Web server (www.i-u.de) and a further offer comes from the local file system. These three offers all refer to the book *The Name of the Rose*, but use different currencies. One file contains an error message as the book is not available at this fictitious shop. A further offer is on an imaginary Web server, which cannot be accessed. Figure 17.4 shows the agent's output. If all large online bookshops had such an XML interface, you would only have to adapt the XML file to the URLs, to find the cheapest book worldwide at the touch of a button.

Chapter 18

Business-to-business applications

After the unbelievable success of business-to-consumer applications such as E-Bay and Amazon, *business-to-business* applications (B2B) are now gaining ground. The objective here is developing processes related to business management such as purchase order processing, advertising, or accounting over the Internet. For example, the chip manufacturer Intel already handles 25 percent of its purchasing over the Internet, yet this is a notable exception. It is therefore not surprising that huge growth rates have been predicted for B2B. For example, the Gartner Group projects a total turnover of US $7,290 billion by 2004. Seals GmbH discovered through a survey launched among leading managers that the German economy could save DM 20 billion in postage costs of invoices alone.

The most popular B2B applications include trade-specific marketplaces. Examples of such marketplaces are `www.e-steel.com` (steel), `www.glomedix.com` (hospital supplies), `www.telcobuy.com` (telecommunication), or `www.chemconnect.com` (chemical industry). These marketplaces are operated by independent companies, and make virtual trade available to subscribers for a small fee. The advantages are obvious: orders for goods or services required can be processed in seconds. The marketplace operator usually ensures that only trustworthy subscribers are authorized, i.e. subscribers that pay their bills and meet their deadlines. As well as those independent organizations mentioned, other models are possible. Especially in the car industry where a manufacturer is dependent on an entire network of suppliers, B2B systems also often are operated by the firm being supplied. In the meantime there is a range of software solutions for providing B2B functionality. Leading suppliers include SAP, Intershop, and Ariba. However, apart from these standard solutions, there also are many individual systems in use.

18.1 Interfaces and data structures of the marketplace application

In this chapter we will show how Books Online can subscribe to an auction system for books and supplies. The standard solution here is a Web application on which auctions can be searched according to certain criteria, and bids can be placed. We will venture a step further, and implement the marketplace as a SOAP-based distributed system. This means that clients can participate via a program, without the need for manual intervention. In our example the marketplace client functions as a type of auction agent that automatically buys a certain amount of a product at auction for the lowest possible price.

We will now look at the functions implemented by the marketplace. We have used Java syntax here; however, it should be noted that SOAP mappings are defined for all data types and constructs used, and methods written in other programming languages easily can be used by clients.

```
Auction[] search(String productID)
Auction[] getAuctionsWhereLeading(String buyerID)
String placeBid(String auctionID, String buyerID, float newBid)
```

The first two methods enable information on current auctions to be retrieved. `search` provides all auctions in which the product with the identification quoted is offered. If the client calls `getAuctionsWhereLeading`, it receives a list of all auctions at which it has currently placed the highest bid. Finally, `placeBid` enables bids to be placed when the amount, bidder identification, and auction identification are entered. Any error messages encountered will be delivered to the client via a returned message text.

It should be noted that we concentrate on core functionality in this example. In a real system, the client has to be prevented from querying auctions under a competitor's buyer ID. This could be achieved by entering a login and password, and using SSL during the transfer, for example.

An array with auction structures is returned by both search methods. In Java this structure is represented as a bean. This means that corresponding get and set methods are defined for the six attributes of an auction. The attributes save the auction identification, the products to be purchased by auction, the product names, the amount, the highest current offer, and the remaining auction time in milliseconds.

```
package soapb2b;

public class Auction
{

    private String auctionID;
    private String productID;
    private String productName;
    private int quantity;
    private float currentBid;
    private long timeRemaining;
```

```java
public Auction() {
}

public Auction(String auctionID, String productID,
               String productName, int quantity,
               float currentBid, long timeRemaining) {
   this.auctionID = auctionID;
   this.productID = productID;
   this.productName = productName;
   this.quantity = quantity;
   this.currentBid = currentBid;
   this.timeRemaining = timeRemaining;
}

public void setAuctionID(String auctionID) {
   this.auctionID = auctionID;
}

public String getAuctionID() {
   return auctionID;
}

public void setProductID(String productID) {
   this.productID = productID;
}

public String getProductID() {
   return productID;
}

public void setProductName(String productName) {
   this.productName = productName;
}

public String getProductName() {
   return productName;
}

public void setQuantity(int quantity) {
   this.quantity = quantity;
}

public int getQuantity() {
   return quantity;
}

public void setCurrentBid(float currentBid) {
   this.currentBid = currentBid;
}

public float getCurrentBid() {
   return currentBid;
}
```

```
    public void setTimeRemaining(long timeRemaining) {
       this.timeRemaining = timeRemaining;
    }

    public long getTimeRemaining() {
       return timeRemaining;
    }

    public String toString() {
       return auctionID + "," + productID + "," + productName + "," +
             quantity + "," + currentBid + "," +
             timeRemaining / 1000 / 3600;
    }
}
```

18.2 The marketplace client

The client is divided into two classes. The application logic is contained in the client class. ClientStub assumes the SOAP-specific communication, and offers to the main class precisely those three methods also implemented by the server. In order to keep the program as simple as possible, it is implemented as a command line application. As well as the individual identification, the user also enters the desired product and quantity. The URL of the Web services is coded into the program. As the marketplace is implemented with a Tomcat SOAP listener on the local computer, the URL is http://localhost:8080/soap/servlet/rpcrouter.

```
    package soapb2b;

    import java.util.Vector;

    public class Client {

       public static void main(String[] args) throws Exception {
          if (args.length != 3) {
             System.out.println(
                      "usage: java Client productID buyerId quantity");
             return;
          }

          ClientStub server = new ClientStub(
                      "http://localhost:8080/soap/servlet/rpcrouter");

          String productID = args[0];
          String buyerID = args[1];
          int quantity = Integer.parseInt(args[2]);
```

First, the agent has to determine how many items would currently be purchased if competitors did not bid anymore. The getAuctionsWhereLeading method is called for this. The result array is traversed, and the sum of quantities of all auctions containing the desired product is added up. These auctions will be stored intermediately in the mine vector.

```
int quantitySoFar = 0;
Vector mine = new Vector();
Auction[] arr = server.getAuctionsWhereLeading(buyerID);
for (int i=0; i<arr.length; i++)
   if (arr[i].getProductID().equals(productID)) {
      quantitySoFar = quantitySoFar + arr[i].getQuantity();
      mine.addElement(arr[i].getAuctionID());
   }

System.out.println("There are currently" + quantitySoFar + " of " +
                   quantity + " units being auctioned.");
if (quantitySoFar >= quantity) {
   System.out.println("No bid placed.");
   return;
}
```

If there are not enough items being purchased, the agent now obtains information about all auctions offering the desired product. Here the result is already pre-sorted by the marketplace in ascending order, according to price. If the auction is not yet contained in the mine vector, the agent bids. If the bid is accepted by the marketplace, the agent increases the variable quantitySoFar, which indicates the quantity bought.

```
arr = server.search(productID);
for (int i=0; i<arr.length; i++) {
   if (!mine.contains(arr[i].getAuctionID())) {
      float newbid = arr[i].getCurrentBid() * (float)1.1;
      System.out.print("Bid " + newbid + " for auction" +
                 arr[i].getAuctionID() + " with " +
                 arr[i].getQuantity() + " Units...");
      String msg = server.placeBid(arr[i].getAuctionID(),
                                   buyerID, newbid);
      if (msg == null) {
         quantitySoFar = quantitySoFar + arr[i].getQuantity();
         System.out.println("ok");
      }
      else
         System.out.println(msg);

      if (quantitySoFar >= quantity) {
         System.out.println("No further bid placed.");
         return;
      }
   }
}
}
```

As previously mentioned, the stub assumes the SOAP-specific communication. Many of the entries made in the deployment of services described in the *Apache SOAP* section on page 352 are also found again here. The marketplace can be reached under the resource name auctions-international. In contrast to the simple example, the BeanSerializer has to be used here, which selects the information of the class auction via the reflection API, and transfers it into the corresponding SOAP format with the name auction and namespace urn:auction. Figure 18.1 shows the information used on deployment. The BeansSerializer class is also used on the receiver side for deserializing, and for the conversion of XML into Java objects. As this functionality goes beyond the support of base types in the SOAP library, serializers and deserializers have to be explicitly indicated.

```
package soapb2b;

import java.net.*;
import java.util.Vector;

import org.apache.soap.SOAPException;
import org.apache.soap.Constants;
import org.apache.soap.Fault;
import org.apache.soap.rpc.Call;
import org.apache.soap.rpc.Response;
import org.apache.soap.rpc.Parameter;
import org.apache.soap.encoding.SOAPMappingRegistry;
import org.apache.soap.encoding.soapenc.BeanSerializer;
import org.apache.soap.util.xml.QName;

public class ClientStub {

    private String url;

    public ClientStub(String url) {
        this.url = url;
    }

    public Auction[] search(String productID) throws SOAPException,
                                            MalformedURLException {
        SOAPMappingRegistry smr = new SOAPMappingRegistry();
        BeanSerializer ser = new BeanSerializer();
        smr.mapTypes(Constants.NS_URI_SOAP_ENC,
                  new QName("urn:auction", "auction"),
                  Auction.class, ser, ser);

        Call call = new Call();
        call.setSOAPMappingRegistry(smr);
        call.setTargetObjectURI("urn:auctions-international");
        call.setMethodName("search");
        call.setEncodingStyleURI(Constants.NS_URI_SOAP_ENC);

        Vector params = new Vector();
        params.addElement(new Parameter("productID", String.class,
                                    productID, null));
```

```
      call.setParams(params);

      Response resp = call.invoke(new URL(url), "");

      if (resp.generatedFault()) {
         Fault fault = resp.getFault();
         System.out.println("Error: ");
         System.out.println(" Code = " + fault.getFaultCode());
         System.out.println(" String = " + fault.getFaultString());
         return null;
      }
      else {
         Parameter result = resp.getReturnValue();
         Auction[] arr = (Auction[])result.getValue();
         return arr;
      }
   }

   public Auction[] getAuctionsWhereLeading(String buyerID)
                     throws SOAPException, MalformedURLException {
      SOAPMappingRegistry smr = new SOAPMappingRegistry();
      BeanSerializer ser = new BeanSerializer();
      smr.mapTypes(Constants.NS_URI_SOAP_ENC,
               new QName("urn:auction", "auction"),
               Auction.class, ser, ser);

      Call call = new Call();
      call.setSOAPMappingRegistry(smr);
      call.setTargetObjectURI("urn:auctions-international");
      call.setMethodName("getAuctionsWhereLeading");
      call.setEncodingStyleURI(Constants.NS_URI_SOAP_ENC);

      Vector params = new Vector();
      params.addElement(new Parameter("buyerID", String.class,
                                     buyerID, null));
      call.setParams(params);

      Response resp = call.invoke(new URL(url), "");

      if (resp.generatedFault()) {
         Fault fault = resp.getFault();
         System.out.println("Error: ");
         System.out.println(" Code = " + fault.getFaultCode());
         System.out.println(" String = " + fault.getFaultString());
         return null;
      }
      else {
         Parameter result = resp.getReturnValue();
         Auction[] arr = (Auction[])result.getValue();
         return arr;
      }
   }
```

```java
public String placeBid(String auctionID, String buyerID,
                       float newBid)
                throws SOAPException, MalformedURLException {
   Call call = new Call();
   call.setTargetObjectURI("urn:auctions-international");
   call.setMethodName("placeBid");
   call.setEncodingStyleURI(Constants.NS_URI_SOAP_ENC);

   Vector params = new Vector();
   params.addElement(new Parameter("productID", String.class,
                                   auctionID, null));
   params.addElement(new Parameter("buyerID", String.class,
                                   buyerID, null));
   params.addElement(new Parameter("newBid", float.class,
                                   new Float(newBid), null));
   call.setParams(params);

   Response resp = call.invoke(new URL(url), "");

   if (resp.generatedFault()) {
      Fault fault = resp.getFault();
      System.out.println("Error: ");
      System.out.println(" Code = " + fault.getFaultCode());
      System.out.println(" String = " + fault.getFaultString());
      return null;
   }
   else {
      Parameter result = resp.getReturnValue();
      String msg = (String)result.getValue();
      return msg;
   }
}
```

18.3 The marketplace server

Only the application logic needs to be implemented on the server side. The server saves the auction information in a database table. The scheme roughly corresponds to the information contained in the auction class. Instead of the remaining auction time, the time is given in hours since 1970. Who auctions and who has currently placed the highest bid is also saved. It also should be noted here that it would, for example, make sense to save all bids in order to be able to trace back the course of the auction. This feature was omitted in favor of simplicity.

```sql
create table Auctions(
   auctionID char(50) primary key,
   productID char(50),
   productName char(100),
   quantity int,
```

```
currentBid float,
dueTime long,
sellerID char(50),
buyerID char(50)
);
```

The `search` and `getAuctionsWhereLeading` methods both access the private method `queryToAuctions`, which executes the SQL select query and returns the results table as an array of auction objects. In order to guarantee that items are sorted according to price, search uses the order-by clause as follows: `order by quantity/currentBid desc`. When the results are converted, hours since 1970 are converted into milliseconds. The interval until the end of the auction can be calculated by subtracting from the system time.

```
package soapb2b;

import java.sql.Connection;
import java.sql.Statement;
import java.sql.ResultSet;
import java.sql.SQLException;
import java.util.Vector;

public class Server {

    public Auction[] search(String productID)
                    throws ClassNotFoundException, SQLException {
      String query = "select * from auctions where productID = '" +
                    productID + "' order by quantity/currentBid desc";
      return queryToAuctions(query);
    }

    public Auction[] getAuctionsWhereLeading(String buyerID)
                    throws ClassNotFoundException, SQLException {
      String query = "select * from auctions where buyerID = '" +
                    buyerID + "'";
      return queryToAuctions(query);
    }

    private Auction[] queryToAuctions(String query)
                    throws ClassNotFoundException, SQLException {
      Class.forName("sun.jdbc.odbc.JdbcOdbcDriver");
      Connection con = java.sql.DriverManager.getConnection(
                    "jdbc:odbc:auctions", "", "");
      Statement stmt = con.createStatement();
      System.out.println(query);
      ResultSet res = stmt.executeQuery(query);
      Vector v = new Vector();
      while (res.next()) {
         String auctionID = res.getString("auctionID").trim();
         String productID = res.getString("productID").trim();
         String productName = res.getString("productName").trim();
```

```
        int quantity = res.getInt("quantity");
        float currentBid = res.getFloat("currentBid");
        long timeRemaining = res.getLong("dueTime") * 1000 * 3600 -
                             System.currentTimeMillis();

        Auction a = new Auction(auctionID, productID, productName,
                            quantity, currentBid, timeRemaining);
        v.addElement(a);
    }

    Auction[] arr = new Auction[v.size()];
    for (int i=0; i<arr.length; i++) {
        arr[i] = (Auction)v.elementAt(i);
    }
    return arr;
}
```

If a bid is submitted, the following criteria have to be met: on the one hand the auction has to exist, and on the other hand the bid has to exceed the previous one. We will assume that expired auctions are no longer available in the table. These two conditions are examined with the select query. If this does not return an auction which satisfies the criteria, an error message is created. Otherwise the new bid and bidder are entered into the auction by means of an update instruction.

```
    public String placeBid(String auctionID, String buyerID,
            float newBid) throws ClassNotFoundException, SQLException
{
        Class.forName("sun.jdbc.odbc.JdbcOdbcDriver");
        Connection con = java.sql.DriverManager.getConnection(
                            "jdbc:odbc:auctions", "", "");
        Statement stmt = con.createStatement();
        String query = "select * from auctions where auctionID = '" +
                    auctionID + "' and currentBid < " + newBid;
        System.out.println(query);
        ResultSet res = stmt.executeQuery(query);
        if (res.next()) {
            query = "update auctions set currentBid = " + newBid +
                    ", buyerID = '" + buyerID +
                    "' where auctionID = '" + auctionID + "'";
            System.out.println(query);
            stmt.executeUpdate(query);
            stmt.close();
            con.close();
            return null;
        }
        else {
            return "ERROR: Invalid auctionID or insufficient funds.";
        }
    }
}
```

18.4 Deployment of marketplace services

In order to compile the classes, the SOAP library *soap.jar* of the Apache SOAP SDK has to be located in the classpath. Several steps are required on the server side. First, the SOAP router has to be installed as a Tomcat Web application. Follow the instructions contained in the SDK. In order to be able to execute the marketplace application, the soapb2b package has to be located in the Tomcat server classpath. It should be noted here that it is not the soapb2b directory itself which is to be entered, but the subordinate directory:

```
set CLASSPATH=%CLASSPATH%;C:\book\booksonline
```

Once entered, the application has to be logged on at the RPC router. Figure 18.1 shows the deployment form. The name of the application, the server class, method names, and classes for reading and writing the auction data type are given. This information need only be entered once.

18.5 Starting the client

Once the server has started and the application is registered, the client can be started. Figure 18.2 shows the initial status of the auction database. Four auctions are in process for the desired product ISBN 3446133631, where auctions 1 and 3 currently have the lowest price. Client b999 wishes to buy at least 250 items at auction. First, the agent bids for auctions 1 and 3, purchases 300 items temporarily and then stops at this point. The application can be started periodically in case the bids are exceeded by other bidders.

```
C:\book\booksonline>java soapb2b.Client ISBN-3446133631 b999 250
There are currently 0 of 250 items bought.
Bid 1980.0 for auction 3 with 200 items...ok
Bid 1100.0 for auction 1 with 100 items...ok
No bids were placed.
```

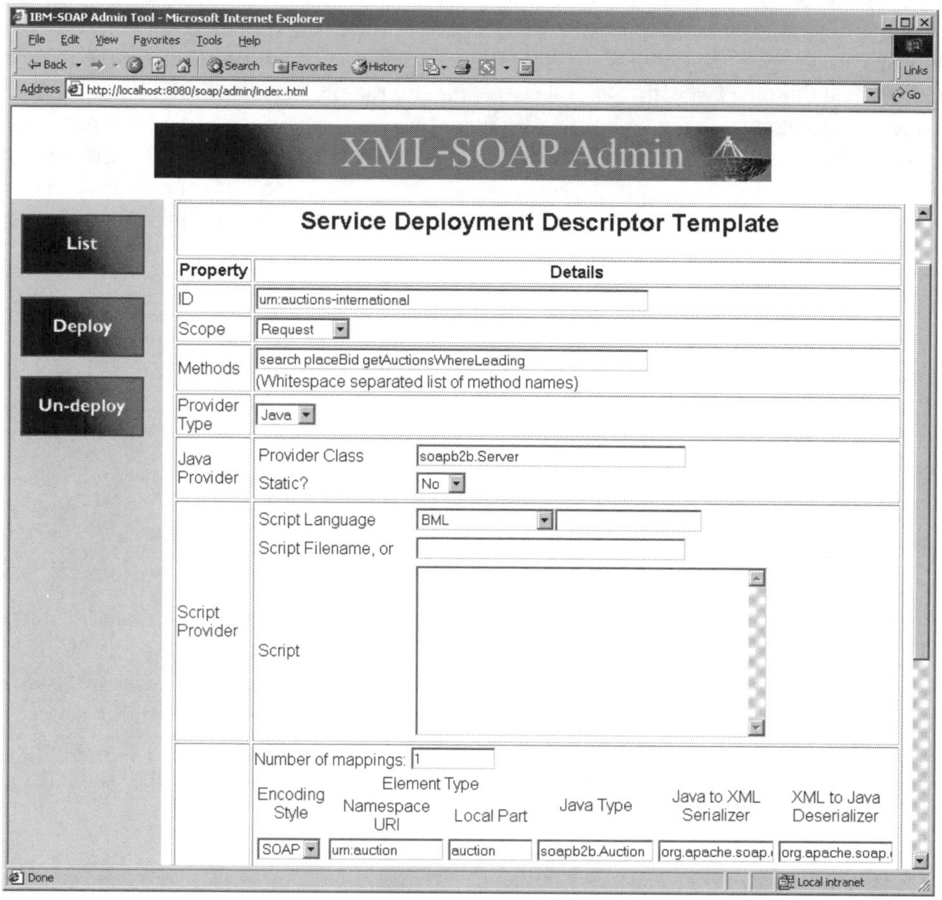

Figure 18.1: Deployment of marketplace services.

The server outputs the SQL queries sent to the database on the console. This can be seen in Fig. 18.3. The sequence of calls is also recognizable here. The first two select queries stem from the search over the auctions led by b999 and the product ISBN 3446133631. The two select–update pairs are the bids for auctions 1 and 3. Figure 18.4 shows the auction database after the agent performed the bidding. The minimum bid for auctions 1 and 3 increased by 10 percent, and b999 is entered as the buyer.

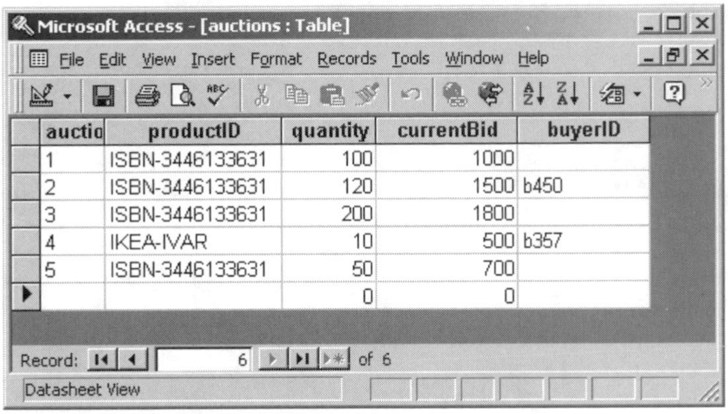

auctio	productID	quantity	currentBid	buyerID
1	ISBN-3446133631	100	1000	
2	ISBN-3446133631	120	1500	b450
3	ISBN-3446133631	200	1800	
4	IKEA-IVAR	10	500	b357
5	ISBN-3446133631	50	700	
		0	0	

Figure 18.2: Output status of the auction database of the marketplace.

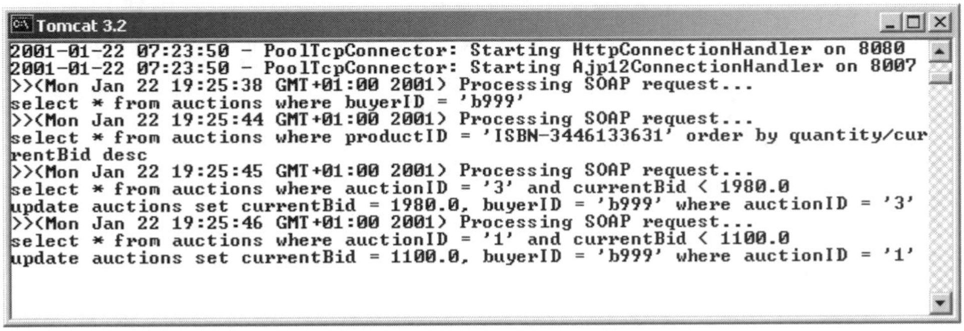

Figure 18.3: The SQL queries to the auction database are displayed on the console of the Tomcat SOAP server. Both update commands enter the bids of Books Online.

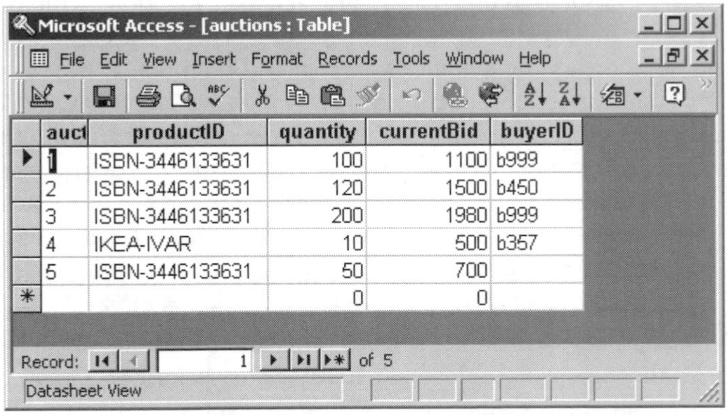

aucti	productID	quantity	currentBid	buyerID
1	ISBN-3446133631	100	1100	b999
2	ISBN-3446133631	120	1500	b450
3	ISBN-3446133631	200	1980	b999
4	IKEA-IVAR	10	500	b357
5	ISBN-3446133631	50	700	
		0	0	

Figure 18.4: The Books Online automatic auction client (buyer ID b999) has bid for auctions 1 and 3.

If the client is started again to buy 300 items at auction, the program interrupts, as the desired quantity is covered by auctions 1 and 3.

```
C:\book\booksonline>java soapb2b.Client ISBN-3446133631 b999 300
There are currently 300 of 300 items bought.
No bids placed.
```

If the amount is increased further, the agent bids for the next best auction. In this case it is auction 2. Buyer b450 is in turn outbid by 10 percent.

```
C:\book\bookonline>java soapb2b.Client ISBN-3446133631 b999 350
There are currently 300 of 350 items.
Bid 1650.0 for auction 2 with 120 items...ok
No bids were placed.
```

In the following test run the agent bids, starting from the original database for all four auctions, aiming to reach as close to 1000 purchased items as possible.

```
C:\book\booksonline>java soapb2b.Client ISBN-3446133631 b999 1000
There are currently 0 of 1000 items bought.
Bid 1980.0 for auction 3 with 200 items...ok
Bid 1100.0 for auction 1 with 100 items...ok
Bid 1650.0 for auction 2 with 120 items...ok
Bid 770.0 for auction 5 with 50 items...ok
```

18.6 B2B standards

This relatively simple application shows how easily a rudimentary B2B solution can be implemented. As the marketplace offers a SOAP interface, so clients can implement an agent-like functionality, support the buying or selling process and partly automate things. SOAP is an attractive solution on a technical level, as it functions without problems in highly heterogeneous systems. However, there is still much to be done on an organizational level regarding standards, so that B2B can reach its full potential. For instance, our example used a product identification, on which all participants of course have to agree. Furthermore, participants have to agree on the signatures of the interface. Here we can refer to many experiences from EDI, yet there is a certain proliferation, causing the interoperability of different B2B systems to suffer. You simply have to wait and see whether initiatives such as UDDI standards will gain widespread support.

Our marketplace could, for example, use the Universal Standard Products and Services Classification (UNSPSC) coding for product identification. UNSPSC is one of the options which can be used for registration in the UDDI directory for the classification of products and services. Furthermore, you could imagine that the marketplace interface conforms to a predefined consortium specification. This concerns the syntax, i.e. names, parameters, data types, and semantics, of a specific call. For example, it is determined here that the search sorts auction information according to item price in ascending order, and that UNSPSC product identification is used. A corresponding UDDI identifier, or tModel, would then be assigned to such a specification. The marketplace can then register its auction service, and advertise to clients how the marketplace is to be called.

Chapter 19

Related solutions – differences and similarities

In this chapter we will shed more light on the jungle of abbreviations of different technologies for the development of distributed applications. Our example, Books Online, showed the whole spectrum of functionality, from retrieving information from a central database, the use of an external credit card service, the implementation of a user's interface with HTML, to an automatic search agent with XML. We have limited our example to Java solutions. From the conceptional point of view, nothing changes when, for example, Microsoft solutions are applied. However, some differences become apparent, from a practical perspective.

Therefore, the aim of the following section is to convey a general idea about common peculiarities and differences of related solutions. Some brief examples help us to explain the advantages and disadvantages of the alternatives shown in comparison with the implementation we chose with Java, CORBA, servlets, and XML.

19.1 Creating dynamic Web pages

The Java variant on the creation of dynamic Web pages is servlets and Java Server Pages. Servlets have been discussed extensively. They represent a simple, easy-to-learn option. In practice, the good support of servlets through the combination of the Tomcat and Apache servers is very important, as Apache is the market leader in this segment. It is also relevant that Apache and Tomcat are available for all major operating systems.

Java Server Pages are converted to servlets internally but offer the programmer an HTML-based view. Java commands are embedded in the HTML text instead of issuing HTML tags from the Java program. The relevant advantage is that HTML-based pages can be processed using Web design tools. With the Tomcat reference implementation, wide support is guaranteed.

Let us now consider the most well-known alternatives to the Java solutions.

19.1.1 Common Gateway Interface (CGI)

The oldest and furthest spread variant of the programming of dynamic Internet applications is the Common Gateway Interface. The Web application is implemented either as a compiled program or as an interpretable script. Here Perl is usually used as a script language. Communication with the Web server is carried out via the standard input and output streams of the program.

The considerable advantage is that this variant works on any Web server. However, we should notice that the correct configuration of the Perl interpreter, Web server, and Perl script under Windows is sometimes laborious. For instance, for the Internet Information Server you need the Perl interpreter module *Active Perl* (www.activestate.com). The programmer has to parse the form values. These are supplied to the CGI program in a character sequence, consisting of parameter names and values, in which characters are separated with the symbols & and =.

Perl offers countless libraries which undertake this task. However, the work becomes much more comfortable with servlets, since all parameters easily are obtainable from the request object. Perl offers also a very wide functionality for working with strings, but the syntax requires habituation in any case.

The following Perl example reads the GET form parameter name and sends it back to the result page again.

```perl
#!/usr/local/bin/perl

@pairs = split(/&/, $ENV{'QUERY_STRING'});
foreach $pair (@pairs) {
    local($name, $value) = split(/=/, $pair);
    $name =~ tr/+/ /;
    $name =~ s/%([a-fA-F0-9][a-fA-F0-9])/pack("C", hex($1))/eg;
    $value =~ tr/+/ /;
    $value =~ s/%([a-fA-F0-9][a-fA-F0-9])/pack("C", hex($1))/eg;
    $value =~ tr/,/ /;
    $value =~ s/<!--(.|\n)*-->//g;
    $INPUT{$name} = $value;
}
print "Content-type: text/html\n\n";
print "<html>";
print "the name given is: ";
print $INPUT{'name'};
print "</html>";
```

The print statements at the end of the script correspond to the out.println applications of a servlet. The form value is saved in the INPUT data structure which gives the developer access to the form values of their name by means of the term $INPUT{'name'}. Unlike with servlets, it is the programmer's responsibility to fill the data structure. This is done in the first part of the script, in which some of the previously mentioned string operations of Perl are used. The instruction $value =~ tr/+/ /;, for instance, causes all + characters in the string value to be replaced with blank characters.

19.1.2 Internet Server Application Programming Interface (ISAPI)

With ISAPI and ASP, Microsoft offers two techniques which, regarding their functionality, can be compared with servlets and JSP. In ISAPI the Web application is typically implemented in C++ and compiled as a DLL. The Web server calls a function in the DLL with the form values as parameters.

ISAPI probably offers the most high-speed Web applications. In comparison with servlets, ISAPI works without a virtual machine, since the DLLs are compiled directly for the respective hardware. ISAPI is also quicker than CGI, because a thread of the Web server executes the function and no separate process needs to be started. Similar to servlets, ISAPI programs can be created in a comfortable way by means of tools such as Visual C++.

The disadvantage is that only the Microsoft Internet Information Server (IIS) and the Personal Web Server support ISAPI.

The following C++ program code shows the ISAPI equivalent to the doGet method in a servlet. The structural similarity to servlets here is recognizable through the HTML text printed and the naming of the method.

```
DWORD WINAPI HttpExtensionProc(EXTENSION_CONTROL_BLOCK *pEcb) {
    SendHTMLHeader(pEcb);

    Output(pEcb, "<html>");
    Output(pEcb, "<head><title>Skeleton DLL</title></head>");
    Output(pEcb, "<body bgcolor=#FFFFFF>This is a test.</body>");
    Output(pEcb, "</html>");

    return HSE_STATUS_SUCCESS;
}
```

19.1.3 Active Server Pages

Active Server Pages are HTML based, as the similarity in name to JSP suggests. The Visual Basic commands can be embedded in an existing HTML page. Then they are executed on the Web server and create dynamic output at the corresponding place on the page. As in JSP, some objects are available to retrieve the values submitted by HTML forms and to create the result page. Communication with databases and mail servers is handled via COM components.

It is very easy to obtain results quickly using ASP. An ASP-capable personal Web server is enclosed with Windows 95 and 98 and a Hello World sample program is three lines long. However, the Visual Basic syntax requires some practice. Like ISAPI, ASP is supported only by the Internet Information Server (IIS) and the Personal Web Server of Microsoft ISAPI.

The following example shows a typical ASP application: displaying the result of a select-query in the form of an HTML table. The similarities to JSP also are easily recognizable in this case. The program looks like an HTML file. The ASP commands are embedded between the characters <% and %>. The outputs of the ASP code are replaced dynamically at the right place in the HTML text using the ASP engine of the Web server. The form value is read with the term `request.querystring("title")` and inserted in the database query. Some details of the ADO database connection are explained in Section 19.3.5 on page 401.

```
<html>
Result of query:
<table border='1'>

<%
    s = request.querystring("title")
    stmt = "select * from cds where title like '%" & s & "%'"
    Set con = Server.CreateObject("ADODB.Connection")
    con.Open "test"
    Set res = con.Execute(stmt)

    Do While Not res.EOF
        response.write("<tr>")
        response.write("<td>" & res("id") & "</td>")
        response.write("<td>" & res("title") & "</td>")
        response.write("<td>" & res("composer") & "</td>")
        response.write("<td>" & res("price") & "</td>")
        response.write("</tr>")
        res.MoveNext
    Loop
%>

</table>
</html>
```

19.1.4 ASP.NET

ASP.NET describes the Active Server Pages section of the new .NET strategy from Microsoft. Under the ASP.NET framework programs are written in Visual Basic, C#, and JScript, based on a common runtime environment and class libraries. In this way the ASP.NET programs are not limited to Visual Basic as they were up to now. But one particular advantage is the powerful class libraries which enable access to the databases and message queues as well as a straightforward integration in the Microsoft transaction server.

The following brief C# example issues the data:

```
<%@Page Language="C#"%>
<html>
<%Response.Write(DateTime.Now.ToString()); %>
</html>
```

Besides the well-known dynamic Web pages, SOAP-based Web services also easily can be implemented, as this brief example shows:

```
<%@ WebService Language="C#" Class="HelloWorld" %>

using System;
using System.Web.Services;

public class HelloWorld {
    [WebMethod] public String SayHello() {
        return "Hello World";
    }
}
```

Notice here that the Web service is described automatically, using a Service Description Language (SDL) file. Using this file Visual Studio can automatically generate a corresponding stub for the client.

All in all, .NET and ASP.NET are very interesting techniques. Microsoft took an overdue step and eliminated a lot of burdens for programmers that had accumulated over time. Due to the extensive class libraries and good integration with MTS, MSMQ, and SQL Server, the result is a very easy to use and powerful alternative to Java.

19.1.5 Hypertext preprocessor (PHP)

PHP is an alternative from the Open Source Community. As in JSP and ASP, PHP commands are embedded directly in the HTML text. The language is somewhat similar to C, Java, and Perl. The Apache Web server is made PHP-capable with the Apache PHP module. Here Apache's large installation base and the availability of PHP are an advantage on many platforms.

With the combination of Linux, Apache, PHP, and MySQL you can create a complete database-driven Web application free of charge, at least as far as the price of the software packages used is concerned.

The following example shows how form values can be read and how a small Web page is created dynamically.

```
<html>
<center>
<?
    PRINT "Hello, $name.";
    PRINT "We will send you further information by $email.";
?>
</center>
</html>
```

The PRINT function corresponds to the out.println commands in servlets. As usual, the form values can be obtained via the name of the HTML entry field, eg. $email. If MySQL or the frequently used mailserver Sendmail are installed under UNIX, PHP enables you to use these directly on predefined functions. You can establish a database connection or send an e-mail with the following simple instructions:

```
MYSQL_CONNECT($hostname,$username,$password)
   OR DIE("No connection to the database.");

mail("$email", "Customer information.",
          "Hello $name, here there is the required information: ...");
```

19.1.6 Client-side scripts

In the previous sections we mentioned the most important common features among ASP, JSP, ISAPI, PHP, and servlets. Their considerable similarities easily can be explained by the fact that programs of all language dialects are executed on the server. This enables us to access the central database or to send out e-mails.

However, client-side scripts are embedded in HTML code and executed by the browser. In this way, functionality is not aimed at the typical functions of a server, but to the interaction with the browser. Client-side scripts are also used for graphical effects such as moving text and animations. Furthermore, with scripts you can often check which browser you are dealing with and correspondingly branch to different versions of the Web page whose design is optimized for the respective browser version.

In essence, we find two language variants: JavaScript and Visual Basic Script (VBScript). Apart from similarities in the syntax, JavaScript has little to do with Java. You can define and inherit classes, but you usually only work with the objects given by the browser such as document and window, and access elements displayed on the current page. VBScript provides similar functionality, but its syntax differs considerably from JavaScript.

Client-side scripts are often a good addition to Web applications. They can never replace any component on the server, but enable you to create Web pages that are both interactive and graphically appealing. The choice between the two dialects ultimately depends on your preference alone. Note that development using JavaScript and VBScript can sometimes be very laborious. Programs often work on one browser but not on another. Furthermore, browsers rarely help you to find errors, and even syntax and semantics are often anything but logical.

Our example shows a frequently occurring application: the checking of form values. In order to keep the number of requests to the server as low as possible, it is better if false inputs are intercepted by the browser before reaching the Web server. In the HTML form listed below, the attribute onsubmit="return alterOK()" indicates that the method alterOK has to be called to establish whether the form is sent or not. In our example, the age entered has to be greater than zero.

```
<html>
<script language="javascript">
    function ageOK() {
        var s = document.frm.age.value;
        var alter = parseInt(s);
        if (isNaN(alter) || (age<= 0)) {
            alert("The age has to be higher than zero.");
            return false;
        }
        return true;
    }
</script>

<form name="frm" action="handler.php" onsubmit="return ageK()">
    <input type="text" name="age">
    <input type="submit">
</form>
</html>
```

The term `document.from.age.value` returns the value of the text field. In this case, document is an object given by the browser which enables access to the document. frm is the name of the HTML form, which is fixed with `<form name="frm" ...>`. The text element is identified with age again. Like an XML document, the HTML text also defines a hierarchical structure.

The value is checked and in case of errors the warning shown in Fig. 19.1 appears. Only when the return value of the method is true is the form sent to handler.php.

Figure 19.1: A warning created using the JavaScript instruction alert.

19.2 Remote procedure calls

CORBA enables the programmer to call application objects which run on another computer. Moreover, there are countless products which enable the development of Java–CORBA projects. A considerable advantage of CORBA is that neither the platform nor the programming language is fixed. Therefore, it is also possible to call a C program under Linux from a client written in Java and running under Solaris. Unfortunately, we have to point out here the serious practical problems in the combination of different CORBA products.

19.2.1 RPC with sockets

Instead of using CORBA, you can implement your own RPC mechanism with sockets. Here sockets undertake only the absolute base functionality in order to send an array of bytes from A to B. The package `java.net` contained in the JDK encloses the classes required here, such as `java.net.DatagramSocket`. The corresponding class libraries are also available for other programming languages, such as Pascal or C++.

The advantage is obvious: if the required RPC functionality is quite simple with respect to the number of methods and parameters, you do not have to struggle with the CORBA APIs and its tools. However, the following brief socket example shows how CORBA relieves the developer of many details of the implementation. With the high flexibility of CORBA and the low programming and maintenance expense on less self-written source code, we believe that an initial investment to learn CORBA pays in the long run.

This example shows a minimal implementation of RPCs based on sockets. The server offers two simple methods to add and multiply two numbers. This is not particularly surprising, and we therefore draw attention to the communication: client and server communicate directly. The client is given the IP address of the server on the command line. The server can determine the IP address of the client from the package received. The server receives on Port 952, and the client gets the result on Port 951. This is the first difference compared to CORBA. Functionality as provided by the name server would have to be self-developed.

```java
import java.net.*;
import java.io.*;

public class Client {

    public static void main(String[] args) throws Exception {
        byte[] buffer = new byte[3];
        DatagramSocket datagramSocket = new DatagramSocket(951);
        InetAddress addr = InetAddress.getByName(args[0]);
        DatagramPackage in;
        DatagramPackage out;
        buffer[0] = Byte.parseByte(args[1]);
        buffer[1] = Byte.parseByte(args[2]);
        buffer[2] = Byte.parseByte(args[3]);
        out = new DatagramPackage(buffer, buffer.length, addr, 952);
```

Since it is only possible to send one data array, the functional call is packed in a self-defined coding. Three bytes are sent each time: the operand and the first argument followed by the second argument. This causes a method with the signature byte f (byte a, byte b) to be called. Obviously, any modification of this signature requires further considerable modifications in the program code. This is not necessary in CORBA, as stubs and skeletons perform the encoding. The transmission of the object reference, the method to be called, and its parameters in a byte array is completely transparent to the user.

```
                datagramSocket.send(out);
                in = new DatagramPackage(buffer, buffer.length);
                datagramSocket.receive(in);
                buffer = in.getData();
                System.out.println(buffer[0]);
        }
    }
```

Once the operand and the parameters are packed, our socket-client sends the byte array to the server and waits for its answer. The server writes the result at the first position in the buffer. Finally, the client outputs it.

The server is built as follows: Two methods implement addition and multiplication. These two methods are called by the `main` method. The server waits for the client's calls in an endless loop.

```
import java.net.*;
import java.io.*;

public class Server {

    public static byte add(byte a, byte b) {
        System.out.println("add called);
        return ((byte)(a + b));
    }

    public static byte multiply(byte a, byte b) {
        System.out.println("multiply a called);
        return ((byte)(a * b));
    }

    public static void main(String[] args) throws Exception {
        byte[] buffer = new byte[3];
        DatagramSocket datagramSocket = new DatagramSocket(952);
        InetAddress addr;
        DatagramPackage in;
        DatagramPackage out;
        System.out.println("Server ready ...");
        while (true) {
            in = new DatagramPackage(buffer, buffer.length);
            datagramSocket.receive(in);
            buffer = in.getData();
            addr = in.getAddress();
```

When a message arrives, operand and argument are read from the byte array and the corresponding method is called. Therefore client and server should agree on the coding. Finally, the result is sent back.

```
                    if (buffer[0] == 0)
                        buffer[0] = add(buffer[1], buffer[2]);
                    else
                        buffer[0] = multiply(buffer[1], buffer[2]);
                    out = new DatagramPackage(buffer, buffer.length, addr, 951);
                    datagramSocket.send(out);
                }
            }
        }
```

19.2.2 Remote Method Invocation (RMI)

RMI is a Java-based alternative to CORBA. As Java can run on different platforms, interoperability between operating systems is given, but it is not possible to communicate with a server written in C.

As regards functionality, there is a fundamental difference from CORBA: with RMI it is possible to shift entire Java objects on the network. You can send not only data in the form of parameters, but also objects with their methods. At the same time, the class file is sent transparently to the programmer on the network. This enables you, for instance, to write agents which not only retrieve data from other servers, as our XML agent does, but can be executed on the servers. However, this functionality is usually unnecessary and makes the programming very complex.

Since RMI is a pure Java-based solution, you do not have to rely on a separate language to define the interface. This is possible with the definition of an interface based on `java.rmi.Remote`. The following example shows the RMI variant of the date server from Chapter 10.

```
import java.rmi.*;
import java.util.Date

public interface DateServer extends java.rmi.Remote {
    Date getTime() throws RemoteException;
}
```

The interface `DateServer` is implemented by the class `DateServerImpl` which consequently embodies the server. A name server is also used in this case, in which the RMI server is registered under a name. This is done in the class constructor.

```
import java.rmi.*;
import java.rmi.server.UnicastRemoteObject;
import java.util.Date;

public class DateServerImpl extends UnicastRemoteObject implements Data
{

    public DateServerImpl(String name) throws RemoteException {
        super();
```

```
        try {
            Naming.rebind(name, this);
        }
        catch (Exception e) {
            System.out.println(e);
        }
    }

    public Date getTime() throws RemoteException {
        System.out.println("getTime called");
        return new Date();
    }
}
```

The actual server object need only be instanced. This happens in the `main` method of this class. The string ("date") is also given here, under which the client can retrieve the reference to the server object at the name server.

```
import java.rmi.*;
import java.rmi.server.*;

public class Server {

    public static void main(String[] args) throws Exception {
        System.setSecurityManager(new RMISecurityManager());
        DateServerImpl ds = new DateServerImpl("date");
    }
}
```

The client receives a reference to the local stub of the server object from the name server. Here it is interesting to note that the name server is referenced via an URL. In our example the URL is contained in the same machine (`localhost`). The "directory" date then corresponds to the registration name.

Finally, the client can call the object. As in CORBA, there also is no recognizable difference here to a local method call, as the local RMI stub which undertakes communication is called. As in CORBA, the stub and the skeleton are created by a special compiler. In the JDK the program `rmic` executes this operation.

```
import java.rmi.*;
import java.rmi.registry.*;
import java.rmi.server.*;

public class Client {

    public static void main(String[] args) throws Exception {
        System.setSecurityManager(new RMISecurityManager());
        Data data = (Data)Naming.lookup("rmi://localhost/date);
        System.out.println(data getTime());
    }
}
```

In order to explain the example, a further file is required. Different security levels are provided here. As in CORBA, you have to start the name server initially (rmiregistry), followed by server and client.

```
grant {
    permission java.net.SocketPermission "*:1024-65535",
        "connect,accept";
    permission java.net.SocketPermission "*:80",
        "connect";
};
```

19.2.3 Distributed Component Object Model (DCOM)

DCOM, recently called COM+, is the extension of the successful *Component Object Model* (COM) architecture from Microsoft. Even if there are DCOM implementations for other platforms, we can say that DCOM represents a highly competitive and simple alternative to CORBA on the Windows platform. You can choose from the comfortable programming tools of the Visual Studio family, Visual J++, Visual C++, and Visual Basic. Furthermore, you can work with distributed DCOM components on ASP.

We will now introduce a brief, very simplified DCOM example, developed with Visual J++. Also, DCOM, like CORBA, works with an Interface Definition Language. Even if the syntax differs greatly from the CORBA IDL, some common elements such as the definition of the server interface can be found. Please note that some details have been omitted so as to retain clarity.

```
library Tester {
    ...
    interface ITest : IUnknown {
        HRESULT getValue([in] int val);
    };
    ...
};
```

The server implements the defined ITest interface. As with RMI, methods called on the network are defined with throws ComException.

```
import com.ms.com.*;
import test.*;

class Test implements ITest {
    public int getValue() throws ComException {
        ...
    }
}
```

Finally, a DCOM client can call an object contained in another computer as if it were local. This example does not use a name server, but a wired object reference. With the Stringified Object References, this possibility also exists in CORBA.

```
import test.*;

class DCOMClient {
    public static void main(String args[]) throws Exception {
        ITest t = (ITest)new test.Test();
        int value = t.getValue();
        ...
    }
}
```

19.2.4 MTS

Like the Enterprise Java Beans (EJB) specification, the Microsoft Transaction Server (MTS) also offers an architecture based on components to develop distributed systems. While EJB is based on many Java standards mentioned in this book, such as CORBA, RMI, or JDBC, MTS obviously uses the Microsoft pendants DCOM and ODBC.

Using EJB or MTS application servers, you can tie operations of different databases into one transaction, in order to guarantee data integrity in case of errors. Moreover, such systems relieve the developer of tasks such as pooling database connections, load balancing, and session management. This functionality was partly self-implemented in Chapter 8 on page 125. Finally, application servers offer further tools for security management.

19.3 Databases

Normally the database server software cannot be chosen, since a particular solution usually is already installed as a central point in the information infrastructure. If a new system is created or installed, the required functionality of the application should be considered when a product is chosen. MySQL is a quick and, above all, cheap solution. As long as you access the databases as read-only, MySQL can definitely keep up with commercial databases. Databases such as SQL Server, Oracle8i, or IBM DB2 guarantee full transaction support which enables you to execute thousands of read and write actions simultaneously on the data, without the separate actions interfering with each other.

The following sections deal with the different ways of accessing relational databases from an application.

19.3.1 Dynamic SQL

ODBC and/or JDBC are flexible, simple interfaces for the programming of SQL with Java. But with the standardization of the interface, some product-specific optimizations cannot be used. If you are obliged to optimize your applications, the product-specific interface should be used. However, this usually requires a certain amount familiarization time.

As the SQL query is at first checked in ODBC and JDBC, these two interfaces are called dynamic.

19.3.2 Embedded SQL

The SQLJ standard is an interesting development, available, for instance, for the Oracle server. Using it, you can integrate SQL queries closer in the Java program text and even make a compiler check the syntax of the SQL statements. Furthermore, the result of a select query can be saved directly in a Java variable without using a ResultSet. The approach is also called *Embedded SQL*.

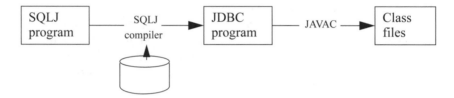

Figure 19.2: The SQLJ compiler checks the source code using the information of the database to be accessed, and creates a corresponding JDBC program automatically.

The following brief example shows the advantages of SQLJ. Let's asume that the name of the collaborator has to be determined with the ID 24372. PreparedStatement and ResultSet objects would be necessary with JDBC. With SQLJ, this can be written in a few lines:

```
String name;
int id = 24372;
#sql {select name into :name from collaborator where id=:id);
System.out.println("The name is" + name);
```

For instance, if the name of the table is not collaborator but staff, the compiler intercepts this error immediately, as it tests the information about the database schema. Figure 19.1 shows this process. In a JDBC program, a similar error would only be noticed when the program is run and an SQLException is thrown. Clearly, this simplifies the development considerably.

19.3.3 Stored procedures

Stored procedures enable you to transfer the application logic from the database client directly to the database server. This offers the advantage that it is not necessary to transfer the result table via the network. This brief example illustrates the SQL instruction for the creation of a stored procedure `turnover` that calculates the daily sales returns.

```
CREATE PROCEDURE turnover
    @tag char(3), @sum int output
    AS
    BEGIN
        SELECT @sum = sum (number* price)
        FROM order
        WHERE tag = @tag
    END
```

Obviously, stored procedures can undertake far more complex operations. In case of the Books Online Web page, the review of prices in the shopping basket, for example, is a good candidate for a stored procedure. The Java program can call a stored procedure, like a prepared statement, on the `CallableStatement` class.

The Oracle database server also enables you to write stored procedures with SQLJ and Java. Therefore it is always worth considering stored procedures as an alternative in the creation of a database application.

19.3.4 JDBC 2.0

The new version of the Java Database Connectivity API offers interesting new features. For instance, distributed transactions and connection pooling are directly supported. Moreover, some optimizations regarding speed are carried out. So it is possible, for example, to send several update instructions to the database all at once. The classes are contained in the package `javax.sql`.

19.3.5 ActiveX Data Objects

ActiveX Data Objects, called also ADODB, is the database interface propagated by Microsoft. On the OLE DB provider for ODBC it is possible to create connections to the ODBC data sources. ADODB supersedes the Remote Data Objects (RDO) and Data Access Objects (DAO) interfaces. The ASP example in Section 19.1.3 on page 389 shows the similarity to JDBC. There are also Connection and ResultSet Objects which work exactly as their JDBC pendants here.

Chapter 20

Technology interaction

In the previous chapter we introduced different alternatives, for example to create dynamic Web pages. In this chapter we do not want to compare the products and specifications of different manufacturers, but discuss meaningful combinations of Web applications, databases, communication with Remote Procedure Calls (RPC), HTML, and XML independently of special software.

In the development of a distributed system, we face a question of principle, i.e. in which form the information has to be transferred via the network. Figure 17.1 on page 357 illustrates different ways in which clients, servers, and databases communicate. Let us explain the terminology again: clients can be browsers as well as individual programs with a user interface. But using the word "servers," we mean components that answer queries and do not offer a user interface. Servers can also call each other. For instance, the credit card server is called by a servlet of the Books Online Web application. Figure 20.1 extends this graphic to two more XML options and uses the general concept in place of the Java terminology. Here we wish to convey a general idea about these two scenarios.

20.1 HTML on HTTP

The furthest spread variant is the transmission of information as an HTML page. Each Web page performing a search function belongs to this category. HTML is easy to learn and browsers tolerate many errors in the HTML text. This variant is an excellent solution when, on the client side, the information only has to be presented to the user.

However, there are problems when computations have to be carried out. Even a simple sorting of a table can no longer be carried out with the data coded in HTML. This operation must be propagated back to the server which holds the information in a structured form and therefore can perform calculations on the data without any problems. For instance, the result of a JDBC database query is such a data structure. For the servlet it is easy to pick out and sort the data. The database server itself implements SQL operations such as ORDER BY and can do calculations with the stored information. The shopping basket object, created in the user session, is also a structured data type which enables simple access to the values. However, as soon as this data, formatted as HTML, reaches the browser, it is almost impossible to retrieve the underlying data.

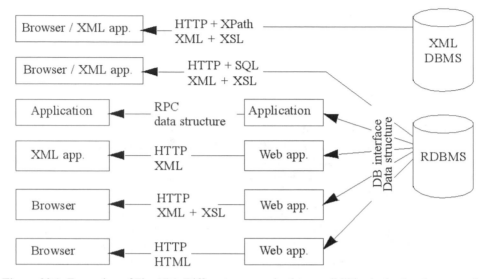

Figure 20.1: Expansion of Fig. 17.1. Different communication possibilities in the development of a Web-based database application.

20.2 XML and XSL on HTTP

Unlike HTML, XML is based on a hierarchical data structure which easily is accessible to any software containing an XML parser. Such applications can be very different. It can be a Java application, as in the example of the price comparison agents. But it is also possible to access the XML data from a common browser.

You can work with a clear data structure if you separate the layout from the content. The layout (i.e. how XML data is presented) is saved in an XSL stylesheet. XSL is a very expressive language, which not only enables the developer to establish how a price element has to be represented. Elements also can be treated in different ways, according to their position in the document. You also can make the representation of the price dependent on the product to which the price refers. However, here it is important that the information that we are dealing with prices remains visible in any case.

A further fundamental advantage offered by the separation of the content from the layout is that different publications such as booklets and Web pages are based on one and the same document. This avoids the redundant storage of data. Modifications have to be carried out just once, thus avoiding any inconsistency between the different publication forms.

An XML-based solution requires discipline on the part of the developer, as the XML parser rejects the work even with simple errors. On the other hand, such "clean" data can serve as a basis for computations. As already mentioned, a simple JavaScript function can sort, for instance, a table according to different criteria, without contacting the server again. Even if, on the one hand, those who create XML documents feel the need to avoid errors as a burden, on the other hand this obligation makes the developer's work easier. Today, browser software is based on very complex source code that must deal with, and interpret, all common HTML errors. However, as we have seen, it is not difficult to program an efficient XML application.

But XML offers further interesting options. In this way, the same Web application can supply a browser and also a program such as our agent with data. Browsers display data with a stylesheet in a graphic form for the user, while the agent processes it further. Both applications are used by the same Web application, even if they are very different. This shows the enormous flexibility of XML and clarifies that the complete Web application can be created with a limited programming effort.

20.3 Solutions without logic on the Web server

Going a step further into Web applications, you realize that it is possible to get by without servlets or other programs on the Web server. Servlets, ASP scripts, and so on often just convert data from one representation to another. In our example, data is saved with the dbLoad method from a JDBC result into book objects and written into very similarly structured XML data records with the toXML method.

```
public void dbLoad(ResultSet res) throws SQLException {
    isbn = res.getString("isbn").trim();
    title = res.getString("title").trim();
    price = res.getFloat("price");
    number = res.getInt("number");
}

public String toXML() {
    return
        ....
    "  <book>" +
    "    <isbn>" + isbn + "</isbn>" +
    "    <title>" + title + "</title>" +
    "    <price>" +
    ...
}
```

The Active Server Pages example in the previous chapter is a very typical example. While our Books Online servlet implements relatively complex application logic such as the shopping basket, only one result table is transformed into HTML there.

Nowadays, many relational databases can supply the results of an SQL query already formatted in XML. As the second communication model above (Figure 20.1) shows, the browser could send the SQL query directly to the database as the parameter of a URL and represent the result coded in XML. In this case the DTD can be directly derived from the table definition.

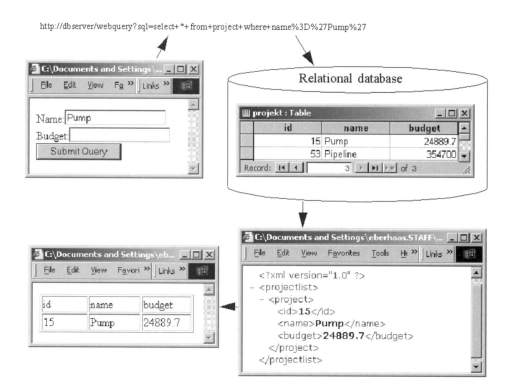

Figure 20.2: The database server is able to carry out queries on a table on the WWW even without programming.

As shown in Fig. 20.2, as a user interface you could use a form in which the search parameters are given. Here you should test the information on the pump project. A little JavaScript function, included with the form as an add-on, can read the search criteria, work in the required SQL query and send them to the database server via HTTP. In this case the JavaScript function could be generated with some sort of Wizard tool, provided with the database software. Finally, a stylesheet supplies the representation of the XML result in table form.

Compared to this solution, the XSQL approach introduced in Chapter 15 on page 283 represents a more server-oriented variant. But with XSQL, neither servlets nor other programs need to be developed.

The advantage is obvious: it is not particularly difficult to develop programs able to convert data from one representation to another, but experience shows that companies usually pay dearly for developing their own source code. Just take into account what happens if a further attribute is inserted into the database. This requires reworking all programs that deal with the data conversion. If these are implemented in a confused manner and badly documented, such an apparently easy task can take quite a long time.

A further and often decisive advantage over a conventional database application is that XML-based solutions work completely with the existing, very elaborated and widely spread Internet infrastructure. These include DNS *Name Servers*, the fact that in practice each user has a browser and each firm a Web server, open HTTP ports on firewalls, and the wide XML (and soon XSL) support in browsers, document management systems, and databases. Now the development of stylesheets and simple JavaScript components for the choice of data and form evaluation is still relatively costly. As we briefly mentioned in the example of the Web database wizard, with an increasing number of applications it will soon be possible to generate scripts and stylesheets for the distribution of data in a certain schema automatically.

In such a system, separate program components such as servlets do not have to be used for simple tasks such as reading and adding form parameters in SQL queries and reformatting JDBC results to HTML. The programmer can concentrate on the programming of the fundamental tasks, for instance transaction handling or the description of more complex business operations.

20.4 XPath-based solutions

More and more database and document management systems support XPath. Here the scenario looks like the SQL-based solution in the previous section: the user sends an XPath query via HTTP to an XPath database and is given back dynamically generated XML.

The Tamino Server of Software AG is an information management system that puts these variants into effect. While the XML interface to relational database servers just presented encodes only tabular structures in XML, and is therefore restricted by the relational data model, XML builds an ideal platform in combination with XPath for the storage and retieval of semi-structured data.

An interesting aspect of the Tamino package is that besides XML documents you also can integrate relational databases. If a firm has implemented an address management system and some related applications under SQL Server, for instance, Tamino can be configured so that addresses contained in XML documents are saved in the relational data model. However, this internal storage is transparent from the outside. A user who receives a document with a call for project proposals will not realize that the addresses contained in the document were not originally available in XML. This option allows XML to be introduced step by step into an operation for suitable areas of responsibility and the new software to be integrated with the existing infrastructure.

20.5 Remote procedure calls

After the explanations in the last section, one could wonder why XML is not used in all apects of communication and why RPC solutions such as CORBA and database interfaces such as JDBC are still used.

As a developer of such a distributed system, you should be careful to combine different techniques in the right way and to bring the advantages of the respective solutions to the overall system. Generally speaking, it is very difficult to give recommendations since there are many parameters, such as the network architecture, the installed operating systems, and individual requirements of the system, which influence the choice of technique.

In our Books Online project, for instance, it is definitely appropriate to convert the search functionality into XML completely, since very limited application logic is required in this case. However, there are also numerous scenarios in which an RPC solution can be implemented in a more efficient and easy way. The advantages of XML consist in the use of very heterogeneous systems over the Internet and in the management of semi-structured data. In the Books Online system this is reflected by the XML search interface.

RPC solutions are advantageous if closely cooperating program components have to communicate, but the architecture of the system does not enable the components to run on the same computer. Let us consider the credit card server as an example, which has to be available for many components. It would be possible to initiate the transfer by sending an XML message. However, CORBA is more suitable in the case because it is more integrated in the Java program. The call of a method on the server appears to the programmer like a call of a local method. The data types remain unchanged and the communication speed is substantially higher. The possibilities offered by XML through stylesheets and its support in many tools are not useful here.

The situation would be different, if there were an XML standard for the handling of a credit card booking and our *commerce service provider,* Easy Commerce, had installed the software with the corresponding XML interface. However, this is not the case, as CORBA is the best variant here. With respect to JDBC, we can say the same for transaction handling. In this case the whole JDBC repertoire is exhausted and XML is not an alternative.

A further example of a meaningful use of RPCs is systems such as Microsoft Transaction Server or Enterprise Java Beans, which enable the user to develop applications able to process many parallel queries easily. Internally, these systems work with RPC mechanisms such as DCOM, CORBA, or RMI, in order to distribute the load among many computers.

In the previous discussion, SOAP has not yet been mentioned as a hybrid solution between the consignment of XML documents and RPC calls. SOAP is based on XML as transport format but its functionality is similar to that of DCOM and CORBA. As happens with other very new tecniques, there are not many applications based on SOAP. Nevertheless, there is a point in favor of SOAP which makes it successful: neither CORBA, RMI nor DCOM is suitable for very heterogeneous systems. Chapter 10 describes some of the problems that occur when CORBA programs are developed and tested with ORBs and name servers from different manufacturers. RMI and DCOM are usually limited to Java or Windows. As far as communication speed is concerned, SOAP cannot compete with any alternative, but as already noticed in Section 20.3, SOAP works easily with firewalls and does not need its own name server. SOAP simply uses the proven DNS infrastructure of the WWW. On the basis of initiatives such as UDDI and the specification of interfaces to SOAP-based Web services, it will be soon possible to call up information and services not only by means of manual browsers but also using programs.

20.6 Scalable design of Web applications

Besides the different means of communication between clients and servers, it also is interesting to know how application servers can be applied. In this book two different configurations are introduced: Chapter 14 on page 261 introduces the EJB solution, based on an application server, while in Chapter 8 on page 125 it is shown that servlets construct the middle tier using their own helper classes.

Application servers relieve the developer of some tasks, such as the instantiation of new server objects or connection pooling. In the high-end field functionality is important, as well as the safe processing of distributed transactions and the support of server clusters. The use of corresponding application server software is therefore a great advantage. However, the use of application servers also brings some disadvantages. Besides the purchase costs, we also have to take into consideration the expediture for configuration and administration. If the load is relatively low, the additional software layer also slows down the system.

An ideal solution is a software design which, with limited effort, can be adapted to an application server. In order to fulfill this purpose, possibly a large amount of functionality should be packed into separate classes which are used by servlets. These helper classes can be converted into session and entity beans and transferred from the servlet container to the application server.

Appendix A

JDBC reference

This appendix addresses the JDBC interface for database connectivity in Java programs. First we consider the Java interface. The following two sections describe the transaction support and the database error messages generated my MySQL, Access 97, and SQL Server 7. The appendix is concluded by a mapping of SQL and Java datatypes.

A.1 The JDBC interface

A complete representation of the JDBC interface would be out of context in this case. We refer to the Web page of this book presented in Appendix H on page 467, which contains a link to the JDBC API documentation. Otherwise the documentation can also be seen directly at `http://java.sun.com/products/jdk/1.3/docs/api/java/sql/package-summary.html`. We will briefly mention the most important classes again:

- `DriverManager` selects a database driver and establishes the connection to a database. The most important method is `getConnection()` which sends back a `Connection` object that encapsulates the database connection.
- `Connection` represents a connection to the database.
- `PreparedStatement` enables you to prepare and execute an SQL command in the database (method execute).
- `ResultSet` is a container for all results which the database provides. The user of this object will normally iterate over all result rows by means of a cursor.

A.2 Transaction support in database products

Table A.1 conveys a general idea of transaction support in the database products used in this book, i.e. Microsoft Access 97, Microsoft SQL Server 7.0, and MySQL.

Database	MS SQL Server 7.0	MS Access 97	MySQL 3.22 win32
JDBC driver	JDBC-ODBC	JDBC-ODBC	mm.mysql.jdbc1.2b
Transaction supports (commit and rollback are implemented not only as empty methods)	yes	yes	no
TRANSACTION_READ_ UNCOMMITTED	yes	no	no
TRANSACTION_READ_ COMMITTED (dirty reads do not occur)	yes	yes	no
TRANSACTION_REPEATABLE _ READ (dirty and non-repeatable reads do not occur)	yes	no	no
TRANSACTION_ SERIALIZABLE (dirty, non-repeatable, and phantom reads do not occur)	yes	no	no

Table A.1: transaction support of different data bases.

A.3 Error messages of different database products

Table A.2 shows possible error messages of the considered database products executing different actions on the database.

Database		MS SQL Server 7.0	MS Access 97	MySQL 3.22 win32
JDBC driver		JDBC-ODBC	JDBC-ODBC	mm.mysql.jdbc 1.2b
ODBC driver		3.70.	4.00	
Action				
Insertion of an existing primary key	Text	[Microsoft][ODBC SQL Server Driver][SQL Server]Violation of PRIMARY KEY constraint 'PK__order__1BC8 21DD'. Cannot insert duplicate key in object 'order'.	General error	Error during query: Unexpected Exception: java.sql.SQLExcepti on message given: Invalid argument value: Duplicate entry 'wehw-ew262-4724742' for key 1
	SQL state	23000	S1000	S1000
	Error code	2627	0	0

Table A.2: Error messages of different database servers.

Database		MS SQL Server 7.0	MS Access 97	MySQL 3.22 win32
Violation of a foreign key constraint	Text	[Microsoft][ODBC SQL Server Driver][SQL Server]INSERT statement conflicted with COLUMN FOREIGN KEY constraint 'FK__order__customer__1CBC46 16'. The conflict occurred in the 'book' database , 'customer' table, 'email' column.	java.sql.SQLE xception: [Microsoft][O DBC Microsoft Access Driver] You cannot add or change a record because a related record is required in the 'book' table .	No error as this functionality is not yet implemented in MySQL.
	SQL state	23000	23000	
	Error code	547	1613	
Violation of the (number > 0) costraint	Text	[Microsoft][ODBC SQL Server Driver][SQL Server]INSERT statement conflicted with COLUMN CHECK constraint 'CK__book__numbe r__17F790F9'. The conflict occurred in the 'book' database , 'book' table, 'number' column .	[Microsoft][O DBC Microsoft Access Driver]Option al feature not implemented	No error as this functionality is not yet implemented in MySQL.
	SQL state	23000	S1C00	
	Error code	547	106	

Table A.2: Error messages of different database servers.

Database		MS SQL Server 7.0	MS Access 97	MySQL 3.22 win32
False table name	Text	[Microsoft][ODBC SQL Server Driver][SQL Server]Invalid object name 'order'.	[Microsoft][ODBC Microsoft Access Driver] Could not find output table 'order'.	Error during query: Unexpected Exception: java.sql.SQLException message given: General error: Table 'test.order' does not exist
	SQL state	S0002	S0002	S1000
	Error code	208	1305	0
Auto commit turned off	Text	no error	no error	Cannot disable AUTO_COMMIT
	SQL state			8003
	Error code			0
Set transaction isolation level to TRANSACTION_READ_UNCOMMITTED	Text	no error	[Microsoft][ODBC Microsoft Access Driver]Optional feature not implemented	Transaction Isolation Levels are not supported.
	SQL state		S1C00	S1C00
	Error code		106	0

Table A.2: Error messages of different database servers.

Database		MS SQL Server 7.0	MS Access 97	MySQL 3.22 win32
Set transaction isolation level to TRANSAC TION_SER IALIZABL E	Text	no error	[Microsoft][O DBC Microsoft Access Driver]Option al feature not implemented	Transaction Isolation Levels are not supported.
	SQL state		S1C00	S1C00
	Error code		106	0
Call commit and rollback		no error	no error	no error
Two queries are open simultaneo usly on the same connection	Text	[Microsoft][ODBC SQL Server Driver]Connection is busy with results for another hstmt	no error	no error
	SQL state	S1000		
	Error code	0		

Table A.2: Error messages of different database servers.

A.4 Mapping SQL data types to Java types

Tables A.3 and A.4 show how SQL data types are mapped to Java types. This happens when the results are selected from a Resultset result table by means of the getXXX methods, for example `res.getInt("number")` or when the parameters of a PreparedStatement are set with a setXXX method, for instance in `pstmt.setString(2, book.title)`. When the table is created in the database, the SQL data type is set. The application uses the data type which is assigned to the SQL type in this table. A column defined in the table as Time is presented to the Java program as a java.sql.Time object.

Table A.3 describes the simple data type. Table A.4 explains the complex types such as *Binary Large Object* (BLOB), *Character Large Object* (CLOB), arrays, structured types, and references on structured types, defined in SQL3 Standard.

SQL data type	Java data type	getXXX method	setXXX method
CHAR	String	getString	setString
VARCHAR	String	getString	setString
LONG VARCHAR	String	getString	setString
NUMERIC	java.math.Big Decimal	getBigDecimal	setBigDecimal
DECIMAL	java.math.Big Decimal	getBigDecimal	setBigDecimal
BIT	boolean	getBoolean	setBoolean
TINYINT	byte	getByte	setByte
SMALLINT	short	getShort	setShort
INTEGER	int	getInt	setInt
BIGINT	long	getLong	setLong
REAL	float	getFloat	setFloat
FLOAT	double	getDouble	setDouble
DOUBLE	double	getDouble	setDouble
BINARY	byte[]	getBytes	setBytes
VARBINARY	byte[]	getBytes	setBytes
LONGVAR-BINARY	byte[]	getBytes	setBytes
DATE	java.sql.Date	getDate	setDate
TIME	java.sql.Time	getTime	setTime

Table A.3: Mapping of SQL data types in Java

SQL data type	Java data type	getXXX method	setXXX method
TIMESTAMP	java.sql. Timestamp	getTimestamp	setTimestamp

Table A.3: Mapping of SQL data types in Java

SQL3 data type	Java data type	getXXX method	setXXX method
BLOB	java.sql.Blob	getBlob	setBlob
CLOB	java.sql.Clob	getClob	setClob
ARRAY	java.sql.Array	getArray	setArray
Structured type	java.sql.Struct	getObject	setObject
REF (structured type)	java.sql.Ref	getRef	setRef

Table A.4: Mapping of SQL3 data types in Java

Appendix B

Servlet objects

The class libraries `javax.servlet` or `java.servlet.http` contain a large number of predefined classes and interfaces which have to be used to develop servlets. This appendix lists their methods and what the methods are used for.

B.1 The interface `Servlet`

Each servlet has to implement the interface `Servlet` either directly or by extending the class `GenericServlet` or `HttpServlet`. The interface defines some fundamental functions that each servlet normally owns. We refer fundamentally to the realization of the life cycle of a servlet. We list here the individual methods.

- `void destroy()`
  is called by the servlet container (in principle by the servlet engine), in order to show the servlet that it is no longer available. The method can be used to "tidy up," such as to close open database connections, etc.
- `ServletConfig getServletConfig()`
  provides an object of the ServletConfig type (see Section B.10 on page 432) which includes the initialization parameters and their values for this servlet.
- `java.lang.String getServletInfo()`
  supplies a piece of information about the servlet as a character string. The contents of the character string are e.g. author of the servlet, version or copyright remarks.
- `void init(ServletConfig config)`
  is called by the servlet container in order to execute the initialization of a servlet.
- `void service(ServletRequest req, ServletResponse res)`
  is also called by the servlet container when the servlet has to process a client query. This is the central method of a servlet.

B.2 The abstract class `GenericServlet`

`GenericServlet` is an abstract class that implements the servlet interface. In order to use this class, you have to write a new class inherited from `GenericServlet` and implement at least the method `service()`.

- `void destroy()`
  is called by the servlet container (in principle by the servlet engine), to show the servlet that it is no longer available. The method can be used to "tidy up," such as to close open database connections, etc.
- `java.lang.String getInitParameter (java.lang.String name)`
  provides a string which contains the value of the initialization parameter identified by name. If the parameter does not exist, the method retuns null.
- `java.util.Enumeration getInitParameterNames()`
  provides the names of all initialization parameters of the servlet as an enumeration of string objects. If the servlet does not own any similar parameter, the method supplies an empty enumeration.
- `ServletConfig getServletConfig()`
  returns a ServletConfig object which describes the configuration of the servlet. Details on this object can be found in Section B.10 on page 432.
- `ServletContext getServletContext()`
  returns a reference to the ServletContext object that describes in which context the servlet works. Details on this object can be found in Section B.10 on page 432.
- `java.lang.String getServletInfo()`
  sends back information about the servlet as a character string. The contents of the character string are e.g. the author of the servlet, version or copyright remarks.
- `java.lang.String getServletName()`
  returns the name of this servlet instance.
- `void init()`
  this method can be overridden for easier use, avoiding calling the method `super.init` (config).
- `void init(ServletConfig config)`
  is called by the servlet container to execute the intialization of a servlet.
- `void log(java.lang.String msg)`
  writes the message given in a protocol file in which the name of the servlet is set before the message.
- `void log(java.lang.String message,java.lang.Throwablet)`
  writes the message that has to be explained as well as a stack trace for a throwable exception in the protocol file of the servlet in which the method indicates the servlet name again.
- `abstract void service(ServletRequest request, ServletResponse response)`
  is called by the servlet container when the servlet has to process a client query. This is the central method of a servlet.

B.3 The interface `ServletRequest`

`ServletRequest` is an interface implemented by the servlet engine. An object of this type is submitted to the servlet calling the `service()` method and includes information about the data sent by the client and the environment variables.

- `java.lang.Object getAttribute(java.lang.String name)`
  gives the value of the parameter/attribute identified by `name` as a reference of the generalized type object. If this parameter is not available the method returns null. A Servlet uses this method to read the values of form fields as provided by the user.
- `java.util.Enumeration getAttributeNames()`
  provides an enumeration containing the names of all available parameters/attributes.
- `java.lang.String getCharacterEncoding()`
  indicates the name of the character coding that is used for this client query.
- `int getContentLength()`
  indicates the length of the client query (only that of the content) in bytes. If the length is not known, the value −1 is sent back.
- `java.lang.String getContentType()`
  returns the MIME type of the content of the query. If the type is not known, the value −1 is sent back.
- `ServletInputStream getInputStream()`
  picks up the content of the query as binary data on a `ServletInputStream`.
- `java.util.Locale getLocale()`
  provides the preferential locale in which the client receives the contents. The return value is based on the *Accept Language Header*.
- `java.util.Enumeration getLocales()`
  supplies an enumeration of local objects that shows the preferential local settings in descending order. This information is based on the *Accept Language Header*.
- `java.lang.String getParameter(java.lang.String name)`
  gives the value of the parameter defined by `name` as a string. If the parameter does not exist, the method gives the value null.
- `java.util.Enumeration getParameterNames()`
  returns an enumeration of string objects which contains the names of all parameters available in this client query.
- `java.lang.String[] getParameterValues(String name)`
  returns an array of string objects that contains all values for the parameter identified by `name`. If the parameter does not exist, the method returns null.
- `java.lang.String getProtocol()`
  returns the name of the protocol used for the query, in which the text has the form *protocol/majorVersion.minorVersion*, for instance HTTP/1.1.
- `java.io.BufferedReader getReader()`
  returns the content of the query character-based (ASCII) on a BufferedReader.

- `java.lang.String getRealPath(java.lang.String path)`
  obsolete method. From Version 2.1 of Servlet-API the method `ServletContext.getRealPath(java.lang.String)` should be used.
- `java.lang.String getRemoteAddr()`
  returns the Internet address (IP address) of the client computer that sent the query.
- `java.lang.String getRemoteHost()`
  gives the complete Internet host name of the computer that generated the query. If the name cannot be determined, the IP address of the computer is given.
- `RequestDispatcher getRequestDispatcher(String path)`
  returns an object of the RequestDispatcher type that functions as wrapping for the resource obtainable under the given path.
- `java.lang.String getScheme()`
  returns the name of the protocol to which this query was transmitted, i.e. http, https, or ftp.
- `java.lang.String getServerName()`
  supplies the host name of the server that has received this query.
- `int getServerPort()`
  indicates the port number on which the query was given.
- `boolean isSecure()`
  returns a boolean value that shows whether the query was transferred on a safe connection.
- `void removeAttribute(java.lang.String name)`
  deletes a parameter/an attribute in this query.
- `void setAttribute(String name, java.lang.Object o)`
  saves a parameter/an attribute in the query object.

B.4 The interface `ServletResponse`

The counterpart of `ServletRequest` is the interface `ServletResponse`, which is also implemented by the servlet engine. On an object of this type a servlet returns above all its output to the client.

- `void flushBuffer()`
  finally sends the data to the client, in case it has remained in the buffer.
- `int getBufferSize()`
  indicates the size of the buffer that is used to answer the client.
- `java.lang.String getCharacterEncoding()`
  gives the name of the character coding that is used for the content of the answer.
- `java.util.Locale getLocale()`
  returns the local adaptation that is used for the answer.

- `ServletOutputStream getOutputStream()`
  supplies a `ServletOutputStream`, suitable for the transmission of binary data as an answer.
- `java.io.PrintWriter getWriter()`
  provides an object of type PrintWriter with which the ASCII text can be sent to the client.
- `boolean isCommitted()`
  returns a boolean value that shows whether the answer has already been submitted.
- `void reset()`
  deletes all data from the buffer and initializes the status code as well as all header fields.
- `void setBufferSize(int size)`
  sets the preferential buffer size for the content of the answer to the client.
- `void setContentLength(int len)`
  sets the length of the content of the answer. With HTTP servlets the method sets the *HTTP Content Length Header*.
- `void setContentType(java.lang.String type)`
  sets the content type of the answer that has to be sent to the client.
- `void setLocale(java.util.Locale loc)`
  sets the local adaptation of the answer, fixing the header field accordingly.

B.5 The class `HttpServlet`

`HttpServlet` is an abstract class that inherits from the class `GenericServlet`. The user has to override at least one of the methods `doGet()`, `doPut()`, `doPost()`, or `doDelete()`, which are available especially for the treatment of HTTP queries.

- `void service(ServletRequest req, ServletResponse res)`
  treats all the queries that reach a client, not like `GenericServlet` but by passing the queries on to the other methods as HTTP queries. Therefore the methods are not overridden.
- `void doDelete(HttpServletRequest, HttpServletResponse)`
  executes the HTTP DELETE operation. If the method is not overridden, it returns HTTP BAD REQUEST.
- `void doGet(HttpServletRequest, HttpServletResponse)`
  executes the HTTP GET operation. If the method is not overridden, it returns HTTP BAD REQUEST.
- `void doOptions(HttpServletRequest, HttpServletResponse)`
  carries out the HTTP OPTIONS operation. If the method is not overridden, it establishes automatically which options are supported by HTTP. Normally, this method should not be overtyped.

- ▨ void doPost(HttpServletRequest, HttpServletResponse)
  executes the HTTP POST operation. If not overridden, the method returns HTTP
  BAD REQUEST.
- ▨ void doPut(HttpServletRequest, HttpServletResponse)
  executes the HTTP PUT operation. If not overridden, the method returns HTTP BAD
  REQUEST.
- ▨ void doTrace(HttpServletRequest, HttpServletResponse)
  executes the HTTP TRACE operation. If the method is not overridden, an answer is
  generated which returns all headfields to which the query referred. Normally, this
  method should not be overridden.

B.6 The interface **HttpServletRequest**

HttpServletRequest inherits the features of ServletRequest and performs
similar tasks, namely providing the features of the client, such as information about the
environment, for the servlet. The interface extends the possibilities, with HTTP-specific
queries being supported.

- ▨ java.lang.String getAuthType()
  returns the name of the authentication schemes which protect the servlet. Possible
  values are, for instance, "BASIC", "SSL" (when *Secure Socket Layer* is used), or
  zero, if the servlet is not protected.
- ▨ java.lang.String getContextPath()
  enters the URL which provides the context of the query.
- ▨ Cookie[] getCookies()
  returns an array containing all objects of the Cookie type enclosed by the client of the
  query.
- ▨ long getDateHeader(java.lang.String name)
  provides the value of the query header identified by name as a value of type long that
  represents an object of type Date.
- ▨ java.lang.String getHeader(java.lang.String name)
  returns the header of the query as a string.
- ▨ java.util.Enumeration getHeaderNames()
  returns all header names contained in this query as an enumeration.
- ▨ java.util.Enumeration getHeaders(java.lang.String name)
  returns all values of a query header identified by name as an enumeration of string
  objects.
- ▨ int getIntHeader(java.lang.String name)
  returns the value of the query header identified by name as an int.
- ▨ java.lang.String getMethod()
  returns the name of the HTTP method (GET, POST, PUT, etc.) on which this query
  was transmitted as a string.

■   `java.lang.String getPathInfo()`
provides the path specified with the URL by the client.

■   `java.lang.String getPathTranslated()`
enters the path of the URL that follows the name of the servlet but preceeds the query character string. Before being returned, the path is converted into a "genuine" path.

■   `java.lang.String getQueryString()`
returns the query character string given in the query URL after the path.

■   `java.lang.String getRemoteUser()`
returns the user's login name to the client computer, provided that the user was identified. Otherwise the value zero is returned.

■   `java.lang.String getRequestedSessionId()`
returns the session ID specified by the client.

■   `java.lang.String getRequestURI()`
returns the URL which serves the protocol names as well as the query character string.

■   `java.lang.String getServletPath()`
returns that part of the path from the query URL that calls the servlet.

■   `HttpSession getSession()`
returns a reference to the session connected with the query. If this query owns no session, one is created calling the method.

■   `HttpSession getSession(boolean create)`
returns a reference to the session connected with the query. If this query has no session, one is created calling the method, provided that the value of the boolean variable is true.

■   `java.security.Principal getUserPrincipal()`
returns an object of type `java.security.Principal` which contains the identified user.

■   `boolean isRequestedSessionIdFromCookie()`
checks if the required session ID was transmitted as a cookie.

■   `boolean isRequestedSessionIdFromUrl()`
obsolete method. It should be replaced with the method `isRequestedSessionIdFromURL()`.

■   `boolean isRequestedSessionIdFromURL()`
checks if the required session ID is received in the servlet as part of the URL.

■   `boolean isRequestedSessionIdValid()`
checks if the session ID is still valid.

■   `boolean isUserInRole(java.lang.String role)`
returns a boolean value which indicates if the authenticated user is part of the logic role (identified by `role`).

B.7 The interface `HttpServletResponse`

`HttpServletResponse` is the counterpart of `HttpServletRequest`. It enables the server to send the answer to the client. In comparison with interface ServletResponse, inherited from this interface, it contains HTTP-specific status messages. The interface is implemented by the servlet engine.

■   `static int SC_ACCEPTED`
    Status-Code (202) indicates that a query for the processing was accepted but not completely executed.
■   `static int SC_BAD_GATEWAY`
    Status-Code (502) indicates that the HTTP server (Web server) has received an invalid answer from a server that has contacted it in its role as a proxy or gateway.
■   `static int SC_BAD_REQUEST`
    Status-Code (400) indicates that the query sent by the client was not correct from the syntactically incorrect.
■   `static int SC_CONFLICT`
    Status-Code (409) indicates that the query could not be completely executed because it conflicted with the current substance of the resource.
■   `static int SC_CONTINUE`
    Status-Code (100) tells the client that it can continue.
■   `static int SC_CREATED`
    Status-Code (201) indicates that the query was succesful and a new resource was created on the server.
■   `static int SC_EXPECTATION_FAILED`
    Status-Code (417) indicates that the server could not fulfile the expectations that the client expressed in its query header.
■   `static int SC_FORBIDDEN`
    Status-Code (403) indicates that the server understood the query but refused to execute it.
■   `static int SC_GATEWAY_TIMEOUT`
    Status-Code (504) indicates that the server has received no answer in the time allowed from another server it had contacted as proxy or gateway.
■   `static int SC_GONE`
    Status-Code (410) indicates that the required resource is not available on the server anymore and that no forwarding address is known.
■   `static int SC_HTTP_VERSION_NOT_SUPPORTED`
    Status-Code (505) indicates that the HTTP version used to transmit the query does not support or at least refuses to support the query.
■   `static int SC_INTERNAL_SERVER_ERROR`
    Status-Code (500) shows an internal error of the HTTP server that impedes the execution of the query.

- `static int SC_LENGTH_REQUIRED`
  Status-Code (411) indicates that the query cannot be dealt with, since no defined *Content-Length* exists.
- `static int SC_METHOD_NOT_ALLOWED`
  Status-Code (405) indicates that the method given in the *Request Line* is not scheduled for access to the resource given with the URL.
- `static int SC_MOVED_PERMANENTLY`
  Status-Code (301) indicates that the addressed resource has been permanently transferred to a different place. From here on, you should use the new URL.
- `static int SC_MOVED_TEMPORARILY`
  Status-Code (302) indicates that a resource has been temporary transferred to another place. To access to the resource again, you have to use the old URL.
- `static int SC_MULTIPLE_CHOICES`
  Status-Code (300) indicates that the required resource corresponds to a series of representations, and each of them has its own storage location.
- `static int SC_NO_CONTENT`
  Status-Code (204) indicates that the query was successful but no information is available.
- `static int SC_NON_AUTHORITATIVE_INFORMATION`
  Status-Code (203) indicates that the meta-information presented by the client does not date from this server.
- `static int SC_NOT_ACCEPTABLE`
  Status-Code (406) indicates that the resource identified by the query can only generate answers that do not agree with the default given in the header.
- `static int SC_NOT_FOUND`
  Status-Code (404) indicates that the required resource is not available.
- `static int SC_NOT_IMPLEMENTED`
  Status-Code (501) indicates that the HTTP server does not have the necessary functionality to fulfill the query.
- `static int SC_NOT_MODIFIED`
  Status-Code (304) indicates that a contingent GET operation has found the resource but could not carry out any modifications.
- `static int SC_OK`
  Status-Code (200) indicates that the query could be executed normally and was successfully concluded.
- `static int SC_PARTIAL_CONTENT`
  Status-Code (206) indicates that an HTTP server could process a partial GET query successfully.
- `static int SC_PAYMENT_REQUIRED`
  Status-Code (402) is reserved for future use.
- `static int SC_PRECONDITION_FAILED`
  Status-Code (412) indicates that the preconditions for the execution of a query, which were specified in one or more header fields, were not fulfilled when they were tested on the server.

- `static int SC_PROXY_AUTHENTICATION_REQUIRED`
  Status-Code (407) indicates that the client has to be authenticated by a proxy before the query can be processed.
- `static int SC_REQUEST_ENTITY_TOO_LARGE`
  Status-Code (413) indicates that the server refuses to process the query because it is too large.
- `static int SC_REQUEST_TIMEOUT`
  Status-Code (408) indicates that the client has not sent any query during the time that the server was waiting.
- `static int SC_REQUEST_URI_TOO_LONG`
  Status-Code (414) indicates that the server refuses to treat the query, because the length of the URL transmitted is greater than the maximum length accepted by the server.
- `static int SC_REQUESTED_RANGE_NOT_SATISFIABLE`
  Status-Code (416) indicates that the server cannot use the required byte area.
- `static int SC_RESET_CONTENT`
  Status-Code (205) asks the client to return to the document view that led to this status code.
- `static int SC_SEE_OTHER`
  Status-Code (303) indicates that the answer to the query indicated can be found under another URL.
- `static int SC_SERVICE_UNAVAILABLE`
  Status-Code (503) indicates that the HTTP server is overloaded at times and therefore the query cannot be processed.
- `static int SC_SWITCHING_PROTOCOLS`
  Status-Code (101) indicates that the server uses another protocol given in the *Upgrade-Header*.
- `static int SC_UNAUTHORIZED`
  Status-Code (401) indicates that an HTTP authentication is required to execute this query.
- `static int SC_UNSUPPORTED_MEDIA_TYPE`
  Status-Code (415) indicates that the server refuses to treat the query because it is coded in a format which is not supported for the method used with the required resource.
- `static int SC_USE_PROXY`
  Status-Code (305) indicates that the required resource can be used on the *Location* field of the given proxy only.
- `void addCookie(Cookie cookie)`
  adds the cookie identified by `cookie` to the answer.
- `void addDateHeader(java.lang.String name, long date)`
  adds an answer header which has the given name and data values.
- `void addHeader(String name, java.lang.String value)`
  adds an answer header which has the given name and value.

- `void addIntHeader(java.lang.String name, int value)`
  adds an answer header which has the given name and integer value.
- `boolean containsHeader(java.lang.String name)`
  returns a boolean value which shows if the answer header identified by `name` has already been set.
- `java.lang.String encodeRedirectUrl(java.lang.String url)`
  obsolete method. From version 2.1 of the servlet API the method `encodeRedirectURL(String url)` should be used.
- `java.lang.String encodeRedirectURL(java.lang.String url)`
  codes the given URL to enable its use in the method `sendRedirect`. If no coding is required the URL is returned unchanged.
- `java.lang.String encodeUrl(java.lang.String url)`
  obsolete method. From Version 2.1 of Servlet-API the method `sencodeURL(String url)` should be used.
- `java.lang.String encodeURL(java.lang.String url)`
  codes the given URL adding the session ID. If this kind of coding is not necessary the URL is returned unchanged.
- `void sendError(int sc)`
  sends an error message to the client. The field `sc` is set on the corresponding status code.
- `void sendError(int sc, java.lang.String msg)`
  sends an error message to the client in which the given status code as well as a descriptive message are used.
- `void sendRedirect(java.lang.String location)`
  sends a message that informs the client about the temporary shifting of a resource to another place, including the new URL.
- `void setDateHeader(java.lang.String name, long date)`
  sets an answer header with the given name and data value.
- `void setHeader(java.lang.String name, java.lang.String value)`
  sets an answer header with the given name and data value.
- `void setIntHeader(java.lang.String name, int value)`
  sets an answer header with the given name and integer value.
- `void setStatus(int sc)`
  sets the status code for this answer.
- `void setStatus(int sc, java.lang.String sm)`
  obsolete method. It should be replaced either with the method `setStatus(int)` to set a status code or with `sendError(int, String)` to send an error message together with a description. The method sets the status code and the content of a descriptive message.

B.8 The interface `HttpSession`

`HttpSession` saves the parameters and values that belong to the session. This interface is implemented by the servlet engine.

- `java.lang.Object getAttribute(java.lang.String name)`
  returns the object tied to the given name in this session. If the name is unknown the method returns the value zero.
- `java.util.Enumeration getAttributeNames()`
  provides an enumeration of string objects that contains the names of all objects that are tied to this session.
- `long getCreationTime()`
  supplies the time at which this session was created. Time is calculated in milliseconds since midnight on the 1 Jannuary 1970 GMT.
- `java.lang.String getId()`
  supplies a character string which contains the definite identification number of the session.
- `long getLastAccessedTime()`
  returns the time at which the client sent the last query belonging to the session. Time is calculated in milliseconds since midnight on the 1 Jannuary 1970 GMT.
- `int getMaxInactiveInterval()`
  gives the long time interval during which the servlet engine maintains the session between two client queries.
- `HttpSessionContext getSessionContext()`
  obsolete method. Since the availability of Version 2.1 of Servlet-API it has been removed and not replaced.
- `java.lang.Object getValue(java.lang.String name)`
  obsolete method. From Version 2.2 of Servlet-API it is replaced with the method `getAttribute(java.lang.String)`.
- `java.lang.String[] getValueNames()`
  obsolete method. From Version 2.2 of Servlet-API it is replaced with the method `getAttributeNames()`.
- `void invalidate()`
  makes the session invalid and dissolves all associations of parameter names to objects.
- `boolean isNew()`
  returns the boolean value true if the client does not yet know the session or does not want to use it.
- `void putValue(String name, java.lang.Object value)`
  obsolete method. From Version 2.1 of Servlet-API the method is replaced with `setAttribute(java.lang.String, java.lang.Object)`.
- `void removeAttribute(java.lang.String name)`
  removes the parameter identified by `name`, including its values, from the session.

- `void removeValue(java.lang.String name)`
  obsolete method. From Version 2.2 of Servlet-API the method is replaced with `setAttribute (java.lang.String, java.lang.Object)`.
- `void setAttribute (java.lang.String name, java.lang.Object value)`
  binds an object with the parameter name `name` at the session.
- `void setMaxInactiveInterval(int interval)`
  gives the time, in seconds, that can clapse between two client queries before the session is made invalid.

B.9 The class `Cookie`

A cookie contains server-side information that is passed by the client and, if necessary, used by the server. The class `Cookie` represents this information.

- `Cookie(java.lang.String name, java.lang.String value)`
  creates a cookie with the given parameter names and value.
- `java.lang.Object clone()`
  overtypes the standard method `java.lang.Object.clone`, in order to return a copy of the cookie.
- `java.lang.String getComment()`
  returns the comment as a character string that decribes the purpose of this cookie. If there is no comment, zero is returned.
- `java.lang.String getDomain()`
  returns the name of the domain that was set for this cookie.
- `int getMaxAge()`
  gives the maximum age of the cookie in seconds. If the standard value −1 is not changed, the Cookie lasts as long as the browser is closed down.
- `java.lang.String getName()`
  returns the name of the cookie.
- `java.lang.String getPath()`
  gives the path to the server on which the client returns the cookie.
- `boolean getSecure()`
  returns the boolean value true provided that the client sends back cookies on a safe protocol only. If the client wants to use any arbitrary protocol, false is sent back.
- `java.lang.String getValue()`
  returns the value of the cookie.
- `int getVersion()`
  gives the version of protocol this cookie agrees with.
- `void setComment(java.lang.String purpose)`
  gives a comment that describes the purpose of the cookie.

- `void setDomain(java.lang.String pattern)`
  gives the domains in which the cookie can be presented.
- `void setMaxAge(int expiry)`
  gives the maximum age of a cookie in seconds.
- `void setPath(java.lang.String uri)`
  gives the path, on the server, to which the client should send back the cookie.
- `void setSecure(boolean flag)`
  tells the client if the cookie has to be transferred to a safe protocol only, such as HTTPS or SSL.
- `void setValue(java.lang.String newValue)`
  assigns the cookie a new value after it was created.
- `void setVersion(int v)`
  sets the version of the cookie protocol to which this cookie holds.

B.10 The interface `ServletConfig`

With `ServletConfig` you can describe the configuration of the servlet. The interface is implemented by the servlet engine.

- `java.lang.String getInitParameter(java.lang.String name)`
  returns the value of the initialization parameter identified by `name` as a character string. If the parameter does not exist the value zero is returned.
- `java.util.Enumeration getInitParameterNames()`
  returns the names of all initialization parameters of the servlet as an enumeration of string objects. The enumeration is empty when there is no initialization parameter.
- `ServletContext getServletContext()`
  returns a reference to the `ServletContext` in which the servlet is executed.
- `java.lang.String getServletName()`
  returns the name of the servlet instance as a character string.

B.11 The interface `ServletContext`

Finally, `ServletContext` describes the context in which the servlet is executed. If necessary, this servlet interface also is implemented by the servlet engine.

- `java.lang.Object getAttribute(java.lang.String name)`
  returns the name of the attribute of the server engine. If the attribute identified by `name` does not exist, zero is returned.
- `java.util.Enumeration getAttributeNames()`
  returns an enumeration that lists all attribute names listed in this context.

■ ServletContext getContext(java.lang.String uripath)
returns an object of type ServletContext belonging to a URL given on the server.

■ java.lang.String getInitParameter(java.lang.String name)
returns a character string that contains the value of the initialization parameter identified by name. Zero is returned if no parameter exists.

■ java.util.Enumeration getInitParameterNames()
gives all names of the initialization parameters of the context as an enumeration of string objects. The enumeration is empty when the context owns no similar parameters.

■ int getMajorVersion()
returns the main version of the Servlet API that supports the servlet engine.

■ java.lang.String getMimeType(java.lang.String file)
returns the MIME type of the file given. If the type is unknown and the file does not exist, zero is returned.

■ int getMinorVersion()
returns the supplementary version of Servlet API that supports the servlet engine.

■ RequestDispatcher getNamedDispatcher(String name)
returns an object of type RequestDispatcher that functions as a wrapping for the servlet identifed by name.

■ java.lang.String getRealPath(java.lang.String path)
gives a character string that contains the genuine path for the specific virtual path.

■ RequestDispatcher getRequestDispatcher(String path)
returns an object of type RequestDispatcher that functions as a wrapping for the resource which has to be found under the given path.

■ java.net.URL getResource(java.lang.String path)
returns a URL that results from the given path.

■ java.io.InputStream getResourceAsStream(String path)
returns the resource you can find at the place identified with the given path as an object of type InputStream.

■ java.lang.String getServerInfo()
returns the name and the version of the servlet engine on which the servlet is executed.

■ Servlet getServlet(java.lang.String name)
obsolete method. Since Version 2.1 of Servlet-API this method is not supported anymore.

■ java.util.Enumeration getServletNames()
obsolete method. Since Version 2.1 of Servlet-API this method is not supported anymore.

■ java.util.Enumeration getServlets()
obsolete method. Since Version 2.0 of Servlet-API this method is not supported anymore.

- ■ `void log(java.lang.Exception exception, String msg)`
  obsolete method. From Servlet-API Version 2.1 the method `log(String message, Throwable throwable)` should be used.
- ■ `void log(java.lang.String msg)`
  writes the given message in the protocol file of the servlet.
- ■ `void log (String message, java.lang.Throwable throwable)`
  writes an explanatory message as well as a stack trace for a given exception of type `Throwable` in the protocol file of the servlet.
- ■ `void removeAttribute(java.lang.String name)`
  removes the attribute with the given name from the context of the servlet.
- ■ `void setAttribute(String name, java.lang.Object object)`
  binds an object in this context at the given attribute.

Appendix C

Java Server Pages (JSP)

C.1 Implicitly defined Java objects

Java Server Pages differ from servlets as well as HTML-based program text, particularly because of the implicitly defined Java objects. These are required because on the JSP pages there are no doGet or doPost methods, with which the request and response contexts are usually passed by the Web server. Table C.1 lists these objects, and describes their use and scope.

Implicitly available objects	Use	Data type	Scope	Frequently used methods
request	Getting the form values	javax.servlet.ServletRequest	On the entire JSP page	getParameter, getParameterNames, getParameterValues
response	The out-object is normally used.	javax.servlet.ServletResponse	On the entire JSP page	

Table C.1:implicitly available JSP objects

Implicitly available objects	Use	Data type	Scope	Frequently used methods
page Context	Access to page attributes, assigned name-spaces and features of the JSP implemen-tation	javax. servlet. jsp. Page Context	On the entire JSP page	find Attribute, getAttribute getAttributes Scope, getAttribute NamesInScope
session	Storage of session-spe-cific infor-mation	javax.serv let.http.H ttp session	For the duration of a session	getId, getValue, getValue Names, putValue
applica-tion	Communi-cation with the servlet engine	javax. servlet. Servlet Context	In entire Web application	getMimeType, getRealPath
out	Output of the result page	javax.serv let.jsp.Js pWriter	On entire JSP page	clear, clearBuffer, flush, getBuffer Size, get-Remaining
config	Reading of externally defined con-figuration parameters	javax. servlet. ServletCon fig	On entire JSP page	getInit Parameter, getInit ParameterNames
page		java.lang. object	On entire JSP page	

Table C.1: implicitly available JSP objects

Implicitly available objects	Use	Data type	Scope	Frequently used methods
excep-tion	Error han-dling	`java.lang.Throwable`	On entire JSP page	`getMessage, getLocalized Message, printStackTrac e`

Table C.1: implicitly available JSP objects

Appendix D

Interface Description Language (IDL)

In this appendix we will briefly describe the constructs available in the IDL as well as equivalent constructs in Java.

D.1 The most important components in IDL

- The module combines logically related object descriptions in a group and simplifies their management.
- Simple data types such as short, long, string, etc. serve the same purposes as in the programming language, i.e. data modeling in principle. The following section lists the most important of these types.
- The struct helps model more complex data structures which also consist of simple data types.
- By means of typedef you can define new data types, i.e. they can be referenced to a name.
- By means of sequence you can define a sequence of data elements of the same type, the length of which is unknown and unlimited.
- The array [] describes a sequence of elements of the same type having fixed length.
- Union describes a data type which can adopt various forms if necessary.
- Exception is an error which can be caused by calling the methods of an object interface.
- Enumerations can be defined using enum.
- Variables marked with constant have invariable values.
- Interface describes the interface of an object using methods and variables. A method has a name as well as input and output parameters whose data types are described using the constructs above.
- For a more detailed description of the parameters in a method, you can use the supplements in, out and inout which establish whether we are dealing with a genuine input, a genuine output, or an input and output parameter.

D.2 Description of the IDL data types in Java

As CORBA is a standard that is independent of any programming language, the mapping of IDL data types also has to be specified. Table D.1 shows the simple IDL types in the first column and the corresponding Java types in the second column. The third column specifies which errors can occur during conversion.

IDL data types	Java data types	Exception
boolean	boolean	
char	char	CORBA::DATA_CONVERSION
wchar	char	
octet	byte	
string	java.lang.String	CORBA::MARSHAL, CORBA::DATA_CONVERSION
wstring	java.lang.String	CORBA::MARSHAL
short	short	
unsigned short	short	
long	int	
unsigned long	int	
long long	long	
unsigned long long	long	
float	float	
double	double	
fixed	java.math.BigDecimal	CORBA::DATA_CONVERSION

Table D.1: Mapping of simple IDL data types. in Java.

We will now explain briefly how the more complex IDL constructs are transformed in Java, module, dealing with interface and struct in particular.

D.2.1 Module

`idlj` transforms an IDL module into a Java package. All interfaces defined within a module are inserted in the corresponding Java package. This also means that the files containing the interface description (and their implementation) have to be saved in a directory whose name corresponds to that of the package. If a module Sample is defined, each file generated starts with `package Sample`.

D.2.2 Interface

An interface in Java corresponds to an interface in IDL. As a result, the implementation of an IDL interface in Java has to implement the corresponding Java interface generated. For example, from

```
interface test {
   CustomerInformation output(in short id);
};
```

the following Java code is generated:

```
public interface test
   extends org.omg.CORBA.Object {
   Sample.CustomerInformation output(short id);
}
```

We notice that the parameter `CustomerInformation` also has the package name as prefix, in order to avoid any possible error.

D.2.3 Struct

A struct is translated into a class which has the same name. The components of the struct are converted into public class variables which can be read and written directly without get and set methods. Let us consider the following example: the struct

```
struct CustomerInformation {
   string name;
   string address;
   short age;
};
```

is converted into the following class:

```
public final class CustomerInformation {
    // instance variables
    public String name;
    public String address;
    public short age;
    // constructors
    public CustomerInformation() { }
    public CustomerInformation(String __name, String __address, short
                                                    __age) {
        name = __name;
        address = __address;
        age = __age;
    }
}
```

We see that two more constructors are created.

Appendix E

Document Object Model (DOM) Level 2

This appendix introduces the required details of the Document Object Model (DOM). To begin with, we will consider the inheritance tree of the DOM interfaces and then the methods of the most important interfaces.

E.1 Inheritance tree of the DOM interfaces

Figure E.1 shows a graphic representation of the inheritance tree. All DOM interfaces are derived from Node. Most of the sample programs we have introduced work with this interface.

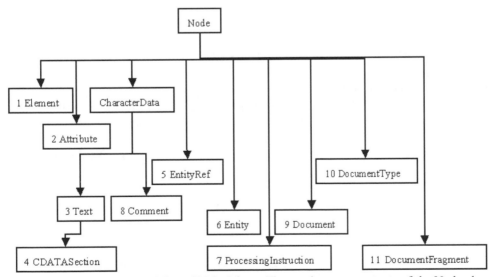

Figure E.1: Inheritance tree of the DOM interfaces. The numbers are constants of the Node class that define the type of the node.

E.2 Description of the DOM data types in Java

The Document Object Model also can be implemented for different programming languages. Therefore the W3C reference does not refer to the Java data types but defines some DOM data types. Table E.1 shows how these types are mapped in Java.

The Java package `org.w3c.dom` only contains Java interfaces and some exceptions. The implementation is left to other manufacturers.

DOM data type	Java data type
DOMString	`java.lang.String`
DOMString	`java.lang.String`
unsigned short	`short`
Node	`org.w3c.dom.Node`
NodeList	`org.w3c.dom.NodeList`
NamedNodeMap	`org.w3c.dom.NamedNodeMap`
Document	`org.w3c.dom.Document`

Table E.1: Description of the DOM data type in Java

E.3 Constants for the identification of the node type

Figure E.1 shows that each DOM interface extends Node. In order to understand whether we are dealing with an element, a document, or an attribute you can use a constant which is available in all DOM objects. This constant is read by the method `getNodeType`. Table E.2 shows which value corresponds to which DOM type.

It is advisable to use the constant in place of the number value, as shown in the following line. This makes the code more readable:

```
if (n.getNodeType() == Node.DOCUMENT_NODE)
```

Data type	Name	Value
short	ELEMENT_NODE	1
short	ATTRIBUTE_NODE	2
short	TEXT_NODE	3
short	CDATA_SECTION_NODE	4
short	ENTITY_REFERENCE_NODE	5
short	ENTITY_NODE	6
short	PROCESSING_INSTRUCTION_NODE	7
short	COMMENT_NODE	8
short	DOCUMENT_NODE	9
short	DOCUMENT_TYPE_NODE	10
short	DOCUMENT_FRAGMENT_NODE	11
short	NOTATION_NODE	12

Table E.2: Constants of the node interface

E.4 The Node interface

This section shows the attributes (Table E.3) and methods (Table E.4) of the Node interface. The term attributes refers to variables defined in the Node class. The DOM specification also uses attributes which are read-only. In Java an attribute can be defined as an instance variable:

```
public class NodeImpl implements org.w3c.dom.Node {
    public String attribute;
```

However, it is not possible to control the access. Therefore get and set methods have to be used. A single get method is defined for the only legible attributes. In fact, in this interface just one single set method exists: with `setNodeValue` the text saved in the node can be modified.

Return type	get / set XXX methods	Description
`String`	`getNodeName`	returns the name of the node
`void`	`setNode-Value(String)`	sets the value of the node
`String`	`getNodeValue`	returns the name of the node
`short`	`getNodeType`	returns the type constant of the node (see Fig. E.1)
`Node`	`getParentNode`	returns the superordinated nodes
`NodeList`	`getChildNodes`	returns the children
`Node`	`getFirstChild`	returns the first child node
`Node`	`getLastChild`	returns the last child node
`Node`	`getPreviousSibling`	returns the left neighbor of the node
`String`	`getNamespaceURI`	returns the namespace of this node
`String`	`getPrefix`	returns the prefix of the node name
`String`	`getLocalName`	returns the node name without prefix
`Node`	`getNextSibling`	returns the right neighbour of the node
`NamedNodeMap`	`getAttributes`	returns the attributes of the node
`Document`	`getOwnerDocument`	returns the document the node belongs to

Table E.3: Attributes of a node object

Return type	Method names and parameters	Description
Node	insertBefore(Node newChild, Node refChild)	inserts newChild before refChild and returns newChild
Node	replaceChild(Node newChild, Node oldChild)	replaces oldChild with newChild and returns oldChild
Node	removeChild(Node oldChild)	deletes oldChild and returns oldChild
Node	appendChild(Node newChild)	inserts newChild as last Child of this object and returns newChild
boolean	hasChildNodes()	returns true, if this object has children
boolean	hasAttributes()	returns true, if this object has attributes
Node	cloneNode(boolean deep)	generates a copy of this object and returns it. If deep is true, children are also copied.
void	normalize()	inserts all text nodes of the partial tree under this node
boolean	isSupported (String feature, String version)	tests if this implementation supports the feature

Table E.4: Methods of a node object

In addition to the attributes, the DOM recommendation also specifies methods which can be converted 1:1 their Java counterparts. The methods are listed in Table E.4.

Return type	Method names and parameters	Description
int	getLength()	returns the number of the nodes in the list
Node	item(int index)	returns the nodes at index

Table E.5: methods and attributes of a NodeList object

E.5 Names and values of different DOM objects

Table E.6 shows what the methods getNodeName, getNodeValue, and getAttributes return if they are called on different DOM objects. Normally, getNodeName and getAttributes are used to get the tag names of elements or the name of their attributes. GetNodeValue determines the value of the text node.

	getNode Name()	getNode Value()	getAttrib utes()
Element	Name of the tag	zero	Named NodeMap
Attr	Name of the attribute	value of attribute	zero
Text	#text	Content of text nodes	zero
CDATASec-tion	#cdata section	Content of CDATA section	zero
EntityRefer-ence	Name of referenced entities	zero	zero
Entity	Name of entity	zero	zero

Table E.6: Names and values of the node objects according to the XML constituent

	getNode Name()	getNode Value()	getAttrib utes()
Processing Instruction	purpose	Content of processing instruction	zero
Comment	#comment	content of comment	zero
Document	#document	zero	zero
Document type	name of document type	zero	zero
Document-Fragment	#document fragment	zero	zero
Notation	name of notation	zero	zero

Table E.6: Names and values of the node objects according to the XML constituent

E.6 The NamedNodeMap interface

NamedNodeMap objects serve mainly as containers for a list of attributes. As attributes are unordered and the attribute name within the start tag has to be clear, attributes are referenced to the name and not to the index, as is the case with elements.

Return type	Method names and parameters	Description
int	getLength()	returns the number of nodes in the list
Node	item(int index)	returns the node at index
Node	getNamedItem (String name)	returns the node with name name

Table E.7: Methods and attributes of a NamedNodeMap object

Return type	Method names and parameters	Description
Node	`setNamedItem` `(Node arg)`	inserts the node `arg` in the list. A node with the same name is replaced and returned.
Node	`removeNamedItem` `(String name)`	deletes the node with name `name` and returns it.
Node	`getNamedItemNS(` `String name-` `spaceURI, String` `localName)`	removes the node with the given name and namespace.
Node	`setNamedItemURI` `(Node arg)`	inserts the node `arg` in the list with the same name and namespace or null.
Node	`removeNamed-` `ItemNS(String` `namespaceURI,` `String` `localName)`	removes the node with the name and namespace given and returns it.

Table E.7: Methods and attributes of a `NamedNodeMap` object

E.7 The document interface

The document interface represents the whole document and not only a single node. The method `getDocument` of the XML parser sends back a document object. The most important method is `getElementsByTagName` which provides a list of all elements of acertain name, `getDocumentElement` which returns the root element, and the createXXX methods which insert new elements.

Return type	Method names and parameters	Description
Document Type	`getDoctype()`	returns the document type assigned
DOM Implementa-tion	`get Implementation ()`	returns the DOM implementation which revises this document
Element	`getDocument Element()`	returns the element at the root
Element	`createElement (String tagName)`	creates a new element
Document Fragment	`createDocument Fragment()`	creates a new document fragment
Text	`createTextNode (String data)`	creates a new text node
Comment	`createComment (String data)`	creates a new comment
CDATA Section	`createCDATA Section (String data)`	creates a new CDATA section
Processing Instruction	`createProcessing Instruction (String target, String data)`	creates a new processing instruction
Attr	`createAttribute (String name)`	creates a new attribute
Entity Reference	`createEntity Reference (String name)`	creates a new entity reference

Table E.8: Methods and attributes of a document object

Return type	Method names and parameters	Description
NodeList	`getElementsBy TagName( String tagname)`	returns a list of all nodes which have the name `tagname`. The sequence corresponds to that in an XML file
Node	`importNode(Node importedNode, boolean deep)`	import a node / a partial tree of another document
Element	`createElementNS (String namespaceURI, String qualifiedName)`	creates a node with the prefix of the given namespaces and the given name
Attr	`createAttribute NS(String namespaceURI, String qualifiedName)`	creates an attribute with the prefix of the given namespaces and name
NodeList	`getElementsByTa gNameNS(String namespaceURI, String localName)`	returns a list of all nodes which have the name `tagname` and the given namespace. The sequence corresponds to that in an XML file
Element	`getElementById (String elementId)`	returns a list of all nodes with the given ID

Table E.8: Methods and attributes of a document object

E.8 The `CharacterData` interface

Methods for text manipulation represent the fundamental functionality of the `CharacterData` interface. The further DOM interfaces rarely contain necessary methods or extend the node interface only insignificantly, and so are not listed here.

Return type	Method names and parameters	Description
String	getData()	returns the value
void	setData(String s)	sets the value to s
int	getLength()	returns the number of the characters
String	substringData(int offset, int length)	returns the partial string of length characters starting at offset
void	appendData(String arg)	appends arg to the current string
void	insertData(int offset, String arg)	inserts arg in offset
void	deleteData(int offset, int count)	deletes count characters from offset
void	replaceData(int offset, int count, String arg)	replace count characters in offset with arg

Table E.9: Methods and attributes of a CharacterData object

Appendix F

XPath

This appendix shows the possibilities of XPath. These can be used with XPointer and XSL. The first table shows the detailed, the second the abbreviated XPath syntax. The terminology is as follows: child elements of an element are *directly* subordinated to it. Subordinate elements can be child elements, grandchild elements, great-grandchild elements, and so on. The element itself is a subordinate element to its ancestors.

F.1 Detailed XPath syntax

Expression	Description
child::para	selects the para child elements of the context element
child::*	selects all child elements of the context element
child::text()	selects all child text-elements of the context element
child::node()	selects all child elements of the context element
attribute::name	selects the name attribute of the context element
attribute::*	selects all attributes of the context element
descendant::para	selects all para elements subordinated to the context element
ancestor::div	selects all div ancestors of the context element
ancestor-or-self::div	selects all div ancestors of the context element and the context element, provided that this is a div element.

Table F1: Detailed XPath syntax

Expression	Description
descendant-or-self::para	selects all para elements subordinated to the context element, and the context element, provided it is a para element
self::para	selects the context element, if this is a para element
child::chapter/descendant::para	selects the para elements subordinated to a chapter child element of the context element
child::*/child::para	selects the para-great-grandchild of the context element
/	selects the root element in the document
/descendant::para	selects all para elements in the document
/descendant::olist/child::item	selects all item elements in the document which have an olist parent element.
child::para[position()=1]	selects the first para child element of the context element

Expression	Description
child::para[position()=last()]	selects the last para child element of the context element
child::para[position()=last()-1]	selects the second to last para child element of the context element
child::para[position()>1]	selects all para child elements of the context element except for the first one
following-sibling::chapter[position()=1]	selects the following chapter element on the level of the context element
preceding-sibling::chapter[position()=1]	selects the previous chapter element on the level of the context element
/descendant::figure[position()=42]	selects the 42nd figure element in the document
/child::doc/child::chapter[position()=5]/child::section[position()=2]	selects the second section element of the fifth chapter element of the doc element under the root
child::para[attribute::type="warning"]	selects all para child elements of the context element whose type attribute have the warning value
child::para[attribute::type='warning'][position()=5]	selects the fifth para child element of the context element whose type attribute has the warning value
child::para[position()=5][attribute::type="warning"]	selects the fifth para child element of the context element if this has a type attribute with warning value
child::chapter[child::title='Introduction']	selects the fifth para child element of the context element which has one or more child elements with the text introduction.
child::chapter[child::title]	selects the chapter child elements of the context element which have one or more title child elements
child::*[self::chapter or self::appendix]	selects the chapter and appendix child elements of the context element

Table F1: Detailed XPath syntax

Expression	Description
child::*[self::chapter or self::appendix][position()=last()]	selects the last chapter or appendix child element of the context element

Table F1: Detailed XPath syntax

F.2 Abbreviated XPath syntax

para	Description
para	selects all para child elements of the context element
*	selects all child elements of the context element
text()	selects all subordinated text elements of the context element
@name	selects the name attribute of the context element
@*	selects all attributes of the context element
para[1]	selects the first para child element of the context element
para[last()]	selects the last para child element of the context element
*/para	selects all para grandchild elements of the context element
/doc/chapter[5]/section[2]	Selects the second element section of the fifth element chapter of all doc elements under the root
chapter//para	selects all para elements subordinated to an element chapter, which is in turn a child of the context element
//para	selects all para elements of the whole document
//olist/item	selects all olist elements in the document which have an olist parent element
.	selects the context element
.//para	selects all the para elements subordinated to the contex element
..	selects all parent elements of the context element
../@lang	selects the lang attribute of the parent element of the context element
para[@type="warning"]	selects all para child elements of the context element whose type attribute have the warning value

Table F.2: Abbreviated XPath syntax

para	Description
para[@type="warning"][5]	selects the fifth para child element of the context element whose type attribute has the warning value
para[5][@type="warning"]	selects the fifth para child element of the context element provided that its type attribute has the warning-value
chapter[title="Introduction"]	selects the chapter child elements of the context element which have one or more child elements with text introduction
chapter[title]	selects the chapter child elements of the context element which have one or more title child elements
employee[@secretary and @assistant]	selects all employee child elements of the context element which have both a secretary attribute and an assistant attribute

Table F.2: Abbreviated XPath syntax

Appendix G

Bibliography

The purpose of this book is not to consider each theme down to the last detail. Therefore, the reader may not find particular information required to solve a peculiar task here. For this reason, in this appendix we will give some suggestions about further basic and especially more specialized publications. A section is dedicated to each important topic.

G.1 Distributed systems and applications

- Johann Schlichter: Verteilte Anwendungen. Vorlesung an der TU München im Sommersemester 1999, http://www11.informatik.tu-muenchen.de/lehre/lectures/va-SS99/VA-top-SS1999.html
- Günther Bengel: Verteilte Systeme — Client-Server-Computing für Studenten und Praktiker. Vieweg textbook, 2000.
- George Coulouris, Jean Dollimore and Tim Kindberg: *Distributed Systems — Concepts and Design*. Second edition, Addison-Wesley, 1994.

G.2 HTML

- Stefan Münz and Wolfgang Nefzger: *HTML 4.0 manual*, Franzis, 1998.
- Thomas Kobert: *Das Einsteigerseminar HTML 4*, BHV, 1998.
- Peter Müller: *Eigene Homepage erstellen*, DATA Becker, 1999.
- Laura Lemay: *HTML 4 in 14 Tagen*, Markt&Technik, 1998.

G.3 Java

- David Flanagan: *Java in a Nutshell*, third edition, O'Reilly, 1999.
- Ernst-Erich Doberkat and Stefan Dißmann: *Einführung in die objektorientierte Programmierung mit Java*, Oldenbourg, 1999.
- Harvey and Paul Deitel: *Java How To Program*, third edition, Prentice Hall, 1999.
- Laura Lemay and Charles Perkins: *Java 2 in 21 Tagen*, Markt&Technik 1999.
- Java-Seiten von Sun: `http://java.sun.com`

G.4 Servlets

- Peter Roßbach and Hendrik Schreiber: *Java Server und Servlets*, Addison-Wesley, 1999.
- Jason Hunter and William Crawford: *Java Servlet Programming*, O'Reilly, 1998.
- Johannes Plachy and Jürgen Schmidt: *Dynamischer Service, C'T 2000 Heft 2*, Heise, 2000.

G.5 CORBA

- Jeremy Rosenberger: *CORBA in 14 Tagen*, Markt&Technik, 1998.
- Robert Orfali, Dan Harkey and Jeri Edwards: *Instant CORBA — Führung durch die CORBA-Welt*, Addison-Wesley, 1998.
- Robert Orfali and Dan Harkey: *Client-Server Programming with Java and CORBA*, second edition, Wiley, 1998.
- Suhail M. Ahmed: *CORBA Programming Unleashed,* Sams, 1998.

G.6 EJB

- Nicolas Kassem et al.: *Designing Enterprise Applications with the Java 2 Platform, Enterprise Edition*, Addison Wesley, 2000.
- Ed Roman: *Mastering Enterprise JavaBeans and the Java 2 Platform, Enterprise Edition*, Wiley, 1999.

G.7 XML

▓ North, Hermans: *Teach yourself XML in 21 days*, Sams Net, 1999.

▓ McGrath: *XML by Example: Building E-Commerce Applications*, Prentice Hall, 1998.

▓ Finkelstein, Aiken: *Building Corporate Portals with XML*, McGraw-Hill, 1999.

▓ Leventhal, Lewis, Fuchs: *Designing XML Internet Applications*, Prentice Hall, 1998.

▓ World Wide Web Consortium: Extensible Markup Language (XML) 1.0, W3C Recommendation 10-February-1998, `http://www.w3.org/TR/1998/REC-xml-19980210`

▓ World Wide Web Consortium: Namespaces in XML, 14-January-1999, `http://www.w3.org/TR/1999/REC-xml-names-19990114/`

▓ World Wide Web Consortium: XSL Transformations (XSLT) Version 1.0, W3C Recommendation 16 November 1999, `http://www.w3.org/TR/xslt`

▓ World Wide Web Consortium: XML Path Language (XPath) Version 1.0, W3C Recommendation 16 November 1999, `http://www.w3.org/TR/xpath`

▓ World Wide Web Consortium: XML Linking Language (XLink), W3C Working Draft 21-February-2000, `http://www.w3.org/TR/xlink/`

▓ World Wide Web Consortium: XML Schema Part 0: Primer, W3C Working Draft, 25 February 2000, `http://www.w3.org/TR/xmlschema-0/`

▓ World Wide Web Consortium: XML Pointer Language (XPointer), W3C Working Draft 6 December 1999, `http://www.w3.org/TR/xptr`

▓ World Wide Web Consortium: Extensible Stylesheet Language (XSL) Version 1.0, W3C Working Draft 27 March 2000, `http://www.w3.org/TR/xsl/`

▓ World Wide Web Consortium: Document Object Model (Core) Level 1, `http://www.w3.org/TR/REC-DOM-Level-1/level-one-core.html`

Appendix H

How to use the Web site for this book

On the Internet you will find a Web site which provides all relevant material about the cotents of this book. The Internet address of the site is

`http://www.i-u.de/schools/eberhart/book/`

In particular, on this site you can find the following information:

- source code of all examples;
- an implementation of all examples which can be tested online;
- hyperlinks on all relevant program packages;
- errata, i.e. corrections of the errors found after the book has been printed;
- up-to-date information about further developments of the techniques explained in the text, new Java versions, new tools etc.

We suggest that you download the file `book.zip` from the Web site for this book. All files on the Web site are contained in this archive. In this way you can read and try out all examples and information, thus avoiding connecting to the Internet all the time. The file `program.html` enables you to see the examples ordered according to each chapter. The file structure of our Books Online project is built so that the servlets can be tested immediately using a local Web server.

H.1 Automated demos

The chapters contain numerous batch programs which enable you to call all demos directly, provided you are using Windows. In detail, the software and operating systems you need for the use of automated demos are:

- Windows 95, 98, ME, NT, or 2000 is installed on your computer. A browser must be installed. We suggest Internet Explorer 5 to display the XML files. However, this is not compulsory.
- The JDK 1.3 or a more recent version is installed.
- A Microsoft ODBC access driver is installed.
- `jdk1.3\bin` is registered in the PATH environment.

Working with another platform, you can orient yourself by the batch programs to start the examples. In place of Access you can use further databases. To create a table, use the corresponding create table instructions and modify the name of the JDBC driver used in the examples.

H.2 Installing the sample program

Some files have to be copied for installation. Installations of different Web servers, XML Parser, etc. are not influenced. In order to try out the examples shown in this book in Windows, you have to go through the following stages:

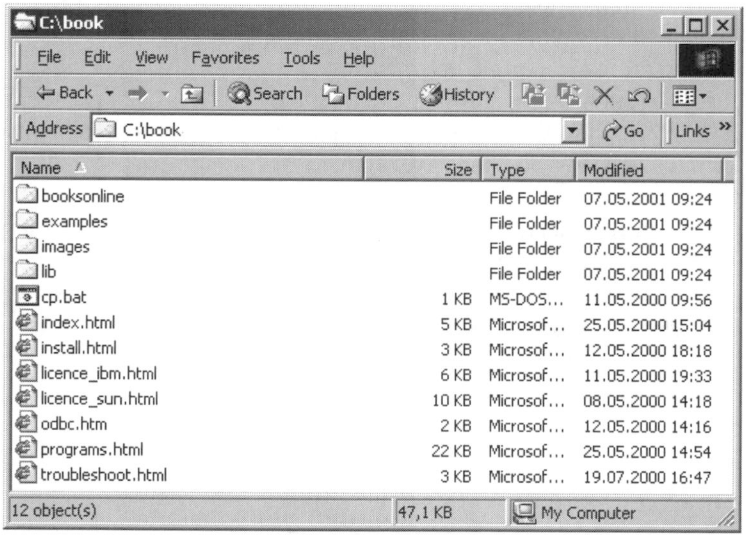

Figure H.1 The unpacked file `book.zip`.

- Load the file `book.zip` from the Web site.
- If possible, unpack the files in the directory `C:\book`. Figure H.1 shows the files contained in the archive. If this operation is not possible on your system you have to edit the file `cp.bat`. This file is called by all batch files in order to set the class path

for the demos. If files in your system are contained in `D:\wiley\demos`, set the base directory variable from `C:\book` to `D:\wiley\demos` in `cp.bat`.

■ In the directory structure two access databases are contained in
`C:\book\examples\jdbc\project.mdb` and
`C:\book\booksonline\database\access97\book.mdb`
The file `project.mdb` contains the sample data base from the section on The Relational Data Model on page 84. `book.mdb` contains the database of our bookshop. Establish an ODBC connection for both databases, as shown in Figure H.2 and in the section on Establishing an ODBC Connection. Choose the system DSN and the Microsoft access driver (`*.mdb`). Set the name of the ODBC connection to project or book.

■ All examples as well as the Books Online Web site can now be called locally. Start only the file `run.bat` in the respective directory.

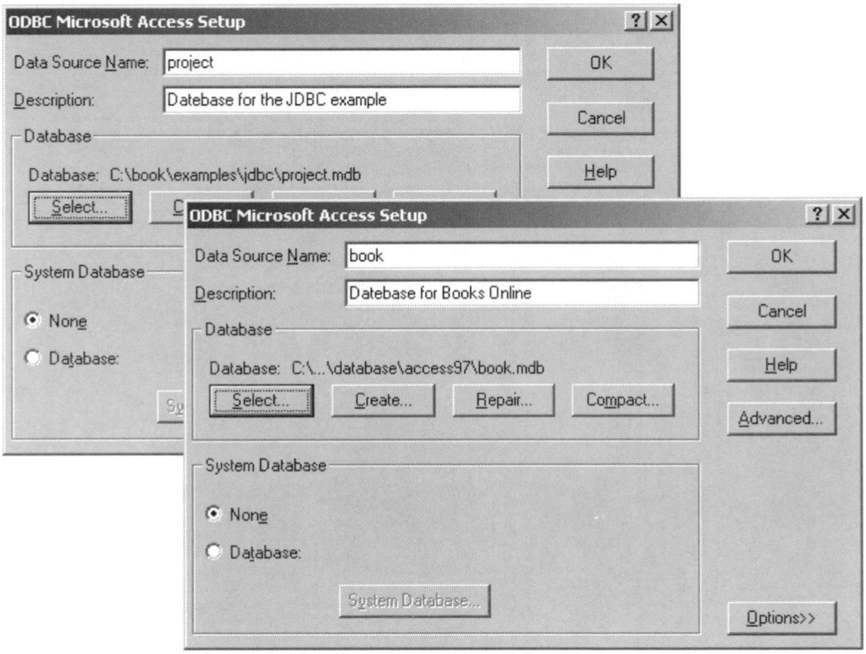

Figure H.2: Establish an ODBC connection to both Access files.